Endogenous Money and the Supermultiplier

This book explores the Supermultiplier model which has rapidly evolved into a key analytical framework, embraced and debated by post-Keynesian economists across various schools of thought. At its core, the model extends Keynesian principles to the long run, asserting that economic growth and productive capacity are fundamentally shaped by effective demand. Central to this framework is the concept of autonomous demand—components of aggregate demand such as government spending, exports, and residential investment and credit-financed consumption that operate independently of income flows, driving growth and capital accumulation.

This book ventures into the relatively uncharted territory of how these autonomous demand components are financed. It highlights the indispensable role of endogenous money creation—credit expansion, state money, and external sector financing—in sustaining demand-led growth. Drawing from recent contributions, the book integrates credit and debt dynamics into the Supermultiplier model, offering insights into the financial underpinnings of autonomous demand.

A vital resource for understanding modern monetary economies, this book bridges theoretical advancements and practical policy implications, making it essential reading for economists, policymakers, and those intrigued by the intersection of demand, finance, and growth.

The chapters in this book were originally published in *Review of Political Economy*.

Maria Cristina Barbieri Góes is Assistant Professor at the LINK Campus University, Rome, Italy, and the co-editor of the *Review of Political Economy*. Her research activity is focused on post-Keynesian economics, growth theory, fiscal and monetary policies, and income distribution. Her scientific contributions were published in various journals.

Óscar Dejuán Asenjo is Full Professor of Economics at the University of Castilla–La Mancha (FCEE of Albacete, Spain). His research has been focused on: growth and crisis, unemployment, Sraffian economics, post-Keynesian economics, input-output analysis, and the Supermultiplier model.

Riccardo Pariboni is Associate Professor at the University of Siena, Italy. After three years as a postdoctoral fellow at the Department of Economics of Roma Tre University, Italy, he was appointed Visiting Professor at the Freie Universität in Berlin, Germany. Then, he joined the Max Planck Institute for the Study of Societies (Cologne) as a postdoctoral fellow. His research interests are growth theory, income distribution, and post-Keynesian economics, but he has also worked on environmental issues and labor market dynamics.

Ricardo Summa is Associate Professor at the Federal University of Rio de Janeiro, Brazil, and co-editor of the *Review of Keynesian Economics*. His research interests are growth theory, conflict inflation and income distribution, endogenous money in open economies, and macroeconomic policies.

Endogenous Money and the Supermultiplier

Edited by
Maria Cristina Barbieri Góes, Óscar Dejuán Asenjo, Riccardo Pariboni and Ricardo Summa

Routledge
Taylor & Francis Group
LONDON AND NEW YORK

First published 2025
by Routledge
4 Park Square, Milton Park, Abingdon, Oxon OX14 4RN

and by Routledge
605 Third Avenue, New York, NY 10158

Routledge is an imprint of the Taylor & Francis Group, an informa business

British Library Cataloguing in Publication Data
A catalogue record for this book is available from the British Library

ISBN13: 978-1-041-05378-1 (hbk)
ISBN13: 978-1-041-05380-4 (pbk)
ISBN13: 978-1-003-63252-8 (ebk)

DOI: 10.4324/9781003632528

Typeset in Minion Pro
by Newgen Publishing UK

Publisher's Note
The publisher accepts responsibility for any inconsistencies that may have arisen during the conversion of this book from journal articles to book chapters, namely the inclusion of journal terminology.

Contents

Citation Information

The chapters in this book were originally published in *Review of Political Economy*, volume 36, issue 5 (2024) along with some additional articles from the same journal. When citing this material, please use the original page numbering for each article, as follows:

Introduction

Introduction to the Symposium on: The Supermultiplier and Endogenous Money
Maria Cristina Barbieri Góes, Óscar Dejuán Asenjo, Riccardo Pariboni and Ricardo Summa
Review of Political Economy, volume 36, issue 5 (2024), pp. 1717–1721

Chapter 1

Finance, Financial Adjustments and Alternative Closures in Neo-Kaleckian Models: The Paradoxes of Thrift and Costs in the Long-Run
Brett Fiebiger
Review of Political Economy, volume 36, issue 5 (2024), pp. 1722–1745

Chapter 2

The Monetary Theory of Production and the Supermultiplier: What Determines Savings?
Lorenzo Di Domenico, Giovanna Ciaffi and Davide Romaniello
Review of Political Economy, volume 36, issue 5 (2024), pp. 1746–1774

Chapter 3

Fiscal Supermultiplier and Endogenous Money in the United States: The COVID-19 Pandemic vs. the Global Financial Crisis
Juan Matias De Lucchi
Review of Political Economy, volume 36, issue 5 (2024), pp. 1775–1800

Chapter 4

Supermultiplier Models, Demand Stagnation, and Monetary Policy: Inevitable March to the Lower Bound for Interest Rates?
Steven Fazzari
Review of Political Economy, volume 36, issue 5 (2024), pp. 1801–1826

Chapter 5

The Supermultiplier-Cum-Finance. An Application to the Credit-Led Boom before the 2008 Crash
Óscar Dejuán and Daniel Dejuán-Bitriá
Review of Political Economy, volume 36, issue 5 (2024), pp. 1827–1849

Chapter 6

Pensions as an Engine of Growth. An Approach to the Spanish Case, Based on the Sraffian Supermultiplier
Eladio Febrero and Fernando Bermejo
Review of Political Economy, volume 36, issue 5 (2024), pp. 1850–1875

Chapter 7

Components of Autonomous Demand Growth and Financial Feedbacks: Implications for Growth Drivers and Growth Regime Analysis
Ryan Woodgate, Eckhard Hein and Ricardo Summa
Review of Political Economy, volume 36, issue 5 (2024), pp. 1876–1893

Chapter 8

Debt-credit Flows and Stocks in a Supermultiplier Model with Two Autonomous Demand Components: Consequences for Growth
Stefano Di Bucchianico, Ettore Gallo and Antonino Lofaro
Review of Political Economy, volume 36, issue 5 (2024), pp. 1894–1914

Chapter 9

Limits to Fiscal and Monetary Policy in Small Open Economies
Ariel Dvoskin and Matías Torchinsky Landau
Review of Political Economy, volume 36, issue 5 (2024), pp. 1915–1942

Chapter 10

Impacts of US Interest Rates on Growth, Income Distribution, and Macroeconomic Policy Space in Developing Countries: A SFC Supermultiplier Model
João Emboava Vaz
Review of Political Economy, volume 36, issue 5 (2024), pp. 1943–1963

Notes on Contributors

Maria Cristina Barbieri Góes, LINK Campus University, Rome, Italy.

Fernando Bermejo, University of Castilla–La Mancha, Cuenca, Spain.

Giovanna Ciaffi, University of Bari 'Aldo Moro', Bari, Italy.

Juan Matias De Lucchi, Central Bank of Argentina (BCRA), Buenos Aires, Argentina.

Óscar Dejuán Asenjo, University of Castilla–La Mancha, Albacete, Spain.

Daniel Dejuán-Bitriá, University Pompeu Fabra, Barcelona, Spain.

Stefano Di Bucchianico, University of Salerno, Fisciano, Italy.

Lorenzo Di Domenico, University of Trieste, Trieste, Italy.

Ariel Dvoskin, CONICET-UNSAM, San Martín, Argentina.

João Emboava Vaz, Federal University of Rio de Janeiro (UFRJ), Rio de Janeiro, Brazil.

Steven Fazzari, Washington University in St. Louis, St. Louis, MO, USA.

Eladio Febrero, University of Castilla–La Mancha, Cuenca, Spain.

Brett Fiebiger, Independent Analyst.

Ettore Gallo, University of Parma, Parma, Italy.

Eckhard Hein, Berlin School of Economics and Law, Berlin, Germany; Institute for International Political Economy (IPE), Berlin, Germany.

Antonino Lofaro, University of Bari 'Aldo Moro', Bari, Italy.

Riccardo Pariboni, University of Siena, Siena, Italy.

Davide Romaniello, Vanvitelli University, Caserta, Italy.

Ricardo Summa, Federal University of Rio de Janeiro (UFRJ), Rio de Janeiro, Brazil.

Matías Torchinsky Landau, EIDAES-CONICET, San Martín, Argentina.

Ryan Woodgate, Forward College Berlin, Berlin, Germany; Institute for International Political Economy (IPE), Berlin, Germany.

Introduction: The Supermultiplier and Endogenous Money

Maria Cristina Barbieri Góes, Óscar Dejuán Asenjo, Riccardo Pariboni and Ricardo Summa

In recent years, the supermultiplier model has emerged as a widely used analytical tool, capable of trespassing the narrow boundaries of Sraffian scholars to be discussed, adopted and extended (and criticized) by post-Keynesians of various orientations (Dejuán 2023). In hindsight, this comes as no surprise, given the inherently Keynesian main purpose of the model, that is to say the extension to the long run of the principle of effective demand (Serrano 1995; Lavoie 2016). In fact, the defining mechanism behind the supermultiplier framework is the proposition that the trajectories of both output and productive capacity are shaped by effective demand within monetary economies of production.

As it is well-known, at the very heart of this hypothesis there is the idea that a part of aggregate demand is independent from the circular flow of income and is not systematically related to the production requirements. This is what has been labeled as autonomous (or semi-autonomous) demand — comprising components such as government spending, exports, autonomous consumption, private residential investment and modernization investment (aimed at transforming productive capacity instead of enlarging it). Such autonomous elements represent the main engine of growth and capital accumulation within the model.

A relatively less explored (with the notable exceptions of Cesaratto 2017 and Cesaratto and Di Bucchianico 2020) feature of the supermultiplier is how these autonomous components of demand are to be financed. If it is true that savings and the pre-existing level of income do not represent a constraint on the spending capacity of the economy, then the very functioning of an autonomous demand-led economy has to rely on the creation and injection of new monetary purchasing power. Hence, it seems uncontroversial to claim that the endogenous credit-money approach is a natural financial counterpart of a real analysis based on the supermultiplier, even in its baseline formulation. At the same time, however, it is also undeniable that the issue has not received a systematic attention so far, in spite of recent contributions that have incorporated credit and debt dynamics related to consumer credit, residential investment, government spending and the external sector (Pariboni 2016; Mandarino, Dos Santos, and e Silva 2020; Hein and Woodgate 2021; Morlin 2022; Pedrosa, Brochier, and Freitas 2023, just to mention some of them) and without forgetting other attempts at integrating financial aspects into supermultiplier-like models, such as the role of the interest rate in influencing autonomous demand (Deleidi and Mazzucato 2019; Serrano, Summa, and Moreira 2020; Petrini and Teixeira 2023; Barbieri Góes 2023).

This special issue of the *Review of Political Economy*, hence, can be thought as a first attempt at a systematic exploration of the multifaceted interconnections between a supermultiplier-based explanation of the growth process and endogenous money. The idea to make a special issue came up from discussions with Louis-Philippe Rochon and the guest-editors about how to reconcile the Supermultiplier with endogenous money in 2022. These discussions took place notably during the Fifth Nordic Post-Keynesian Conference, in Aalborg, in the 19th Annual STOREP Conference in Viterbo, and in the occasion of a visit of Louis-Philippe Rochon to Spain.

Hopefully, the fruitfulness of this Special Issue will not be limited to an explicit connection of two naturally complementary strands of post-Keynesian theory, but it can lead to building bridges within the post-Keynesian community. Starting from Keynes' concept of *finance* to the notion of semi-autonomous components used by Kalecki (1967) making reference to Luxemburg's external markets (Luxemburg 1913 [2015]), and arriving at the Monetary Circuit insight that every economic circuit must start with money creation and end with money destruction (Rochon 1999), with the related concepts of initial and final finance, a common thread emerges. Moreover, as the supermultiplier deals with a growing economy, credit creation also plays an important role to finance the growing wage bill necessary for production, which feeds back into the system as induced consumption and the multiplier. The injection of new monetary purchasing power — whether it comes from the creation of credit-money by banks, State money or the external sector — represents the only avenue through which an economy can be demand-led. The articles that comprise this special issue build upon this premise and advance in several directions.

The papers by Fiebiger (2024) and Di Domenico, Ciaffi and Romaniello (2024) discuss the difference between saving and credit in the supermultiplier model. Fiebiger (2024) incorporates the circuitist intra-period endogenous money financing relations, and the financial adjustments that increase the elasticity of household portfolio adjustments and firm liability-side management, providing a clear distinction between the concepts of finance and thrift. The author uses this approach to criticize the Neo-Marxian/neo-Harrodian approach (NMNH), in which thrift has a positive effect on the 'equilibrium' warranted growth rate. Di Domenico, Ciaffi and Romaniello (2024) explore how savings are created in the economy as a result of liabilities creation when autonomous spending and investments are financed, and compare different sources of initial financing of investments and autonomous components, showing that the endogenous process of money creation is the only structural mechanism guaranteeing the existence of autonomous components of demand and their independence from current income in the long-run, and the independence of investments from saving.

The papers by De Lucchi (2024) and Fazzari (2024) incorporate monetary elements into the supermultiplier via policy. De Lucchi (2024) integrates the supermultiplier with endogenous money to discuss the dynamics of the quantity of money (M2) and the monetary base in the US economy as a result of fiscal and monetary policy implemented during the great financial crisis of 2008 and the Covid-19 Pandemic. Fazzari

(2024) introduces monetary policy via interest rate setting by the Central bank into a supermultiplier model with a flexible supply side, and shows that Taylor rule-guided monetary policy can prove ineffective in counteracting permanent negative demand shocks, even when the lower bound for interest rates is not a limiting factor.

Dejuán and Dejuán-Bitriá (2022) also introduce endogenous money into the supermultiplier model, by including autonomous banks which are able to change the pace of credit expansion. The authors explore the effect of credit expansion in financing non-output transactions (land, old houses, shares) and its speculative bias to generate financial instability, demand depression and asset inflation.

The two papers by Febrero and Bermejo (2024) and Woodgate, Hein, and Summa (2024) explore the role of state money in financing autonomous demand. Febrero and Bermejo (2024) include consumption out of government transfers — more specifically pensions — into the supermultiplier, to check the impact of pensioners' spending on output and employment in the Spanish economy. Woodgate, Hein, and Summa (2024) integrate the role of another kind of government transfers — interest paid on the public debt — via rentiers' consumption into the supermultiplier model. They show that, under certain conditions, an endogenous stock-flow interaction aligns the growth rates of the autonomous consumption out of interest rate to the exogenous growth rate of government spending, and they explore the consequence of these results to the demand-led growth decomposition analysis. The paper attempts to demonstrate the interdependence of two autonomous demand components, providing a mechanism to tackle the question raised by Allain's (2022) on how two (or more) non-capacity-generating autonomous demand components growing at different rates may coexist in the supermultiplier.

Also as an attempt to address Allain's (2022) question, Di Buchianico, Gallo and Lofaro (2024) propose a solution in which growth is driven by workers' debt accumulation as well as rentier's consumption out of interest. They show that, under specific conditions, there is a steady-state solution in which growth ultimately converges toward that of the fastest-growing component, but the other does not disappear due to the presence of endogenous stock-flow relations, with endogenous money creation surrounding this process of growth driven by credit to households.

Finally, the articles by Dvoskin and Landau (2024) and Vaz (2024) explore the role of monetary elements and capital flows in open economies in supermultiplier models. Dvoskin and Landau (2024) investigate with a supermultiplier model the impact of the balance-of-payments constraint on output, income distribution and policy space, both fiscal and monetary policies. They also examine the effects of the currency denomination of debt, and find that, in case of a depreciation, debt in domestic currency allows for a less contractionary adjustment than foreign currency-denominated debt but does not lead to higher economic growth. In the same vein, Vaz (2024) builds a supermultiplier model to investigate the effects of interest rate hikes abroad that may impact growth and income distribution domestically in developing countries.

Less than 10 years ago, also in a symposium in Review of Political Economy, Freitas and Serrano (2015) stated that a promising research agenda on the supermultiplier 'should focus on the determinants and dynamics (particularly financial) of the trend of growth of the different "unproductive" autonomous components of demand' (Freitas and Serrano 2015, p. 280). We are glad to see that the papers described above provide interesting and creative attempts to tackle this challenge. We hope the result of the advances in this research agenda contained in this symposium will provide questions and ideas for much further investigation. It is important to remember that this was a result of a collective work which involved more than forty scholars — authors, reviewers and the editor Louis-Philippe Rochon — to whom we would like to thank, as they helped a lot to improve the quality of the final result. Without further ado, we wish all an excellent reading.

Disclosure Statement

No potential conflict of interest was reported by the author(s).

ORCID

Maria Cristina Barbieri Góes http://orcid.org/0000-0001-8953-5412
Óscar Dejuán Asenjo http://orcid.org/0000-0002-9319-6609
Riccardo Pariboni http://orcid.org/0000-0002-5275-9559
Ricardo Summa http://orcid.org/0000-0002-4769-8974

References

Allain, O. 2022. 'A Supermultiplier Model with Two Non-Capacity-Generating Semi-Autonomous Demand Components.' *Structural Change and Economic Dynamics* 63: 91–103.

Barbieri Góes, M. C. 2023. 'A Tale of Three Prices: Monetary Policy and Autonomous Consumption in the US.' *Structural Change and Economic Dynamics* 67: 115–127.

Cesaratto, S. 2017. 'Initial and Final Finance in the Monetary Circuit and the Theory of Effective Demand.' *Metreoconomica* 68 (2): 228–258.

Cesaratto, S., and S. Di Bucchianico. 2020. 'Endogenous Money and the Theory of Long-Period Effective Demand.' *Bulletin of Political Economy* 14 (1): 1–38.

De Lucchi, J. M. 2024. 'Fiscal Supermultiplier and Endogenous Money in the United States: The COVID-19 Pandemic vs. the Global Financial Crisis.' *Review of Political Economy* 36 (5): 1775–1800.

Dejuán, Ó. 2023. *The Supermultiplier: A Cornerstone of the New Macroeconomics.* Cheltenham: Edward Elgar Publishing.

Dejuán, Ó., and D. Dejuán-Bitriá. 2022. 'The Supermultiplier-Cum-Finance. An Application to the Credit-Led Boom Before the 2008 Crash.' *Review of Political Economy* 36 (5): 1827–1849.

Deleidi, M., and M. Mazzucato. 2019. 'Putting Austerity to Bed: Technical Progress, Aggregate Demand and the Supermultiplier.' *Review of Political Economy* 31 (3): 315–335.

Di Buchianico, S., E. Gallo, and A. Lofaro. 2024. 'Debt-Credit Flows and Stocks in a Supermultiplier Model with two Autonomous Demand Components: Consequences for Growth.' *Review of Political Economy* 36 (5): 1894–1914. https://doi.org/10.1080/09538259.2024.2375298.

Di Domenico, L., G. Ciaffi, and D. Romaniello 2024. 'The Monetary Theory of Production and the Supermultiplier: What Determines Savings?' *Review of Political Economy* 36 (5): 1746–1774.

Dvoskin, A., and M. T. Landau. 2024. 'Limits to Fiscal and Monetary Policy in Small Open Economies.' *Review of Political Economy* 36 (5): 1915–1942.

Fazzari, S. 2024. 'Supermultiplier Models, Demand Stagnation, and Monetary Policy: Inevitable March to the Lower Bound for Interest Rates?' *Review of Political Economy* 36 (5): 1801–1826.

Febrero, E., and F. Bermejo. 2024. 'Pensions as an Engine of Growth. An Approach to the Spanish Case Based on the Multiplier-Accelerator Model (a Sraffian Supermultiplier).' *Review of Political Economy* 36 (5): 1850–1875.

Fiebiger, B. 2024. 'Finance, Financial Adjustments and Alternative Closures in Neo-Kaleckian Models: The Paradoxes of Thrift and Costs in the Long-Run.' *Review of Political Economy* 36 (5): 1722–1745.

Freitas, F., and F. Serrano. 2015. 'Growth Rate and Level Effects, the Stability of the Adjustment of Capacity to Demand and the Sraffian Supermultiplier.' *Review of Political Economy* 27 (3): 258–281.

Hein, E., and R. Woodgate. 2021. 'Stability Issues in Kaleckian Models Driven by Autonomous Demand Growth — Harrodian Instability and Debt Dynamics.' *Metroeconomica* 72 (2): 388–404.

Kalecki, M. 1967. 'The Problem of Effective Demand with Tugan-Baranovsky and Rosa Luxemburg.' *Collected Works of Michał Kalecki*, 2.

Lavoie, M. 2016. 'Convergence Towards the Normal Rate of Capacity Utilization in Neo-K Aleckian Models: The Role of Non-Capacity Creating Autonomous Expenditures.' *Metroeconomica* 67 (1): 172–201.

Luxemburg, R. 1913 [2015]. *The Accumulation of Capital*. New York: Routledge.

Mandarino, G. V., C. H. Dos Santos, and A. C. M. e Silva. 2020. 'Workers' Debt-Financed Consumption: A Supermultiplier Stock–Flow Consistent Model.' *Review of Keynesian Economics* 8 (3): 339–364.

Morlin, G. S. 2022. 'Growth Led by Government Expenditure and Exports: Public and External Debt Stability in a Supermultiplier Model.' *Structural Change and Economic Dynamics* 62 (C): 586–598.

Pariboni, R. 2016. 'Household Consumer Debt, Endogenous Money and Growth: A Supermultiplier-Based Analysis.' *PSL Quarterly Review* 69 (278): 211–233.

Pedrosa, Í., L. Brochier, and F. Freitas. 2023. 'Debt Hierarchy: Autonomous Demand Composition, Growth and Indebtedness in a Supermultiplier Model.' *Economic Modelling* 126: 1–5.

Petrini, G., and L. Teixeira. 2023. 'Determinants of Residential Investment Growth Rate in the US Economy (1992–2019).' *Review of Political Economy* 35 (3): 702–719.

Rochon, L. P. 1999. 'The Creation and Circulation of Endogenous Money: A Circuit Dynamique Approach.' *Journal of Economic Issues* 33 (1): 1–21.

Serrano, F. 1995. 'Long Period Effective Demand and the Sraffian Supermultiplier.' *Contributions to Political Economy* 14 (1): 67–90.

Serrano, F., R. Summa, and V. G. Moreira. 2020. 'Stagnation and Unnaturally Low Interest Rates: A Simple Critique of the Amended New Consensus and the Sraffian Supermultiplier Alternative.' *Review of Keynesian Economics* 8 (3): 365–384.

Vaz, J. E. 2024. 'Impacts of US Interest Rates on Growth, Income Distribution, and Macroeconomic Policy Space in Developing Countries: A SFC Supermultiplier Model.' *Review of Political Economy* 36 (5): 1943–1963.

Woodgate, R., E. Hein, and R. Summa. 2024. 'Components of Autonomous Demand Growth and Financial Feedbacks: Implications for Growth Drivers and Growth Regime Analysis.' *Review of Political Economy* 36 (5): 2105–2115.

Finance, Financial Adjustments and Alternative Closures in Neo-Kaleckian Models: The Paradoxes of Thrift and Costs in the Long-Run

Brett Fiebiger

ABSTRACT
Heterodox economists debate if Keynesian/Kaleckian or Marxian/Harrodian results apply in the long-run. This paper explores different financial mechanisms in neo-Kaleckian models with the: (1) traditional closure of an endogenous utilisation rate; and, (2) supermultiplier closure where the utilisation rate is restored to its normal degree in the long-run. Keynesian/Kaleckian results are obtained regardless of the assumptions on the utilisation rate. Attention is also given to circuitist intra-period endogenous money financing relations, and to financial adjustments that increase the elasticity of household portfolio adjustments and firm liability-side management.

1. Introduction

Keynes's (1930) parable of the 'widow's cruse' is the forerunner to the 'paradox of thrift' of the *General Theory*. The widow's cruse appears in Kalecki's (1935) macrodynamics as a proposition that profits are generated by firm investment and capitalist consumption. For the neo-Kaleckian (NK) branch of post-Keynesian economics, the paradox of thrift and the paradox of costs are not just results with applicability to the real world, but also provide a yardstick to access whether an approach to macro modelling is consistent with the Keynes/Kalecki principle of effective demand (Lavoie 2014).

Neo-Marxian/neo-Harrodian (NMNH) authors advance the contrarian view that higher rates of capital accumulation require a higher saving rate and/or higher profit share (at least in the long-run).[1] Following Harrod (1939, 1960) those authors insist that the long-run is a realm where the actual utilisation rate must be at its desired cost-minimisation degree. The traditional NK closure of an endogenous utilisation rate is therefore criticised on the basis that it is only an unstable equilibrium. For critics, as the long-run equilibrium utilisation rate is the normal one, the canonical neo- and post-Kaleckian models are vulnerable to the problem of 'long-run Harrodian instability' aka the prospect that firms will instigate a strong and potentially destabilising

[1] See Duménil and Lévy (1999), Moudud (2009), Shaikh (2009) and the Harrodian "dual" economy of Skott and Ryoo (2008) and Skott (2010, 2020).

investment response whenever there is a non-trivial discrepancy between the actual and normal utilisation rates (hereafter the utilisation gap).[2]

The Sraffian branch of post-Keynesian economics is divided on whether the utilisation rate should be an accommodating variable in the long-run.[3] What matters here is that heterodox proponents of a classical-styled long-run equilibrium differ on whether effective demand is a determining variable of macroeconomic outcomes. NMNH hail so-called fully-adjusted positions as entailing the demise of Keynesian/Kaleckian results. Those who write under the banner of the Sraffian supermultiplier (SM) instead emphasise the key role played by semi-autonomous non-capacity generating expenditures in driving effective demand, and thereby the macro economy, towards its fully-adjusted position.[4]

The debate over the utilisation rate originates in the aspiration of Kaleckians to project certain modelling results into the long-run. The canonical NK model combines exogenous distribution with an endogenous utilisation rate. The novel result is the 'paradox of costs' where a higher wage share leads to higher rates of capacity utilisation, capital accumulation and profits. The NK model also obtains the 'paradox of thrift' that was a novelty of the neo-Keynesian model (Kaldor 1955–56; Robinson 1956). Yet, as the latter model combines endogenous distribution with an exogenous utilisation rate, it yields a negative relation between capital accumulation and the wage share. The paradox of costs drops out.

Kaleckians have offered a number of replies to their critics. One reply is that the normal utilisation rate could adjust to the actual rate (Lavoie 1995). A second reply formalises a range for the utilisation gap wherein firms do not alter their investment behaviour (Setterfield 2019). A third reply modifies the canonical NK model to allow for a convergence between the utilisation rate and a structurally-determined normal rate, through the combination of the SM adjustment mechanism that endogenises the output share of capacity investment, and a Harrodian adjustment mechanism that brings firms' expectations of the secular trend in sales growth in line with the long-run equilibrium rate of capital accumulation.[5] One motivation for the third reply is to allay the concerns of those who worry that a persistently large utilisation gap is akin to a missing feedback mechanism.

NMNH authors and some Kaleckians have in turn criticised the simplifying assumption in the canonical SM model of an exogenously-given growth rate of semi-autonomous demand expenditures. Skott (2019) doubts that the SM adjustment mechanism could take long-run Harrodian instability. Nikiforos (2018) and Blecker and Setterfield (2019) lament that the paradoxes of thrift and costs hold in Lavoie's (2016) NK-SM model only as 'level effects' (during the transition between steady-states), rather than as permanent growth effects, as in Kaleckian models that assume either an endogenous actual utilisation rate or that the normal utilisation rate adjusts endogenously to the actual rate.[6]

---

[2]The closure of an endogenous utilisation rate is shared by the canonical neo-Kaleckian model (Rowthorn 1981; Dutt 1984) and the canonical post-Kaleckian model (Bhaduri and Marglin 1990).

[3]See Palumbo and Trezzini (2003) for a critical Sraffian perspective on fully-adjusted positions.

[4]See Cesaratto (2015), Freitas and Serrano (2015), Serrano and Freitas (2017), Brochier and Macedo e Silva (2019), Girardi and Pariboni (2019), Brochier and Freitas (2020).

[5]See Allain (2015), Lavoie (2016), Dutt (2019), Cassetti (2020), Lavoie and Nah (2020), Fiebiger (2021, 2022), Hein and Woodgate (2021).

[6]Note that, while Nikiforos (2016, 2018) labels his approach endogeneity in the normal utilisation rate, he uses an unconventional definition of the utilisation rate. In conventional definitions his approach implies an *exogenous* utilisation rate and *endogenous* capital-to-full-capacity output ratio. See Fiebiger (2020) for a critical discussion.

Recent SM contributions have shown that the growth rate of semi-autonomous non-capacity generating expenditures can be easily endogenised, while Keynesian/Kaleckian results still apply in the long-run. Brochier and Macedo e Silva (2019) recover the paradoxes of thrift and costs as permanent growth effects in a Sraffian SM model that endogenises the semi-autonomous consumption expenditures of the household sector via wealth effects. Fiebiger (2021) obtains the same results in a NK-SM model that endogenises the growth rate of a Lernerian government's pure expenditures to an endogenous natural rate of employment. The integration of the demand-led SM closure into NK models has gone some way to resolving the utilisation debate. It is now clear that Keynesian/Kaleckian results do require any particular assumptions on the utilisation rate.

This paper reproduces the celebrated Keynesian/Kaleckian results with a focus on the concept of finance as well as portfolio and equity issuance adjustments. The analysis proceeds in Section Two with an overview of contemporary heterodox debates. Section Three presents a stock-flow consistent NK model with the traditional closure of an endogenous utilisation rate. Attention is given to circuitist intra-period endogenous money financing relations, ex-ante financial constraints and to extensions that increase both the elasticity of household portfolio adjustments and firm liability-side management. Section Four integrates the alternative SM closure. Concluding remarks are offered in Section Five.

2. Contemporary Heterodox Debates

As is well-known Bhaduri and Marglin's (1990) post-Kaleckian model — with its wage-led and profit-led demand regimes — was the neo-Marxian reply to the NK paradox of costs. An extensive literature has explored the empirics of wage-/profit-led demand regimes, albeit there is no consensus, due in part to differences in econometric techniques (Blecker and Setterfield 2019; Cauvel 2019). The protagonists are neo-Goodwinians and NK who utilise the post-Keynesian model (Stockhammer 2017). The former can be segmented into two groups: 'structuralist'[7] and 'Harrodian'.[8] Neo-Goodwinian (NK) empirical studies tend to report results that confirm their theoretical perspective that a faster rate of output growth is promoted by a more regressive (progressive) distribution of functional income.

Much of the literature has proceeded under the assumption that a pro-cyclical relation between the profit share and the utilisation rate and/or employment rate confirms neo-Goodwinian profit-led theory and discredits NK wage-led theory (von Arnim and Barrales 2015, p. 326). It is oft overlooked that NK models with overhead labour can generate a pro-cyclical profit share.[9] The abstraction from overhead labour points to a broader concern: are the causal chains of the wage-/profit-led models sufficiently complex to capture real world economic phenomena? Fiebiger and Lavoie (2019) point to the driving role in post-WWII US business cycles of Kalecki/Luxemburg 'external markets' in the form of dwelling investment and debt-financed consumption as one

---

[7]See Barbosa-Filho and Taylor (2006), von Arnim and Barrales (2015), Taylor et al. (2016), Tavani and Petach (2019, 2020), Barrales-Ruiz et al. (2020), Tavani and Zamparelli (2021).
[8]See Skott (1989, 2010), Skott and Zipperer (2012).
[9]See Rowthorn (1981), Lavoie (2014, Ch. 5), Lavoie and Nah (2020), Fiebiger (2022).

important missing causal chain. We wish to explore in more detail the issue of structural realism (or lack thereof).

2.1. Real Analysis with No Financial Assets and Harrod/Goodwin Loanable Funds

A large neo-Marxian literature has followed Harrod (1939, 1960) and Goodwin (1967) in considering a macro economy with no explicit financial relations let alone a financial sector. Such models have only one asset: the capital stock K. The working hypothesis is that 'saving' (somehow) finances investment. For Harrod (1939, 1960) it is aggregate saving. For Goodwin (1967) it is saving out of profits. He posits the classical saving assumptions: 'all wages consumed, all profits saved and invested' (Goodwin 1967, p. 54):

$$I_K = s_\pi \cdot \Pi = \Pi_U, \qquad s_\pi = 1 \tag{i}$$

where I_K is capacity investment, s_π is the saving rate, Π is profits and Π_U is retained profits. Models with equation i advance the limiting behavioural hypothesis that each sector always has zero net lending/borrowing (Fiebiger 2022). Here we can make some inroads by relaying that the net lending/borrowing aka net financial saving $\Delta NFA_i^f \cdot$ of any domestic sector i is equal to its net acquisition of financial assets ΔFA_i^f minus its net issuance of liabilities ΔL_i^f (with both flows before revaluation gains)[10] and, conceptually equivalent, to its revenues R_i minus expenditures E_i.

$$\Delta NFA_i^f \stackrel{\text{def}}{=} \Delta FA_i^f - \Delta L_i^f \equiv R_i - E_i \tag{ii}$$

Summed over all sectors aggregate net lending/borrowing is zero:

$$\sum_i \Delta NFA_i^f \stackrel{\text{def}}{=} \sum_i \Delta FA_i^f - \sum_i \Delta L_i^f \equiv \sum_i R_i - \sum_i E_i \equiv 0 \tag{iii}$$

Next we define a domestic sectors' saving S_i as its investment I_i plus it net financial saving:

$$S_i \stackrel{\text{def}}{=} I_i + \Delta NFA_i^f \tag{iv}$$

For firms its saving S_f is its investment I_f; in fixed investment I_K and inventory investment ΔIN, plus its net lending/borrowing ΔNFA_f^f. In a closed economy the firm sector's saving is also equal to its undistributed profits Π_U (and plus foreign earnings retained abroad in an open economy). Thus:

$$S_f \stackrel{\text{def}}{=} I_f + \Delta NFA_f^f \equiv \Pi_U, \quad I_f = I_K + \Delta IN \tag{v}$$

Now, if inventory investment is zero (i.e., $\Delta IN = 0$), then:

$$\Pi_U \equiv I_K + \Delta NFA_f^f \tag{vi}$$

The classical saving assumption that $I_K = \Pi_U$ can only hold if $\Delta NFA_f^f = 0$. The one real asset neo-Goodwinian models describe an economy without any financial assets and

[10] The superscript f is used to denote *flows* before revaluation changes. See Lindner (2015).

counterpart liabilities. An assumption that *each* individual sector *always* has $\Delta NFA_i^f \stackrel{\text{def}}{=} \Delta FA_i^f - \Delta L_i^f \equiv R_i - E_i = 0$ is a strong behavioural hypothesis that lacks empirical support (Fiebiger 2022). It also lacks theoretical support:

> The absurd ... idea that an act of individual saving is just as good for effective demand as an act of individual consumption, has been fostered by the fallacy ... that an increased desire to hold wealth, being much the same thing as an increased desire to hold investments, must ... provide a stimulus to their production ... [Yet,] there is always an alternative to the ownership of real capital-assets, namely the ownership of money and debts. (Keynes 1936, pp. 211–212)

Modelling demand leakages requires formal attention to the net lending/borrowing of sectors. Thrift in the sense of not spending a portion on income is necessarily a sectoral-level phenomenon (i.e., $\Delta NFA_i^f \stackrel{\text{def}}{=} FA_i^f - \Delta L_i^f \equiv R_i - E_i > 0$) that has no counterpart at the aggregate-level (as $\sum_i \Delta NFA_i^f \stackrel{\text{def}}{=} \sum_i \Delta FA_i^f - \sum_i \Delta L_i^f \equiv \sum_i R_i - \sum_i E_i \equiv 0$). At the aggregate-level the net financial saving of all sectors must net out to zero such that aggregate saving is a *literal* accounting record of aggregate investment.

$$\sum_i S_i \stackrel{\text{def}}{=} \sum_i I_i + \sum_i \Delta NFA_i^f \stackrel{\text{def}}{=} \sum_i I_i + 0 \Rightarrow S \stackrel{\text{def}}{=} I, \quad \sum_i \Delta NFA_i^f \equiv 0 \qquad \text{(vii)}$$

We have interpreted the classical saving assumptions as implying that capacity investment equals undistributed profits. Some neo-Goodwinians entertain other assumptions. Taylor et al. (2016), Tavani and Petach (2019, 2020) and Tavani and Zamparelli (2021) suppose that households realise saving in the form of physical capital. A Keynesian monetary production economy requires money and debt relations.

2.2. Monetary Analysis with Explicit Financial Relations and Endogenous Money

The Cambridge growth models of the 1950s and 1960s gave insufficient attention to the financial side of the macro economy. Since then many post-Keynesian have sought to fill in the gaps. In this respect Godley and Lavoie's (2007) stock-flow consistent (SFC) modelling methodology is a seminal contribution. The SFC approach has allowed post-Keynesians to explore endogenous money financing relations and complex portfolio considerations. One debated issue is whether or not to include Tobin's q in the investment function.[11] High parameter values for Tobin q wealth effects in the investment and consumption functions can lead to neoclassical results. The relative strength of parameter values is also contested in the literature that explores various phenomena attributed to 'financialisation'.[12]

Lavoie and Godley's (2001–02) first SFC modelling foray came with an interesting result on the paradox of thrift. The authors utilised a complicated investment function with positive parameters for animal spirits, the utilisation rate, Tobin's q and cash flow (i.e., undistributed profits-to-capital ratio), and a negative parameter for firm interest payments. In the 'normal' ('puzzling') regime, where the investment function is more (less) responsive

[11]Tobin (1969) supposes that firm fixed investment is a positive function of q; the ratio of the market value of the capital stock (as proxied by corporate equities) divided by its replacement cost, and especially if q exceeds unity.

[12]See Lavoie (2008), Skott and Ryoo (2008), van Treeck (2009), Bernardo, Stockhammer, and Martínez (2015).

to the utilisation rate than Tobin's q, a decrease in the household sector's propensity to save in net financial terms out of disposable income has a positive (negative) long-run effect on the rate of capital accumulation. The normal (puzzling) regime thus lends support to the Keynesian/Kaleckian (Marxian/Harrodian) theoretical position.

Taylor (2004, Ch. 8) used the terminology of 'debt-led/debt-burdened' to specify whether an increase in the debt-to-capital ratio (aka leverage ratio) has a positive or negative effect on the utilisation rate. Lavoie and Godley's (2001–02) normal regime was interpreted as the case when a higher utilisation rate has a negative effect on the change in the leverage ratio. The alternative case was associated with the writings of Minsky (1975), and was also seen as more likely on the empirical front. Brochier and Freitas (2020) instead use the terminology of Steindlian (Minskyan) to denote whether a change in the utilisation rate (or rate of capital accumulation) has a negative (positive) effect on the leverage ratio. The terminology of Steindlian/Minskyan regimes is more cogent.[13]

Franke (2016, p. 535) refers to debt-led/debt-burdened demand regimes, although as his analytical model refers to the effect of an increase in Tobin's q on the rate of capital accumulation, the terminology of q-led/q-burdened is more appropriate. With rentiers maintaining a constant portfolio composition between bonds and equities, and firms paying a fixed dividend rate on equities, he finds that long-run macro stability requires the q-led accumulation regime. An implication is that the paradox of thrift does not hold in the long-run. Taylor (2004, p. 277) can be interpreted similarly as he notes that his 'model behaves in Keynesian fashion in the short run, but is more classically inclined in the steady state'. As no further remarks are made, and a reference is given to Duménil and Lévy (1999), it seems that he has in mind a long-run thrift-driven profit-led accumulation regime. Ryoo (2013) likewise points to Minsky (1975) in support of debt-led and q-led utilisation and accumulation regimes.

The causal chains of the debt-led (or q-led) utilisation regime or accumulation regime are theoretically ambiguous. A higher leverage ratio could occur due to a higher interest rate, a lower profit retention rate, a lower profit share, a lower household consumption propensity, an increase in the proportion of debt issues in firms' funding requirements, a lower rate of price inflation or a change in output growth. Tobin's q could increase, besides some of the points just mentioned, due to a shift in the household's sector portfolio composition towards equities. Unless we know what variables are causing firms to incur higher leverage (or inflate q), it cannot be known if the causal mechanisms of the debt-led (q-led) utilisation/accumulation regimes are Keynesian/Kaleckian or Marxian/Harrodian.

Skott (1988) presents a NMNH model where firms issue equities at a constant growth rate and households maintain a constant portfolio composition between deposits and equities. He considers an anti-Keynesian causal chain that runs from an increase in household thrift → higher equity demand → higher equity prices → higher Tobin's q → lower cost of finance → lower desired utilisation rate → faster rate of capital accumulation. Keynesian/Kaleckian intuition would suggest that a thrift-induced decrease in sales, by reducing profits and thus future dividends, would prompt a bear market shift away from equities into fixed-income instruments (and a flight to safety from

[13]Taylor's (2004, p. 276) interpretation of Lavoie and Godley (2001–02) is odd given that their two regimes refer to the relative strength of investment function parameters for the utilisation rate and Tobin's q. One could therefore say that the normal (puzzling) regime is more likely to generate results that are "q-burdened" ("q-led").

riskier corporate bonds into safe government bonds and foreign assets). Further, with a given monetary policy stance for the base interest rate, the thrift campaign will make it all the harder for firms to obtain external financing on reasonable terms due to the increased default and bankruptcy risks that attend lower sales.

There is a neoclassical flavour to Tobin q wealth effects. As Moore (1973, p. 543) observes on the inclusion of q into the investment function: '[it] leads back to the neoclassical conclusions of the control of the rate of accumulation by [household] saver preferences'.[14] Godley and Lavoie's (2007) 'normal' regime embeds the empirical finding that firm fixed investment is more responsive to changes in the quantity of real output (i.e., the utilisation rate) than to changes in the cost of finance (e.g., Tobin's q). Anti-Keynesian modelling results obtained via Tobin q wealth effects also tend to assume perverse valuation effects. Normal (perverse) valuation effects occur when the market value of corporate equities moves in the same (opposite) direction to the book value of the firm. The models in Section Three and Section Four will show that Keynesian/Kaleckian results are more likely with normal valuation effects. An extension will discard the restrictive assumptions of a fixed equity supply and an inelastic household portfolio composition.

Another modelling focus will be endogenous money financial relations along the lines of the Franco-Italian circuit schools (Section 3.1.1).[15] A circuitist approach to finance will be sketched that includes intra-period repayments of bank loans and *ex-ante* financial constraints on firm investment. The approach can be contrasted with the *ex-post* financial constraints of NMNH models. Skott (1988) and Skott and Ryoo (2008) present the following equation (and Ryoo (2013) a rearranged version):

$$I_K = \phi \cdot (\Pi - i \cdot \mathcal{L}) + \Delta\mathcal{L} + p_e \cdot \Delta e, \qquad \phi \cdot (\Pi - i \cdot \mathcal{L}) = \Pi_U$$

where the new variables are the retention rate ϕ, the interest rate i, loans $\mathcal{L}$, the price of firm equities p_e and the quantity issued e. For NMNH the above equation is meant to be interpreted as an ex-ante financial constraint on firm investment. Apparently, when households or firms are thriftier, this will increase the financial resources available to firms to invest. The equation is, however, just an ex-post budget identity. Firm' access to finance is not governed by household thrift. Nor are the household sector's net financial saving and firm sector's undistributed profits independent sources of 'loanable funds' that finance investment. Changes in $\Delta\mathcal{L} + p_e \cdot \Delta e$ must have an equal offsetting effect on the *same side* of the NMNH financial constraint equation (rather than in firm investment on the right-hand side) because $\phi \cdot (\Pi - i \cdot \mathcal{L}) = \Pi_U$, $\Pi_U \equiv I_K + \Delta NFA_f^f$ and $\Delta NFA_f^f \stackrel{def}{=} -(\Delta\mathcal{L} + p_e \cdot \Delta e)$.

3. A Traditional Neo-Kaleckian Model

This section presents a NK model with the traditional closure of an endogenous utilisation rate of productive capacity. The traditional NK model is cast in the short- to medium-run where the forces of gravitation towards a normal degree of capacity utilisation are assumed to not apply.

[14] See Petri (2004) for a critical discussion of how the integration of Tobin's q into mainstream models tends to replicate the neoclassical assumption of an inverse relation between firm fixed investment and the interest rate.

[15] The important task of integrating the SM approach with the post-Keynesian endogenous money approach has also received development from Cesaratto and Di Bucchianico (2020) and Cesaratto and Pariboni (2022).

Table 1. Transaction matrix for simple NK model.

	Households	Firms: Current	Firms: Capital	Banks: Current	Banks: Capital	Σ
Consumption	$-C$	$+C$				0
Gross Investment		$+I_K$	$-I_K$			0
Wage Bill	$+WB$	$-WB$				0
Depreciation Allow.		$-DA$	$+DA$			0
Entrep. Net Profits	$+\Pi^n_{D,f}$	$-\Pi^n_f$	$+\Pi^n_{U,f}$			0
Bank Profits	$+\Pi_{D,b}$			$-\Pi_b$	$+\Pi_{U,b}$	0
Interest on Deposits	$+i_{\mathcal{D},-1} \cdot \mathcal{D}_{-1}$			$-i_{\mathcal{D},-1} \cdot \mathcal{D}_{-1}$		0
Interest on Loans		$-i_{\mathcal{L},-1} \cdot \mathcal{L}_{-1}$		$+i_{\mathcal{L},-1} \cdot \mathcal{L}_{-1}$		0
Δ Deposits	$-\Delta\mathcal{D}$				$+\Delta\mathcal{D}$	0
Δ Loans			$+\Delta\mathcal{L}$		$-\Delta\mathcal{L}$	0
Δ Firm Equities	$-p_e \cdot \Delta e$		$+p_e \cdot \Delta e$			0
Σ	0	0	0	0	0	0

3.1. NK Baseline Model

The baseline NK model describes a closed economy with no public sector. It has three sectors: households, firms and banks. For simplicity we assume there is no inflation, productivity growth or population growth. The transaction matrix and balance sheet are shown in Tables 1 and 2.

Equations 1–9 define output Y, gross investment I_K, net investment I^n_K, the capital stock K, the rate of capital accumulation g_K, the utilisation rate u, full-capacity output Y_{fc}, gross profits Π and the wage bill WB. Fixed capital depreciates at the rate δ. Full-capacity output evolves over time with K and a constant capital-to-full-capacity-output ratio v. The investment function has two parameters: γ for 'animal spirts' and γ_u for the utilisation gap. As a simplification the wage share ϖ is constant.[16]

$$Y = C + I_K \qquad \text{Output} \qquad (1)$$

$$I_K = I^n_K + \delta \cdot K_{-1}, \quad \bar{\delta} > 0 \qquad \text{Gross capacity investment} \qquad (2)$$

$$I^n_K = K_{-1} \cdot g_K \qquad \text{Net capacity investment} \qquad (3)$$

$$K = K_{-1} \cdot (1 + g_K) \qquad \text{Capital stock} \qquad (4)$$

$$g_K = \gamma + \gamma_u \cdot u_{-1}, \quad \bar{\gamma} > 0, \bar{\gamma}_u > 0 \qquad \text{Growth of capital stock} \qquad (5)$$

$$u = Y/Y_{fc} \qquad \text{Capacity utilisation rate} \qquad (6)$$

$$Y_{fc} = K_{-1}/v, \quad \bar{v} > 0 \qquad \text{Full-capacity output} \qquad (7)$$

$$\Pi = Y - WB \qquad \text{Gross profits} \qquad (8)$$

$$WB = \varpi \cdot Y, \quad 0 < \bar{\varpi} < 1 \qquad \text{Wage bill} \qquad (9)$$

[16]The model implicitly assumes that firms set prices as a constant mark-up over production costs. An explicit pricing equation could be easily added; however, doing so would just add complexity (as output variables would need to be distinguished into real and nominal magnitudes) while making no difference to the modelling dynamics. See Lavoie and Nah (2020) and Fiebiger (2022) for NK-SM models that can generate an endogenous and pro-cyclical profit share through the addition of fixed overhead labour. The latter also extends the model to include a conflicting-claims approach to inflation that assumes the radical price adjustment mechanism.

Table 2. Balance sheet for simple NK model.

	Households	Firms	Banks	Σ
Capital Stock		$+K$		$+K$
Deposits	$+\mathcal{D}$		$-\mathcal{D}$	0
Loans		$-\mathcal{L}$	$+\mathcal{L}$	0
Firm Equities	$+p_e \cdot e$	$-p_e \cdot e$		0
Bank Equity	$+\mathcal{E}_b$		$-\mathcal{E}_b$	0
Balance (net worth)	$-V$	0	0	$-K$
Σ	0	0	0	0

Next we list the equations of the firm sector. Equations 10–16 define respectively entrepreneurial net profits Π_f^n, depreciation allowances DA, firms' distributed profits $\Pi_{D,f}$, firms' net undistributed profits $\Pi_{U,f}^n$, firms' deficit DEF, loans $\mathcal{L}$ and the equity supply e_s. Firms pay interest on the period opening stock of loans at the loan rate $i_\mathcal{L}$ contracted in the previous period. Dividends are also lagged: set as a fixed portion $1 - \phi$ of last period's net profits. As per Lavoie and Godley (2001–02) firms issue equities as a fixed share χ of the net investment undertaken in the last period.

$$\Pi_f^n = \Pi - DA - i_{\mathcal{L},-1} \cdot \mathcal{L}_{-1}, \quad \bar{i}_\mathcal{L} > 0 \quad \text{Entrepreneurial net profits} \tag{10}$$

$$DA = \delta \cdot K_{-1} \quad \text{Firm depreciation allowances} \tag{11}$$

$$\Pi_{D,f} = (1 - \phi) \cdot \Pi_{f,-1}^n, \quad \bar{\phi} > 0 \quad \text{Firm distributed profits} \tag{12}$$

$$\Pi_{U,f}^n = \Pi_f^n - \Pi_{D,f} \quad \text{Firm net undistributed profits} \tag{13}$$

$$DEF = I_K^n - \Pi_{U,f}^n \quad \text{Firm deficit} \tag{14}$$

$$\mathcal{L} = \mathcal{L}_{-1} + DEF - p_e \cdot \Delta e_s \quad \text{Bank loans} \tag{15}$$

$$e_s = e_{s,-1} + \chi \cdot I_{K,-1}^n / p_e, \quad \bar{\chi} > 0 \quad \text{Firm equities supply} \tag{16}$$

Firms are corporate businesses while banks are noncorporate businesses. Equations 17–23 define respectively bank profits Π_b, the loan rate $i_\mathcal{L}$ as a fixed mark-up $m_\mathcal{D}$ on the deposit rate $i_\mathcal{D}$, banks' dividend $\Pi_{D,b}$, banks' undistributed profits $\Pi_{U,b}$, bank equity $\mathcal{E}_b$, the deposit supply $\mathcal{D}_s$ and the demand for deposits $\mathcal{D}_d$. Banks retain a portion of profits κ to meet regulatory capital requirements.[17]

$$\Pi_b = i_{\mathcal{L}-1} \cdot \mathcal{L}_{-1} - i_{\mathcal{D},-1} \cdot \mathcal{D}_{s,-1} \quad \text{Bank profits} \tag{17}$$

$$i_\mathcal{L} = i_\mathcal{D} + m_\mathcal{L}, \quad \bar{i}_\mathcal{D} > 0, \bar{m}_\mathcal{L} > 0 \quad \text{Bank loan rate} \tag{18}$$

$$\Pi_{D,b} = \Pi_b - \Pi_{U,b} \quad \text{Bank distributed profits} \tag{19}$$

$$\Pi_{U,b} = \mathcal{E}_b - \mathcal{E}_{b,-1} \quad \text{Bank undistributed profits} \tag{20}$$

$$\mathcal{E}_b = \kappa \cdot \mathcal{L}, \quad \bar{\kappa} > 0 \quad \text{Proprietors' equity in banks} \tag{21}$$

$$\mathcal{D}_s = \mathcal{L} - \mathcal{E}_b \quad \text{Bank deposit supply} \tag{22}$$

[17]The model thus overlooks banks' operating costs and fixed investment, which while unrealistic, is a standard simplifying assumption in SFC models that include banks.

$$\mathcal{D}_d = \mathcal{D}_{d,-1} + \Delta NFA_h^f - p_e \cdot \Delta e_d \quad \text{Bank deposit demand} \tag{23}$$

Equations 24–31 list the household sector's equations; respectively, disposable income YD, consumption C as a positive function of disposable income α_1 and the period start stock of wealth α_2, household net financial saving ΔNFA_h^f, household wealth V, the equity share in household wealth net of bank equity λ, the equity yield r_e, the price of equities p_e and equity demand e_d. Household sector portfolio demand for equities depends on a constant parameter λ_0 and another parameter λ_1 for the net return differential between the equity yield and the deposit rate. As is standard in SFC models the redundant equation is that which equates the supply of, and demand for, deposits.

$$YD = WB + \Pi_{D,f} + \Pi_{D,b} + i_{\mathcal{D},-1} \cdot \mathcal{D}_{d,-1} \quad \text{Household income} \tag{24}$$

$$C = \alpha_1 \cdot YD + \alpha_2 \cdot V_{-1}, \quad 0 < \bar{\alpha}_2 < \bar{\alpha}_1 < 1 \quad \text{Household induced consumption} \tag{25}$$

$$\Delta NFA_h^f = YD - C \quad \text{Household net financial saving} \tag{26}$$

$$V = V_{-1} + \Delta NFA_h^f + \Delta p_e \cdot e_{d,-1} + \Pi_{U,b} \quad \text{Household wealth} \tag{27}$$

$$\lambda = \lambda_0 + \lambda_1 \cdot (r_{e,-1} - i_{\mathcal{D}}), \quad \bar{\lambda}_0 > 0, \bar{\lambda}_1 > 0 \quad \text{Household equity demand} \tag{28}$$

$$r_e = (\Pi_{D,f} + \Delta p_e \cdot i_{d,-1})/(p_{e,-1} \cdot e_{d,-1}) \quad \text{Return on firm equities} \tag{29}$$

$$p_e = \lambda \cdot (V - \mathcal{E}_b)/e_d \quad \text{Price of firm equities} \tag{30}$$

$$e_d = e_s \quad \text{Firm equities demand} \tag{31}$$

3.1.1. Extension 1: Initial Finance and Credit Constraints

Kalecki (1935) and Keynes (1937) contemplate a production process with intra-period effluxes and refluxes of bank money. The monetary circuit tradition followed suit. In the simplest circuit model banks supply initial finance to firms only for production costs. Seccareccia (1996), Rochon (1999) and Parguez and Seccareccia (2000) all recognise that banks may also supply initial finance for final purchases of capital-goods. The first extension will integrate a circuitist approach to investment finance along those lines. We will also build on Le Heron and Mouakil's (2008) modelling of ex-ante financial constraints.

Equations 32–15a define respectively firms' desired finance demand $\mathcal{F}_I^d$, desired net capacity investment $I_K^{n,d}$, net capacity investment I_K^n, the supply of initial finance $\mathcal{F}_I$, an ex-ante credit-constraining function for Kalecki's (1937) principle of 'lenders' risk' LR, the net undistributed profit-to-capital ratio r_U^n, intra-period loan repayments $\mathcal{F}_R$ and the stock of loans $\mathcal{L}$. We will refer shorthand to the baseline and extension one models, respectively, as BL and E1. In the E1 model the amount of initial finance that banks supply to firms for their fixed investment depends on an evaluation of creditworthiness. Lenders' risk is a positive function of the current loan rate and a negative function of the net undistributed profit rate.[18] In Circuit theory, firms issues liabilities that households can acquire after the sales period, and do so to obtain monetary liquidity to pay down the initial finance. Intra-period loan repayments are therefore given by the monetary liquidity embodied in firms' gross undistributed profits plus the proceeds from new equity issues $p_e \cdot \Delta_{e_S}$.

$$\mathcal{F}_I^d = I_K^n + \delta \cdot K_{-1} \quad \text{Desired finance demand} \quad (32)$$

$$I_K^{n,d} = K_{-1} \cdot g_K \quad \text{Desired net capacity investment} \quad (33)$$

$$I_K^n = \mathcal{F}_I - \delta \cdot K_{-1} \quad \text{Net capacity investment} \quad (3a)$$

$$\mathcal{F}_I = \mathcal{F}_I^d \cdot (1 - LR) \quad \text{Finance supply (capacity investment)} \quad (34)$$

$$LR = \tau_0 + \tau_1 \cdot i_{\mathcal{L}} - \tau_2 \cdot r_{U,-1}^n, \quad \bar{\tau}_0 < 0, 0 < \bar{\tau}_1 < \bar{\tau}_2 \quad \text{Lenders risk} \quad (35)$$

$$r_U^n = \Pi_{U,f}^n / K_{-1} \quad \text{Net undistributed profit rate} \quad (36)$$

$$\mathcal{F}_R = \Pi_{U,f}^n + DA + p_e \cdot \Delta_{e_S} \quad \text{Intra-period loan repayments} \quad (37)$$

$$\mathcal{L} = \mathcal{L}_{-1} + \mathcal{F}_I - \mathcal{F}_R \quad \text{Bank loans} \quad (15a)$$

3.1.2. Extension 2: A Profitability Effect on Equity Demand

In the second extension (E2) model a profitability effect on equity demand is incorporated, by adding into the household sector's portfolio equation, a parameter for the entrepreneurial net profit rate r_E^n. The rationale is that the corporate sector's profit reporting season typically sees financial markets respond strongly to announcements of future dividends and the anticipated capital gains (losses).

$$\lambda = \lambda_0 + \lambda_1 \cdot (r_{e,-1} - i_D) + \lambda_2 \cdot r_E^n, \quad \bar{\lambda}_2 > 0 \quad \text{Household equity demand} \quad (28a)$$

$$r_E^n = \Pi_f^n / K_{-1} \quad \text{Entrepreneurial net profit rate} \quad (38)$$

3.1.3. Extension 3: Enhanced Household Portfolio Elasticity and Firm Liability-Side Management

The E2 model permits greater elasticity in the household sector's financial portfolio composition than the BL and E1 models. In the third extension (E3) model we augment that elasticity by subjecting the λ_0 parameter in the household equity demand portfolio equation to bounded endogeneity. It is now being supposed that the demand for equities, as captured by the λ_0 parameter, is a positive function of the discrepancy between the equity yield and a conventional equity yield r_e^C.[19] The latter is a fixed mark-up $\mathfrak{m}_e$ over the deposit rate. Equations 39–42 enhance portfolio elasticity within the boundaries given by specified minimum and maximum portfolio compositions of equities, respectively, λ^L and λ^H. Increasing the λ_1 parameter is another option although that can lead to

[18] The importance of firms' "internal funds" to fixed investment has received attention from Kalecki (1937), Steindl (1952 [1976]), Minsky (1975) and Fazzari, Hubbard, and Petersen (1988).

[19] The conventional equity yield is that which households use as a benchmark to inform portfolio decisions; in the model r_e^C is held constant for pedagogical purposes, but would in reality be a slow-adjusting variable that is informed by recent experiences of a normal financial return and the future expectations thereof.

excessive volatility.

$$\lambda_0 = \lambda_{0,-1} + \eta \cdot \mathfrak{b}_1 \cdot \mathfrak{b}_2 \cdot (r_{e,-1} - r_e^C), \quad \bar{\eta} > 0 \quad \text{Household equity demand parameters} \tag{39}$$

$$r_e^C = i_{\mathcal{D}} + \mathfrak{m}_e, \quad \bar{\mathfrak{m}}_e > 0 \quad \text{Conventional equity yield} \tag{40}$$

$$\mathfrak{b}_1 = \begin{cases} 1, & \textit{iff } \lambda_{-1} > \lambda^L \\ 0, & \textit{iff } \lambda_{-1} \leq \lambda^L \end{cases}, \quad \bar{\lambda}^L > 0 \tag{41}$$

Logical functions for composition of equity demand in household portfolio

$$\mathfrak{b}_2 = \begin{cases} 1, & \textit{iff } \lambda_{-1} < \lambda^H \\ 0, & \textit{iff } \lambda_{-1} \geq \lambda^H \end{cases}, \quad \bar{\lambda}^H > 0 \tag{42}$$

Next we allow firms to adjust equity issuance to support the financial valuation of the company subject to the net earnings-to-equity price ratio *epr*. Equation 43 supposes that firms will always seek to defend the financial value of the company whenever q fall bellows the low threshold q^L, and do so by reducing the proportion of equity issues in its ex-post funding requirements. Firms will also lower χ if q is below the higher threshold value q^* but only if epr_{-1} is above a conventional benchmark epr^C. Finally, if $q > q^*$ and $epr_{-1} < epr^C$, firms will then increase χ. The rationale is that if q is at an acceptable value (that prevents an undervalued takeover), the firm will seek to push *epr* up to its conventional benchmark by reducing the proportion of debt issues in its funding requirements, which will increase entrepreneurial net profits by lowering firm interest payments.[20] The conventional net earnings-to-equity price ratio is set at the conventional equity yield.

$$\chi = \chi_{-1} + \beta \cdot [\mathfrak{c}_1 \cdot (q_{-1} - q^L) + (\mathfrak{c}_2 \cdot \mathfrak{c}_3 + \mathfrak{c}_4 \cdot \mathfrak{c}_5) \cdot (q_{-1} - q^*)], \quad \bar{\beta} > 0 \tag{43}$$

Proportion of equity issuance in firms' funding requirements

$$q = (\mathcal{L} + p_e \cdot e_s)/K \quad \text{Tobin's } q \tag{44}$$

$$\mathfrak{c}_1 = \begin{cases} 1, & \textit{iff } q_{-1} < q^L \\ 0, & \textit{iff } q_{-1} \geq q^L \end{cases}, \quad \bar{q}^L > 0 \tag{45}$$

$$\mathfrak{c}_2 = \begin{cases} 1, & \textit{iff } q_{-1} < q^* \\ 0, & \textit{iff } q_{-1} \geq q^* \end{cases}, \quad \bar{q}^* = 1 \tag{46}$$

$$\mathfrak{c}_3 = \begin{cases} 1, & \textit{iff } epr_{-1} > epr^C \\ 0, & \textit{iff } epr_{-1} \leq epr^C \end{cases} \quad \text{Logical functions for firm equity issues} \tag{47}$$

[20]Reducing debt issues by increasing equity issues will also put downward pressures on equity prices.

$$c_4 = \begin{cases} 1, & iff\ q_{-1} > q^* \\ 0, & iff\ q_{-1} \leq q^* \end{cases} \tag{48}$$

$$c_5 = \begin{cases} 1, & iff\ epr_{-1} < epr^C \\ 0, & iff\ epr_{-1} \geq epr^C \end{cases} \tag{49}$$

$$epr = \Pi_f^n/(p_{e,-1} \cdot e_{d,-1}) \quad \text{Net earnings-to-equity price ratio} \tag{50}$$

$$epr^C = r_e^C \quad \text{Conventional } epr \tag{51}$$

3.2. Simulation A: Positive Shock to Alpha1 Consumption Propensity

The first simulation is a positive shock to the α_1 disposable income consumption propensity (Figure 1).[21] Looking first at the BL and E1 NK models, the increases in the rates of capacity utilisation (Panel A) and capital accumulation (Panel B) are greater in the E1 NK model, as the higher household consumption by boosting firms' net undistributed profits, thereby lessens the financial constraints on firm investment. The increases in u and g_K are even greater in the E2 NK model, as the increased profitability of firms spurs a higher demand for equities that pushes up Tobin's q (Panel C) and the equity-to-capital ratio e (Panel D), which impels a faster growth rate of output through induced-consumption wealth effects.

The results of the E3 NK model are strikingly different. The initial trajectories of u, g_K and q are broadly similar, albeit more elevated in the E3 NK model. Further, in contrast to the other models, u, g_K and q all stabilise at a significantly higher value in the E3 NK model. Part of the answer is that the greater elasticity of equity demand in the E3 NK model further lifts equity prices, which raises output growth through induced-consumption wealth effects, and that in turn contributes to a lower leverage ratio l (Panel E). The proportion of equities in the household sector's financial portfolio (Panel F) increases on account of the equity yield being higher than before the α_1 shock (Panel G).

Additionally, in the E3 NK model, firms decrease the rate of equity issues (Panel H) in view of Tobin's q falling below the high target q^* while the net earnings-to-equity price ratio is above its conventional benchmark (Panel I). Essentially, when $epr_{-1} > epr^C$, the firm regards the company as undervalued when q is less than q^* and intervenes by decreasing χ. If instead $epr_{-1} < epr^C$ the firm accepts that the company is overvalued and defends only the lower target q^L.

3.3. Simulation B: Positive Shock to Alpha1 Consumption Propensity with Tobin's q in the Investment Function

In Section 2.2 it was remarked that including Tobin's q into the investment function can lead to Marxian/Harrodian results. To explore this possibility we amend the investment

[21] Results reported are the percentage point deviations from the baseline scenario of a constant growth rate. Simulations were run with Joao Macalos's R software package: https://joaomacalos.github.io/sfcr/index.html.

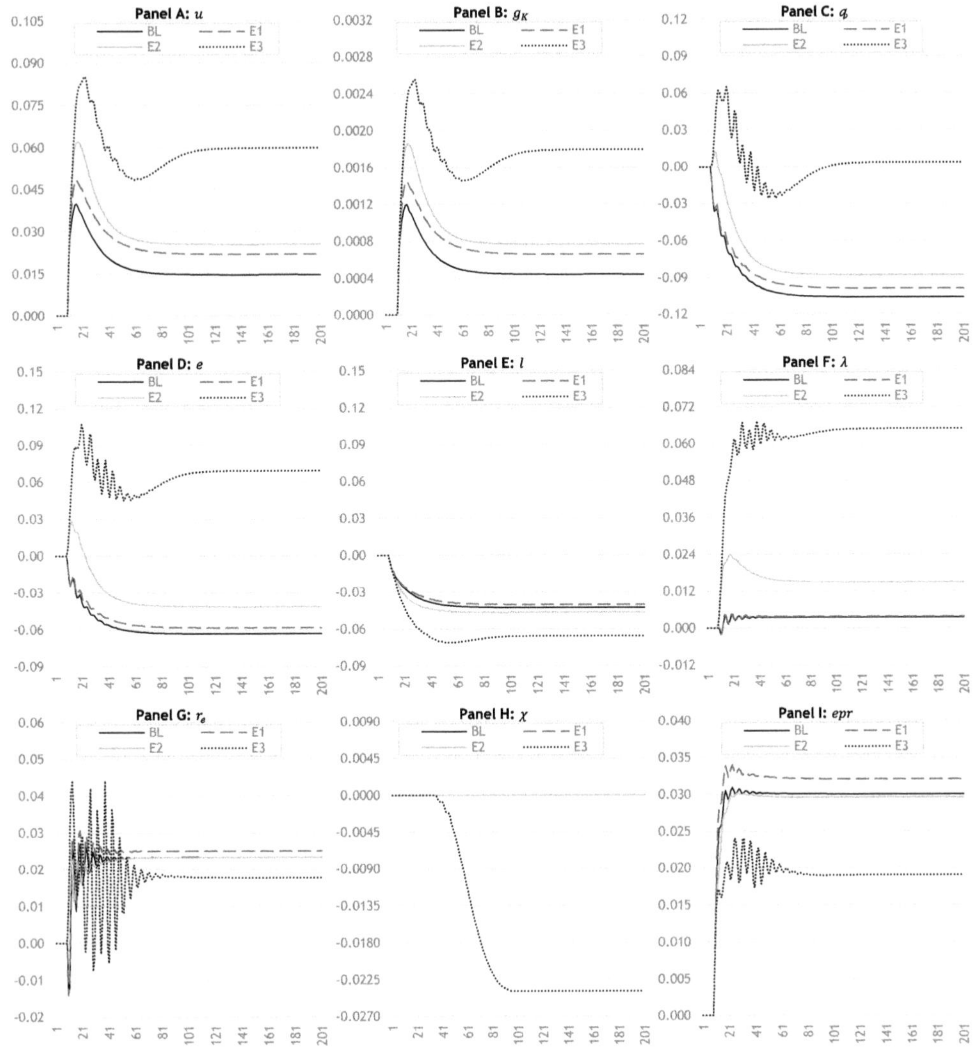

Figure 1. Positive shock to Alpha1 consumption propensity.

function as follows:

$$g_K = \gamma + \gamma_u \cdot u_{-1} + \gamma_q \cdot q_{-1}, \quad \bar{\gamma}_q > 0 \quad \text{Growth of capital stock} \tag{5a}$$

We now repeat the simulation of a positive shock to the α_1 consumption propensity with the new investment function (Figure 2). The BL, E1 and E2 NK models all yield Lavoie and Godley's (2001–02) puzzling regime, where a higher consumption propensity has a positive effect on the utilisation rate (Panel A), but a negative effect on the rate of capital accumulation (Panel B). In contrast the results of the E3 NK model for u, g_K and Tobin's q (Panel C) are very similar to the previous simulation; notably, the paradox of thrift still holds. We are not convinced that Tobin's q should even be included in the investment function let alone assigned a strong parameter value; nonetheless, the simulation shows that Keynesian/Kaleckian results can still be obtained so long as there is

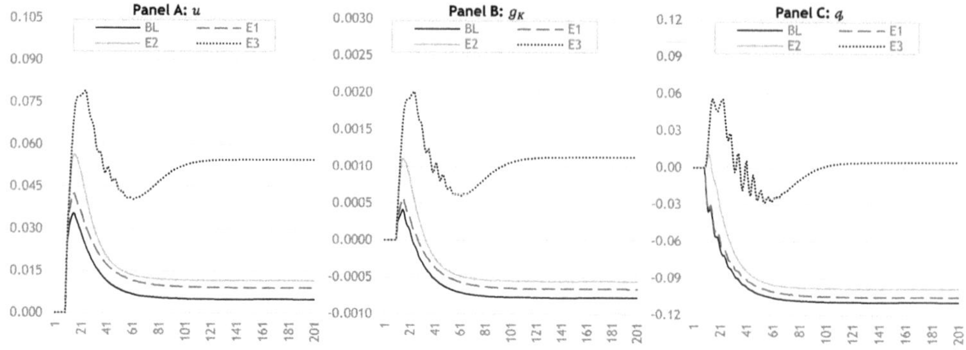

Figure 2. Positive shock to Alpha1 consumption propensity with Tobin's q in the investment function.

sufficient elasticity in household portfolio compositions and firms undertake liability-side management.

4. A Neo-Kaleckian Supermultiplier Model

The growing popularity of SM models can be attributed to the fact that the restoration of a normal utilisation rate occurs via a demand-led closure. This section begins by modifying the Section Three model, it then investigates if the paradoxes of thrift and costs hold, before examining the cyclical dynamics.

The inclusion of semi-autonomous consumption Z requires new equations for output and household net financial saving. The growth rate of semi-autonomous consumption g_Z depends on an exogenous parameter ψ_0 and an endogenous parameter ψ_1 that is responsive to the growth rate of disposable income g_{YD}.[22] Equations 56–57 specify that ψ_1 will change only if the discrepancy between the lagged growth rates of g_{YD} and g_Z exceeds a small threshold given by the term ε.

$$Y = C + Z + I_K \quad \text{Output} \tag{1a}$$

$$\Delta NFA_h^f = YD - C - Z \quad \text{Household net financial saving} \tag{28a}$$

$$Z = Z_{-1} \cdot (1 + g_Z) \quad \text{Semi-autonomous consumption} \tag{52}$$

$$g_Z = \psi_0 + \psi_1, \quad \bar{\psi}_0 > 0 \quad \text{Semi-autonomous consumption growth} \tag{53}$$

$$\psi_1 = \psi_{1,-1} + \zeta \cdot (\eth_1 + \eth_2) \cdot (g_{YD,-1} - g_{Z,-1}), \quad \bar{\zeta} > 0 \quad \text{Endogenous component of } g_Z \tag{54}$$

$$g_{YD} = \Delta YD / YD_{-1} \quad \text{Household disposable income growth} \tag{55}$$

[22]The rationale for making g_Z partially responsive to g_{YD} would seem to find some intellectual support from Keynes's (1936, p. 96) psychological law for consumption: '[people] are disposed, as a rule and on the average, to increase their consumption as their income increases, but not by as much as the increase in their income'.

$$\eth_1 = \begin{cases} 1, & iff\ g_{YD,-1} - g_{Z,-1} > \varepsilon \\ 0, & iff\ g_{YD,-1} - g_{Z,-1} < \varepsilon \end{cases}, \quad \bar{\varepsilon} > 0 \tag{56}$$

Logical functions for the growth rate of semi-autonomous consumption

$$\eth_2 = \begin{cases} 1, & iff\ g_{YD,-1} - g_{Z,-1} < \varepsilon \\ 0, & iff\ g_{YD,-1} - g_{Z,-1} > \varepsilon \end{cases} \tag{57}$$

Following Allain (2015) and Lavoie (2016) the investment function is now sensitive to the utilisation gap. The γ parameter must be reinterpreted as the trend in expected sales growth: it is now an endogenous variable that responds positively to the utilisation gap.[23]

$$g_K = \gamma + \gamma_u \cdot (u_{-1} - u_n), \quad \bar{\gamma}_u > 0, \bar{u}_n > 0 \quad \text{Growth of capital stock} \tag{5b}$$

$$\gamma = \gamma_{-1} + \mu \cdot \gamma_u \cdot (u_{-1} - u_n), \quad \bar{\mu} > 0 \quad \text{Expected sales} \tag{58}$$

Moving beyond an aggregated household sector, the wage share is divided into two portions; non-supervisory (NS) workers ϖ_w and managers ϖ_m. The consumption function now allows for a higher consumption propensity out of non-supervisory wage income α_{1w} *vis-à-vis* other disposable income α_{1m}.

$$WB = (\varpi_w + \varpi_m) \cdot Y, \quad 0 > \bar{\varpi}_m > \bar{\varpi}_w > 1 \quad \text{Wage bill} \tag{9a}$$

$$C = \alpha_{1w} \cdot \varpi_w \cdot Y + \alpha_{1m} \cdot (YD - \varpi_w \cdot Y) + \alpha_2 \cdot V_{-1}, \quad 0 < \bar{\alpha}_2 < \bar{\alpha}_{1m} < \bar{\alpha}_{1w} < 1 \quad \text{Household induced consumption} \tag{25a}$$

We are also interested in personal income distribution shifts that do not affect the profit share. In such simulations equation 9 for the wage bill $WB = \varpi \cdot Y$ is reinserted. We also add an equation for the consumption function with a term for the share of NS workers in the wage bill φ.

$$C = \alpha_{1w} \cdot \varpi \cdot \varphi \cdot Y + \alpha_{1m} \cdot (YD - \varpi \cdot \varphi \cdot Y) + \alpha_2 \cdot V_{-1} \quad \bar{\varphi} > 0 \quad \text{Household induced consumption} \tag{25b}$$

Another amendment is that the λ_2 parameter in the household portfolio equation is changed to a discrepancy between the entrepreneurial net profit rate and its trend rate $\tilde{r}^n_E$. The loan rate and net undistributed net profit rate in the lenders' risk equation are likewise changed to actual vs trend gaps.

$$\lambda = \lambda_0 + \lambda_1 \cdot (r_{e,-1} - i_{\mathcal{D}}) + \lambda_2 \cdot (r^n_E - \tilde{r}^n_E) \quad \text{Household portfolio parameters} \tag{28b}$$

$$LR = \tau_1 \cdot (i_{\mathcal{L}} - \tilde{i}_{\mathcal{L}}) - \tau_2 \cdot (r^n_{U,-1} - \tilde{r}^n_{U,-1}) \quad \text{Lenders risk} \tag{35a}$$

The NK-SM model is the equations of the E3 NK model subject to the above amendments.[24]

[23]See Fiebiger (2021, 2022) for other formulations of the expected sales adjustment mechanism.
[24]Some of the parameter and threshold variables are also modified.

4.1. Simulation C: Shocks to Wage Variables

The simulations of shocks to wage variables have four cases: (1) a higher wage share for NS workers ϖ_w; (2) a higher wage share for managers ϖ_m; (3) a higher φ that increases (decreases) the wage share of NS workers (managers); and, (4) a lower φ. The reports are shown in Figure 3. With the utilisation rate returning to its normal rate (Panel A), the more interesting results are those for the growth rates of capital accumulation (Panel B) and semi-autonomous consumption (Panel C). Increases in ϖ_w and φ have the greatest positive effect on the equilibrium growth rate, which is expected, given the higher consumption propensity of NS workers. A higher ϖ_m is also expansionary such that the paradox of costs holds even for managers; conversely, a lower φ that increases the manager wage share at the expense of the NS worker wage share has a contractionary effect on the equilibrium growth rate.

Tobin's q gravitates back towards its initial value in all of the cases (Panel D) through the workings of the model's financial-side adjustments (rather than through neoclassical real-side investment function adjustments).[25] The cases where the profit share is reduced lead initially to a lower equity yield (Panel E) that in turn impels a sustained portfolio shift away from equities (Panel F); in contrast, the portfolio composition gradually returns to its initial value in the cases of changes to φ. Kaleckians acknowledge that the paradox of costs may get diminished in an open-economy setting (Blecker and Setterfield 2019). Our findings on the expansionary effects of a higher φ are interesting as it implies that, if NS workers could gain a higher wage share at the expense of managers, there would be no detrimental implications for external competiveness. Reversing the post-1980 shift in wage income from NS workers to managers would go a long way towards overcoming stagnationist tendencies.

4.2. Simulation D: Positive Shocks to Consumption Propensities

The next simulation is a positive shock to the consumption propensities for NS worker wage income, other disposable income and lagged wealth. The results are broadly similar although there is greater cyclical oscillation in the case of the α_2 parameter (Figure 4). In all cases the paradox of thrift holds in the long-run as permanent growth effects. Those results reflect in part how we have endogenised the growth rate of semi-autonomous consumption. Equations 53–57 tend to ensure that, if a change in a variable has an initial expansionary output effect, then that will persist into the long-run.

4.3. Simulation E: Positive Alpha1 Shock with High Expected Sales Adjustment Speed

Our final simulation will reveal the cyclical patterns of the NK-SM model. We again subject the α_{1w} consumption propensity to a positive stock. Although this time the adjustment speed parameter μ for excepted sales is set at a sufficiently high level to generate persistent cyclical oscillations.

[25]Greater variation in the long-run equilibrium value of Tobin's q could be obtained by introducing low and high parameter thresholds for the equity yield in equation 39 and into the logical functions for the net earnings-to-equity price ratio in equation 43. However, as such extensions have only a comparatively minor influence on the equilibrium growth rate, we limit ourselves to the case given by equations 39–51.

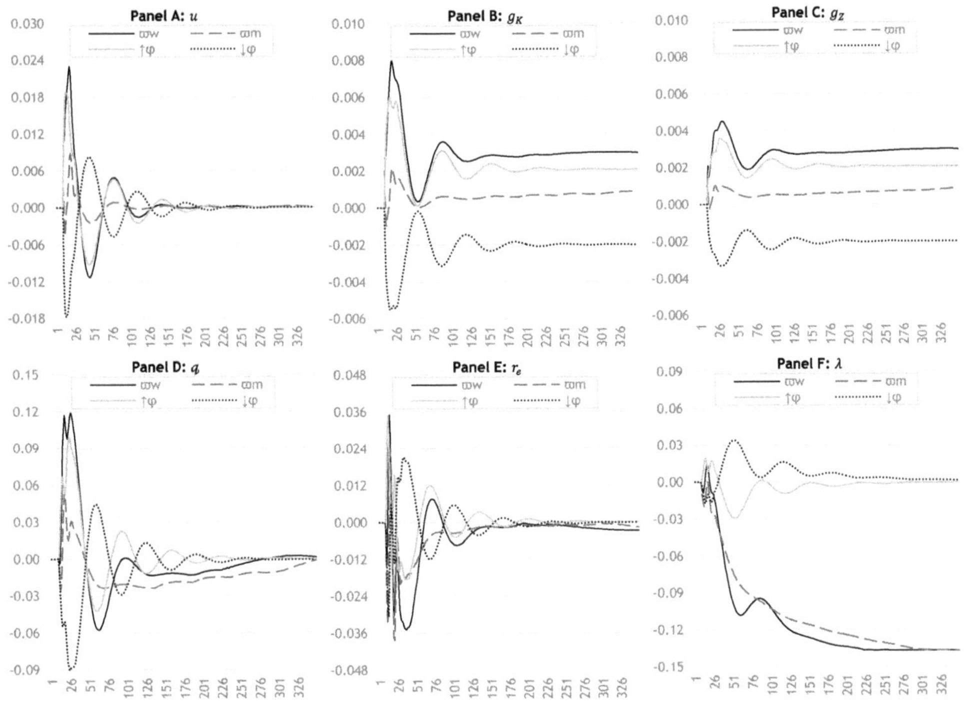

Figure 3. Shocks to wage variables.

The results are shown in Figure 5. Increases in the utilisation rate lower the leverage ratio (Panel A); hence, the patterns fit the Steindlian utilisation regime and 'paradox of debt'. In contrast, as the leverage ratio increases (decreases) when g_K is above (below) the equilibrium growth rate (Panel B) determined by g_Z (which shifts outwards and also oscillates in the simulation), the patterns fit the Minskyan accumulation regime. Although the story differs from Minsky (1975), who assumes that increases in firm leverage are initially an expansionary force (via Tobin q investment and consumption wealth effects), but by increasing financial fragility eventually prompt a shift from a debt-led to a debt-burdened accumulation regime. In the NK-SM model the leverage ratio increases when households become thriftier and thus constrain upward instability in growth processes.[26] Macro stability prevails as the household net financial saving rate $s_h^f = \Delta NFA_h^f / YD$ moves in the same direction, albeit with a lag, as the rate of capital accumulation (Panel C). In essence: g_Z endogenises s_h^f which bounds g_K.[27]

The output shares of fixed investment h (Panel D) and household net financial saving Δnfa_h^f (Panel E) both lag the utilisation rate; in contrast, the output share of semi-autonomous consumption z leads the utilisation rate (Panel F). The dynamics of SM models differ from neo-Goodwinian models where capacity investment leads the utilisation Rate. Another difference is that the latter also predict that the net lending/borrowing

[26]Debt-burdened patterns emerge, not as a result of negative investment function parameters for I (or $i \cdot \mathcal{L}/K$), but due to a casual chain that runs an increase in g_K relative to $g_Z \rightarrow$ higher s_h^f (and I) $\rightarrow$ lower $u \rightarrow$ slower g_K.

[27]The NK model endogenises s_h^f through the α_2 parameter; however, the inclusion of Z drastically increases the NK-SM model's stabilising properties by making s_h^f increase (decrease) the further that g_K is above (below) g_Z.

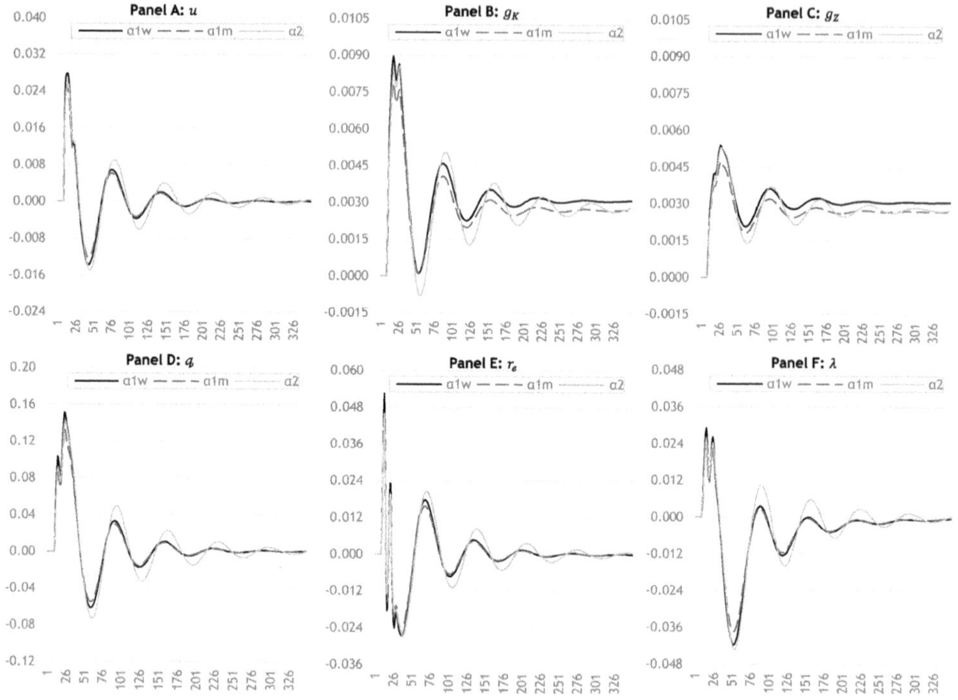

Figure 4. Positive shocks to consumption propensities.

output share of each sector is always zero. There is empirical support for the SM approach in respect to the induced nature of capacity investment and the cyclical patterns for the net lending/borrowing output shares of the firm and non-firm sectors (Fiebiger 2022).

5. Conclusion

Post-Keynesians widely celebrate Keynes's (1930, 1936) widow's cruse / paradox of thrift because it exposes fundamental errors in the household thrift-determined orthodox view of capital accumulation. Household thrift is a societal vice that has a self-defeating effect on household net worth, and by reducing sales, sets in motion a contraction. The post-1980 slowdown in capital accumulation amidst a declining wage share and widening in personal income inequality is in line with Kaleckian concerns on functional income distribution and the division of wage income between managers and NS workers.

The results of the NK-SM model with its semi-endogenous/semi-autonomous consumption should go some way to appeasing the critics of SM models; and at least the Kaleckians, who believe that the paradox of thrift and paradox of costs should generate long-run permanent growth effects. Skott (2019, p. 244) expresses the view that 'the safeguarding of specific, desirable conclusions — whether Keynesian, Marxian or neoliberal — is not a good criterion for model selection'. It is true that Keynesian/Kaleckian modelling inputs yield Keynesian/Kaleckian modelling outputs and likewise for Marxian theory and neoliberal theory. It is also the case that many of the characteristic inputs

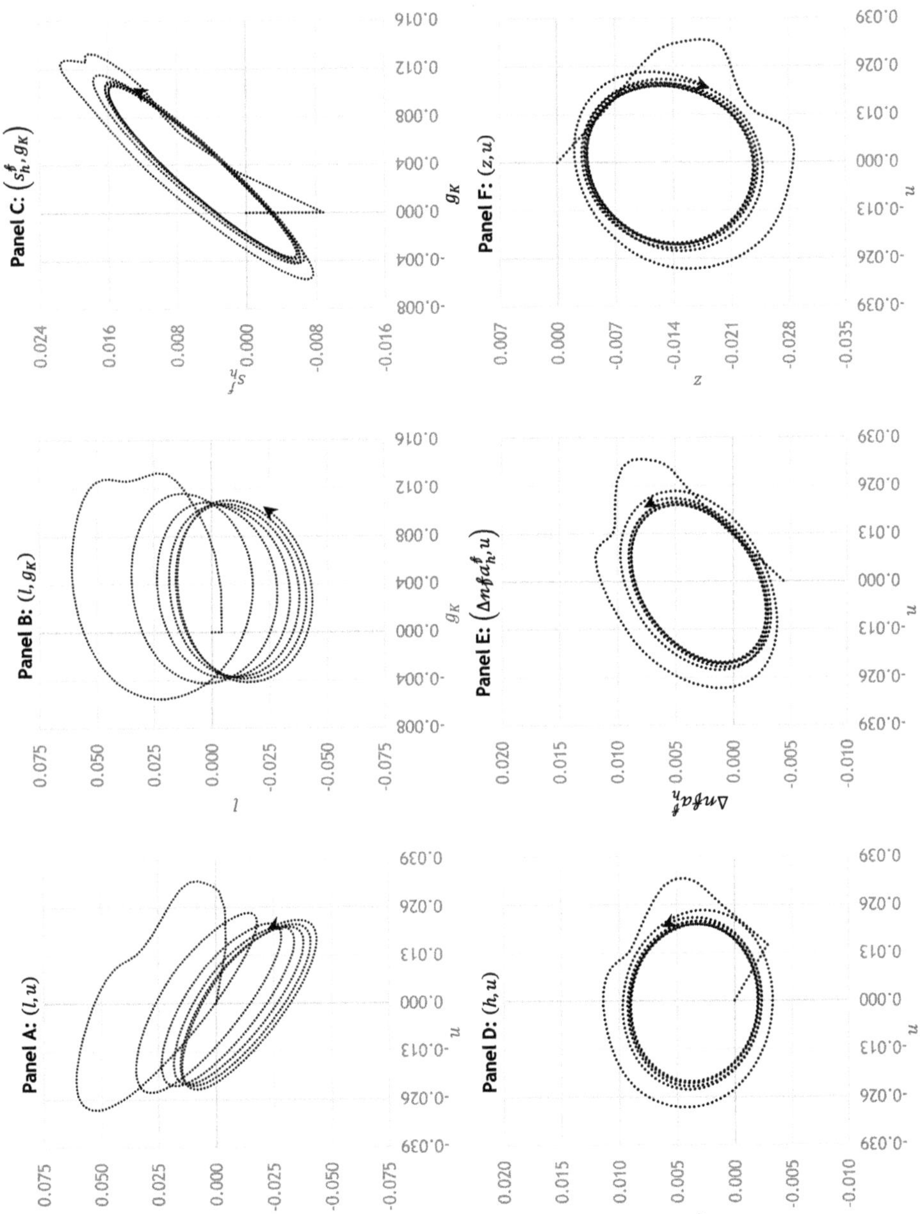

Figure 5. Positive Alpha1 shock with high expected sales adjustment speed.

into Marxian models lack theoretical intuition and empirical support. The complete abstraction from the financial sphere in the neo-Goodwinian limit cycle models is one example. Assuming that each sector always has revenues equal to expenditures is a Say's Law type assumption that no one should ponder.

NMNH reach the same conclusion as neoclassical economists on the alleged merits of thrift in developing economies with 'dual' unconstrained labour markets. And likewise for 'mature' economies with constrained labour markets so long as the path of the 'warranted growth rate' is stable. If instead the warranted growth rate is unstable, thrift may have contractionary level effects, but only if the 'valuation effects' from Tobin's q on the desired utilisation rate are comparatively weak (Skott 1988). In NMNH theory thrift has a positive effect on the 'equilibrium' warranted growth rate. The latter is a 'metaphysical concept' (Robinson 1971, p. 111) as it supposes that thrift would not have a negative effect on the utilisation rate which is (somehow) kept constant. In NMNH mature economies the rate of capital accumulation invariably returns to an exogenously-given natural growth rate. Needless to say that such an assumption cannot furnish us with an explanation of the long-run growth rate.

The short story is that the NMNH framework that Skott (2019) urges post-Keynesians to adopt does safeguard neoclassical conclusions by adopting neoclassical positions: a positive effect for thrift on a metaphysical equilibrium growth rate, an exogenous natural growth rate and an assumption that household thrift eases the financial constraints on firms by increasing the supply of loanable funds.[28] The alternative circuitist approach to investment finance presented in this paper has the benefit of providing a clear distinction between the concepts of finance and thrift. Endogenous money and complex financial-side mechanisms can be merged with the demand-led SM approach and its emphasis on the capital stock adjustment principle. This paper has also provided another way to endogenise the growth rate of semi-autonomous demand expenditures; indeed, the SM closure can be easily integrated into Sraffian or NK models in such a way that the economy becomes path-dependent while replicating 'results familiar from earlier neo-Kaleckian growth models' (Blecker and Setterfield 2019, p. 364).

Acknowledgements

I would like to use this opportunity to acknowledge and thank the reviewers who reviewed this article and aided in its publication.

Disclosure Statement

No potential conflict of interest was reported by the author(s).

References

Allain, O. 2015. 'Tackling the Instability of Growth: A Kaleckian-Harrodian Model with an Autonomous Expenditure Component.' *Cambridge Journal of Economics* 39 (5): 1351–1371.

[28]We shall also mention that Skott's (1988, 1989, 2010) NMNH models rule out the NK paradox of costs due to the assumption of a "profit-led" output expansion function.

Barbosa-Filho, N., and L. Taylor. 2006. 'Distributive and Demand Cycles in the US Economy — a Structuralist Goodwin Model.' *Metroeconomica* 57 (3): 389–411.

Barrales-Ruiz, J., I. Mendieta-Muñoz, C. Rada, D. Tavani, and R. von Arnim. 2020. 'The Distributive Cycle: Evidence and Current Debates.' Department of Economics, University of Utah, Working Paper No. 2020-07.

Bernardo, J. L., E. Stockhammer, and F. L. Martínez. 2015. 'A Post-Keynesian Theory for Tobin's q in a Stock-Flow Consistent Framework.' Post Keynesian Economics Society, Working Paper No. 1509.

Bhaduri, A., and S. Marglin. 1990. 'Unemployment and the Real Wage.' *Cambridge Journal of Economics* 14 (4): 375–393.

Blecker, A. R., and M. Setterfield. 2019. *Heterodox Macroeconomics: Models of Demand, Distribution and Growth*. Cheltenham: Edward Elgar.

Brochier, L., and F. Freitas. 2020. 'Debt and Demand Regimes in Canonical Growth Models: A Comparison of Neo-Kaleckian and Supermultiplier Models.' IE-UFRJ Discussion Paper No. 035-2020.

Brochier, L., and A. C. Macedo e Silva. 2019. 'A Supermultiplier Stock-Flow Consistent Model: The "Return" of the Paradoxes of Thrift and Costs in the Long Run?' *Cambridge Journal of Economics* 43 (2): 413–442.

Cassetti, M. 2020. 'Fiscal Policy as a Long-Run Stabilization Tool. Simulations with a Stock-Flow Consistent Model.' Post Keynesian Economics Society, Working Paper No. 2003.

Cauvel, M. 2019. 'The Neo-Goodwinian Model Reconsidered.' Post-Keynesian Economics Society, Working Paper No. 1915.

Cesaratto, S. 2015. 'Neo-Kaleckian and Sraffian Controversies on the Theory of Accumulation.' *Review of Political Economy* 27 (2): 154–182.

Cesaratto, S., and S. Di Bucchianico. 2020. 'Endogenous Money and the Theory of Long-Period Effective Demand.' *Bulletin of Political Economy* 14 (1): 1–38.

Cesaratto, S., and R. Pariboni. 2022. 'The Relation Between Keynesian Monetary Theory and Demand-Led Growth: A Sraffian Exploration.' *Review of Keynesian Economics* 10 (3): 291–315.

Duménil, G., and D. Lévy. 1999. 'Being Keynesian in the Short Term and Classical in the Long Term: The Traverse to Classical Long-Term Equilibrium.' *The Manchester School* 67 (6): 684–716.

Dutt, A. K. 1984. 'Stagnation, Income Distribution and Monopoly Power.' *Cambridge Journal of Economics* 8 (1): 25–40.

Dutt, A. K. 2019. 'Some Observations on Models of Growth and Distribution with Autonomous Demand Growth.' *Metroeconomica* 70 (2): 288–301.

Fazzari, S., R. G. Hubbard, and B. Petersen. 1988. 'Investment, Financing Decisions, and Tax Policy.' *The American Economic Review* 78 (2): 200–205.

Fiebiger, B. 2020. 'Some Observations on Endogeneity in the Normal Rate of Capacity Utilisation.' *Review of Keynesian Economics* 8 (3): 385–406.

Fiebiger, B. 2021. 'The Post-Keynesian "Crowding-In" Policy Meme: Government-Led Semi-Autonomous Demand Growth.' IMK Macroeconomic Policy Institute, Düsseldorf, FMM Working Papers No. 67.

Fiebiger, B. 2022. 'An Evaluation of Neo-Kaleckian Supermultiplier and Neo-Goodwinian Models: Pseudo-Goodwin Cycles, External Markets and Pro-Cyclical Labour Productivity.' IMK Macroeconomic Policy Institute, Düsseldorf, FMM Working Papers No. 78.

Fiebiger, B., and M. Lavoie. 2019. 'Trend and Business Cycles with External Markets: Non-Capacity Generating Semi-Autonomous Expenditures and Effective Demand.' *Metroeconomica* 70 (2): 247–262.

Franke, R. 2016. 'A Supplementary Note on Professor Hein's (2013) Version of a Kaleckian Debt Accumulation.' *Metroeconomica* 67 (3): 529–550.

Freitas, F., and F. Serrano. 2015. 'Growth Rate and Level Effects: The Adjustment of Capacity to Demand and the Sraffian Supermultiplier.' *Review of Political Economy* 27 (3): 257–281.

Girardi, D., and R. Pariboni. 2019. 'Normal Utilization as the Adjusting Variable in Neo-Kaleckian Growth Models: A Critique.' *Metroeconomica* 70 (2): 341–358.
Godley, W., and M. Lavoie. 2007. *Monetary Economics: An Integrated Approach to Credit, Money, Income, Production and Wealth*. Basingstoke: Palgrave Macmillan.
Goodwin, R. M. 1967. 'A Growth Cycle.' In *Socialism, Capitalism and Economic Growth*, edited by C. H. Feinstein. Cambridge: Cambridge University Press.
Harrod, R. F. 1939. 'An Essay in Dynamic Theory.' *Economic Journal* 49 (193): 14–33.
Harrod, R. F. 1960. 'Second Essay in Dynamic Theory.' *Economic Journal* 70 (278): 277–293.
Hein, E., and R. Woodgate. 2021. 'Stability Issues in Kaleckian Models Driven by Autonomous Demand Growth — Harrodian Instability and Debt Dynamics.' *Metroeconomica* 72 (2): 388–404.
Kaldor, N. 1955–56. 'Alternative Theories of Distribution.' *Review of Economic Studies* 23 (2): 83–100.
Kalecki, M. 1935. 'A Macrodynamic Theory of Business Cycles.' *Econometrica* 3 (3): 327–344.
Kalecki, M. 1937. 'The Principle of Increasing Risk.' *Economica* 4 (16): 440–447.
Keynes, J. M. 1930. *A Treatise on Money, Volume 1: The Pure Theory of Money*. New York: Harcourt Brace and Company.
Keynes, J. M. 1936. *The General Theory of Employment, Interest and Money*. London: Macmillan.
Keynes, J. M. 1937. 'The "Ex-Ante" Theory of the Rate of Interest.' *Economic Journal* 47 (188): 663–669.
Lavoie, M. 1995. 'The Kaleckian Model of Growth and Distribution and Its Neo-Ricardian and Neo-Marxian Critiques.' *Cambridge Journal of Economics* 19 (6): 789–818.
Lavoie, M. 2008. 'Financialisation Issues in a Post-Keynesian Stock-Flow Consistent Model.' *Intervention. European Journal of Economics and Economic Policies: Intervention* 5 (2): 331–356.
Lavoie, M. 2014. *Post-Keynesian Economics: New Foundations*. Cheltenham: Edward Elgar.
Lavoie, M. 2016. 'Convergence Towards the Normal Rate of Capacity Utilization in Neo-Kaleckian Models: The Role of Non-Capacity Creating Autonomous Expenditures.' *Metroeconomica* 67 (1): 172–201.
Lavoie, M., and W. Godley. 2001–02. 'Kaleckian Models of Growth in a Coherent Stock-Flow Monetary Framework: A Kaldorian View.' *Journal of Post Keynesian Economics* 24 (2): 277–311.
Lavoie, M., and W. J. Nah. 2020. 'Overhead Labour Costs in a Neo-Kaleckian Growth Model with Autonomous Non-Capacity Creating Expenditures.' *Review of Political Economy* 32 (4): 511–537.
Le Heron, E., and T. Mouakil. 2008. 'Post-Keynesian Stock-Flow Consistent Model for Dynamic Analysis of Monetary Policy Shock on Banking Behaviour.' *Metroeconomica* 59 (3): 405–440.
Lindner, F. 2015. 'Does Saving increase the Supply of Credit? A Critique of Loanable Funds Theory.' *World Economic Review* 4: 1–28.
Minsky, H. P. 1975. *John Maynard Keynes*. New York: Columbia University Press.
Moore, B. J. 1973. 'Some Macroeconomic Consequences of Corporate Equities.' *Canadian Journal of Economics* 6 (4): 529–544.
Moudud, J. K. 2009. 'The Role of the State and Harrod's Economic Dynamics.' *International Journal of Political Economy* 38 (1): 35–57.
Nikiforos, M. 2016. 'On the "Utilisation Controversy": A Theoretical and Empirical Discussion of the Kaleckian Model of Growth and Distribution.' *Cambridge Journal of Economics* 40 (2): 437–467.
Nikiforos, M. 2018. 'Some Comments on the Sraffian Supermultiplier Approach to Growth and Distribution.' *Journal of Post Keynesian Economics* 41 (4): 659–667.
Palumbo, A., and A. Trezzini. 2003. 'Growth Without Normal Capacity Utilization.' *European Journal of the History of Economic Thought* 10 (1): 109–135.
Parguez, A., and M. Seccareccia. 2000. 'The Credit Theory of Money: The Monetary Circuit Approach.' In *What is Money?*, edited by J. Smithin. London: Routledge.
Petri, F. 2004. *General Equilibrium, Capital and Macroeconomics: A Key to Recent Controversies in Equilibrium Theory*. Cheltenham: Edward Elgar.
Robinson, J. 1956. *The Accumulation of Capital*. London: Macmillan.

Robinson, J. 1971. *Economic Heresies*. London: Macmillan.
Rochon, L.-P. 1999. *Credit, Money and Production: An Alternative Post-Keynesian Approach*. Cheltenham: Edward Elgar.
Rowthorn, B. 1981. 'Demand, Real Wages and Economic Growth.' *Thames Papers in Political Economy* (Autumn): 1–39.
Ryoo, S. 2013. 'The Paradox of Debt and Minsky's Financial Instability Hypothesis.' *Metroeconomica* 64 (1): 1–24.
Seccareccia, M. 1996. 'Post Keynesian Fundism and Monetary Circulation.' In *Money in Motion*, edited by G. Deleplace and E. J. Nell. London: Macmillan.
Serrano, F., and F. Freitas. 2017. 'The Sraffian Supermultiplier as an Alternative Closure for Heterodox Growth Theory.' *European Journal of Economics and Economic Policies: Intervention* 14 (1): 70–91.
Setterfield, M. 2019. 'Long-Run Variation in Capacity Utilization in the Presence of a Fixed Normal Rate.' *Cambridge Journal of Economics* 43 (2): 443–463.
Shaikh, A. 2009. 'Economic Policy in a Growth Context: A Classical Synthesis of Keynes and Harrod.' *Metroeconomica* 60 (3): 455–494.
Skott, P. 1988. 'Finance, Saving and Accumulation.' *Cambridge Journal of Economics* 12 (3): 339–354.
Skott, P. 1989. 'Effective Demand, Class Struggle and Cyclical Growth.' *International Economic Review* 30 (1): 231–247.
Skott, P. 2010. 'Growth, Instability and Cycles.' In *Handbook of Alternative Theories of Economic Growth*, edited by M. Setterfield. Cheltenham: Edward Elgar.
Skott, P. 2019. 'Autonomous Demand, Harrodian Instability and the Supply Side.' *Metroeconomica* 70 (2): 233–246.
Skott, P. 2020. 'Fiscal Policy and Structural Transformation in Developing Economies.' UMass Economics Working Paper No. 294.
Skott, P., and S. Ryoo. 2008. 'Macroeconomic Implications of Financialisation.' *Cambridge Journal of Economics* 32 (6): 827–862.
Skott, P., and Zipperer B.. 2012. 'An Empirical Evaluation of Three post-Keynesian Models.' *European Journal of Economics and Economic Policies: Intervention* 9 (2): 277–308.
Steindl, J. 1952 [1976]. *Maturity and Stagnation in American Capitalism*. New York: Monthly Review Press.
Stockhammer, E. 2017. 'Wage-Led Versus Profit-Led Demand: What Have We Learned? A Kaleckian-Minskyan View.' *Review of Keynesian Economics* 5 (1): 25–42.
Tavani, D., and L. Petach. 2019. 'No One is Alone: Strategic Complementarities, Capacity Utilization, Growth, and Distribution.' *Structural Change and Economic Dynamics* 50 (September): 203–215.
Tavani, D., and L. Petach. 2020. 'Firm Beliefs and Long-Run Demand Effects in a Labor-Constrained Model of Growth and Distribution.' *Journal of Evolutionary Economics* 31: 353–377.
Tavani, D., and L. Zamparelli. 2021. 'Labor-Augmenting Technical Change and the Labor Share: New Microeconomic Foundations.' *Structural Change and Economic Dynamics* 56 (March): 27–34.
Taylor, L. 2004. *Reconstructing Macroeconomics*. Cambridge, MA: Harvard University Press.
Taylor, L., D. K. Foley, A. Rezai, L. Pires, O. Ömer, and E. Scharfenaker. 2016. 'Demand Drives Growth All the Way.' New School for Social Research, Working Paper No. 2016-4.
Tobin, J. 1969. 'A General Equilibrium Approach to Monetary Theory.' *Journal of Money, Credit and Banking* 1 (1): 15–29.
van Treeck, T. 2009. 'A Synthetic, Stock–Flow Consistent Macroeconomic Model of "Financialisation".' *Cambridge Journal of Economics* 33 (3): 467–493.
von Arnim, R., and J. Barrales. 2015. 'Demand-Driven Goodwin Cycles with Kaldorian and Kaleckian Features.' *Review of Keynesian Economics* 3 (3): 351–373.

The Monetary Theory of Production and the Supermultiplier: What Determines Savings?

Lorenzo Di Domenico, Giovanna Ciaffi and Davide Romaniello

ABSTRACT

The paper presents a closed-economy stock-flow consistent model aimed at outlining the natural synthesis between two fundamental pillars of the post-Keynesian approach: the supermultiplier (SM) model and the monetary theory of production based on the notion of endogenous money. Such integration allows the defining of the whole economic mechanism describing the financing of autonomous components and investments, as well as the determination of output and saving within a monetary economy of production. Our contribution argues that the endogenous money theory plays a non-ancillary role within the SM approach. By comparing different scenarios describing the financing of autonomous components of demand and investments (bank loans, retained profits, CB, and equity emissions), we point out that the endogenous process of money creation is the only structural mechanism through which the autonomous components can exist and be independent of current income, and Keynesian causality materializes in the long-run. In general, it is the initial finance of investments and autonomous components through endogenous money that allows them to be ex-post founded by household saving. Conversely, the initial finance through the existing stock of wealth, although it does not intact the investments-saving causality, can be considered only a temporary spin-off of the endogenous money process.

1. Introduction

The Classical-Keynesian approach has yet to establish a clear integration between demand-led growth models and endogenous money theory (EMT) (Cesaratto 2017). In this paper, we refer to demand-led growth models as multiplier-accelerator models that incorporate at least one autonomous component of demand. Our reference point is the Supermultiplier model (SM) (Freitas and Serrano 2015). Notably, two key features of the SM model are closely connected to the endogenous money theory: autonomous spending does not depend on the current circulation of income, and investments do not depend on ex-ante saving formation. Conversely, as long as deposits are created

Supplemental data for this article can be accessed online at https://doi.org/10.1080/09538259.2024.2378373.

by loans in the EMT, saving is created by investments in the SM approach. A few theoretical contributions have sought to integrate the SM models with the PK-EMT (Cesaratto 2017; Cesaratto and Di Bucchianico 2020; Pariboni 2016). Pariboni (2016) examines the macroeconomic implications of debt-financed consumption within an extended SM model that incorporates endogenous credit money. Cesaratto and Di Bucchianico (2020) present a first attempt to complement the Supermultiplier with the endogenous money theory, demonstrating that credit-money creation pertains to autonomous consumption fueled by consumer credit, government spending that precedes taxation and saving, and investments that are only founded ex-post by saving. Drawing on the circuitist approach, they emphasize that endogenous money finances both investments and the autonomous components of aggregate demand (initial finance), which are later funded by saving (final finance).

Our contribution is strictly related to the so-called (implicit) classical-Keynesian received view, as defined in Cesaratto (2017). With the latter, the author refers to the apparently surprising absence of the financial and monetary dimension within the Classical-Keynesian theory of output, which, instead, necessarily requires an endogenous money theory. According to the author, since it is characteristic of autonomous expenditure not to be financed out of income revenues, unlike induced consumption, it must therefore be financed by endogenous money. Thus, the received view of the SM posits that endogenous money finances autonomous spending and investments which in turn generate induced spending, and both determine output. In this depiction, the separation between monetary and real analysis in macroeconomic systems disappears. As Cesaratto (2017) argues, there is no dualism between real and monetary sectors in the Classical-Keynesian approach which 'metaphorically represent the skeleton and circulation apparatus, respectively, while serving the muscles' (Cesaratto 2017, p. 229). Our paper provides an analytical framework to support this narrative. By employing the Stock-Flow Consistent (SFC) macroeconomic accounting, we further expand Cesaratto's thesis by showing how saving is generated as a result of liabilities creation when autonomous spending and investments are financed. Unlike Cesaratto (2017), we delve deeper into the connections between autonomous components, investments, and endogenous money, specifically examining the relationship between saving and investment, and deficit autonomous spending. In particular, we further investigate the implication of the financing of autonomous components and investments through the existing stock of savings.

We compare different sources of initial finance — such as loans, retained profits, and equity financing for investments, as well as central bank or household wealth financing for deficit public spending — to study whether they can be considered long-run mechanisms for affirming the Keynesian principle and the independence of autonomous components from current circulation. The discussion about the different methods of initial finance will be kept separate from the analysis of the final financing of these components through household savings.

Through this analysis, we show that the endogenous process of money creation is the sole structural mechanism that guarantees the existence of autonomous components of demand and their independence from current income in the long-run, as well as the independence of investments from saving. Alternative ways of financing, such as utilizing the existing stock of wealth can be understood only as subordinated mechanisms to the endogenous process of money creation.

The paper investigates these issues making explicit the monetary dimension of the SM model to highlight why this approach implicitly contains an endogenous theory of money and, in particular, how this theory plays a non-ancillary role in such a framework, conversely to the neoclassic theory where it is auxiliary (Wicksell 1935). With this aim, we develop a Stock Flow Consistent (SFC) — SM model (see, among others, Brochier 2020; Brochier and Macedo e Silva 2019; Carnevali et al. 2024; Di Domenico, Góes, and Gallo 2023; Mandarino, Dos Santos, and Macedo e Silva 2020; Pedrosa, Brochier, and Freitas 2023; Teixeira and Petrini 2023) as the SFC approach has proven highly effective in illustrating the relationships between assets and liabilities across different sectors and how they are created (for a revised version, see Caverzasi and Godin 2013; 2015; Nikiforos and Zezza 2017). In this regard, this paper also relates to the literature on monetary circuit theory and developing SFC models where the initial and final finance are explicitly addressed (see Berr and Monvoisin 2023; Lavoie 2004; Sawyer and Passarella 2017; Zezza 2012).

On the one hand, the model provides a sound macroeconomic and monetary framework explaining the financing of the autonomous component of demand and underlying stock-flow relationships. It describes how exogenous purchasing power injections are realized and how current income circulation is created. On the other hand, it clarifies how monetary savings are ex-post determined symmetrically to the bookkeeping of the aggregate debt generated when financing such components.

In this sense, the integration of the SM model with EMT allows to shed light on two main issues: (i) how monetary savings are generated; (ii) how autonomous components and investments are financed.

The first point can be well understood by looking at the sequential analysis adopted by the monetary circuit approach (Graziani 1990; 2003; Lavoie 1987; Nell 1996; Parguez 1981; Poulon 1982), and the idea of 'initial' and 'final finance'. In this framework, deposits exist as a result of loans generation, and the generation of monetary savings ultimately depends on debt creation. In a monetary economy, unlike real assets, monetary/financial assets held by an agent or sector have an accounting counterpart in the liability side of the balance sheets of other agents or sectors (Fontana, Realfonzo, and Passarella 2020). Additionally, deposits are also created when the Central Bank (CB) or commercial banks finance deficit public spending (Godley and Lavoie 2007). More in general, one sector can hold positive wealth or monetary savings if one or more other sectors have incurred a debt creation. At the same time, when a loan is reimbursed, a corresponding amount of deposits is destroyed. To this extent, the ex-ante financing of production decisions and investments (initial finance) through endogenous money allows them to be ex-post founded by saving (final finance). It is the initial finance of bank loans that, generating a corresponding amount of deposits, allows investments to be ex-post founded by household equities. In a second step, households can convert a share of deposits created by bank loans to acquire firm equities, creating the illusion that the investments were financed by equity.

Within this wisdom, investments or other autonomous components of demand represent the form and reason for the realization of the lending process, and they are, in substance, the 'economic decision' through which newly created purchasing power is injected into the system and because of which a liability is created. When a bank loan is created to finance investments or any autonomous component of demand, a corresponding amount of deposits is generated. Similarly, when the CB provides an overdraft or buys public bonds to finance public deficit spending, an equivalent amount of deposits is created. As for the ex-post financing of investments through equity, households can convert the deposit created by CB into public bonds, giving the illusion that the public deficit has been financed by collecting household savings. In short, it is the 'initial finance' of such expenditures that allows for their ex-post founding through household saving (final finance). Consistently with this causal relationship, investments create a corresponding amount of saving when financed by loans.

Regarding the second point, we show that different methods of financing autonomous components and investments are ultimately subordinate to the endogenous money-creation process. This process underlies the Keynesian principle of investment-driven saving, making the two points inherently interconnected. Integrating the Supermultiplier model with Endogenous Money Theory (EMT) provides a comprehensive framework for understanding the financing of autonomous components and investments, as well as the determination of output and saving in a monetary production economy. Autonomous components, such as public spending, serve as exogenous injections of purchasing power that, through the multiplier-accelerator interaction, determine long-run GDP. Their debt financing, alongside investments, determines the saving formation in the economy. Monetary savings emerge as a residual of this multiplicative process, with household saving decisions influencing the final net debts of each sector. Money enters circulation when autonomous demand or investment decisions are financed by the central bank or commercial banks. Consequently, the stock of wealth and changes in aggregate debt are determined by household saving and portfolio decisions. The close interconnection between the SM and the PK-EMT can be summed up in the following terms: as deposits cannot exist without prior loan creation, monetary savings cannot materialize without ex-ante investments.

Along these lines, the paper raises three main points: (i) investments and other autonomous components demand generate a corresponding amount of monetary saving only when financed out-of-debt creation; (ii) the long-run independence of investments from monetary saving, and more broadly, the Keynesian causality, can be revealed only through an endogenous process of money creation; (iii) the endogenous money causality, that goes from loans to deposits, is the substance of the causality that goes from investments to saving. While the first point doesn't necessarily imply the second, and the second doesn't preclude financing investments with existing wealth, these arguments are interconnected. Regarding the second point, the creation of liability-asset linkages does not necessarily entail endogenous money creation. For instance, a liability-asset linkage can be created through existing wealth, such as when investments are financed by equity or households acquire public bonds with existing deposits (initial finance). However, while any liability creation generates a corresponding amount of monetary saving, endogenous money creation is the structural mechanism ensuring the long-run independence of savings from investment and the 'autonomy' of the autonomous components. Any secondary mode of financing, like equity emissions or public bonds financed out of household wealth, does not create deposits but relies on them. Only bank loans or CB bond purchases create money and deposits, making the endogenous money process the sole engine of direct and indirect (via secondary financing) monetary saving creation.

In the short-run, autonomous components of demand or investments could be financed through equities or bonds acquired by households, leading to an increase in debt and savings. However, this depends on the existing deposit stock. On the one hand, deposits can exist only as a result of the endogenous money creation process. Therefore, financing current investments through equities ultimately depends on past investments financed by bank loans, which created the current stock of deposits. On the other hand, a given amount of deposits can continue to exist only if the corresponding amount of bank (or CB) debt keeps existing. If this debt must be repaid, the corresponding deposits are destroyed. Then, the structural substitution of bank financing with equity financing implies a constant destruction of deposits, making the same equity financing of investments non-feasible. Alternatively, short-run equity financing necessarily requires assuming that debts previously created are perpetual and, therefore, do not have to be repaid. This reasoning can also be applied to the discussion on financing autonomous demand components.

Lastly, even if we consider the existing stock of deposits as a 'manna from heaven', it would not be possible to assume that, in a growing economy or an economy with positive inflation, a growing amount of nominal investments would be financed out of a fixed amount of deposits. A fixed amount of deposits can purchase only a fixed amount of equities. Therefore, it would not be possible to do without the creation of new spending capacity by means of new monetary creation.

These arguments briefly summarize why the Keynesian principle of investment determining saving and the independence of autonomous components from current income requires an endogens process of money creation.

The remainder of the paper is structured as follows. Section Two reviews the Supermultiplier model and Endogenous Money Theory. Section Three presents the Stock-Flow Consistent — SM model, which is used to examine the Keynesian causality by comparing loan-financed and retained-earnings-financed investments. Section Four further investigates the relationship between investments and saving, considering autonomous investments in place of the traditional SM investment function. In Section Five, we compare cases where the initial finance of autonomous components and investments is implemented out of the existing stock of wealth rather than through a genuine process of monetary creation. Section six concludes.

2. The Supermultiplier and the Endogenous Money Theory

The SM approach argues that a long-run relationship between demand and output exists, where the trend growth rate of output is determined by the growth rate of non-capacity-creating autonomous components of demand. Initially developed by Serrano (1995) and Bortis (1997), this model has been further enriched by several authors (Allain 2015; Cesaratto, Serrano, and Stirati 2003; Deleidi and Mazzucato 2019; 2021; Fazzari, Ferri, and Variato 2020; Freitas and Serrano 2015; Hein 2018; Lavoie 2016; Palley 2019). The SM extends the principle of effective demand to the long-run and introduces the role of non-capacity creating autonomous components of demand within an accelerator-multiplier mechanism (Harrod 1939). Specifically, the model combines the standard multiplier effect on consumption with an investment function grounded on a flexible accelerator principle, where capital accumulation is endogenously shaped by the level of effective demand. Firms try to adjust productive capacity to achieve a normal degree of capacity utilization over time. In this framework, long-run output is the result of the interaction between the multiplier and the accelerator mechanisms, while savings adjust to investments through variations in the level of production and the corresponding production capacity (Garegnani 1992; 2015).

One of the central issues in the SM literature is the notion of non-capacity creating autonomous components of demand, namely those components of aggregate demand that are independent of the current level of income and do not directly affect the capital stock. Among these components, we can include: (i) government expenditure which is affected by policy decisions; (ii) exports which depend on the level of foreign demand; and (iii) autonomous consumption which is financed either in the credit market or through accumulated wealth. Other relevant aspects of the SM are that normal prices and capacity utilization,[1] in the long run, are combined with an exogenously given income distribution determined outside the economic system. Indeed, in line with the theory of the surplus approach grounded on the theory developed by Smith, Ricardo, Marx, and Sraffa (Garegnani 1984), income distribution is determined by social, historical, economic, and institutional factors, customs, and social norms that affect the bargaining power of opposite social classes, namely workers and entrepreneurs (Kalecki 1943; Levrero 2013; Stirati 1994).

Our study is grounded on the post-Keynesian Endogenous Money Theory (PK-EMT) (Deleidi 2020; Fontana 2003; Kaldor 1970; Lavoie 1996; Moore 1988; Rochon 1999; 2001). According to the PK-EMT, the quantity of money in the economic system is endogenously determined by the demand for loans, rather than exogenously determined by the central bank. Commercial banks are 'money producers' and are not mere intermediaries between saving and investment decisions. Following this perspective, commercial banks can create money *ex-nihilo*, that is without a prior volume of savings, the gathering of deposits, and a predetermined creation of monetary reserves by the central bank. In the PK-EMT, monetary aggregates are an outcome of the borrowers' demand for loans and the supply of loans by commercial banks. After the creation of bank loans and deposits, commercial banks demand a certain volume of the monetary base to the central bank, to comply with reserve requirements. Therefore, monetary reserves are a consequence of commercial banks' lending activity, rather than the cause of it. A logic chain exemplifying the PK-EMT can be summarized as follows: (i) the creditworthy borrowers' demand[2] determines the volume of loans granted by commercial banks; (ii) the volume of bank loans provided to borrowers creates an equivalent level of deposits; (iii) the volume of deposits and the value assumed by the credit divisor (Lavoie 1984) — which is the opposite of the money multipliers — affects the volume of reserves demanded by commercial

[1]For a discussion on the on the utilization controversy, see Nikiforos (2016), Girardi and Pariboni (2016), and Gahn and González (2020).

[2]Commercial banks do not merely accommodate all potential demands for loans (Lavoie 1996), but only the effective creditworthy demand for loans (Kaldor 1981; Moore 1988). This implies that banks select good borrowers (Robinson 1952) and ration credit by means of quantitative constraint, e.g., by varying the collateral requirements (Fontana and Setterfield 2009; Wolfson 1996).

banks to the central bank. Within this perspective, central and commercial banks set interest rates that are regarded as exogenous variables, independent of the volume of money demanded and supplied.[3] Once the central bank sets the short-run interest rate on reserves, commercial banks determine their interest rates on loans (Arestis and Eichner 1988), by applying a mark-up over the short-run interest rate pegged by the central bank.[4] The money endogeneity and the creation of bank money are central arguments in the *Theory of the Monetary Circuit*, where money is seen as a necessary tool to activate the production of commodities in a *Monetary Economy of Production* by paying workers and purchasing capital goods (Graziani 2003). In this sense, according to the Circuitists authors, the correct macroeconomic method to integrate money in the economy is to consider money creation (Poulon 1982). The endogenous character of money appears at the first step of the circuit: money creation doesn't depend on a money supply function but on firms' needs and entrepreneurs' anticipations to begin their activities (Accoce and Mouakil 2007). Entrepreneurs need to borrow money from banks to finance investments and production decisions. This is what Graziani (1990) calls initial finance. Money is created by banks when they grant loans to creditworthy economic agents. At the end of the production process firms recover part of the income generated by production through the consumption of workers and issuing securities. This is what Graziani (1990) defines as final finance. At this stage, entrepreneurs pay back a share of their loans. Workers' portfolio decisions determine the residual stock of money.

The PK-EMT has been extensively acknowledged and gained momentum in the international debate. This perspective disregards two main ideas of the marginalist perspective: (i) the Monetarist idea of a money supply exogenously determined by the central bank through changes in the monetary base and the money multiplier, and (ii) the marginalist Loanable Funds Theory (LFT) according to which saving determines investment. Recently, academics from different schools of thought (Ryan-Collins, Werner, and Castle 2016; Werner 2014), as well as monetary authorities (ECB 2011; Jakab and Kumhof 2015; 2019; McLeay, Radia, and Thomas 2014), have endorsed the view of an endogenous money creation process. In its first quarterly bulletin of 2014, the Bank of England (BoE) stated:

> In the modern economy, most money takes the form of bank deposits. But how these bank deposits are created is often misunderstood: the principal way is through commercial banks making loans. Whenever a bank makes a loan, it simultaneously creates a matching deposit in the borrower's bank account, thereby creating new money. (McLeay, Radia, and Thomas 2014, p. 1)

Within this depiction, since money is created when financing investments, the causal relation between saving and investments is reversed compared to the one described in the LFT (Bertocco and Kalajzić 2022). Just as in a corn (neoclassical) economy saving presupposes the production of corn, in an economy based on the use of bank

[3] Within the PK-EMT, a twofold perspective on the determination of interest rates exists, namely the horizontalist (Deleidi 2020; Lavoie 1996; Moore 1988; Rochon 1999; 2001) and the structuralist (Dow 1996; Palley 1994; 1996; 2017; Wray 1990; 1992) views. For an in-depth review of these issues, see, among others, Lavoie (1996), Rochon (2001), Fontana (2003; 2004), and Deleidi (2019; 2020). In this paper, following both the recent literature on SFC modelling and on the EMT, we endorse the horizontalist perspective.

[4] For a discussion on the determinants of the mark-up, see among others Eichner (1987) and Deleidi (2020).

money, saving decisions presuppose the production of money that will be accumulated by savers.

3. The Supermultiplier and the Post-Keynesian Endogenous Money Theory: A Stock-flow Consistent Model

This section presents an analytically solvable SFC — Supermultiplier model. The model considers a closed economy with public spending as the sole autonomous component of demand. Consumption and investments are fully induced. In line with the SFC approach, we make explicit the source of financing of autonomous components of demand and investments, including debt repayments. Firms invest according to the principle of capacity adjustment, households consume a fraction of disposable income and hold their wealth as deposits and public bonds. Central Bank acts as lender of last resort, commercial bank collects deposits and grants loans to firms to finance investment decisions. The difference between deposits and loans is held as reserves by commercial banks.

In this section, we highlight the natural interdependency between the Keynesian hypothesis of investments determining saving and the theory of endogenous money. In particular, we show that if investments are fully financed by loans, a corresponding amount of monetary saving originates. Conversely, if investments are financed through retained profits, they do not generate a corresponding amount of monetary saving and they figure as an increase in the average propensity to consume. In this case, the public deficit decreases and, with that, the flow of household saving[5] (see Di Domenico 2022 about the relationships between saving rate, public debt, and private savings).

For the sake of the discussion, we are considering two versions of the SM-SFC model. The first one rigorously reproduces the traditional version in which consumption depends only on disposable income. In the second one, consumption depends also on the stock of wealth. Latter is a typical feature of post-Keynesian SFC models (Godley and Lavoie 2007) and allows us to analyze the stationary state values of stock variables.[6] The SFC-SM model is described by the following system, from equation (1) to (17):

$$Y_t = C_t + \bar{G} + I_t \tag{1}$$

$$C_t = YD_{t-1}c_1 + V^h_{t-1}c_2 \tag{2}$$

$$YD_t = (Y_t - D_t - I_t\alpha)(1 - \theta) \tag{3}$$

$$D_t = L_t\delta \tag{4}$$

$$I_t = Y^e_t v - K_t(1 - \delta) \tag{5}$$

$$Y^e_t = Y_{t-1} \tag{6}$$

$$B_t = B_{t-1} + G_t - \theta(Y_t - D_t - I_t\alpha) \tag{7}$$

[5]In general, the debt-financing can occur through a money creation process (bank loans) or from the existing wealth stock when firms issue equities. Section Five is devoted to the latter aspect, studying the implications for the macroeconomic theory.

[6]In models with a propensity to consume out-of-wealth equal to zero and constant level of public spending, the public debt has a positive growth rate in the stationary state. Then, the public debt-to-GDP ratio constantly grows.

$$V_t^h = V_{t-1}^h(1 - c_2) + YD_{t-1}(1 - c_1) \tag{8}$$

$$K_t = K_{t-1}(1 - \delta) + I_{t-1} \tag{9}$$

$$L_t = L_{t-1}(1 - \delta) + I_t(1 - \alpha) \tag{10}$$

$$B_t^h = \min(\beta V_t^h, B_t) \tag{11}$$

$$M_t^h = V_t^h - B_t^h \tag{12}$$

$$M_t^c = YD_t \tag{13}$$

$$B_t^{CB} = B_t - B_t^h \tag{14}$$

$$M_t = M_t^c + M_t^h \tag{15}$$

$$H_t = M_t - L_t \tag{16}$$

$$H_t = B_t^{CB} \tag{17}$$

where Y_t is the national income, C_t is the consumption, $\bar{G}$ is the primary public spending, I_t is the flow of gross investments, YD_t is the disposable income of households, Y_t^e is expected demand, D_t is the debt repayment, V_t^h is the stock of household wealth, L_t is the stock of loans, B_t is the public debt, B_t^{CB} is the amount of public bonds held by the Central Bank, B_t^h is the amount of public bonds held by households, I_t^n is the net investment, K_t is the capital stock, M_t^h is the stock of time deposits, M_t^c is the stock of check deposits, H_t is the amount of reserves, δ is the capital depreciation rate, θ is the tax rate, c_1 is the propensity to consume out-of-income, c_2 is the propensity to consume out-of-wealth, α is the share of investments financed by retained profits, v is the normal capital-to-output ratio, β is the share of household savings held in the form of public bonds. For the sake of simplicity, we are assuming an interest rate equal to zero. However, relaxing this assumption does not modify our results. Model results with positive interest rates can be sent upon request.

Equation 1 defines GDP as the sum of investments, public spending, and consumption. Current consumption (equation 2) depends on the disposable income distributed at the end of the previous period and the stock of household savings.[7] The income before tax of households in equation (3) is net of debt repayment and retained profit used to finance a share of gross investments. That is, the income before tax is net of depreciation allowances and retained profits used to finance a share of net investments (See Godley and Lavoie 2007, Chapter 7 for a similar treatment).[8] Since investments can be financed through a mix of loans and retained profits, depreciation allowances

[7] In the balance sheet, the disposable income distributed by firms to households at the end of the period figures as check deposits. Such income is held in the bank account but does not formally constitute savings.

[8] Note that disposable income can be rewritten as $YD_t = (Y_t - K_t\delta - I_t^n\alpha)(1 - \theta)$, where I_t^n is net investmetns. Indeed, depreciation allowances are equal to $K_t\delta = [K_t(1 - \alpha) + K_t\alpha]\delta = (L_t + K_t\alpha)\delta = D_t + K_t\alpha\delta$. Since a share of retained profit is used for replacing the corresponding depreciated capital ($K_t\alpha\delta$), and the remaining part is used to finance a share of capital expansion (net investments) we have that: $I_t^n\alpha = I_t\alpha - K_t\alpha\delta$. Then, $D_t + I_t\alpha = K_t\delta + I_t^n\alpha$.

consists of debt repayment (D_t) and retained profits needed to replace the depreciated capital. Note that if the leverage is equal to one ($\alpha = 0$), the amortization corresponds to the debt repayment and the income before tax corresponds to NDP. In equation (4) the dynamic of debt repayment is consistent with capital depreciation and interest rates are equal to zero.[9] As a result, the capital stock is equal to the stock of loans plus accumulated retained profits.

The SM investment function is expressed in equation (5), firms adjust capacity to match expected demand at the normal degree of capacity utilization.[10] Expected demand is equal to the demand realized in the previous period (equation 6). Equations 7–10 express the dynamic of stocks. As expressed by equation (11), the amount of public bonds held by households is a fixed share of wealth (β) which cannot exceed the supply of government bonds, and the remaining amount of wealth is held in terms of deposits (equation 12). Check deposits are equal to the income distributed to households at the end of the period (equation 13). CB acts as lender of last resort (equation 14) and the commercial bank holds the difference between the stock of deposits and loans as reserves at the CB (equation 16). Total deposits are equal to the sum of check and time deposits (equation 15). Equation (1) is the redundant equation that ensures the stock-flow consistency of the model, and states that the amount of reserves is equal to the amount of public bonds held by CB. The balance sheet and the transaction matrixes describing the economy are reported in Tables 1 and 2.

The dynamic of production and demand works as follows. Production depends on consumption demand, investments, and public spending. Consumption, in turn, depends on the disposable income distributed at the end of the previous period. Each period represents one production cycle. Public expenditure sets in motion the economic system, it represents the exogenous injection of purchasing power realized in each period and that triggers the income-expenditure sequence realized over the following periods. Investments financed by loans represent the second source of purchasing power injection. Investments are fully induced and respond to the capacity adjustment principle. The expected demand is equal to the demand from the previous period. A portion of the income distributed in period t is retained by firms to finance investments. The long-run income is the result of the overlapping of multiplier sequences triggered by the investments and public spending realized in each period.

First, we consider the traditional formulation of the SM, with the propensity to consume out-of-wealth equal to zero ($c_2 = 0$ in equations 2 and 8). By solving the system, we can derive the values of stock and flow variables in the stationary state (see Appendix B for mathematical derivations)[11]:

$$Y^* = \frac{G}{1 - c_1[(1-\theta) - \alpha v\delta - v(1-\alpha)\delta(1-\theta)] - v\delta} \tag{18}$$

[9]Being α the share of investments financed by retained profits, $K_t(1-\alpha)$ corresponds to the stock of debt.

[10]The investment function is the out-of-the stationary state version on the function adopted in the traditional SM model. In the stationary state, when the realized degree of capacity utilization is equal to normal, we can substitute $K_t = Y_t^e v$ and the investment function becomes $I_t = Y_t^e v\delta$.

[11]For the sake of analytical simplicity, we are assuming that also retained profit are taxed. In this way, it is possible to simplify investments and get manageable results. In this sense, equation (3) becomes: $YD_t = (Y_t - D_t)(1-\theta) - I_t\alpha$. Also equation (7) changes accordingly. Such an assumption does not modify the conclusion of the paper.

Table 1. Balance sheet matrix.

Assets	Household	Production	Bank	Government	CB	$\sum$
Check deposits	$+M^h$		$-M$			0
Time deposits	$+M^c$		$-M^c$			0
HPM			$+H_b$		$-H$	0
Loans		$-L$	$+L$			0
Fixed Capital		$+K$				$+K$
Public bonds	$-B_h$			$-B$	$+B_{cb}$	0
Net wealth	$-V^h$	$-V^f$	0	$+V^g$	0	$-K$
$\sum$	0	0	0	0	0	0

Table 2. Transaction matrix.

	Households	Production		Government	Bank		CB		$\sum$
		Current	Capital		Current	Capital	Current	Capital	
Consumption	$-C$	$+C$							0
Income	$+Y^N$	$-Y^N$							0
Ret. profits	$-FU$		$+FU$						
Investments		$+I$	$-I$						0
Public expenditure		$+G$		$-G$					0
Taxes	$-T$			$+T$					0
Debt rep.		$-L_t\delta$	$+L_t\delta$						0
Δ Deposits time	$-\Delta M$					$+\Delta M$			0
Δ Deposits check	$-\Delta M^c$					$+\Delta M^c$			0
Δ Loans			$+\Delta L$			$-\Delta L$			0
Δ Bonds	$-\Delta B^h$			$+\Delta B$				$-\Delta B^{bc}$	0
Δ Reserves						$-\Delta H$		$+\Delta H$	0
$\sum$	0	0	0	0	0	0	0	0	0

$$I^* = \frac{Gv\delta}{1 - c_1[(1-\theta) - \alpha v\delta - v(1-\alpha)\delta(1-\theta)] - v\delta} \tag{19}$$

$$K^* = \frac{Gv}{1 - c_1[(1-\theta) - \alpha v\delta - v(1-\alpha)\delta(1-\theta)] - v\delta} \tag{20}$$

$$u^* = u_n = \frac{Y^*}{Y^n} = 1 \tag{21}$$

$$\Delta L^* = 0 \tag{22}$$

$$\Delta B^* = \frac{G(1-c)\{1 - \theta - v[\delta + (-1+\alpha)\delta\theta]\}}{1 - c_1[(1-\theta) - \alpha v\delta - v(1-\alpha)\delta(1-\theta)] - v\delta} \tag{23}$$

$$\Delta V^{h*} = \frac{G(1-c)\{1 - \theta - v[\delta + (-1+\alpha)\delta\theta]\}}{1 - c_1[(1-\theta) - \alpha v\delta - v(1-\alpha)\delta(1-\theta)] - v\delta} \tag{24}$$

$$L^* = \frac{Gv(1-\alpha)}{1 - c_1[(1-\theta) - \alpha v\delta - v(1-\alpha)\delta(1-\theta)] - v\delta} \tag{25}$$

$$M_t^{c*} = \frac{G[(1-\theta) - v(1-\alpha)\delta(1-\theta) - \alpha v\delta]}{1 - c_1[(1-\theta) - \alpha v\delta - v(1-\alpha)\delta(1-\theta)] - v\delta} \tag{26}$$

Appendix C reports codes to reproduce both analytical and simulated results and checking their consistency.

Since we are assuming that the growth rate of public spending is zero, the economy reaches a stationary state where GDP is constant.[12] In the stationary state, gross investments are equal to capital depreciation, net investments are zero and the actual degree of capacity utilization is equal to the normal one. Then, the accumulation of household savings is solely due to a positive public deficit ($\Delta B^* = \Delta S^*$).

The initial finance of public spending is realized through CB overdraft. This is the first channel of endogenous money creation. At the end of the period, when the Government realize fiscal revenues and households update their wealth, households can convert a share of deposits to buy back a share of public debt. As a result, public debt is ex-post funded by household savings (final finance). The end of-the period accounting of SFC model may give the illusion that public deficit is financed by households' wealth, however, it is the CB overdraft that allows for the original creation of deposits, from which households can purchase the corresponding public debt.[13] Through the proceeding of the paper, and in particular, in Section Five, the difference between initial and final finance will become clear.

The second channel of money creation is the financing of investments through bank loans. Through the same mechanism, investments can be ex-post founded by households purchasing equities (Graziani 2003). Anyhow, the focus of the paper is to show the relationship between monetary savings and endogenous money, independently from the form they take and portfolio choices of households.

Firstly, to analyze the relationship between investments and saving, we must examine the dynamic of capital accumulation when net investments are positive. To do this, we proceed with our analysis by considering stock rather than flow variables. Figure 1 reports the levels of private and public debt, savings, and capital stocks as the share of investments financed by retained profits increases. In the full-leverage scenario, α is equal to zero and investments are fully financed by bank loans. In the zero-leverage scenario ($\alpha = 1$), investments are fully financed by retained profits. In the partial–leverage scenario α is equal to 0.5.

As shown in Figure 1, the stock of savings (including check deposits) is always equal to the stock of aggregate debt (private plus public debt). Depending on firms' leverage to finance investments, the level and composition of aggregate debt changes. Symmetrically, the level of household savings changes, and is originated by different sources of indebtedness.

When $\alpha = 0$, the capital stock is equal to firms' debt and the stock of savings is equal to the sum of public debt and private debt. Namely, the direct financing of investments through bank loans generates a corresponding amount of saving. When $\alpha = 1$, a share of profits is retained to finance investments, household savings are only generated by public debt.

Notably, the initial finance of investments through bank loans corresponds to an endogenous creation of money generating a corresponding amount of deposits.

[12] We chose a stationary-state model because it allows us to have not very complex analytical formulations of the stock values in the stationary state (see Di Domenico 2022 for a similar exercise with positive growth rates). Such an approach allows us to use the partial derivative of the stock of savings to study their relationship with the methos of financing and other parameters.

[13] In a system with only public spending and fiat money, the stock of deposits is equal to the amount of public bonds held by CB.

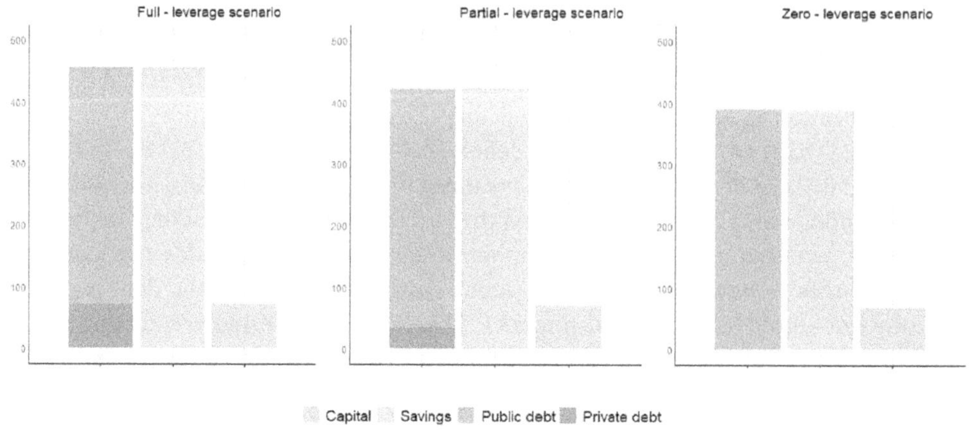

Figure 1. The effect of changes in α on the stock of debt and savings.

Conversely, when the initial finance of investments is realized through retained profits, the expansion of investment does not coincide with an exogenous injection of purchasing power into the system and does not generate any saving. Indeed, investment spending simply corresponds to a recirculation of existing income without affecting the liability-assets relationships of the system. Such difference is also understandable looking at the reduction in the output level as the share of investments financed out of retained profits increase. In the first step, the initial finance through retained profit corresponds to a reduction in households' disposable income and consumption (compared to the case of $\alpha = 0$). However, this amount is recirculated due to the investment and still leads to higher spending than if the income were distributed entirely to households and used only for consumption. In this sense, it is easy to verify that:

$$(YD_t - I_t)c_1 + I_t > YD_t c_1 \tag{27}$$

Hence, when calculated in terms of spending on disposable income, investment financed through retained profits figures as an increase in the average propensity to consume. In contrast, when investment is financed through debt it figures as an 'exogenous' addition to existing demand and has a greater expansionary effect. Indeed:

$$YD_t c_1 + I_t > (YD_t - I_t)c_1 + I_t \tag{28}$$

In this regard, it is possible to verify that the value of the (super) multiplier is maximum when $\alpha = 0$ and it is at the minimum level when $\alpha = 1$. The (super) multiplier when $\alpha = 0$ is:

$$m_{\alpha=0} = \frac{1}{1 - c_1[1 - \theta - v\delta(1 - \theta)] - v\delta} \tag{29}$$

The (super) multiplier when $\alpha = 1$ is:

$$m_{\alpha=1} = \frac{1}{1 - c_1(1 - \theta - v\delta) - v\delta} \tag{30}$$

Where:

$$\frac{1}{1-c_1[1-\theta-v\delta(1-\theta)]-v\delta} > \frac{1}{1-c_1(1-\theta-v\delta)-v\delta} \tag{31}$$

When investments are financed through retained profits, the reduction in consumption has a cascade effect on investments and aggregate demand, ultimately resulting in lower levels of income, debt, and savings (compared to the case of investments financed by loans). In this scenario, saving is primarily generated through the public deficit. Conversely, the model suggests that the maximum level of GDP and savings is achieved when investments are fully financed through loans. In this case, household savings are generated by both public debt and firms' debt.

To better highlight such relationships, we can consider the system with a positive propensity to consume out-of-wealth ($c_2 > 0$ in equations 2 and 8). In this scenario, it is possible to determine the stationary state values of stocks (debts and savings) and apply the partial derivatives of the stationary stock of savings with respect to α to study the impact of different types of investment financing. The stationary values of stock and flow variables are:

$$Y^* = \frac{G}{\theta[1-\delta v(1-\alpha)]} \tag{32}$$

$$I^* = \frac{Gv\delta}{\theta[1-\delta v(1-\alpha)]} \tag{33}$$

$$K^* = \frac{Gv}{\theta[1-\delta v(1-\alpha)]} \tag{34}$$

$$L^* = \frac{Gv(1-\alpha)}{\theta[1-\delta v(1-\alpha)]} \tag{35}$$

$$M_c^* = \frac{G}{\theta}(1-\theta) \tag{36}$$

$$V^{h*} = \frac{(1-c_1)G(1-\theta-\delta v(1-\theta(1-\alpha)))}{\theta[1-\delta v(1-\alpha)]c_2} \tag{37}$$

$$B^* = G\frac{(1-c_1)\{1-\theta-\delta v[1-\theta(1-\alpha)]\}+c_2\{(1-\theta)[1-\delta v(1-\alpha)]-v(1-\alpha)\}}{\theta[1-\delta v(1-\alpha)]c_2} \tag{38}$$

The partial derivative of savings with respect to α is negative:

$$\frac{\partial V^{h*}}{\partial \alpha} = -\frac{(1-c_2)Gv\delta(1-v\delta)}{c_2[1-v(1-\alpha)\delta]^2\theta} < 0 \tag{39}$$

When the share of investments financed by retained profits increases, the amount of savings generated by investments decreases. In particular, when $\alpha = 1$ and investments are fully financed by retained profits, the stock of savings is simply equal to public debt minus current disposable income:

$$B^*_{\alpha=1} - M^*_{c_{\alpha=1}} = B^* = G\frac{(1-c_1)(1-\theta-\delta v)}{\theta c_2} \tag{40}$$

We can verify that the latter is equal to the stock of savings:

$$V^{h*}_{\alpha=1} = \frac{G(1-c_1)(1-\theta-\delta v)}{\theta c_2} \tag{41}$$

That is, investments do not generate any changes in the stock of monetary savings. Conversely, when investments are fully financed by an endogenous process of money creation, they generate a corresponding amount of monetary saving. In this case, the stock of savings is equal to the sum of public debt and private debt. The latter, in turn, is equal to the capital stock.

The sum of public and private debt, net of disposable income is:

$$B^*_{\alpha=0} + L^*_{\alpha=0} - M^*_{c_{\alpha=0}} = G\frac{(1-c_1)(1-\theta)}{c_2\theta} \tag{42}$$

The stock of savings is:

$$V^{h*}_{\alpha=0} = G\frac{(1-c_1)(1-\theta)}{c_2\theta} \tag{43}$$

Finally, it is possible to verify that, given the same initial conditions and the level of public spending, the stock of savings is higher compared to the case when investments are fully financed by retained profits:

$$V^{h*}_{\alpha=0} > V^{h*}_{\alpha=1} \tag{44}$$

Indeed:

$$(1-\theta) > (1-\theta-\delta v) \tag{45}$$

In case $\alpha = 1$, the circular flow of income only depends on the injection of purchasing power realized through public spending. For the same reason, the amount of saving that households retain from this circulation only determines the public deficit and is independent of investments.

In sum, when investments are fully financed by retained profits, they are indirectly financed by the public spending financed through the CB overdraft. In this case, the circular flow of income interlay originates from CB purchasing of public bonds. The latter, being the only mechanisms of endogenous money creation, results to be the only mechanism generating monetary saving. When investments are financed through bank loans, a second mechanism of money and debt creation comes into a play. As a result, investments add a second mechanism of monetary saving generation.

To further examine the relationship between investments and monetary saving and eliminate the effect produced by changes in total output and level of investments when α changes, the next section considers autonomous investments in the system.

This approach allows us to assess the impact on savings of an exogenous shock on investments in the two extreme cases, namely when investments are financed by loans ($\alpha = 0$) or when investments are financed by retained profits ($\alpha = 1$).

4. Autonomous Investments and Monetary Saving

This section considers the same SFC model presented in Section Three, with autonomous investments. Then, $I = \bar{I}$ replaces equation 5. The steady-state solutions of the system are:

$$Y^* = \frac{\bar{G} + \bar{I}\{1 - c_1[1 - \theta(1 - \alpha)]\}}{1 - (1 - \theta)c_1} \tag{46}$$

$$C^* = \frac{c_1\{\bar{G}(1 - \theta) + \bar{I}\alpha\theta\}}{1 - c_1(1 - \theta)} \tag{47}$$

$$K^* = \frac{I}{\delta} \tag{48}$$

$$L^* = \frac{\bar{I}(1 - \alpha)}{\delta} \tag{49}$$

$$\Delta L^* = 0 \tag{50}$$

$$\Delta V^{h*} = \frac{(1 - c)[\bar{G}(1 - \theta) - \bar{I}\alpha\theta]}{1 - c_1(1 - \theta)} \tag{51}$$

$$\Delta B^* = \frac{(1 - c)[\bar{G}(1 - \theta) - \bar{I}\alpha\theta]}{1 - c_1(1 - \theta)} \tag{52}$$

$$S_t = \bar{G}m^s_G + +\bar{I}m^s_I \tag{53}$$

$$m^s_G = \frac{(1 - c_1)f[(c_1 f)^n + t(1 - c_1 f) - 1]}{(c_1 f - 1)^2} \tag{54}$$

$$m^s_I = \frac{1}{\delta(1 - c_1 f)^2(-1 + \delta + c_1 f)}(1 - c_1) \left\{ \begin{array}{l} (-1 + \delta)f(-1 + c_1 f)[(-1 + (1 - \delta)^t)(-1 + c_1 f) + \delta(-1 + (c_1 f)^t)] \\ +\alpha[(-1 + (1 - \delta)^t)f(-1 + c_1 f)^2 + \delta(-1 + c_1 f)(-1 + (c_1 f)^t \\ +t + f(-1 + c_1 f + (1 - \delta)^n(1 - c_1 f) - t - c_1 t + c_1 f t)) \\ +\delta^2(-1 + (cf)^t + t - f(t + c(f(-1 + (c_1 f)^n - t) + t)))] \end{array} \right\} \tag{55}$$

Where $f = 1 - \theta$. As in the previous system, the stationary-state level of net investments is zero and the flow of saving is generated only by the public deficit. Now, we assess the impact of a positive shock on the permanent level of investments on the flow of saving. Figure 2 reports the effect of a permanent increase in gross investments in both full-leverage ($\alpha = 0$) and zero-leverage scenarios ($\alpha = 1$).

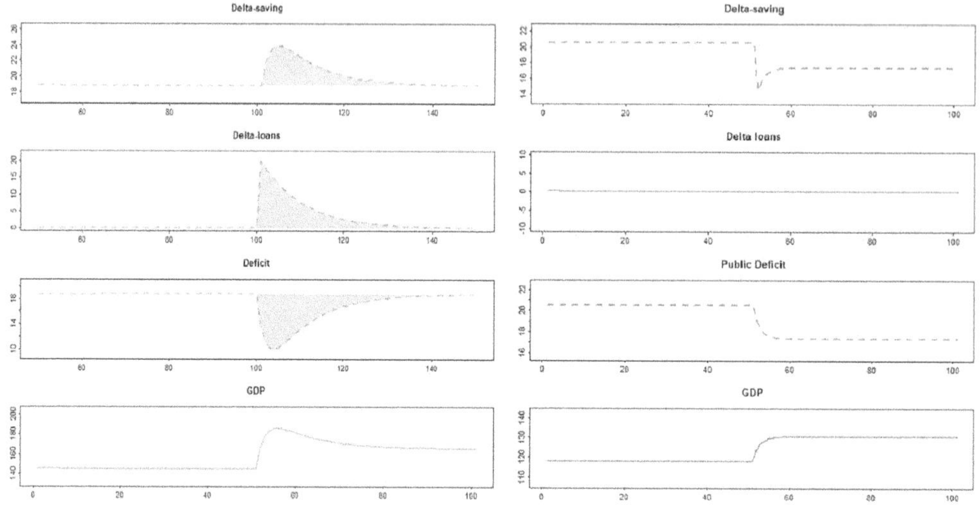

Figure 2. Impact of a persistent increase in gross investments. Left side ($\alpha = 0$). Right side ($\alpha = 1$).

When $\alpha = 0$, the partial derivative of equation (51) with respect to investments is positive and the flow of investments generates a proportional and positive amount of saving:

$$m_I^s > 0 \tag{56}$$

The increase in net investments generates an equal amount of saving that, in turn, is equal to the variation of firms' debt. The flow of investments corresponds to an exogenous injection of purchasing power and the amount of money that is retained by households (as savings/deposits) and the Government (through taxation) from such injection corresponds to the net variation in firms' debt. The flow of saving generated by investments is split into a reduction in the public deficit and an increase in household savings.

$$\sum_{i=s}^{T} \Delta L_i = \sum_{i=s}^{T} \Delta I_i = \sum_{i=s}^{T} \Delta S_i + \sum_{i=s}^{T} \Delta B_i \tag{57}$$

The cumulated flows of saving produced by the variation in net investments correspond to the shaded areas in Figure 2. Given a constant level of public spending, public deficit decreases since a higher amount of fiscal revenues is generated by the taxation on the income produced by the flow of investments. When $\alpha = 1$ the partial derivative is negative and the increase in investments leads to a decrease in the stock of savings:

$$m_I^s < 0 \tag{58}$$

As described in Section Three, the financing of investments through retained profits figures as a higher share of income that is spent and, thus, as an increase in the average propensity to consume. Since all the circular flow of income is financed (or generated) by public debt, a higher average propensity to consume implies a lower public deficit. Therefore, the accumulation of private savings decreases as well.

In detail, the increase in investments partially offset private consumption, but, since $\left|\frac{\partial C^*}{\partial I}\right| < \left|\frac{\partial Y^*}{\partial I}\right|$, GDP increases:

$$\frac{\partial Y^*}{\partial I} = \frac{1 + c_1}{1 - (1 - \theta)c_1} > 0 \tag{59}$$

$$\frac{\partial C^*}{\partial I} = c_1\left[\frac{(1 + c_1)\theta}{1 - c_1(1 - \theta)} - 1\right] < 0 \tag{60}$$

That is, the increase in investments more than offsets the decrease in consumption (this effect is like the one depicted in the Haavelmo theorem)[14] and figures as an increase in the average propensity to consume.

As shown in Di Domenico (2022), the accumulation of public debt is determined, among other factors, by the saving rate of the economy and is positively correlated with it. When investments are financed through retained profits, the public deficit becomes the only source of debt that can generate household saving. If the saving rate decreases, the public deficit also decreases, and the expansion of investment leads to a decrease in the flow of saving.

This analysis leads to an important conclusion: net investment generates a corresponding amount of household saving only when financed through bank loans. In this case, investments represent an exogenous injection of purchasing power into the system, leading to a symmetrical accumulation of debt and savings. Conversely, when investments are financed through retained profits, they are indirectly financed through the already existing income circulation that, in turn, is indirectly financed by public spending. In this case, a positive shock to the level of investments corresponds to an increase in the average propensity to consume and, therefore it produces a decrease in the flow of household saving by reducing public deficit.

5. Initial and Final Finance of Autonomous Components and Investments

In this section, we delve into the mechanism of initial and final finance that underpins the presented model. In particular, we compare the cases where the initial finance of autonomous components and investments is operated through the existing stock of wealth or endogenous money. This exercise is functional to highlight the mechanism by which the SM approach, and, more in general, the Keynesian principle of investment determining saving and the independence of the autonomous components from current income requires an endogens process of money creation.

In the framework we presented, as in the monetary circuit approach, it is the ex-ante financing through endogenous money, of autonomous components and investments (initial finance) that allows them to be ex-post founded by saving (final finance). It is the initial finance of bank loans that, generating a corresponding amount of deposits, allows investments to be ex-post founded by household equities. Households can convert a share of the deposits created by bank loans to purchase firm equities. At the

[14]The amount of income subtracted to consumption and used to finance investments is entirely spent, while only a fraction of such income would be spent if remains in the hand of households.

end of the process, the illusion that the investments have been financed by household saving can appear.

Similarly, government spending, financed by purchasing power creation (initial finance), allows the ex-post funding (final finance) by taxes and household savings. Usually, as pointed out by Modern Monetary Theory (MMT), government spending is typically financed by the CB, later funded by tax collection, and if tax revenues are insufficient, by collecting savings. However, as shown in Cesaratto and Di Bucchianico (2020) and Lavoie (2013), the same mechanism is implemented when the initial finance is performed by commercial banks. Regardless of a specific source of money creation, the point is that it is the act of spending financed by endogenous money that, through the multiplier, generates a residual amount of monetary saving.

For the sake of clarity, let's consider one type of expenditure at a time. As a first step, we consider only public spending by taking the SM model presented in Section Three and removing induced investments. Figure 3 presents numerical simulations in the scenario where households prefer to hold their wealth only in the form of deposits and the propensity to consume out-of-wealth is positive. At the beginning of the period, CB provides an overdraft of 50 to the government to finance public spending. This injection of purchasing power results, in the first period, in an equivalent increase in output, tax revenues of 15, and government debt of 35. At the end of the period, disposable income is distributed to households and recorded as check deposits. In period 2, demand is the sum of government spending and household consumption generated by the disposable income distributed at the end of period 1. At the end of period 2, households can decide to hold savings in the form of public bonds or deposits. In case $\beta = 0$, households desire to hold their wealth in the form of deposits, the change in the stock of deposits equals the change in public bonds held by CB. This sequence repeats in each period. After a number of periods, the economy reaches a stationary state, where GDP and stocks remain constant over time. The stationary value of GDP is the result of the overlapping of multiplier sequences triggered by public spending realized in each period. In each period, the amount of deposits is equal to the amount of public bonds held by CB which, in turn, is equal to the amount of reserves. As illustrated in Figure 3, it is the CB's process of money creation financing public deficit that allows the collection of taxes and generates a corresponding amount of deposits.[15]

In case households desire to hold a share of their wealth in the form of public bonds, at the end of the period, they can convert a share of deposits created by CB into public bonds. In this case, the public debt held by CB and the amount of reserves decrease proportionally. If households desire to hold the wealth completely in the form of public bonds, deposits and public bonds held by CB are zero. The ex-ante financing of public spending by endogenous money allows public deficit to be ex-post financed by household saving. Figure 4 displays such scenario.

Without the initial finance of public spending by CB, it would not be possible to generate deposits through which public debt is ex-post founded by households. This raises the question: is it possible that public spending is ex-ante financed by households? In other words, can the initial financing of a constant level of the autonomous component be structurally carried out through household saving, rather than endogenous money creation?

[15] Such mechanism would be activated also in the case public spending is ex-ante financing by commercial banks.

Time	Gov. exp.	Consumption	GDP	Publid debt	CB bonds	Time deposits	Check dep.	Households bonds	Loans	Reserves
1	50	0	50	28	28	0	28	0	0	28
2	50	25	75	44	44	3	41	0	0	44
3	50	37	87	55	55	7	48	0	0	55
4	50	44	94	62	62	11	52	0	0	62
..	..	..	..	..	..	..	..	..	..	..
48	50	61	111	121	121	60	61	0	0	121
49	50	61	111	121	121	60	61	0	0	121
50	50	61	111	121	121	60	61	0	0	121

Figure 3. Initial and final finance of public spending: households hold the stock of wealth in the form of deposits.

Time	Gov. exp.	Consumption	GDP	Publid debt	CB bonds	Time deposits	Check dep.	Households bonds	Loans	Reserves
1	50	0	50	28	28	0	28	0	0	28
2	50	25	75	44	41	0	41	3	0	41
3	50	37	87	55	48	0	48	7	0	48
4	50	44	94	62	52	0	52	11	0	52
..	..	..	..	..	..	..	..	..	..	..
48	50	61	111	121	61	0	61	60	0	61
49	50	61	111	121	61	0	61	60	0	61
50	50	61	111	121	61	0	61	60	0	61

Figure 4. Initial and final finance of public spending: households hold the stock of wealth in the form of bonds.

Firstly, there must be a pre-existing stock of deposits. Since deposits are only created through endogenous money, which occurs when the central bank or commercial banks finance government spending, investment or consumer credit, it is necessary that for a sufficient number of periods, the autonomous component has been financed through money creation. Then, the initial finance operated by households is eventually possible only after an ex-ante accumulation of public bonds by CB. Moreover, it must be assumed that for a certain number of periods, households prefer to hold their savings in the form of deposits. Only at this point, it is possible to force public spending to be initially financed by household deposits by imposing a change in portfolio preferences. Household deposits act as initial finance.

In the numerical example shown in Figure 5, the propensity to consume and the tax rate have been fixed in such a way as to generate a sufficient accumulation of deposits in

Time	Gov. exp.	Consumption	GDP	Publid debt	CB bonds	Time deposits	Check dep.	Households bonds	Loans	Reserves
49	50	61	111	121	121	60	61	0	0	121
50	50	61	111	121	121	60	61	0	0	121
51	50	61	111	121	121	60	61	0	0	121
52	50	61	111	121	121	60	61	0	0	121
53	50	61	111	122	121	60	61	0	0	121

Figure 5. Initial finance of public spending through household deposits.

the stationary state. In this case, in the stationary-state, the public deficit is zero and public spending generates an equal amount of fiscal revenues. Starting from period 50, we impose the initial finance must be realized through household deposits. At the end of the period, since public spending generates an equal amount of taxes, households do not hold any public bonds, and all their wealth is held in the form of deposits. Ultimately, it is necessary to assume previous financing through endogenous money of government spending to allow interim financing through the existing stock of savings.

Is it possible to finance a fiscal expansion through the existing stock of wealth? Figure 6 reports the case in which the increase in public spending is consistent with the existing stock of wealth. From period 50, the expansion of public spending is ex-ante financed by household wealth. The debt-financing of public deficit generates a corresponding amount of saving. As shown in Figure 6, household wealth increases by 6 (bonds increase by 12, while time deposits decrease by 6) although no process of endogenous money creation has been activated.

It is important to note that, for all the previous cases to be realized, two special hypotheses are required. The first hypothesis considers that the stock of debt financed by CB or commercial bank (namely, the stock that, though the endogenous money process has generated a corresponding amount of deposits) does not have to be reimbursed, or the related bonds must be renewed in perpetuity. Indeed, if this debt were to be repaid and rolled over through the sale of bonds to households, a corresponding amount of deposits would be destroyed. It follows that if all the debt held by the Central Bank were to be repaid at maturity, the stock of deposits would disappear, and it would precisely not be possible to finance government spending from household savings. Hence, an ongoing process of endogenous money creation, i.e., one aimed at renewing maturing securities, is always necessary to imagine some role of the stock of household savings in initial finance operations. The second hypothesis requires that, in correspondence with the fiscal expansion, there is a change in household portfolio preferences. In particular, it is necessary to assume that households preferred to hold wealth in the form of deposits initially and, from the shock onward, in the form of public bonds. The same applies to the scenario of refinancing a constant level of public spending.

These examples show that the initial finance of autonomous components and investments cannot be considered as a structural mechanism of financing. First, as above-mentioned, because the initial finance operated through household wealth requires the pre-existence of a stock of deposits.[16] Since deposits are created only through money creation, that is, when the central bank or commercial bank finances government spending, investment, or consumer credit, it is necessary that for a sufficient number of periods the spending components have been financed through endogenous money. In this sense, initial finance through the existing stock of wealth can exist only as a spin-off of the structural flow of deposit creation generated by expenditures financed through endogenous money. These possibilities will always be tied to the size of the former and cannot exist without it. Second, for a fixed/constant amount of deposits to keep existing, there is a need for an ever-living process of monetary creation aimed at renewing maturing debts.[17]

[16]In addition, such deposits have to be sufficient to finance the autonomous level of public spending or investments.
[17]While it could be realistically assumed that CB, the same do not apply for bank loans.

Time	Gov. exp.	Consumption	GDP	Publid debt	CB bonds	Time deposits	Check dep.	Households bonds	Loans	Reserves
49	50	61	111	121	121	60	61	0	0	121
50	50	61	111	121	121	60	61	0	0	121
51	55	61	116	124	121	58	64	3	0	121
52	55	63	118	126	121	56	65	5	0	121
53	55	65	120	127	121	56	66	6	0	121
...	...	...	...	...	...	...	...	...	...	...
70	55	67	122	133	121	54	67	12	0	121
71	55	67	122	133	121	54	67	12	0	121
72	55	67	122	133	121	54	67	12	0	121

Figure 6. Financing the fiscal expansion through household deposits.

Third, in a growing economy or one with positive inflation, it is not possible to imagine a structural financing of investments and autonomous components through a constant stock of deposits. A positive growth rate of expenditure components unequivocally requires an endogenous process of money creation. As argued by Rochon and Rossi (2004): 'In a monetary economy of production, credit is needed to enable firms to continue and expand production. There is a definitive link between bank credit and economic growth.'

Now, we can extend the analysis to the case of investments financed through the existing stock of savings. In this case, the initial finance is operated through equity emissions. For the sake of clarity, let's consider the income-expenditure model with autonomous investments ($\bar{I}$) and excluding public spending.[18] In this way, we can focus on the investments-saving nexus.

$$Y_t = C_t + \bar{I} \tag{61}$$

$$C_t = YD_{t-1}c_1 + V^h_{t-1}c_2 \tag{62}$$

$$YD_t = Y_t - K_t\delta \tag{63}$$

$$V^h_t = V^h_{t-1}(1 - c_2) + YD_{t-1}(1 - c_1) \tag{64}$$

$$E^h_t = E^h_{t-1} + min(M_t, \bar{I}\,\varepsilon - K^{eq}_t\delta) \tag{65}$$

$$L_t = L_{t-1}(1 - \delta) + I_t(1 - \varepsilon) \tag{66}$$

$$K^{eq}_t = K^{eq}_{t-1}(1 - \delta) + I_t\varepsilon \tag{67}$$

$$M^h_t = V^h_t - E^h_t \tag{68}$$

$$L_t = M_t \tag{69}$$

[18]For the sake of clarity, we are considering a system with autonomous investment in place of the traditional investment function because the latter necessarily require another autonomous component in the system, such as public spending. In that case, since the creation of deposits depends also on the deposits created by CB, the macroeconomic relationships could appear less clear.

With respect to the first system of equation (p. 11), equation (61) defines the GDP as the sum of autonomous investments and consumptions, while equation (62) is the same of equation (2). Disposable income (equation 63) is equal to the NDP.[19] E_t^h is the amount of equity, ε is the percentage of investments financed issuing equities, K_t^{eq} is the stock of capital financed by equity emissions, δ is the capital depreciation rate. According to equation 65, E_t^h is equal to stock of equity from the previous period plus the new amount of equity purchased by household, where this is equal to the minimum between the stock of deposits (M_t) and the new emission of equity by the firms ($\bar{I}\ \varepsilon - K_t^{eq}\delta$) [20]. The stock of loans is equal to the amount carried over from the previous year plus the share of investments financed by loans (equation 66). Equation 68 refers to the stock of deposits, which is equal to household wealth minus equity. Equation (69) is the redundant equation, according to which the stock of loans is equal to the stock of deposits in a closed-economy without public debt.

As before, we must assume that for a sufficient number of periods, investments have been financed through endogenous money (bank loans). In this way, it is possible to accumulate a sufficient stock of deposits. The results are reported in Figure 7.

Starting from period 80, investments are financed by issuing equities, hence households convert a share of deposits into equity. Parallelly, since firms must repay the debt previously incurred, in each period an amount of deposits is destroyed. As a result, after some periods, it is no longer possible to finance investments drawing on household wealth. After period 84, the stock of deposits is lower than the flow of investments. Trivially, a given amount of deposits can only continue to exist if a proportional amount of bank (or CB) debt continues to exist. If the latter must be repaid, the stock of deposits will decrease simultaneously.

Lastly, as done for the case of public spending, we study the case in which the initial finance of investment expansion is realized through equity emission (see Figure 8). First, as before, it is necessary to assume that investments have been financed by bank loans for a number of periods to generate a sufficient amount of deposits. Then, the investment expansion (financed by equity) initially leads to an increase in household savings. It is worth noticing that the fact that investments are financed through the existing stock of savings does not imply that saving determines investments. Indeed, still it is investment decisions that determines a corresponding amount of saving. To this extent, imposing that investments have to be financed by household savings means that savings are constraining investment possibilities, but not determining investments.

However, once the shock is imposed, the existing stock of deposits starts being reduced.[21] Indeed, deposits exist as a counterpart of an equal amount of debt that has to be reimbursed. As firms repay the loan, a proportional amount of deposits is destroyed. As long as net investments are positive (i.e., equity issuance exceeds capital depreciation, which includes a portion equal to the bank installments), they generate a corresponding amount of saving. After some periods, deposits are no longer sufficient to finance the increased level of investments, compromising the possibility of

[19]Please note that $K_t = L_t + K_t^{eq}$ that is the sum of loans plus the stock of capital financed by equity. As for the system at p. 11, the income before tax is net of depreciations allowances. These, in turn, are composed of a share of debt repayment and profits retained to replace the share of capital financed through equity.

[20]According to $\bar{I}\ \varepsilon - K_t^{eq}\delta$, the new amount of equity is equal to the of net investments financed by equity emission.

[21]Firms keep reimbursing the previous debt, this translates into a reduction in disposable income while households keep transforming the accumulated stock of deposits into equities over time. Then, a share of deposits is indirectly destroyed when households keep buying firms' equity and these keep paying back previous loans.

Time	Investments	Consumption	GDP	Publid debt	CB bonds	Time deposits	Check dep.	Households bonds	Loans	Equity	Reserves
2	60	0	60	0	0	0	60	0	60	0	0
3	60	54	114	0	0	6	108	0	114	0	0
4	60	98	158	0	0	16	146	0	163	0	0
...	...	...	...	...	...	...	...	...	...	...	...
79	60	300	360	0	0	300	300	0	600	0	0
80	60	300	360	0	0	300	300	0	600	0	0
81	60	300	360	0	0	240	300	0	540	60	0
82	60	300	360	0	0	180	306	0	486	120	0
83	60	305	365	0	0	120	317	0	437	180	0
84	60	315	375	0	0	62	331	0	394	240	0
85	60	329	389	0	0	5	349	0	354	300	0

Figure 7. Initial finance of investments through equity emission.

Time	Investments	Consumption	GDP	Publid debt	CB bonds	Time deposits	Check dep.	Households bonds	Loans	Equity	Reserves
2	60	0	60	0	0	0	60	0	60	0	0
3	60	54	114	0	0	6	108	0	114	0	0
4	60	98	158	0	0	16	146	0	163	0	0
...	...	...	...	...	...	...	...	...	...	...	...
77	60	300	360	0	0	300	300	0	600	0	0
78	60	300	360	0	0	300	300	0	600	0	0
79	60	300	360	0	0	300	300	0	600	0	0
80	60	300	360	0	0	300	300	0	600	0	0
81	90	300	390	0	0	210	330	0	540	90	0
82	90	327	417	0	0	123	363	0	486	180	0
83	90	357	447	0	0	39	398	0	437	270	0

Figure 8. Financing investments expansion through equity emission.

financing investments through equity emission. In this sense, the financing of investments through equity emissions can be considered only as temporary, as well as subordinated financing to the process of endogenous money.

In general, the financing of investments through equity (that is through the conversion of the existing stock of deposits) does not intact the causality that goes from investments to saving, however, taken alone, it undermines the hypothesis of independence of investments from saving. Namely, an increase in equity-financed investment raises the stock of savings (and debt), but needs ex-ante formation of savings (and, in particular, deposits).

Of course, when we include other autonomous components in the model and assume that these are financed through endogenous money, the possibility of financing investments through equity increases. Indeed, in that case, it is possible to draw on the stock of deposits continually fueled by the endogenous money aimed at financing such autonomous components. If bank loans are excluded, the only remaining source of money creation is the financing of public spending by CB.[22] If investments are fully

[22]In this case, it is necessary to assume that households prefer to hold equity and deposits, while they do not want public securities. Conversely, if they wish to hold public securities, the amount of deposits created by the public securities purchased by the CB would not exist and, therefore, it would not be possible to purchase equity.

financed by equities, they are indirectly financed by deposits generated by CB when financing public spending (assuming that households do not hold their wealth entirely in the form of public bonds).

In the same way, if investments are fully financed by retained profits, they are indirectly financed through the circular flow of income triggered by public spending financed by CB. In both cases, investments cannot be considered completely autonomous since they depend on the path of public spending and saving rate.

In conclusion, this section was intended to highlight how the initial finance realized through household savings, although it generates an equal amount of saving, can be considered only as a transitory way of financing. It cannot be considered as a structural mechanism since it constantly requires a parallel financing of the expenditure components through endogenous money which, by creating a stock of deposits, will allow it to partially exist as an appendage of the latter.

6. Conclusions

The paper contributes to the Post-Keynesian literature taking the first steps in building a monetary theory of demand-driven growth. Our contribution argues that the endogenous money theory plays a non-ancillary role within the Supermultiplier approach. On the one hand, we point out that the Keynesian principle of investments determining saving along with the existence of autonomous components of demand, naturally implies the notion of endogenous money. On the other hand, we demonstrate that integrating the Supermultiplier and the endogenous money theory allows to clearly define the whole economic mechanism describing the financing of autonomous components and investments, as well as the determination of output and saving in a monetary economy of production.

Our derivations stem from the recognition that in a monetary economy of production, monetary savings exist only as the counterpart of liabilities: a sector can have positive financial (or monetary) wealth only if one or more sectors have negative financial wealth. If one sector reduces its debt, the savings of other sectors necessarily decrease, and vice versa.

First, we show that the initial finance of deficit public spending through CB (or commercial banks) and investments through bank loans allows them to be (structurally) ex-post founded by household saving. Specifically, we point out that public deficit spending or investments generate a corresponding amount of monetary saving only when financed through debt creation. When investments are fully financed by loans, they directly activate a process of endogenous money creation, resulting in a higher amount of saving generated through a corresponding expansion in firms' debt. Conversely, when the expansion of investments is fully financed by retained profits, it figures as an increase in the average propensity to consume, while public deficit and household saving decrease.

Second, although debt-financing and liability-asset linkages can also be realized through the existing stock of wealth, the endogenous money creation process is the only structural mechanism that allows investments to be independent of and determine saving in the long-run, enabling autonomous components to be defined as such. In this sense, the initial finance of investments and public spending by issuing equities or selling public bonds to households can only be considered a temporary spin-off of the endogenous money process. The subordination of the financing through the existing stock of wealth (deposits) to the process of endogenous money creation relies on three main points: (i) the pre-existence of a stock of deposits: investments and autonomous components must have been founded by endogenous money for a sufficient span of time to generate a 'sufficient' amount of deposits. (ii) The concept of 'perpetual deposits' and 'perpetual debt': the stock of deposits keeps existing over time only if the corresponding debt is not reimbursed, or if a rollover through endogenous money is continuously operating. (iii) Even in the case the stock of deposits is regarded as a 'manna from heaven', a fixed amount of deposits cannot fuel a growing economy or an economy with positive inflation.

Acknowledgements

The authors would like to thank the reviewers for their helpful and constructive comments and suggestions. All remaining errors are of the authors.

Disclosure Statement

No potential conflict of interest was reported by the author(s).

ORCID

Davide Romaniello http://orcid.org/0000-0001-9960-3036

References

Accoce, J. V., and T. Mouakil. 2007. 'The Monetary Circuit Approach: A StockFlow Consistent Model.' In *Money, Distribution and Economic Policy: Alternatives to Orthodox Macroeconomics*, edited by E. Eckhard Hein and A. Truger. Cheltenham: Edward Elgar Publishing.

Allain, O. 2015. 'Tackling the Instability of Growth: A Kaleckian-Harrodian Model with an Autonomous Expenditure Component.' *Cambridge Journal of Economics* 39 (5): 1351–1371.

Arestis, P., and A. S. Eichner. 1988. 'The Post-Keynesian and Institutionalist Theory of Money and Credit.' *Journal of Economic Issues* 22 (4): 1003–1021.

Berr, É, and V. Monvoisin. 2023. 'Monetary Circuit Theory, Stock-flow Consistent Modeling and Parguez's Analysis.' *International Journal of Political Economy* 52 (3–4): 317–327.

Bertocco, G., and A. Kalajzić. 2022. 'On the Monetary Nature of Savings: A Critical Analysis of the Loanable Funds Theory (No. PKWP2206).'

Bortis, H. 1997. *Institutions, Behaviour and Economic Theory: A Contribution to Classical-Keynesian Political Economy*. Cambridge University Press.

Brochier, L. 2020. 'Conflicting-claims and Labour Market Concerns in a Supermultiplier SFC Model.' *Metroeconomica* 71 (3): 566–603.

Brochier, L., and A. C. Macedo e Silva. 2019. 'A Supermultiplier Stock-flow Consistent Model: The Return of the Paradoxes of Thrift and Costs in the Long Run?' *Cambridge Journal of Economics* 43 (2): 413–442.

Carnevali, E., M. Deleidi, R. Pariboni, and M. Veronese Passarella. 2024. 'Economy-finance-environment-society Interconnections in a Stock-flow Consistent Dynamic Model.' *Review of Political Economy* 36 (2): 844–878.

Caverzasi, E., and A. Godin. 2013. 'Stock-flow Consistent Modeling through the Ages.' Levy Economics Institute of Bard College Working Paper (745).

Caverzasi, E., and A. Godin. 2015. 'Post-Keynesian Stock-flow-consistent Modelling: A Survey.' *Cambridge Journal of Economics* 39 (1): 157–187.
Cesaratto, S. 2017. 'Initial and Final Finance in the Monetary Circuit and the Theory of Effective Demand.' *Metroeconomica* 68 (2): 228–258.
Cesaratto, S., and S. Di Bucchianico. 2020. 'Endogenous Money and the Theory of Long-period Effective Demand.' *Bulletin of Political Economy* 14 (1): 1–38.
Cesaratto, S., F. Serrano, and A. Stirati. 2003. 'Technical Change, Effective Demand and Employment.' *Review of Political Economy* 15 (1): 33–52.
Deleidi, M. 2019. 'Horizontalists, Structuralists and the Credit Market: An Empirical Assessment of Post-Keynesian Endogenous Money Approaches.' *Bulletin of Political Economy* 13 (1): 21–53.
Deleidi, M. 2020. 'Post-Keynesian Endogenous Money Theory: Horizontalists, Structuralists and the Paradox of Illiquidity.' *Metroeconomica* 71 (1): 156–175.
Deleidi, M., and M. Mazzucato. 2019. 'Putting Austerity to Bed: Technical Progress, Aggregate Demand and the Supermultiplier.' *Review of Political Economy* 31 (3): 315–335.
Deleidi, M., and M. Mazzucato. 2021. 'Directed Innovation Policies and the Supermultiplier: An Empirical Assessment of Mission-oriented Policies in the US Economy.' *Research Policy* 50 (2): 104151.
Di Domenico, L. 2022. 'Stability and Determinants of the Public Debt-to-GDP Ratio: A Stock-flow Consistent investigation (No. 888).' Department of Economics, University of Siena.
Di Domenico, L., M. C. B. Góes, and E. Gallo. 2023. 'Distribution, Capital Intensity and Public Debt-to-GDP Ratio: An Input Output — Stock Flow Consistent Model.' *Economia Politica*, 1–22. https://link.springer.com/article/10.1007/s40888-023-00318-7.
Dow, S. C. 1996. 'Horizontalism: A Critique.' *Cambridge Journal of Economics* 20 (4): 497–508.
Eichner, A. S. 1987. *The Macrodynamics of Advanced Market Economies.* Armonk, NY: M.E. Sharpe.
European Central Bank (ECB). 2011. 'Decision of the European Central Bank of 3 November 2011 on the Implementation of the Second Covered Bond Purchase Programme.' *Official Journal of the European Union* ECB/2011/17, 2011/744/EU.
Fazzari, S. M., P. Ferri, and A. M. Variato. 2020. 'Demand-led Growth and Accommodating Supply.' *Cambridge Journal of Economics* 44 (3): 583–605.
Fontana, G. 2003. 'Post Keynesian Approaches to Endogenous Money: A Time Framework Explanation.' *Review of Political Economy* 15 (3): 291–314.
Fontana, G. 2004. 'Rethinking Endogenous Money: A Constructive Interpretation of the Debate between Horizontalists and Structuralists.' *Metroeconomica* 55 (4): 367–385.
Fontana, G., R. Realfonzo, and M. V. Passarella. 2020. 'Monetary Economics After the Global Financial Crisis: What has Happened to the Endogenous Money Theory?' *European Journal of Economics and Economic Policies: Intervention* 17 (3): 339–355.
Fontana, G., and M. Setterfield. 2009. 'Macroeconomics, Endogenous Money and the Contemporary Financial Crisis.' *International Journal of Pluralism and Economic Education* 1 (1–2): 130–147.
Freitas, F., and F. Serrano. 2015. 'Growth Rate and Level Effects, the Stability of the Adjustment of Capacity to Demand and the Sraffian Supermultiplier.' *Review of Political Economy* 27 (3): 258–281.
Gahn, S. J., and A. González. 2020. 'On the "Utilisation Controversy": A Comment.' *Cambridge Journal of Economics* 44 (3): 703–707.
Garegnani, P. 1984. 'Value and Distribution in the Classical Economists and Marx.' *Oxford Economic Papers* 36 (2): 291–325.
Garegnani, P. 1992. 'Some Notes for an Analysis of Accumulation.' In *Beyond the Steady State. A Revival of Growth Theory*, edited by J. Halevi, D. Laibman, and E. Nell. London: Macmillan.
Garegnani, P. 2015. 'The Problem of Effective Demand in Italian Economic Development: On the Factors That Determine the Volume of Investment.' *Review of Political Economy* 27 (2): 111–133.
Girardi, D., and R. Pariboni. 2016. 'Long-run Effective Demand in the US Economy: An Empirical Test of the Sraffian Supermultiplier Model.' *Review of Political Economy* 28 (4): 523–544.

Godley, W., and M. Lavoie. 2007. *Monetary Economics: An Integrated Approach to Credit, Money, Income, Production and Wealth*. Basingstoke, UK: Palgrave Macmillan.

Graziani, A. 1990. 'The Theory of the Monetary Circuit.' *Économies et Sociétés* 24 (6): 7–36.

Graziani, A. 2003. *The Monetary Theory of Production*. Cambridge: Cambridge University Press.

Harrod, R. F. 1939. 'An Essay in Dynamic Theory.' *The Economic Journal* 49 (193): 14–33.

Hein, E. 2018. 'Autonomous Government Expenditure Growth, Deficits, Debt, and Distribution in a Neo-Kaleckian Growth Model.' *Journal of Post Keynesian Economics* 41 (2): 316–338.

Jakab, Z., and M. Kumhof. 2015. 'Banks are not Intermediaries of Loanable Funds–and why this Matters.' Bank of England. Working Paper No. 529.

Jakab, Z., and M. Kumhof. 2019. 'Banks are not Intermediaries of Loanable Funds — Facts, Theory and Evidence.' Bank of England. Working Paper No. 761.

Kaldor, N. 1970. 'The New Monetarism.' *Lloyds Bank Review* 97 (1): 18.

Kaldor, N. 1981. *Origins of the New Monetarism*. Cardiff: University College Cardiff Press.

Kalecki, M. 1943. 'Political Aspects of Full Employment.' *Political Quarterly* 14 (4): 322–331. [Reprinted in Osiatyński (1990), 347–356].

Lavoie, M. 1984. 'The Endogenous Flow of Credit and the Post Keynesian Theory of Money.' *Journal of Economic Issues* 18 (3): 771–797.

Lavoie, M. 1987. 'Monnaie et production: une synthèse de la théorie du circuit.' *Économies et Sociétés* 9:65–101.

Lavoie, M. 1996. 'Horizontalism, Structuralism, Liquidity Preference and the Principle of Increasing Risk.' *Scottish Journal of Political Economy* 43 (3): 275–300.

Lavoie, M. 2004. 'Circuit and Coherent Stock–Flow Accounting.' In *Money, Credit, and the Role of the State*, edited by R. Arena and N. Salvadori, 136–151. Aldershot: Ashgate.

Lavoie, M. 2013. 'The State, the Central Bank and the Monetary Circuit.' In *Monetary Economies of Production: Banking and Financial Circuits and the Role of the State*, edited by L.-P. Rochon and M. Seccareccia, 11–22. Cheltenham: Edward Elgar Publishing.

Lavoie, M. 2016. 'Convergence towards the Normal Rate of Capacity Utilization in Neo-Kaleckian Models: The Role of Non-capacity Creating Autonomous Expenditures.' *Metroeconomica* 67 (1): 172–201.

Levrero, E. S. 2013. 'Marx on Absolute and Relative Wages and the Modern Theory of Distribution.' *Review of Political Economy* 25 (1): 91–116.

Mandarino, G. V., C. H. Dos Santos, and A. C. Macedo e Silva. 2020. 'Workers' Debt-financed Consumption: A Supermultiplier Stock–Flow Consistent Model.' *Review of Keynesian Economics* 8 (3): 339–364.

McLeay, M., A. Radia, and R. Thomas. 2014. 'Money Creation in the Modern Economy.' *Bank of England Quarterly Bulletin Q1*.

Moore, B. J. 1988. *Horizontalists and Verticalists: The Macroeconomics of Credit Money*. Cambridge: Cambridge University Press.

Nell, E. 1996. 'The Circuit of Money in a Production Economy.' In *Money in Motion*, edited by E. Nell and G. Deleplace. London: Macmillan.

Nikiforos, M. 2016. 'On the "Utilization Controversy": A Theoretical and Empirical Discussion of the Kaleckian Model of Growth and Distribution.' *Cambridge Journal of Economics* 40 (2): 437–467.

Nikiforos, M., and G. Zezza. 2017. 'Stock-flow Consistent Macroeconomic Models: A Survey.' *Journal of Economic Surveys* 31 (5): 1204–1239.

Palley, T. I. 1994. 'Competing Views of the Money Supply Process: Theory and Evidence.' *Metroeconomica* 45 (1): 67–88.

Palley, T. I. 1996. 'Accommodationism Versus Structuralism: Time for an Accommodation.' *Journal of Post Keynesian Economics* 18 (4): 585–594.

Palley, T. I. 2017. 'The Theory of Endogenous Money and the LM Schedule: Prelude to a Reconstruction of ISLM.' *Revista de Economia Politica* 37 (1): 3–22.

Palley, T. 2019. 'The Economics of the Super-multiplier: A Comprehensive Treatment with Labor Markets.' *Metroeconomica* 70 (2): 325–340.

Parguez, A. 1981. 'Ordre social, monnaie et régulation.' *Économie appliquée* 34 (2): 383–448.

Pariboni, R. 2016. 'Household Consumer Debt, Endogenous Money and Growth: A Supermultiplier-Based Analysis.' *PSL Quarterly Review* 69 (278): 211–233.

Pedrosa, Í, L. Brochier, and F. Freitas. 2023. 'Debt Hierarchy: Autonomous Demand Composition, Growth and Indebtedness in a Supermultiplier Model.' *Economic Modelling* 126:106369.

Poulon, F. 1982. *Macroéconomie approfondie : équilibre, déséquilibre, circuit.* Paris: Cujas.

Robinson, J. 1952. *The Rate of Interest and Other Essays.* London, UK: Macmillan.

Rochon, L.-P. 1999. *Credit, Money and Production: An Alternative Post-Keynesian Approach.* Cheltenham, UK: Edward Elgar.

Rochon, L.-P. 2001. 'Horizontalism: Setting the Record Straight.' In *Credit, Interest Rates and the Open Economy: Essays on Horizontalism*, edited by L. P. Rochon and M. Vernengo. Cheltenham, UK: Edward Elgar Publishing.

Rochon, L.-P., and S. Rossi. 2004. 'Banking in the Monetary Circuit.' In *Central Banking in the Modern World: Alternative Perspectives*, edited by M. Lavoie and M. Seccareccia. Cheltenham: Edward Elgar.

Ryan-Collins, J., R. A. Werner, and J. Castle. 2016. 'A Half-century Diversion of Monetary Policy? An Empirical Horserace to Identify the UK Variable Most Likely to Deliver the Desired Nominal GDP Growth Rate.' *Journal of International Financial Markets, Institutions & Money* 43:158–176.

Sawyer, M., and M. Veronese Passarella. 2017. 'The Monetary Circuit in the Age of Financialisation: A Stock-flow Consistent Model with a Twofold Banking Sector.' *Metroeconomica* 68 (2): 321–353.

Serrano, F. 1995. 'Long Period Effective Demand and the Sraffian Supermultiplier.' *Contributions to Political Economy* 14 (1): 67–90.

Stirati, A. 1994. *The Theory of Wages in Classical Economics: A Study of Adam Smith, David Ricardo, and their Contemporaries.* Aldershot: Edward Elgar Publishing.

Teixeira, L., and G. Petrini. 2023. 'Long-run Effective Demand and Residential Investment: A Sraffian Supermultiplier Based Analysis.' *Review of Keynesian Economics* 11 (1): 72–99.

Werner, R. A. 2014. 'Can Banks Individually Create Money Out of Nothing? The Theories and the Empirical Evidence.' *International Review of Financial Analysis* 36:1–19.

Wicksell, K. 1935. *Lectures on Political Economy, Vol. II: Money.* London: Routledge and Kegan Paul.

Wolfson, M. H. 1996. 'A Post Keynesian Theory of Credit Rationing.' *Journal of Post Keynesian Economics* 18 (3): 443–470.

Wray, L. R. 1990. *Money and Credit in Capitalist Economies: The Endogenous Money Approach.* Aldershot, Hants, England; Brookfield, VT, USA: Edward Elgar Pub.

Wray, L. R. 1992. 'Alternative Approaches to Money and Interest Rates.' *Journal of Economic Issues* 26 (4): 1145–1178.

Zezza, G. 2012. 'Godley and Graziani: Stock-flow Consistent Monetary Circuits.' In *Contributions in Stock-flow Modeling: Essays in Honor of Wynne Godley*. London: Palgrave Macmillan UK. https://link.springer.com/chapter/10.1057/9780230367357_8.

Fiscal Supermultiplier and Endogenous Money in the United States: The COVID-19 Pandemic vs. the Global Financial Crisis*

Juan Matias De Lucchi

ABSTRACT

The paper examines different real-monetary dynamics and policy responses during the COVID-19 pandemic (C19P) and the Global Financial Crisis (GFC) in the United States through the lens of the Sraffian Supermultiplier model and the endogenous money approach. On the one hand, the C19P triggered a relatively deeper contraction in GDP, but its recovery was relatively faster and more robust. The 'V' shaped recovery from the C19P significantly contrasted the 'L' shaped trajectory of the post-GFC period. On the other hand, the money supply (M2) grew relatively more, and the monetary base expanded relatively less during the C19P. To explain these different real-monetary dynamics, a theoretical framework is developed and analyzed empirically for the United States. The theoretical model and the empirical analysis suggest that money supply is endogenously determined by creditworthy demand derived from the multiplier-accelerator effect of non-capacity generating autonomous demand, in which government spending plays a key role. Therefore, the absence of full hysteresis after the C19P shock had nothing to do with a traditional neoclassical trend reversal mechanism but with the fiscal supermultiplier effect of the extraordinary pandemic-related government spending.

1. Introduction

This paper analyzes the different output and monetary dynamics observed during the COVID-19 pandemic (C19P) and the Global Financial Crisis (GFC) in the United States. The paper builds a real-monetary theoretical framework based on the Sraffian Supermultiplier model (Freitas and Serrano 2015; Serrano 1995; Serrano and Freitas 2017) applied to open economies (Dvoskin and Torchinsky Landau 2022; Freitas, Dweck, and Ligiero 2021; Freitas and Dweck 2013; Gallo and Barbieri Goes 2023), in particular, to the US economy (Girardi and Pariboni 2016; Haluska, Braga, and Summa 2021); and the post-Keynesian endogenous money (Kaldor 1970; Lavoie 1984, 2022; Moore 1988; Rochon 1999), as well as the Sraffian exogenous interest rate (Pivetti 1991; Serrano and Summa 2013).

*The views and opinions expressed in this paper are those of the author and do not necessarily reflect the views and opinions of the Central Bank of Argentina (BCRA).

As it is well known, the C19P and the GFC were different phenomena. On the one hand, the GFC was triggered by an endogenous financial shock in 2007–08. The crisis was initiated in the US subprime housing market, extended to the derivate market for mortgage-backed securities (MBS), and then affected the whole financial system. Finally, it spread to the real economy and the rest of the world. On the other hand, the C19P was an exogenous real shock by definition. The disease outbreak and the mobility restrictions of official lockdowns suddenly affected the supply of goods and services and the financial stability of firms and households. Unlike the GFC, this time, the emergency was the people's health, not the banks' solvency.

Beyond their different causes, these two crises also exhibited different real and monetary dynamics. On the one hand, the C19P shock triggered a relatively deeper contraction in the US gross domestic product (GDP), but the recovery was relatively faster and more robust. The 'V' shaped recovery from the C19P shock significantly contrasted the 'L' shaped trajectory of the post-GFC period, which Setterfield (2022) characterized as 'an exhausted but institutionally entrenched growth regime' (p. 4). On the other hand, although the US Federal Reserve (Fed) responded to both crises similarly by setting the federal funds target range at 0.25–0 percent and conducting large-scale asset purchases, the money supply M2 grew relatively more, and the monetary base expanded relatively less during the C19P.

The paper builds a model that explicitly integrates the Supermultiplier demand-led growth model and the endogenous money approach to explain and empirically analyze those differences. The model states that the money supply is endogenously determined by creditworthy demand derived from the multiplier-accelerator effect of non-capacity generating autonomous demand, in which government spending plays a key role. The paper suggests that, in contrast to the post-GFC, the absence of full hysteresis in the GDP in 2020–21 and the resulting monetary implications had nothing to do with a traditional neoclassical trend reversal mechanism but with the fiscal supermultiplier effect of the extraordinary pandemic-related government spending.

The paper is structured as follows. After this introduction, Section Two presents the different real and monetary dynamics observed in the GFC and the C19P. Section Three builds a real-monetary theoretical framework reconciling the supermultiplier model and the endogenous money approach. Section Three analyses the Fed's monetary policy framework since the GFC and different fiscal policy responses in both crises. Section Five presents the econometric analysis based on long-run cointegration and short-run error correction models. Finally, Section Six presents some concluding remarks.

2. Different real and monetary dynamics

The GFC and the C19P were systemic crises that unprecedentedly affected output and employment levels since the Great Depression of the 1930s. However, these two crises exhibited quantitatively and qualitatively different dynamics. As shown in Figure 1, the decline in GDP was relatively faster and deeper during the C19P. For instance, the annual GDP growth rate dropped to −4 percent in Q2 2009 but plummeted to −8.3 percent in Q2 2020. Moreover, the economic recovery was relatively faster and more robust in the C19P. While the GDP followed an 'L'-shaped trajectory after the GFC, a 'V'-shaped recovery was observed in 2020–21. The GFC recession lasted 18 months

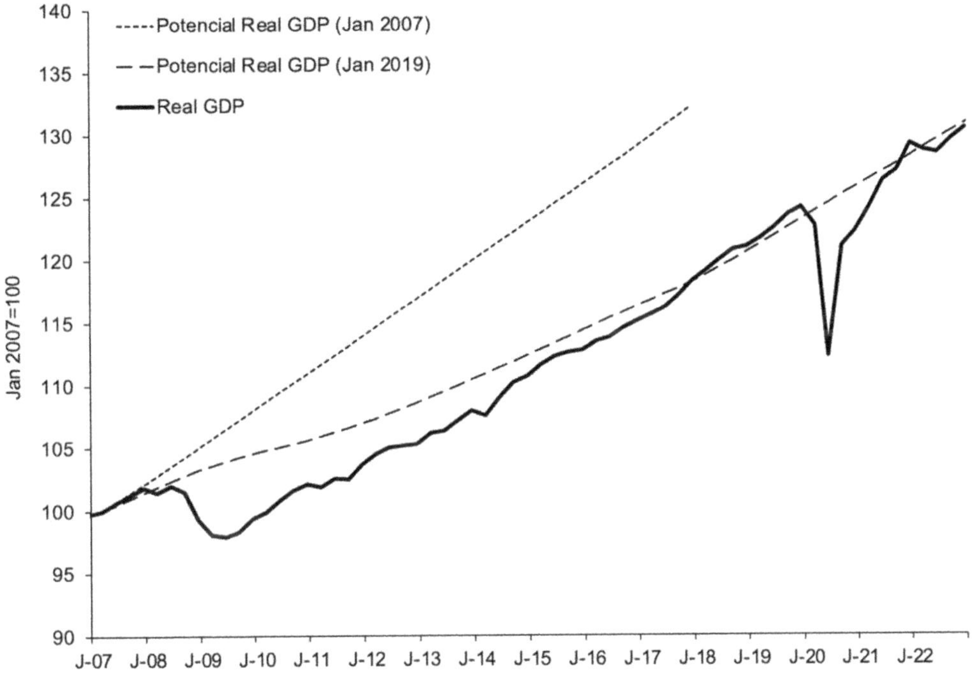

Figure 1. Actual and potential real GDP in the United States (2007–22, Quarterly frequency). Source: Own elaboration based on CBO and FRED.

(from January 2008 to June 2009), and it took eight years for the unemployment rate (which had archived 10 per cent at the end of 2009) to return to its pre-crisis level. However, the C19P recession lasted only two months (March–April 2020), and it took only two years for the unemployment rate (which achieved 15 per cent in April 2020) to return to the pre-pandemic level (see Setterfield 2023, for more details).[1]

More intriguing, the GDP path did not revert to the pre-GFC trend as one should expect from the standard neoclassical supply-led growth theory, in which the actual output growth rate $g = \frac{\dot{Y}}{Y}$ tends to adjust to the 'natural' rate g_n:[2]

$$g \leftleftarrows g_n = q + n \tag{1}$$

where $n = \bar{n}$ is the exogenous growth rate of the population, and $q = \frac{\dot{Q}}{Q}$ (where $Q = \frac{Y}{L}$, being L the employed labor force) is the growth rate of labor productivity which is exogenous in Solow (1956)'s model, $q = \bar{q}$, or endogenously determined by a vector of supply-side variables $q = q(V_S)$ in neoclassical endogenous growth theories.[3]

[1]The unemployment rate is an indicator that should be taken with caution. For example, it excludes discouraged and involuntary part-time workers unless explicitly added. Also, it does not consider the people who give up and stop looking for a job 'actively' and thus are excluded from the 'labor force.' Alternatively, the employment-population ratio is an indicator that provides additional information on the state of the labor market. For example, this ratio has diminished in each recession and has never returned to the pre-crisis level since 2000.

[2]See Lavoie (2016) for a discussion on 'hysteresis' in recent mainstream economics.

[3]The vector of supply-side variables can include tax incentives, saving propensities, intertemporal discount rates, and/or human capital accumulation depending on the modeling version (see Blecker and Setterfield 2019, ch. 1.4)

Figure 1 shows that the actual GDP did not converge to the potential GDP estimated by the US Congressional Budget Office (CBO) in January 2007. In contrast, subsequent CBO's estimations of potential output tended to be closer to the observed GDP. This fact is consistent with heterodox demand-led growth models that rely on path dependency or full hysteresis to shape output dynamics. In the case of the Sraffian Suppermultiplier, for example, Serrano, Summa, and Freitas (2022) state that 'it is realistically assumed that productivity growth depends in part on the rate of growth of the economy and of the capital stock, as technical change tends to be embodied, following some version of the so-called Kaldor-Verdoorn law' (p. 27). Formally:

$$g_n \overset{\leftarrow}{=} q(g) + n \tag{2}$$

where the output growth rate determines the productivity growth rate, $q = q(g)$, and thus the 'natural' rate became endogenously determined by the long-period effective demand (see Blecker and Setterfield 2019; Serrano and Freitas 2017 and Lavoie 2022 for a discussion on heterodox growth models).[4]

However, the economic recovery from the C19P shock was relatively faster and qualitatively different. As also shown in Figure 1, full hysteresis is not visualized this time. The actual GDP 'converged' to the potential GDP estimated by the CBO in January 2019 (although not entirely to the estimation of January 2007) So, does it mean that the standard neoclassical theory worked this time?

Also, different monetary dynamics were observed when comparing the two crises. As shown in Figure 2, the aggregate M2 grew relatively more, and the monetary base expanded relatively less during the C19P.[5] For example, while the 'commercial and industrial loans' fell 10 percent a year after the Fed's first 'quantitative easing' (QE) program began in the second semester of 2008, it increased 10 percent a year after the fourth QE began in the first semester of 2020. In other words, why did the M2-monetary base ratio, interpreted by monetarists as the 'money multiplier,' substantially drop during the GFC and remain relatively stable during the C19P as observed in Figure 2?

Finally, after the C19P, a phenomenon not seen since the end of the 1970s resurged. As shown in Figure 3, the price inflation rate increased substantially in 2021, and it has become a hot public topic since then. In the beginning, the Fed believed that inflation acceleration was 'transitory,' and consequently, it relaxed its traditional 2 percent inflation target to 'an *average* inflation target (AIT) of 2 per cent over the *long run*' (The FRED Blog 2020, emphasis added). Later, as inflation did not slow down as quickly as expected (it started to fall since mid-2022), the Fed adopted a view closer to the mainstream demand-pull inflation.

[4]Note that the population growth rate could eventually be endogenized in an open economy model. Considering Adam Smith's 'perfect liberty' which implies free mobility of capital and labor, immigration could be a solution for potential labor constraints (see Foley 2011).

[5]The M2 expansion referred to during the pandemic has nothing to do with the sudden increase of the aggregate M1 in May 2020. The latter was caused by changes in 'Regulation D,' which specifies how banks must classify deposit accounts. After specific deregulation during the C19P, the US Federal Reserve established that savings accounts must be computed as part of the M1 since they became more liquid. In summary, those changes affected the composition of M2 but not its level.

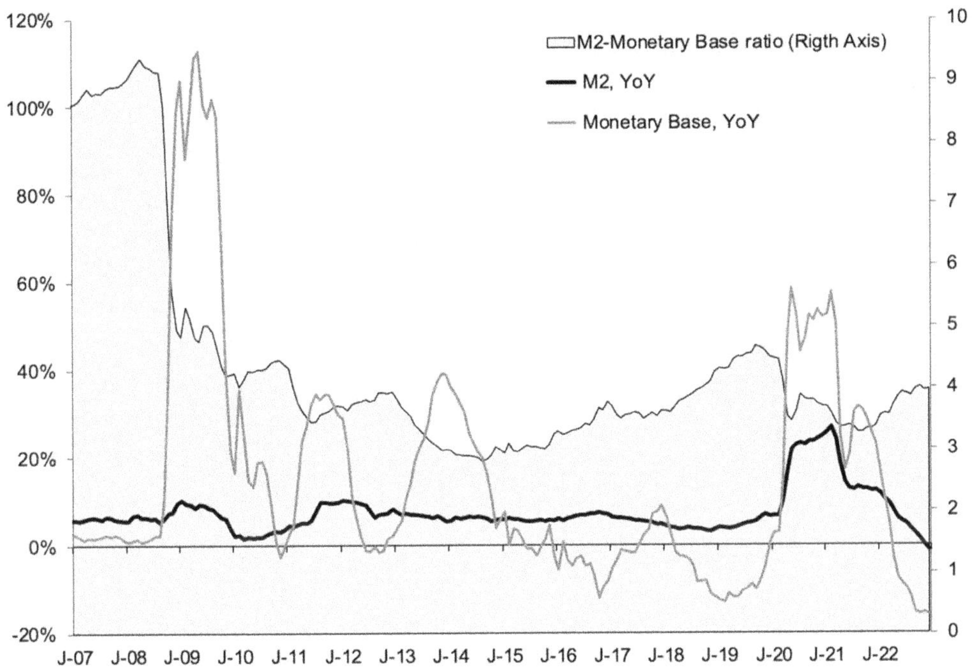

Figure 2. Annual percent changes in the monetary aggregates, and the M2-Monetary Base ratio (2007–22, Monthly frequency). Source: Own elaboration based on FRED.

There was also a rich debate on inflation in heterodox economics.[6] For example, the profit-led inflation or Weber and Wasner's (2023) 'sellers' inflation' view claimed that the surge of inflation was driven by firms that 'propagated' and/or 'amplified' the upward cost pressures by keeping and/or increasing their (real) markup rates. However, Lavoie (2023, 2024) challenged that by emphasizing the role of imported (demand-determined) commodity prices and raw materials in income distribution (particularly the oil price shock of 2021, as shown in Figure 3). The author, who recognized the possibility of higher markup rates in some sectors, explained that increases in the profit share could also occur when unit material costs rise enough, even if markup rates remain unchanged (or, let's add, do not fall enough). It is worth noting that the paper does not aim to discuss the post-pandemic inflation dynamics. However, to complete the real-monetary framework, a cost-push inflation approach based on the Sraffian/post-Keynesian and Latin-American structuralist traditions is modeled in the following theoretical section.

3. Theoretical framework

This section reconciles the Sraffian Supermultiplier with the endogenous money approach. The following real-monetary model formalizes the monetary effect of non-

[6]See the inflation debate in the Monetary Policy Institute Blog, or the debate between Franklin Serrano, Marc Lavoie, Louis-Phillipe Rochon, and Ettore Gallo during the '4th International Workshop on Demand-Led Growth' at the Federal University of Rio de Janeiro (Rio de Janeiro, Brazil) on July 27, 2023.

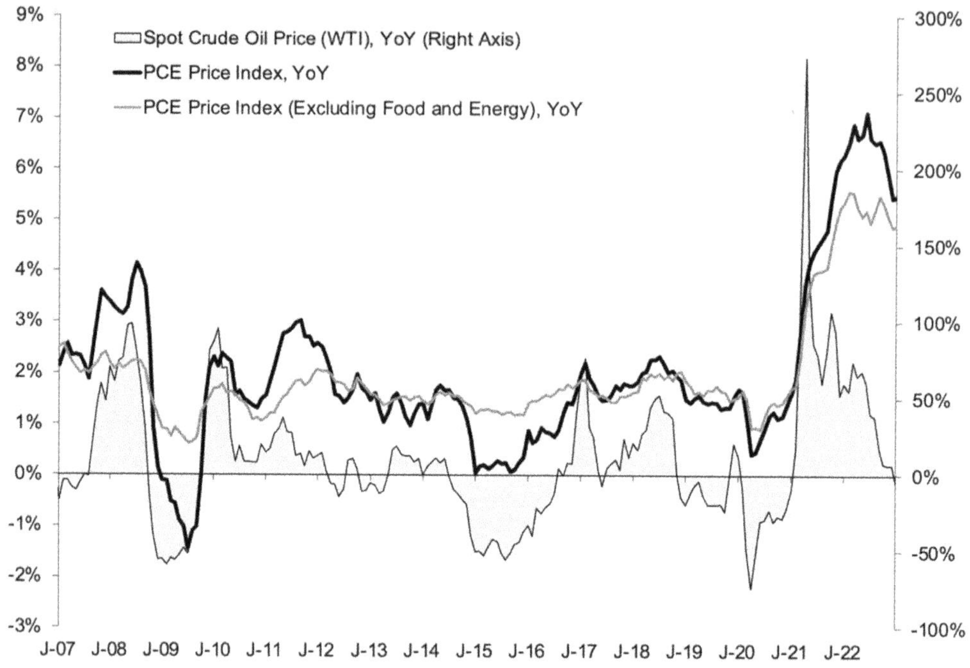

Figure 3. Annual percent changes in the Personal Consumption Expenditures Price Index and the Spot Crude Oil Price (WTI) (2007–22, Monthly frequency). Source: Own elaboration based on FRED.

capacity-generating autonomous demand. Before presenting the model, a brief review of the supermultiplier demand-led growth and the endogenous money approach is necessary.

3.1. Supermultiplier

The Sraffian Supermultiplier is a heterodox demand-led growth model that reconciles the Keynesian long-period effective demand with the classical/Sraffian exogenous income distribution. In this model, the economic growth is driven by the non-capacity generating autonomous demand because the actual capacity utilization rate endogenously adjusts to deviations from its normal rate. Thus, the output growth rate depends on the multiplier-accelerator effect of autonomous demand.

To derive the supermultiplier model, consider the following spending approach to measure the output level in an open economy, without taxation for simplicity:

$$Y + M = C + I + G + X \tag{3}$$

where Y and M are the levels of output and imports, respectively; C is the private consumption, I is the private and public investment, G is the government consumption and X are exports. Note that the left-hand side represents the supply side of goods and services, and the right-hand side represents the demand side.

Assume that imports are induced by the output level:

$$M = bY \tag{4}$$

where b is the import-output ratio or the propensity to import.

Consider that private consumption C is determined by induced and autonomous components. On the one hand, it is induced by households' income Y and the government's social transfers, Γ_G, respectively. On the other hand, private consumption also depends on an autonomous component, C_A, that households finance by issuing new liabilities or selling existing assets. Formally:

$$C = c(Y + \Gamma_G) + C_A \tag{5}$$

where c is the propensity to consume.

The total investment is assumed to be determined by induced and autonomous components. On the one hand, the private non-residential fixed investment is induced by the economic activity, Y. It is crucial to note that this is the only component that creates productive capacity. On the other hand, two types of non-capacity generating autonomous components are considered: the private residential investment I_H and the government investment I_G, which 'is considered autonomous because (a) public gross capital formation does not create productive capacity for the private sector and (b) it is submitted to political decisions, and it is not motivated to adjust capacity do demand' (Haluska, Braga, and Summa 2021, p. 3)[7]

Formally:

$$I = hY + I_H + I_G \tag{6}$$

where h is the propensity to invest in private non-residential fixed capital.

Finally, government consumption G and exports X are the other autonomous variables considered in the model: government consumption depends on policymakers' decisions, and exports depend on the demand from the rest of the world.

Plugging (4), (5) and (6) into (3), follows that:

$$(1 + m)Y = c(Y + \Gamma_G) + C_A + hY + I_H + I_G + X \tag{7}$$

Thus, considering the private autonomous demand, $C_A + I_H$, the public autonomous demand, $G + c\Gamma_G + I_G$, and the external autonomous demand, X, the sum of all non-capacity generating autonomous components is defined as follows:

$$Z = C_A + c\Gamma_G + I_H + I_G + G + X \tag{8}$$

Simplifying (7) with (8) and solving by Y, we get the Sraffian Supermultiplier for an open economy (see Freitas and Dweck 2013; and Freitas, Dweck, and Ligiero 2021 and

[7]It is worth noting that if public investment eventually generates capacity, capital accumulation would not be limited to the private sector. Therefore, the model would need to be adapted to these assumptions.

Haluska, Braga, and Summa 2021, for a complete model with taxation):

$$Y \doteq \left(\frac{1}{1-c-h+m}\right)Z \tag{9}$$

$$\Rightarrow g = \zeta + g_Z \tag{10}$$

where $\dfrac{1}{1-c-h+m}$ is the supermultiplier and ζ, g and g_Z are the growth rates of the supermultiplier, output, and autonomous demand, respectively.

Note that, assuming $\zeta = 0$, which is theoretically reasonable for the 'very long' period, the Supermultiplier model states that the growth rate of autonomous expenditures determines the economic growth and, consequently, the 'natural' rate:

$$g_n \overset{\leftarrow}{=} g \overset{\leftarrow}{=} g_Z \tag{11}$$

This is feasible because the productivity growth rate can be decomposed as the difference between the output growth rate and the employed labor force growth rate, $q = g - l$. Additionally, assuming that the employed labor force and the population grow at the same rate, $l = n$, which implies that the employment-population ratio $\frac{L}{N}$ remains constant over time, it follows that $g_n = g - n + n = g$.

Nevertheless, recognizing the unrealistic nature of the fixed accelerator assumption, Freitas and Serrano (2015) and Serrano and Freitas (2017) proposed a flexible accelerator in which the growth rate of the propensity to invest, $\hat{h}$, increases (decreases) when the actual capacity utilization rate, u, is above (below) its normal rate, u_n:

$$\hat{h} = \frac{\dot{h}}{h} = \gamma(u - u_n),\ \gamma > 0 \tag{12}$$

Therefore, the transition dynamic of economic growth toward the long-run equilibrium is expressed as follows:

$$g = \frac{h\gamma(u - u_n)}{1-c-h+m} + g_Z \tag{13}$$

Finally, considering that h is an endogenous variable, the 'fully adjusted position' of equation 9, is specified as follows (see also Fagundes and Freitas 2017, for more details):

$$Y = \left(\frac{1}{1-c-\left(\frac{v}{u_n}\right)g_Z + m}\right)Z \tag{14}$$

where $h^* = \left(\frac{v}{u_n}\right)g_Z$ if no depreciation rate of the capital stock is assumed for simplicity.[8]

3.2. Endogenous money

According to Lavoie (2022), 'Post-Keynesians of various strands hold views on monetary matters that have a common core, whether they are Sraffians, French and Italian

[8]Considering the growth rate of the capacity utilization rate $\hat{u} = \frac{\dot{u}}{u} = g - g_k$ where $g_K = \hat{K} = \frac{\dot{K}}{K} = \frac{I}{K} = \frac{I}{Y}\frac{Y}{Y_K}\frac{Y_K}{K} = \frac{hu}{v}$ is the growth rate of capital accumulation (and v the technical-capital-to-capacity-output ratio), it follows that $\hat{u} = g - \frac{hu}{v}$. Therefore, assuming that $\hat{u} = 0$ in the long-run, it follows that $h^* = \left(\frac{v}{u_n}\right)g_z$ when $g = g_z$ and $u = u_n$.

circuitists, Kaleckians, Fundamentalist Keynesians or neo-chartalists (...) All these economists agree that the supply of money is endogenous and demand-led' (p. 193). Accordingly, Serrano, Summa, and Freitas (2022) state that 'in the Supermultiplier model, following what is becoming a consensus in the heterodox literature, it is assumed that money is endogenous' (p. 4). Also, Cesaratto and Di Bucchianico (2020) claim that 'one interesting aspect of autonomous spending is that, by definition, it must be financed by endogenous credit/money creation by banks' (p. 3).

The money supply is endogenous because it is credit-driven and demand-determined. First, money is credit-driven because commercial banks create 'deposits' *ex nihilo* when they grant loans. This is possible because firms and households accept those deposits as means of payment and reserve of value. In this sense, banks are not 'financial intermediaries' between the supply of and demand for Wicksellian 'loanable funds'. In contrast, banks are money issuers of IOUs in the form of publicly accepted transferable deposits.

Second, money is demand-determined because commercial banks accommodate the creditworthy demand. However, banks are not passive accommodative institutions but active credit rationers. According to Wolfson (1996), banks' expectations about borrowers' ability to meet their financial commitments determine which portion of total demand is credit-worthy and thus accommodated and which one is 'notional' and thus rationed.

Note that there is a critical moment in the endogenous mechanism of money creation. In contemporary banking systems, money is a 'legal contract' defined by the national state. Banks issue IOUs convertible into a currency they do not control, the legal tender. Bank deposits are denominated in the national state's unit of account and thus the central bank is the monopoly supplier of (electronic) reserves and (physical) banknotes.[9] For this reason, banks can create deposits *ex nihilo*, but they need reserves to meet clients' transfer orders, cash demand, or the central bank's reserve requirements, eventually.

So, is the monetary base endogenous? Although the central bank is the monopoly supplier of reserves, post-Keynesians have always claimed (and this perspective now prevails among central bankers and academics) that the monetary base is endogenous in practice, except since the GFC, as Section Four will discuss. The reason is straightforward: if the central bank does not accommodate the demand for reserves, the overnight rate becomes highly volatile, and the payment system could eventually collapse. For example, the Fed's non-borrowed reserve controls of the period 1979–1982 were, in practice, an upward volatility interest rate policy rather than a Friedman (1968)-based monetary targeting. At least that was clear to former Fed's Chairman Paul Volcker, who recognized 'Fed's seeming inability to assure, week by week, confidence-building control of the money supply, something that we learned is technically impossible to do' (Volcker and Harper 2018, 91).

Considering that central banks' daily function is usually controlling the interest rate (Bindseil 2014), a critical macroeconomic price with distributive and financial implications, it is reasonable to say that the monetary base is also endogenous most of the time. In a nutshell, 'loans make deposits' instantaneously at the micro level, and then

[9]One of the hot topics that central bankers worldwide are currently discussing is the possibility of issuing central bank digital currencies to replace physical notes and coins.

'deposits make reserves' at the macro level, although with some delays eventually (see De Lucchi 2022, ch. 2)

Additionally, as Keynes (1936) suggested in the *General Theory*'s chapter 17, the monetary base is also an 'asset' subject to portfolio decisions. The 'liquidity preference' for precautionary or speculative motives creates another type of monetary base endogeneity that is not directly associated with the flow of bank credit but with the private portfolio management of the stock of money.

In summary, assuming that the change in demand deposit $\dot{D}$ is purely credit-driven, the change in bank reserves $\dot{R}$ is endogenously determined by the change in the creditworthy demand, given the interest rate:

$$\dot{R} \overset{\leftarrow}{=} d\dot{D} \tag{15}$$

where d is Lavoie (1984)'s 'credit divisor', which captures the central bank's reserve requirements and/or commercial banks' liquidity preference (Cardim de Carvalho 2015).

From other perspective, the central bank's reaction function and the endogenous reserves can be represented as follows:

$$\dot{R} \overset{\leftarrow}{=} \alpha(\delta - \delta^T),\ \alpha > 0 \tag{16}$$

where δ is the overnight interest rate, δ^T is the central bank target rate and α is the speed of adjustment of monetary policy or the 'efficiency' of central bank's operation procedures.

Plugging (15) into (16) and solving for δ, follows that:

$$\delta = \delta^T + \frac{d\dot{D}}{\alpha} \tag{17}$$

where $d\dot{D}/\alpha$ captures transitory deviations of the overnight rate from the target rate.

Alternatively:

$$\delta = \delta^T + \varepsilon \tag{18}$$

where $\varepsilon \sim N(0,\ \sigma^2)$ is the market noises or liquidity shocks, which are assumed normally distributed for simplicity. Note again that the higher the central bank's efficiency, the lower the noise (De Lucchi 2022).

3.3. The monetary effect of autonomous demand

The objective of this subsection is to integrate the Supermultiplier model and the endogenous money approach into a single real-monetary framework. First, consider the following accounting identity and solve for the money supply M_2 to get an expression in which it is endogenously determined by the nominal output, PY, adjusted by the velocity of money, V:

$$M_2 V = PY \tag{19}$$

$$\Rightarrow M_2 \overset{\leftarrow}{=} \frac{PY}{V} \tag{20}$$

It is worth noting that, as Kaldor (1970) claimed early, 'the rise in the 'money supply' should precede the rise in income — irrespective of whether the money increase was a cause or an effect' (p.10). The quantity of money depends on the demand for bank credit, but it must precede the spending by definition (this is confirmed by Granger causality tests of Section Four).

Considering the right-hand side of equation (20), the velocity of money and the price level still have to be defined. First, it is reasonable to assume that the velocity growth rate is zero in the 'very long' period, $\hat{V} = 0$. However, it doesn't mean that short-run fluctuations and medium/long-term trends in the velocity of money are negligible, especially for empirical analysis, as they will be taken into account in Section Five. For instance, while the annual percent change of the velocity of M2 was −0.3 on average in the United States from 1960 to 2019, the level of the velocity of M2 showed an upward trend between 1987 and 1997 and a clear downward trend since 1997.[10]

Second, following the classical price theory and the Kaleckian markup pricing (see Bastian and Setterfield 2020; Blecker and Setterfield 2019; Braga and Serrano 2023; De Lucchi 2022; Lavoie 2022; 2023; 2024), the cost-plus pricing is modeled as follows:

$$P = (1 + \tau)(Wa + EP_f b) \tag{21}$$

$$\Rightarrow P = (1 + \tau)(1 + j)Wa \tag{22}$$

where $j = \frac{EP_f b}{Wa}$ is the ratio between the unit imported material cost, $EP_f b$, and the unit labor cost, Wa. Additionally, W is the nominal wage, E is the nominal exchange rate, P_f is the international price level (which includes the crude oil price, for instance) and $a = \frac{L}{Y}$ and $b = \frac{M}{Y}$ (see equation 4 again), are the labor-output and the import-output ratios, respectively. Note that a and b are fixed coefficients under the assumption of a Leontief production function with no import substitution industrialization. Finally, τ is the (real) markup rate, the target rate of return, or the normal rate of return r, depending on the more general approach.

As mentioned in Section Two, it is worth noting some distributive implications derived from equation (22). Considering the profit share in value-added, π, and dividing the numerator and the denominator of (23) by Wa,

$$\pi = \frac{\tau(Wa + EP_f b)}{Wa + \tau(Wa + EP_f b)} \tag{23}$$

$$\Rightarrow \pi = \frac{\tau(1 + j)}{1 + \tau(1 + j)} \tag{24}$$

it is clear that, as emphasized by Lavoie (2023; 2024), π can increase when j increases, even if τ remains unchanged or does not fall enough.

Therefore, considering that $J = (1 + j)$ and assuming that $\hat{\tau} = 0$ for simplicity, or because 'one would not expect the share of profit to increase forever' (Lavoie 2022,

[10]The stability of the velocity of money has been extensively debated in monetary economics. For example, take the debate at the Radcliffe Commission in England in the 50s between the academics who claimed that velocity was a constant or a predictive variable and the central bankers, supported by the post-Keynesians Kaldor and Kahn, who claimed that it was unstable (see Lavoie 2022, chapter 4).

p. 594), the inflation rate is derived as follows:

$$\hat{P} = \hat{J} + \hat{W} + \hat{a} \tag{25}$$

Plugging (9) into (20) follows that the money supply is endogenously determined by the supermultiplier effect of nominal autonomous demand (adjusted by the velocity of money). In other words, the creditworthy demand is derived from the multiplier-accelerator effect of the nominal autonomous demand:

$$M_2 = \left(\frac{1}{1-c-h+m}\right)\frac{PZ}{V} \tag{26}$$

$$\Rightarrow M_2 = \frac{(1+\tau)(Wa + EP_f b)(C_A + c\Gamma_G + I_H + I_G + G + X)}{(1-c-h+m)V} \tag{27}$$

Therefore, assuming a flexible accelerator effect, the money supply growth rate is derived as follows:

$$\hat{M}_2 = \left(\frac{h\gamma(u-u_n)}{1-c-h+m}\right) + \hat{J} + \hat{W} + \hat{a} + g_Z - \hat{V} \tag{28}$$

Or as follows in the 'very long' period:

$$\hat{M}_2 = \hat{P} + g_Z \tag{29}$$

Where $\zeta = \hat{V} = 0$ is assumed.

4. The monetary policy framework since the GFC and different fiscal policy responses to both crises

Through the lens of the theoretical framework presented above, particularly focusing on the role of government spending and the endogenous creation of money supply, this section discusses the similarities and differences of the US policy responses to the GFC and the C19P. The following analysis of the monetary policy framework since the GFC and the extraordinary pandemic-related fiscal policy is thus the starting point for an explanation of the different real and monetary dynamics presented in Section One.

4.1. The monetary policy framework since the GFC

During the GFC, the government's primary objective was to bailout the financial sector that had turned insolvent after a typical 'debt deflation' process. As a result, the 'unconventional monetary policy' was the core of the US policy response to the crisis. From September 2008, the Fed functioned as the lender of last resort of the financial system in a scale, scope, and speed without precedent in contemporary capitalism. As shown in Figure 4, firstly, it provided liquidity and credit facilities to the system. Then, it initiated large-scale asset purchases from 'zombie' financial institutions, the so-called Quantitative Easing (QE) programs. In the beginning, the Fed targeted mortgage-backed securities (MBS) but then increased the purchases of US treasury securities.

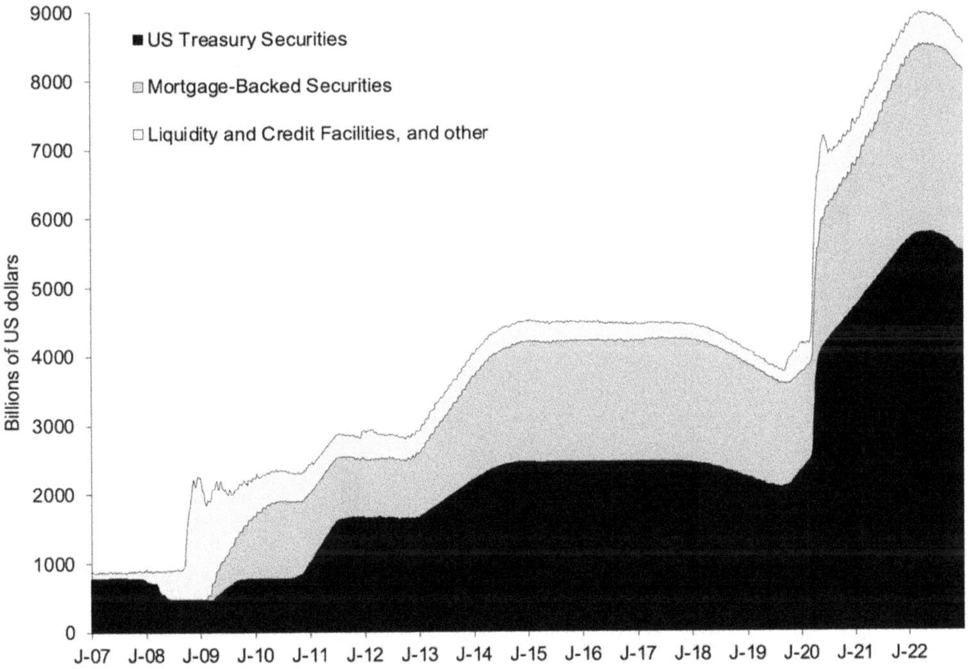

Figure 4. US Federal Reserve's assets: US treasury securities, Mortgage-backed securities, and liquidity and credit facilities (2007–22, Monthly frequency). Source: Own elaboration based on FRED.

As shown in Figure 5, additionally, the Fed started to set an 'interest rate on excess reserves' (IOER) in October 2008, which was replaced by the 'interest rate on reserve balances' (IORB) in July 2021. In a nutshell, the new monetary policy framework turned into a 'floor system' (Lavoie 2022): the Fed created persistent downward pressure on the 'federal funds rate' (FFR), the interbank overnight rate, by supplying huge amounts of reserves (purchasing securities on a large scale) and simultaneously it set a lower bound by remunerating them.

However, as also shown in Figure 5, the FFR has fluctuated below the IOER, not over its level. In fact, from December 2008 to June 2018, the IOER was defined as the upper limit of the 'federal funds target range' instead of a lower bound. The reason why the IOER/IORB worked in practice as a 'ceiling' instead of a floor is straightforward: commercial banks are the only ones eligible to make interest-bearing deposits at the Fed, but they are not the only participants in short-term money markets. As a result, the excess liquidity from non-bank financial institutions such as mutual funds has been putting downward pressure on the FFR below the IOER/IORB.

While the target range was set at 0–0.25 percent, as it was until 2015, that didn't have relevant implications. However, the Fed required additional policy tools when it decided to increase the FFR. Otherwise, the FFR would become very volatile within a wide corridor between zero and some higher IOER, implying a partial loss of monetary policy control. To pave the way for the rate hike cycle that began in December 2015 and ended in 2019, the Fed started to conduct overnight reverse repo facilities (ON RRP) to nonbank financial institutions at positive interest rates but below the IOER. In

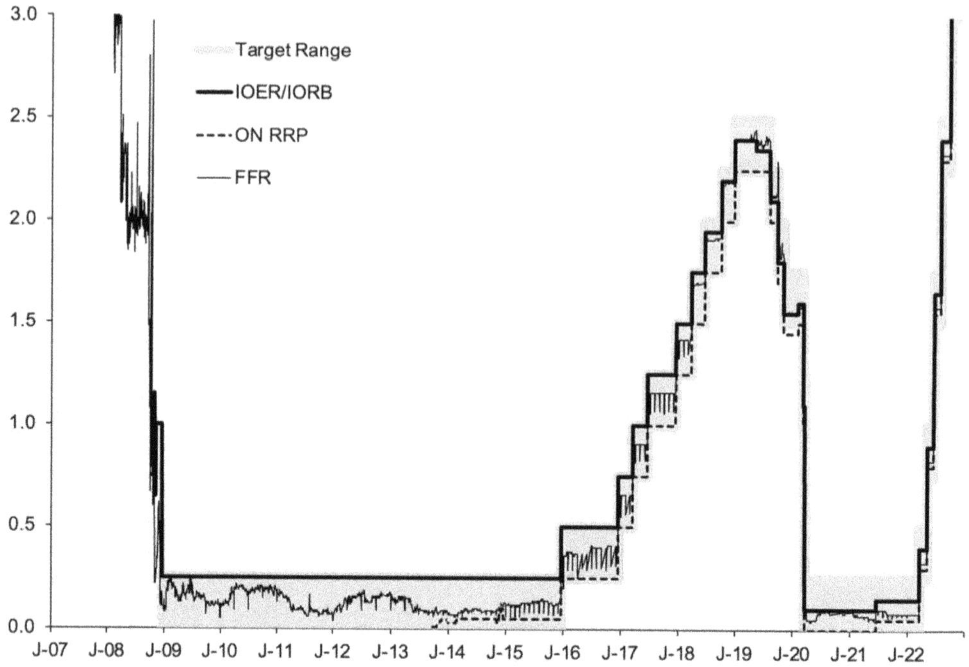

Figure 5. Fed's target range, policy rates and the federal funds rate (2007–22, Daily frequency). Source: Own elaboration based on FRED.

summary, the Fed created an operating corridor based on two deposit rates: the IOER/IORB for banks as a ceiling and the ON RRP for non-banks as a floor.

Also, notice that the IOER/IORB and the ON RRP have not always been set as the upper and lower limits of the target range. The IOER/IORB has been set slightly below the upper limit since June 2018, and the ON RRP has been set slightly above the lower limit since June 2021. As a result, the operating corridor has been narrower than the target range, which has always been 250 basis points wide. In other words, the target range has become a forward guidance of monetary policy without an immediate operational backstop. In summary, the policy framework observed since 2021 has shown the following structure:

$$Lower\ Limit < ON\ RRP < FFR < IORB < Upper\ Limit \tag{30}$$

In principle, the pandemic-related monetary policy was similar to the one of the GFC. From March 2020 to March 2022, for example, the target range was set again at 0–0.25 percent, but this time with a narrowed operating corridor as mentioned above.[11] Additionally, the Fed implemented a new QE program, the fourth since 2008. This time, however, the Fed purchased more long-term U.S. Treasury securities rather than MBS (see Figure 4 again).

[11]In the post-pandemic, however, the Fed initiated a new rate hike cycle to reduce the inflation rate that accelerated during 2021 and the first semester of 2022. Although the Fed had initially claimed that inflationary pressures were 'transitory' derived from pandemic-related supply-chain factors, later, it returned to a more mainstream view by pointing out that the economy was 'overheated'.

During the C19P, the Fed acted more as a 'fiscal agent' rather than a lender of last resort to the financial system. This time, Fed's primary function was to 'monetize' the increasing fiscal deficit caused by the extraordinary expansion of government spending as never seen before in peacetime (see Felipe et al. 2020; and Felipe and Fullwiler 2022, for a discussion on fiscal deficit 'monetization' during the C19P)

It is worth noting that the Fed's purchases of treasury bonds were also probably associated with a novel phenomenon observed in the C19P. As it is well known, US treasury securities are risk-free international liquid assets preferred by global investors for hedging in times of turbulence and used by foreign central banks as foreign reserves. Despite that, between March and April 2020, foreign private investors sold longer-term U.S. Treasury bonds and 'shortened' the duration of their holdings to face the sudden demand for cash. Also, several emerging market economies' central banks, especially from China and oil-exporting countries, became net sellers of US treasury securities (Weiss 2022). Broadly speaking, they exchanged US bonds for US dollars to intervene in their foreign exchange markets. That renewed the debate about the 'collapse of the American power' and the international dollar standard (Fiori, Medeiros, and Serrano 2009). However, a few weeks after the COVID-19 shock of March 2020, most emerging market economies became net buyers of US bonds again while rebuilding foreign reserves.

Additional comments are required to understand the determination of the US monetary base since the GFC. As inferred by Figure 2, the monetary base became 'exogenously' determined by the Fed's QE programs. These significant expansions of bank reserves were not driven by economic activity and the creditworthy demand as expected by the canonical model discussed in Section 3.2. However, there is nothing wrong with the endogenous money approach. Early, Lavoie (2010) explained that:

> 'it is possible for central banks to control the amount of reserves in the system, as long as they are willing to accept that the target rate of interest be set at the deposit rate on bank reserves at the central bank. There can thus be a supply of reserves that far exceeds the amount of required or demanded reserves' (p. 20)

In the same line, Wray (2015) pointed out that 'with what is called Quantitative Easing (QE), the Fed 'exogenously' increases bank reserves far beyond what banks want to hold' (p. 90)

Under such conditions, there is no room for 'sterilization' mechanisms through open market operations or reverse repo agreements. As profit-seekers and portfolio decision-makers, banks prefer to invest their excess reserves in interest-bearing deposits at the Fed instead of purchasing US treasury securities or making repos at lower interest rates. Recall again that the Fed set the interest rate on reserves balances (IOER/IORB) above the reverse repo rate (ON RRP).

However, the bank credit and the money supply (M2) remained tied to economic activity as stated by the endogenous money approach. The QEs did not 'multiply' the M2 as expected by Monetarists but dramatically dropped the M2-monetary base ratio (see in Figure 2 again), which has no multiplying power by definition (see also Koo 2011) Conceptually speaking, we cannot even say that increased the 'credit divisor.' The fall in the M2-monetary base ratio observed since 2008 cannot be fully explained by transitory increases in banks' 'liquidity preference' that usually occurs in times of stress (Cardim de Carvalho 2015, ch. 5). It was simply the result of the unconventional institutional arrangement described above.

However, despite the monetary policy framework being almost the same during both crises, the M2-monetary base ratio remained relatively stable after the C19P, around the post-GFC historical average. To explain that, it is necessary to consider the monetary effect of government spending.

4.2. The extraordinary pandemic-related government spending

The stimulus package of the GFC was not negligible. In February 2008, the US Congress passed the 'Economic Stimulus Act,' a bill of roughly $150 billion that provided tax rebates and tax incentives, as well an increase in the purchase limit of mortgages from government-sponsored enterprises such as Fannie Mae and Freddie Mac. In October 2008, additionally, the US Congress authorized the 'Troubled Asset Relief Program' (TARP), which effectively disbursed $444 billion to support financial firms such as the American International Group (AIG) and the automotive industry. Finally, in February 2009, the US Congress passed the 'American Recovery and Reinvestment Act,' a larger stimulus package of roughly $800 billion in tax credits and tax cuts, infrastructure spending, unemployment benefits and food stamps, subsidies for health insurance, aid to states, and other measures.

However, the fiscal response to the C19P was much bigger and faster. From 2020 to 2021, the IMF (2021) estimated that the US government's 'spending and forgone revenue' was 25.45 percent of GDP, and its support with 'loans, equity and guarantees' was 2.44 percent of GDP. The US fiscal response was the largest in the world, followed by the United Kingdom, Australia, and Japan, with around 16 percent of GDP. According to Romer (2021), 'the fiscal policy response to the pandemic in the United States has been extraordinary (...) As a share of GDP, that is nearly equivalent to what the United States spent on war production in 1943' (pp. 89–19)

In March 2020, the US Congress passed the 'Coronavirus Aid, Recovery, and Economic Security Act' (CARES), a bill of $2.2 trillion for cash payments to people ($1,200 for a single adult, for example), unemployment benefits, the creation of the Paycheck Protection Program (to support small business's payroll costs), loans for firms, and aid to states and local governments. Additionally, in March 2021, the US Congress passed the 'American Rescue Plan Act,' a bill of $1.9 trillion to accelerate the economic recovery. At the time of writing, legislative and administrative actions for spending, tax cuts, loans, subsidies, and other measures achieved more than $ 6 trillion, according to some estimations (covidmoneytracker.org).

Despite the complexity of those fiscal measures, we can easily visualize the extraordinary increase in social transfers during the C19P. As shown in Figures 6 and 7, social benefits to persons achieved almost 30 percent of GDP in the second quarter of 2020 and 27 percent in the first quarter of 2021. In real terms, social benefits to persons that had accumulated $7,558 billion of 2020 chained dollars in 2008–10, increased to $12 trillion in 2020–22. Thus, real social benefits increased by 58 percent between the two crises, going from 36 percent of total real expenditures in the GFC to 46 percent in the C19P.

Government consumption, however, was similar in both crises. For example, it was 16 percent of GDP in 2008 and 15 percent in 2020. In real terms, it accumulated $8,747 billions of 2020 chained dollars in 2008–10 and $9,517 in 2020–22. Similar dynamics are observed in gross government investment. It remained relatively stable at around 4

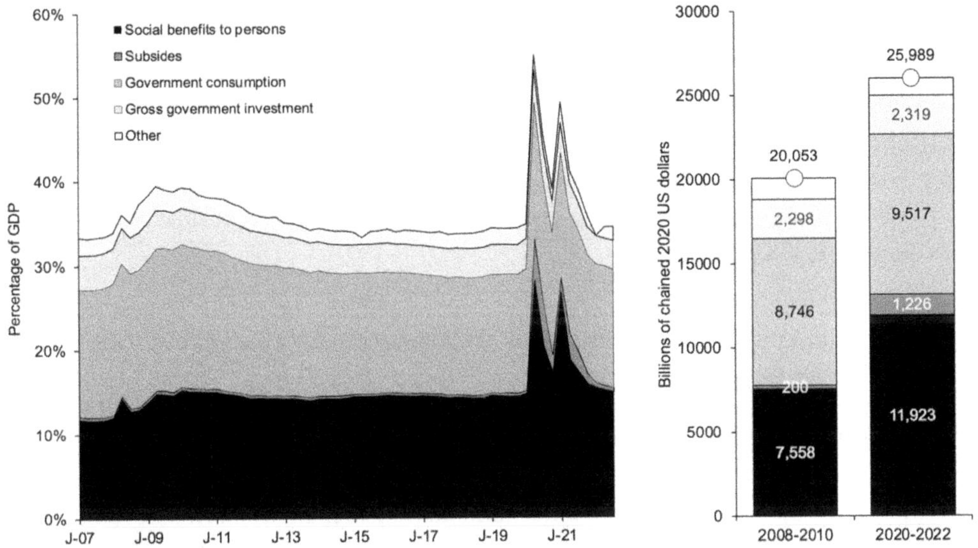

Figure 6 and 7. Decomposition of the US government's expenditures as a percentage of GDP (2007–22, Quarterly frequency). Accumulated real expenditures in 2008–10 and 2020–22. Source: Own elaboration based on FRED.

percent of GDP in 2008 and 2020, and around 2,4 trillion of 2020 chained dollars in 2008–10 and 2020–22. Finally, government subsidies increased substantially during the C19P. It increased to more than 3 percent in 2020, while it was 0.4 percent of GDP in 2008. Subsidies increased from $200 billion in 2020 chained dollars in 2008–10 to $1,2 trillion in 2020–21.

In summary, despite the monetary policy framework being similar during both crises, the extraordinary pandemic-related fiscal policy largely explains the different real and monetary dynamics of the C19P. According to the previous theoretical model based on supermultiplier demand-led growth and endogenous money, the bigger government spending of the C19P would explain the 'V'- shaped economy recovery and the associated M2 growth. To get a more conclusive explanation, the next section will empirically estimate the suggested real-monetary framework.

5. Empirical analysis

The primary goal of this section is to empirically analyze the model of Section 3.3 for the United States. Following Freitas and Dweck (2013) and Haluska, Braga, and Summa (2021), firstly, US data that best fit the accounting analysis of the supermultiplier model was collected from FRED. As summarized by Table 1, the autonomous demand is captured by 'exports of goods and services' for X, the 'personal consumption expenditures in durable goods' for C_A, the 'private residential fixed investments' for I_H and the sum of 'government consumption expenditures,' 'social benefits to persons,' 'subsidies' and 'gross government investment' for $G + c\Gamma_G + I_G$. Note that government's interest payments are excluded under the assumption that they have a near-zero multiplier

Table 1. Data collection for the US autonomous demand.

Autonomous Demand	US Data
Exports	Exports of goods and services
Private autonomous consumption	Personal consumption expenditures in durable goods
Private autonomous investment	Private residential fixed investments
Government spending	Government consumption expenditures
	Social benefits to persons
	Subsidies
	Gross government investment

Source: Own elaboration based on FRED.

effect. However, on average, 94 percent of 'total government expenditures' was considered autonomous government spending.

As observed in Figures 8 and 9, and also analyzed empirically for the United States by Girardi and Pariboni, R. (2016) and Haluska, Braga, and Summa (2021), the growth rates in the real GDP and real autonomous demand are highly correlated, as expected by the Supermultiplier model.[12] However, note that small discrepancies are observed between these two rates. This is, of course, consistent with the Supermultipler model in which $\zeta = 0$ corresponds to the long-run fully adjusted position but $\zeta = g - g_Z \gtrless 0$ to the short-run dynamics. These discrepancies were especially significant during the C19P due to the large increase in the propensity to save, $1 - c$, (see Aladangady et al. 2022) which consequently reduced the supermultiplier.

Despite not being the primary focus of this research, a preliminary empirical analysis of the investment function was also conducted. On the one hand, considering equation (13), the growth rate of the propensity to invest $\hat{h}$ was derived from the share of the 'private non-residential fixed investment' in the GDP. On the other hand, the 'capacity utilization rate: total index' collected from FRED was log-linearized and detrended by using the Hodrick-Prescott (HP) filter, similar to Lavoie, Rodriguez, and Seccareccia (2004) and Setterfield (2017).[13] In principle, the HP cycle can be interpreted as an approximation of deviations of the capacitary utilization rate from its 'normal' $u - u_n$, or, at least, as the direction of the reaction function of capacity-creating expenditures. As shown in Figures 10 and 11, the growth rate of the propensity to invest is positively correlated to the capacity utilization cycle, as expected by the supermultiplier model with a flexible accelerator effect.[14]

[12]Similar to Girardi and Pariboni (2016)'s analyses for the US case, Gallo and Barbieri Goes (2023) also run a vector-error correction model for Euro Area.

[13]As recommended for HP filtering, the lambda value was set at 1600 for quarterly frequency.

[14]Note that it is not the objective to precisely estimate the level of the normal capacity utilization rate but simply in approximating the direction of the reaction function of capacity-creating expenditures. Also note that the use of a data-smoothing technique, such as the HP filter, does not necessarily imply a theoretical endogenous normal rate of capacity utilization as suggested by some neo-Kaleckians (see Lavoie 2022, ch. 6; and Setterfield 2017). Recall that the Sraffian Supermultiplier model assumes an exogenous normal rate determined by historical conventions that can eventually change over time but not with respect to the business cycle. Even so, Serrano, Summa, and Freitas (2022) have already claimed that in the case in which 'there is indeed a definite function that relates the normal degree of capacity utilization directly to the rate of growth of demand (…) this relation in the model would have the consequence of basically making the propensity to invest become somewhat less sensitive to increases in the actual growth rate of demand as less new capacity would now be necessary to meet it. This would, ceteris paribus, reduce the propensity to invest both during the adjustment process and in the fully adjusted position and, in its turn, make the model's equilibrium more prone to be dynamically stable and compatible with higher rates of demand-led growth (…) Therefore, if such endogeneity of the normal degree of utilization were to be established as theoretically and empirically relevant, the main conclusions of the Supermultiplier model would only be reinforced'

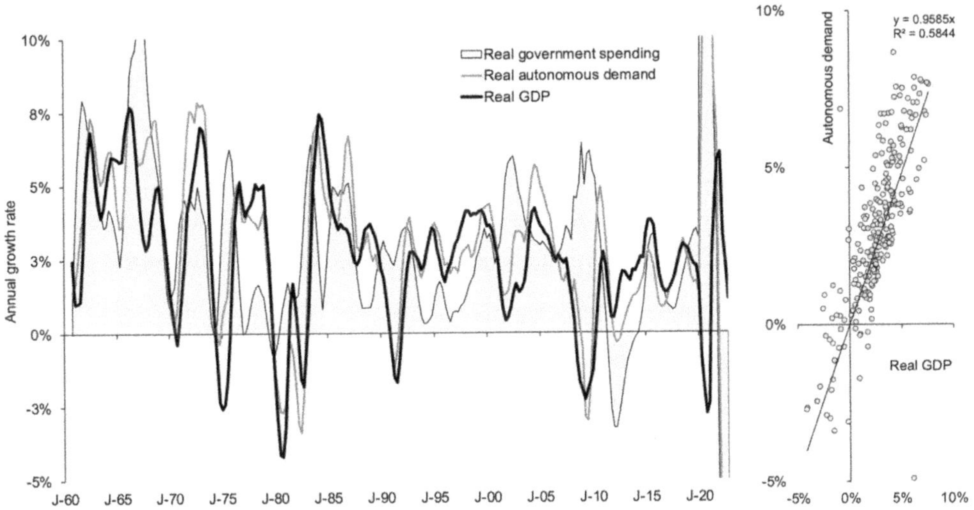

Figure 8 and 9. Demand-led supermultiplier growth in the United States (1960–2022, 1-year moving average, Quarterly frequency). Source: Own elaboration based on FRED.

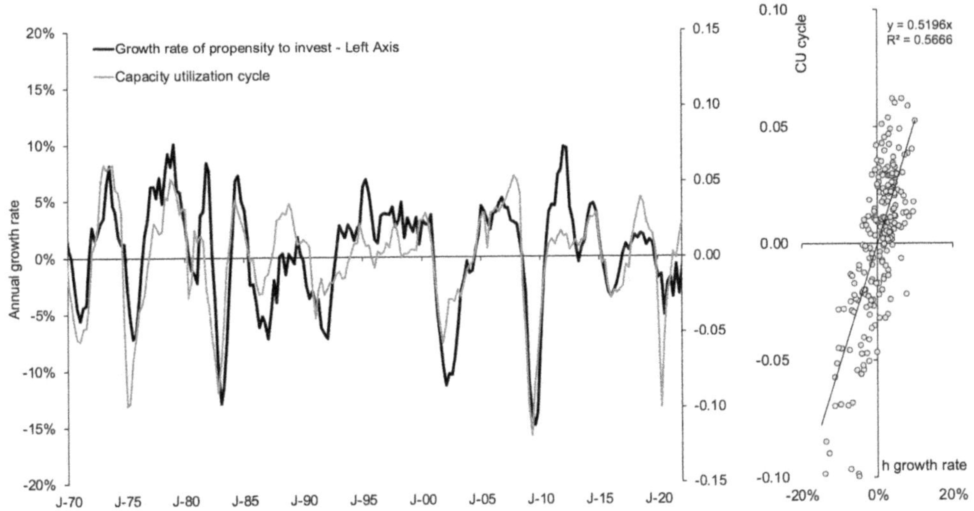

Figure 10 and 11. Flexible accelerator effect in the United States (1970–2022, Quarterly frequency). Source: Own elaboration based on FRED.

Finally, the paper's primary theoretical contribution, represented by equations (28) and (29), is empirically addressed by analyzing the following approximation: $\hat{M}_2 \approx \hat{P} + g_Z - \hat{V}$. Note that this expression approximates equation (28) if ζ is subtracted, or equation (29) if $\hat{V}$ is added. The decision not to directly test equation (28)

(pp. 13–14). Finally, also consider that there are alternative methods to the HF filter if the objective would be to estimate the normal rate of capacity utilization (see Botte 2020 and Gallo and Barbieri Goes 2023, for example). Moreover, eventually, the so-called 'capacity controversy' on using the FRED index as a measure of actual utilization should be considered (see Gahn and Gonzalez 2020; Nikiforos 2016).

stems from the necessity of first estimating short-term fluctuations in the supermultiplier effect, a task that exceeds the paper's scope. Additionally, as previously mentioned, the inclusion of the velocity of money is justified by the relevance of its short-run fluctuations and medium/long-term trends in the case of the United States.

On the one hand, the growth rate of the money supply, $\hat{M}_2$ was calculated from the monetary aggregate 'M2', which was collected from FRED. On the other hand, the sum of the nominal autonomous demand (as specified in Table 1) was divided by the GDP-M2 ratio (the velocity of money) and then its growth rate was calculated, $\hat{P} + g_Z - \hat{V}$.

Figures 12 and 13 show that the $\hat{M}_2$ is certainly a very good approximation of $\hat{P} + g_Z - \hat{V}$. This finding is consistent with the theoretical model in which the money supply is endogenously determined by creditworthy demand derived from the multiplier-accelerator effect of autonomous demand.

Moreover, a cointegration analysis was conducted to avoid relying only on graphical visualization. The objective was to verify the existence of a stationary linear combination between the natural logarithms of M2, $ln(M_2)$, and the nominal autonomous demand adjusted by the velocity of money, $ln(P) + ln(Z) - ln(V) = ln\left(\frac{PZ}{V}\right)$ for the period 1959: Q1-2022: Q4. After log-linearizing the data, the Augmented Dickey-Fuller test was conducted to verify the order of integration of the variables (Dickey and Fuller 1979). Table 2 shows that both variables are stationary in first differences at 1 percent of significance, which means they are $I(1)$ time series as usually required for cointegration analysis.

Granger's (1969) causality test in first differences (using two lags) was also conducted to get additional information on the variables under analysis. As expected from Section 3.3, Table 3 shows that $d(ln(M_2))$ Granger-causes $d\left(ln\left(\frac{PZ}{V}\right)\right)$, which means that the change in money supply precedes the change in nominal autonomous demand (adjusted by the velocity of money). The same result was also found between $d(ln(M_2))$ and $d(ln(GDP))$,

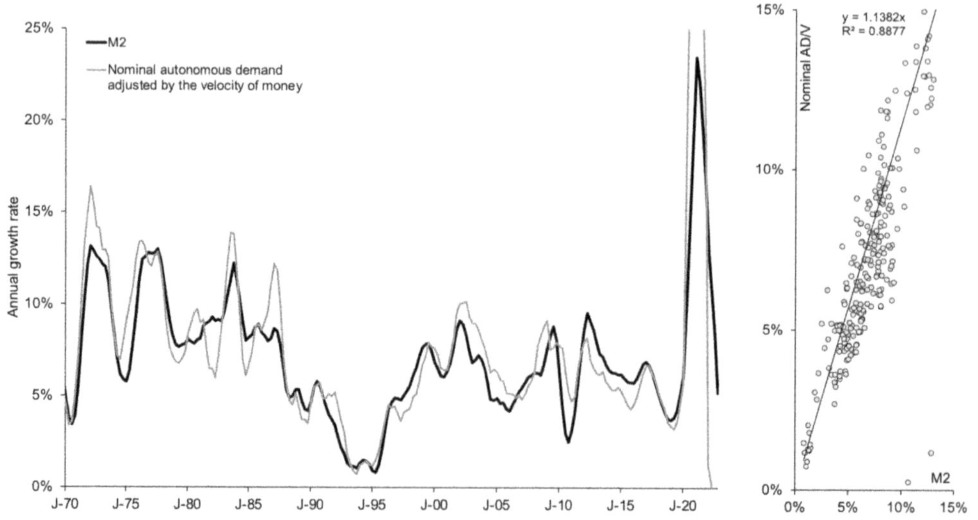

Figure 12 and 13. The monetary effect of autonomous demand in the United States (1970–2022, 1-year moving average, Quarterly frequency). Source: Own elaboration based on FRED.

Table 2. Augmented Dickey-Fuller Test for variables in first differences and residuals.

Null hypothesis	CV at 1% level	t-Statistic	Prob.*
$d(ln(M_2))$ has a unit root	−3.99	−8.55	0.00
$d(ln(\frac{PZ}{V}))$ has a unit root	−3.99	−7.62	0.00

Table 3. Granger causality test.

Null hypothesis	F-Statistic	Prob.
$d(ln(M_2))$ does not Granger Cause $d(ln(\frac{PZ}{V}))$	11.76	0.00
$d(ln(\frac{PZ}{V}))$ does not Granger Cause $d(ln(M_2))$	2.72	0.06
$d(ln(M_2))$ does not Granger Cause $d(ln(GDP))$	26.69	0.00
$d(ln(GDP))$ does not Granger Cause $d(ln(M_2))$	1.65	0.19

Table 4. Johansen cointegration test.

Unrestricted Cointegration Rank Test (Trace)				
No. of CEs	Eigenvalue	Trace Statistic	CV at 5% level	*p*-value
None*	0.09	26.25	15.49	0.00
Unrestricted Cointegration Rank Test (Max-eigenvalue)				
No. of CEs	Eigenvalue	Trace Statistic	CV at 5% level	*p*-value
None*	0.09	25.54	14.26	0.00

*Denotes rejection of the hypothesis at the 5% level.

as Kaldor (1970) knew and correctly understood in terms of the endogenous money approach. In contrast, Monetarists wrongly interpreted it as an argument in favor of the exogeneity of money supply (see Section 3.3).

Then, Johansen's (1988, 1991) cointegration test was set up following Granger causality tests, that is, by normalizing with respect to $ln(\frac{PZ}{V})$. As shown in Table 4, adding a constant and using four lags according to the Schwarz information criterion, a long-run cointegration relationship was found at a 5 percent of significance. The econometric output can be represented as follows:

$$\ln\left(\frac{PZ}{V}\right) = 1.05(\ln(M_2)) - 1.07 \tag{30}$$

The Engle and Granger (1987)'s method for testing long-run cointegration was also conducted. After running a least square regression between both variables, the stationarity of the residuals was analyzed. The ADF test confirmed that residuals are stationary at 5 percent of significance and thus, the variables under analysis are cointegrated (Table 5).

Finally, a vector error-correction model (VECM) was also run to analyze the short-run dynamics. As shown in Table 6, the speed of adjustment of $ln(\frac{PZ}{V})$ is relatively faster and

Table 5. Augmented Dickey-Fuller test for the residuals.

Null hypothesis	CV at 5% level	t-Statistic	Prob.*
Residual has a unit root	−3.42	−3.84	0.01

Table 6. Vector error correction model.

	EC Coeff.	SE	*t*-Statistics
$d(ln(\frac{PZ}{V}))$	−0.23	0.07	−3.18
$d(ln(M_2))$	−0.02	0.02	−1.21

significant. While the error correction coefficient of $ln(M_2)$ is relatively low (2 percent) and not significant (−1.21 of *t*-statistics), the one of $ln(\frac{PZ}{V})$ is significant (−3.18) and it corrects 23 percent in each quarter.

Before concluding, a comment on government spending. Considering that it represented, on average, almost 60 percent of the total autonomous demand since the 1960s, it is reasonable to conclude that it has played a crucial role in driving the economy.[15] However, as shown in Figure 8, government spending has tended to rise during recessions and slow down during recovery, a consistent dynamic with the countercyclical Keynesian policy, which became more or less a consensus among policy-makers since the so-called 'neoclassical synthesis.' The negative correlation between growth rates in government spending and output, particularly during recessions, suggests that countercyclical fiscal policies tend to mitigate, rather than compensate, the short-term contractions in private effective demand. It thus reveals some degree of endogeneity in observed government spending, as Skott (2017) discussed. Additionally, Haluska, Braga, and Summa (2021) have also claimed that 'autonomous expenditures may be exogenous or partially endogenous, depending on if and to which degree they are explained by the output level' (p. 7). In summary, it is important to distinguish between the long-run growth and the economic cycle when analyzing the role of government spending.

6. Final remarks

Beyond the fact that the Global Financial Crisis (GFC) was triggered by an endogenous financial shock and the COVID-19 pandemic (C19P) was, by definition, an exogenous real shock, these two crises exhibited different output and monetary dynamics in the United States. On the one hand, the C19P triggered a relatively deeper contraction in GDP, but its recovery was relatively faster and more robust. The 'V' shaped recovery after the C19P shock significantly contrasted the 'L' shaped trajectory of the post-GFC regime. On the other hand, the money supply (M2) grew relatively more, and the monetary base expanded relatively less during the C19P.

A theoretical framework that integrates the Sraffian Supermultiplier model and the endogenous money approach was developed to explain those different real-monetary dynamics. The model suggested that money supply is endogenously determined by creditworthy demand derived from the multiplier-accelerator effect of autonomous demand, in which government spending plays a key role.

The model was empirically analyzed for the United States during the period 1960–2022. In addition to the graphical visualization, a long-run cointegration relationship between the money supply M2 and the nominal autonomous demand (adjusted by the

[15]Note, however, that it is possible that one component, even if it is smaller than another, could have a relatively larger supermultiplier effect. Theoretically, each component has a particular supermultiplier effect.

velocity of money) was founded. Also, the speeds of short-run adjustments were estimated with a vector-error correction model (VECM).

The paper concluded that the economic recovery was faster during the C19P than in the GFC, as well as the M2 expanded relatively more (and the monetary base expanded relatively less) due to the extraordinary pandemic-related government spending, which was unprecedented in peacetime.

This time, the government put more cash in people's hands rather than reserves in banks' vaults. In fact, it was literal in the case of the social benefits transferred to people's bank accounts directly (which impacted the M2 directly). The US Federal Reserve (Fed) expanded the monetary base relatively more during the GFC because the government's primary objective was to bail out the financial sector. However, during the C19P, the primary objective was to rescue firms and households. In other words, this time, the Fed acted more as a 'fiscal agent' to cover the pandemic-related-fiscal deficit rather than a lender of last resort of banks as in the GFC. The monetary policy framework, however, was similar during both crises. While the monetary base continued to be 'exogenously' determined by the Fed's large-scale asset purchases, the federal funds target range was set at 0.25-zero percent.

The absence of full hysteresis after the C19P shock (but observed after the GFC) had nothing to do with a traditional neoclassical trend reversal mechanism but with the fiscal supermultiplier effect. However, two counteracting forces determined the effectiveness of government spending. On the one hand, the increases in the savings rate after the C19P shock, as the result of the increasing uncertainty and changes in the consumption patterns, among other factors, affected the fiscal supermultiplier effect negatively. On the other hand, the government had greater control over the business cycle during the C19P. This time, the government knew in advance when the supply-side shock generated by the lockdowns would occur, and thus, it was able to implement demand-side policies quickly, something that is difficult to happen in unexpected and endogenous market-based shocks.

Acknowledgements

I would like to use this opportunity to acknowledge and thank the reviewers who reviewed this article and aided in its publication. Moreover, I extend my gratitude to Franklin Serrano, Marc Lavoie, Mark Setterfield and Ricardo Summa for their direct or indirect contributions to this paper.

Disclosure Statement

No potential conflict of interest was reported by the author(s).

References

Aladangady, A, D. Cho, L.; Feiveson, and E. Pinto. 2022. '*Excess Savings During the COVID-19 Pandemic.*' FEDS Notes. Washington: Board of Governors of the Federal Reserve System.

Bastian, E. F., and M. Setterfield. 2020. 'Nominal Exchange Rate Shocks and Inflation in an Open Economy: Towards a Structuralist Inflation Targeting Agenda.' *Cambridge Journal of Economics* 44 (6): 1271–1299.

Bindseil, U. 2014. *Monetary Policy Operations and the Financial System.* Oxford: Oxford University Press.

Blecker, R. A., and M. Setterfield. 2019. *Heterodox Macroeconomics. Models of Demand, Distribution and Growth.* Cheltenham: Edward Elgar Publishing.

Botte, F. 2020. 'Estimating Normal Rates of Capacity Utilisation and Their Tolerable Ranges: A Comment on Mark Setterfield.' *Cambridge Journal of Economics* 2019: 1–8.

Braga, J., and F. Serrano. 2023. 'Post-Keynesian Economics: New Foundations by Marc Lavoie. Chapter 8: Inflation Theory.' *Review of Political Economy* 35 (4): 1096–1108.

Cardim de Carvalho, F. J. 2015. *Liquidity Preference and Monetary Economies.* London: Routledge.

Cesaratto, S., and S. Di Bucchianico. 2020. 'Endogenous Money and the Theory of Long- Period Effective Demand.' *Bulletin of Political Economy* 14 (1): 1–38.

De Lucchi, J. M. 2022. 'Three Essays on Unstable Exchange Markets and Monetary Policy Implications.' PhD. Dissertation. The New School.

Dickey, D. A., and W. A. Fuller. 1979. 'Distribution of the Estimators for Autoregressive Time Series with a Unit Root.' *Journal of the American Statistical Association* 74 (366a): 427–431.

Dvoskin, A., and M. Torchinsky Landau. 2022. 'Income Distribution and Economic Cycles in an Open Economy Supermultiplier Model.' Banco Central de la Republica Argentina, Working Papers 102.

Engle, R. F., and C. Granger. 1987. 'Co-integration and Error Correction: Representation, Estimation, and Testing.' *Econometrica* 55 (2): 251–276.

Gahn, S. J., and A. Gonzalez. 2020. 'On the 'Utilisation Controversy': A Comment.' *Cambridge Journal of Economics* 44 (3): 703–707.

Gallo, E., and M. C. Barbieri Goes. 2023. 'Investment, Autonomous Demand and Long-Run Capacity Utilization: An Empirical Test for the Euro Area.' *Economia Politica* 40 (1): 225–255.

Girardi, D., and R. Pariboni. 2016. 'Long-run Effective Demand in the US Economy: An Empirical Test of the Sraffian Supermultiplier Model.' *Review of Political Economy.* https://doi.org/10.1080/09538259.2016.1209893.

Granger, C. W. J. 1969. 'Investigating Causal Relations by Econometric Models and Cross-Spectral Methods.' *Econometrica* 37 (3): 424–438.

Fagundes, L., and F. Freitas. 2017. 'The Role of Autonomous Non-Capacity Creating Expenditures in Recent Kaleckian Growth Models: An Assessment from the Perspective of the Sraffian Supermultiplier.' *In even3.azureedge.net.*

Felipe, J., S. Fullwiler, G. Estrada, M. H. Jaber, M. A. Magadia, and R. Patagan. 2020. How 'Monetization' Really Works — Examples from Three Asian Nations' Responses to COVID-19. ADB Economics Working Paper Series 627, December 2020.

Felipe, J., and S. Fullwiler. 2022. 'How 'Monetization' Really Works — Examples from Three Asian Nations' Responses to Covid-19.' *Review of Political Economy* 34 (3): 397–419.

Fiori, J. L., C. Medeiros, and F. Serrano. 2009. 'O mito do colapso do peder americano.' Record.

Foley, D. K. 2011. 'The Long-Period Method and Marx's Theory of Value.' In *The Evolution of Economic Theory: Essays in Honour of Bertram Schefold*, edited by V. Caspari, pp. 15-38. 1st ed. London: Routledge.

Freitas, F. N., and E. Dweck. 2013. 'The Pattern of Economic Growth of the Brazilian Economy 1970–2005: A Demand-led Growth Perspective.' In Vol. 2 of *Sraffa and the Reconstruction of Economic Theory*, edited by E. S. Levrero, A. Palumbo, and A. Stirati. London: Palgrave Macmillan.

Freitas, F., and F. Serrano. 2015. 'Growth Rate and Level Effects, the Stability of the Adjustment of Capacity to Demand and the Sraffian Supermultiplier.' *Review of Political Economy* 27 (3): 258–281.

Freitas, F., E. Dweck, and F. Ligiero. 2021. 'Autonomous Demand Composition and Fiscal Policy in a Supermultiplier Simulation Model,' Ensayos Económicos, 78, Noviembre de 2021 Banco Central de la República Argentina.

Friedman, M. 1968. 'The Role of Monetary Policy.' *American Economic Review* 58: 1–17.

Haluska, G., J. Braga, and R. Summa. 2021. 'Growth, Investment Share and the Stability of the Sraffian Supermultiplier Model in the U.S. Economy (1985–2017).' *Metroeconomica* 72 (2): 345–364.

International Monetary Fund. 2021. 'Fiscal Monitor Database of Country Fiscal Measures in Response to the COVID-19 Pandemic,' IMF Fiscal Affairs Department, October 2021, www.imf.org.

Johansen, S. 1988. 'Statistical Analysis of Cointegration Vectors.' *Journal of Economic Dynamics and Control* 12: 231–254.

Johansen, D. 1991. 'Estimation and Hypothesis Testing of Cointegration Vectors in Gaussian Vector Autoregressive Models.' *Econometrica* 59 (6): 1551–1580.

Kaldor N. 1970. 'The new Monetarism,' Lloyds Bank Review, July, 1–17.

Keynes, J. M. 1936. *The General Theory of Employment, Interest and Money*. London: Macmillan.

Koo, R. 2011. 'The World in Balance Sheet Recession,' Ensayos Economicos, 63, September 2011, Banco Central de la República Argentina.

Lavoie, M. 1984. 'The Endogenous Flow of Credit and the Post Keynesian Theory of Money.' *Journal of Economic Issues* 18 (3): 771–797.

Lavoie, M., G. Rodriguez, and M. Seccareccia. 2004. 'Similitudes and Discrepancies in Post-Keynesian and Marxist Theories of Investment: A Theoretical and Empirical Investigation1.' *International Review of Applied Economics* 18 (2): 127–149.

Lavoie, M. 2010. 'Changes in Central Bank Procedures During the Subprime Crisis and Their Repercussions on Monetary Theory.' *International Journal of Political Economy* 39 (3): 3–23.

Lavoie, M. 2016. 'Rethinking Macroeconomic Theory Before the Next Crisis.' Institute for New Economic Thinking, September 23, 2016.

Lavoie, M. 2022. *Post-Keynesian Economics: New Foundations*. 2nd Ed. Cheltenham: Edward Elgar Publishing.

Lavoie, M. 2023. 'Some Controversies in the Causes of Post-Pandemic Inflation.' Monetary Policy Institute blog #77, May 14, 2023.

Lavoie, M. 2024. 'Conflictual Inflation and the Phillips Curve.' *Review of Political Economy* 1–23. https://doi.org/10.1080/09538259.2023.2294305.

Moore, B. J. 1988. *Horizontalists and Verticalists: The Macroeconomics of Credit Money*. Cambridge: Cambridge University Press.

Nikiforos, M. 2016. 'On the 'Utilisation Controversy': A Theoretical and Empirical Discussion of the Kaleckian Model of Growth and Distribution.' *Cambridge Journal of Economics* 40 (2): 437–467.

Pivetti, M. 1991. *An Essay on Money and Distribution*. London: Macmillan.

Rochon, L.-P. 1999. *Credit, Money and Production: An Alternative Post-Keynesian Approach*. Cheltenham and Northampton: Edward Elgar.

Romer, C. D. 2021. 'The Fiscal Policy Response to the Pandemic.' *Brookings Papers on Economic Activity* 2021: 89–110.

Serrano, F. 1995. 'Long Period Effective Demand and the Sraffian Supermultiplier.' *Contributions to Political Economy* 14 (1): 67–90.

Serrano, F., and R. Summa. 2013. 'Uma sugestão para simplificar a teoria da taxa de juros exógena.' *Ensaios FEE, Porto Alegre* 34 (2): 383–406. dez. 2013.

Serrano, F., and F. Freitas. 2017. 'The Sraffian Supermultiplier as an Alternative Closure for Heterodox Growth Theory*.' *European Journal of Economics and Economic Policies: Intervention* 14 (1): 70–91.

Serrano, F., R. Summa, and F. Freitas. 2022. '*Autonomous Demand-led Growth and the Supermultiplier: The Theory, the Model and Applications*.' 26th FMM Conference: Post-Keynesian Economics and Global Challenges, 2022, September 2022.

Setterfield, M. 2017. 'Long-run Variation in Capacity Utilization in the Presence of a Fixed Normal Rate.' New School for Social Research, Department of Economics, Working Papers 1704.

Setterfield, M. 2022. 'Neoliberalism: An Entrenched but Exhausted Growth Regime.' Ensayos Economicos, 79, Mayo 2022, Banco Central de la República Argentina.

Setterfield, M. 2023. 'Inflation and Distribution During the Post-COVID Recovery: A Kaleckian Approach.' *Journal of Post Keynesian Economics* 46 (4): 587–611.

Solow, R. M. 1956. 'A Contribution to the Theory of Economic Growth.' *The Quarterly Journal of Economics* 70 (1): 65–94.

Skott, P. 2017. 'Autonomous Demand and the Harrodian Criticisms of the Kaleckian Model.' *Metroeconomica* 68 (1): 185–193.

The FRED Blog. 2020. 'From Inflation Targeting to Average Inflation Targeting. The Fed's new Long-run Monetary Framework', November 9, 2020.

Volcker, P., and C. Harper. 2018. *Keeping at It: The Quest for Sound Money and Good Government.* New York: Public Affairs.

Weber, I. M., and Wasner, E. (2023) 'Sellers' Inflation, Profits and Conflict: Why can Large Firms Hike Sellers' Inflation, Profits and Conflict: Why can Large Firms Hike Prices in an Emergency?' Economics Department Working Paper Series. 343.

Weiss, C. R. 2022. 'Foreign Demand for U.S. Treasury Securities During the Pandemic.' FEDS Notes. Washington: Board of Governors of the Federal Reserve System. January 28, 2022.

Wolfson, M. 1996. 'A post-Keynesian theory of credit rationing.' *Journal of Post Keynesian Economics* 18 (3): 443–470.

Wray, L. R. 2015. *Modern Money Theory. A Primer on Macroeconomics for Sovereign Monetary Systems.* 2nd ed. New York: Palgrave Macmillan.

Supermultiplier Models, Demand Stagnation, and Monetary Policy: Inevitable March to the Lower Bound for Interest Rates?

Steven Fazzari

ABSTRACT

This article integrates monetary policy into a very simple dynamic supermultiplier model with an accommodating supply side. Results show that monetary policy guided by a mainstream Taylor rule may stabilize an economy around the steady-state path of demand-led growth following temporary demand shocks. However, monetary policy is ineffective in offsetting permanent negative demand shocks even if the lower bound for interest rates is not binding. This outcome contrasts with the prevailing view among policymakers that monetary policy can usually assure full utilization of an economy's resources in the long run. The ineffectiveness of monetary policy is particularly acute if autonomous demand grows more slowly than necessary to generate full employment. In this case, if policymakers recognize the under-utilization of resources, monetary policy leads to interest rates trending necessarily to their lower bound. The analysis also shows how monetary policy may lead to counter-productive responses to supply shocks. The article concludes with observations about how the theoretical results correspond with the history of US monetary policy in recent decades.

1. Introduction

This paper takes a simple step to integrate two important strands of research. First, there has been an explosion of interest in supermultiplier models of demand-led growth pioneered by Serrano (1995). Recent work explores a wide variety of model extensions and policy issues in the supermultiplier framework. However, there has been little attention in supermultiplier models to the second research strand considered here, the effects of monetary policy. There is a wide range of post-Keynesian research and perspectives on monetary policy employing other modeling frameworks (see Lavoie 2014, chapter 4 and Docherty 2021 for example), but consideration of monetary policy has been minimal in supermultiplier research.[1]

More specifically, I consider the implications of mainstream 'Taylor rule' monetary policy in a simple, stylized model of demand-led growth with accommodating supply.

[1]In a detailed analysis of the possible arbitrariness of monetary policy interest rate targets, Aspromourgos (2007) presents a model closely related to the supermultiplier approach.

The baseline model is a simplified version of Fazzari, Ferri, and Variato (2020), as presented in Fazzari and González (2023), with the addition of interest elasticity of aggregate demand. The demand side of this model generates familiar supermultiplier results. Also, it integrates the supply side to show there is no long-run path of potential output or equilibrium rate of unemployment that is independent of the path of demand. Indeed, growth in both actual and potential output is driven by the dynamics of autonomous demand.[2] While resources can constrain the economy from growing arbitrarily fast, there is neither a supply determined path of potential output nor a unique supply determined equilibrium rate of unemployment.

In contrast, most mainstream 'new consensus' or 'new Keynesian' models are based on a view of the economy in which the supply side of tastes, technology, and resources uniquely determines the long-run path of the economy independent of the dynamics of aggregate demand, as discussed by Palley (2007) and Hein and Stockhammer (2010). According to this framework, the job of monetary policy is to offset effects of demand shocks that affect real output and employment because of nominal rigidities. The objective is to return the output to its supply driven 'potential' path and the labor market to its 'natural' rate of unemployment. The maintained assumption in these mainstream models is that monetary policy is sufficient to accomplish this goal unless a negative demand shock is so large that a lower bound on interest rates is binding, a situation usually considered abnormal. This alternative perspective sets up the key question addressed in this article: what can mainstream Taylor rule monetary policy accomplish if the economy is, in fact, driven by demand beyond a short-run horizon defined by nominal rigidity?

Following the presentation of the model (Section Two) and the integration of monetary policy and interest rates (Section Three), the paper presents four key results. First, I consider how the model predicts that Taylor-rule monetary policy can stabilize output and employment around an equilibrium unemployment rate and steady-state growth path following temporary demand shocks (Section Four). But that unemployment rate is not 'natural' as assumed in mainstream models; it depends on the growth rate of autonomous demand. While activist monetary policy can mitigate output loss following a temporary negative demand shock, monetary stabilization that targets an equilibrium unemployment rate may sacrifice output after a temporary positive demand shock.

Second, I consider permanent negative shocks to the *level* of autonomous demand (Section Five). Following a permanent negative shock, monetary policy that targets the equilibrium unemployment rate reduces output loss along the transition path that follows the shock. But if monetary policy follows a Taylor rule it will not prevent the long-run output loss resulting from a permanent downward shift of demand. This result arises even if the interest rate is above its lower bound, and therefore strongly contrasts with the mainstream view that monetary policy can always offset demand shocks (temporary or permanent) if the lower bound is not binding. Symmetrically, restrictive monetary policy following a permanent positive demand shock will slow the transition to a higher long-run output path.

[2] While they do not use the supermultiplier framework explicitly, Setterfield (2011), Palley (2012), and Mason and Jayadev (2023) also present models of demand-led growth with accommodating supply induced by endogenous productivity and labor supply. The implications for monetary policy developed here apply in these alternative models. Also see Hein and Stockhammer (2010), along with the extensive references they provide, for post-Keynesian critiques of the 'natural' or 'NAIRU' rate of unemployment assumptions that are central to the mainstream monetary policy approach.

Third, and perhaps most interesting, I analyze the effect of mainstream monetary policy following a permanent negative shock to the *growth* rate of autonomous demand (Section Six). This shock, other things equal, raises the equilibrium unemployment rate (equivalent in this model to the output gap). Monetary policy will not be able to restore the unemployment rate that prevailed prior to the shock. I propose two possible scenarios for the policy response to this situation. In the first scenario, policymakers guided by a mainstream view of the long run according to which the supply side necessarily drives the output path, will conclude that the 'natural' rate of unemployment has risen and accept an economy that grows more slowly, incorrectly assuming this outcome is the best than can be achieved. However, faster equilibrium growth and a lower equilibrium rate of unemployment would be feasible with faster demand growth. An alternative policy scenario arises if policymakers do understand that economic growth is unacceptably low due to weak aggregate demand. In this case, they may abandon the rigid Taylor rule and keep cutting interest rates. But this policy can only affect the level, not the growth rate, of aggregate demand and it will therefore cause an inevitable march of the interest rate to its lower bound. This outcome corresponds to the resurrected 'secular stagnation' hypothesis proposed most prominently by Summers (2015).

Fourth, although the focus of this paper is on the interaction between monetary policy and the dynamics of aggregate demand, I exploit the integration of the supply side into the simple model and consider how monetary policy affects the response of the economy to supply shocks (Section Seven). The analysis shows that Taylor-rule monetary policy can lead to economic damage following negative shocks to labor productivity, especially following permanent shocks to productivity growth. Furthermore, a positive shock to productivity growth will likely lead the interest rate to its lower bound.

Although the model is very simple, Section Eight considers how the results can be used to interpret important features of the interaction of monetary policy and the path of output over the past several decades. During this period, the US and other countries experienced a persistent downward trend in interest rates, eventually hitting the lower bound for an extended period prior to the pandemic. This history fits broad aspects of the theoretical results here and provides motivation for more detailed research on the theoretical and empirical effects of monetary policy when growth is led by demand beyond the short run as discussed briefly in the concluding Section Nine.

2. A Simple Model of Demand-Led Growth

This section presents a simple supermultiplier model of demand-led growth. The model is designed to explore basic results and build intuition in the most transparent way possible. As such it abstracts away from features of modern economies that must ultimately be incorporated to address critical issues related to the empirical effectiveness of monetary policy. In this sense, the simple model here follows how Summa, Petrini, and Teixeira (2023) describe much of the supermultiplier research as intended to investigate 'general analytical properties' of the model.[3] That said, the results are sufficiently

[3]Serrano, Summa, and Freitas (2023) provide an insightful discussion of the supermultiplier model that identifies and addresses a variety of criticisms of the associated research.

general that they will very likely apply in more realistic models designed for quantitative and empirical research.

The model is based on the simple version of the demand-led growth model for a closed economy designed to develop intuition in Fazzari and González (2023, section 2).[4] It includes just two components of demand: private consumption based on income (C_t) and autonomous demand (Z_t). Autonomous demand can be thought of as a bond-financed government transfer that is fully consumed or government spending on public goods and services, but the specific definition of autonomous demand for the purposes of this paper does not matter. For simplicity, there is no capital or fixed investment in the model, although all results could be easily generalized to include investment and fixed capital in the version of the extended empirical model from Fazzari and González (2023). This simplifying assumption also abstracts from any effect of growth or monetary policy on the investment share. We will return to discuss the relevance of this assumption in assessing the results.

Total output (Y_t) is determined by aggregate demand:

$$Y_t = C_t + Z_t$$

subject to the constraint that output cannot exceed supply (Y_t^s) that will be discussed below. The consumption function is:

$$C_t = (1 - s)Y_t$$

with the saving propensity (s) between zero and one. Autonomous demand grows at a constant rate g_Z. It is immediately obvious that:

$$Y_t = \frac{Z_t}{s} \tag{1}$$

and output grows at rate g_z for a given value of s.[5]

To analyze some basic implications of monetary policy on the economy's capacity to produce and its equilibrium unemployment rate, the supply side must be modeled explicitly. Supply is a linear (Leontief) function of employment (l_t),

$$Y_t^s = A_t l_t$$

Labor productivity (A_t) evolves over time. Assume total labor supply is fixed and normalized to one. Then, employment and unemployment (u_t) can be interpret as rates that sum to unit labor supply,

$$1 = u_t + l_t$$

A simplified version of the productivity growth (g_A) specification from Fazzari, Ferri, and Variato (2020) is:

$$g_A = \phi_0 - \phi_1 u_{t-1} \tag{2}$$

[4]The assumption of a closed economy, while useful given the simple objective of this analysis, excludes effects of monetary policy on exchange rates working through balance-of-payments constraints. See Serrano and Summa (2015) and Dvoskin and Landau (2023) for discussion of monetary policy in an open economy.

[5]In the absence of capital, the supermultiplier becomes the most basic textbook Keynesian multiplier: 1/ s. For example, see Pariboni (2016, equation 11).

The intuition is that productivity (per employed person or per hour worked) will grow faster in a stronger economy with greater incentive to economize on labor and engage in productivity-enhancing R&D. The strength of the economy is proxied by the unemployment rate which creates a key connection between the demand and supply sides of the economy. This relationship is explained in more detail in Fazzari, Ferri, and Variato (2020) with extensive references. The most basic way to interpret this specification is from Dutt (2006) that 'necessity is the mother of invention.' When the economy has little economic slack (a low unemployment rate), the incentive to innovate rises. In addition, as discussed in Brown, Fazzari, and Petersen (2009), a stronger economy generates higher profits and cash flows to finance innovative activity to raise output per hour of labor.

In this very simple framework, equation 1 shows the economy will grow at the rate of growth of autonomous demand, g_Z.[6] The supply side productivity relationship in equation 2 gives the steady-state unemployment rate as[7]:

$$u^* = \frac{\phi_0 - g_z}{\phi_1} \quad (\phi_1 > 0) \tag{3}$$

Equation 3 presents a central result of this research program critical to understanding its implications for monetary policy: *there is no 'natural' rate of unemployment* defined independently of the economy's demand dynamics. The basic intuition for this result is clear. Suppose the economy starts in steady state in period zero and then g_z rises in period one. Higher demand induces greater output which requires more labor input and reduces the unemployment rate in period one, and stimulates faster productivity growth in the period two (equation 2). If the higher rate of productivity growth in period two is not large enough to accommodate the faster growth of autonomous demand, the unemployment rate in period two falls again, causing even faster growth of productivity in period three.[8] The process continues until the unemployment rate converges to u^* such that productivity grows at a rate consistent with the new higher level of g_z. This result is the central message of Fazzari, Ferri, and Variato (2020), that is, the dynamic path of the supply side *accommodates* the demand-determined dynamics, or, more simply: demand leads supply.

This result has two caveats. First, equation 2 has a meaningful solution for the steady-state unemployment rate only if $\phi_1 > 0$, that is, there must be some structural channel in the economy that induces faster supply-side *growth* when the *level* of economic activity rises at any point in time. This specification is somewhat different from the Kaldor-Verdoorn effect, more common in post-Keynesian growth models, relating output *growth* to productivity *growth*,[9] Fazzari and González (2023) provide estimates of the

[6]In Fazzari, Ferri, and Variato (2020) we have a broader set of structural features and dynamics, including capital accumulation and expectation formation. In this environment, as in all other supermultiplier modeling with stable dynamics, the steady-state rate of output growth that converges to the rate of growth of autonomous demand. Deviations from the steady-state path can be significant and persistent, as discussed in detail by Gallo (2022).

[7]Estimates of ϕ_0 and ϕ_1 from Fazzari and González (2023) easily satisfy the parameter restrictions to obtain a positive steady-state unemployment rate.

[8]For high values of ϕ_1, it is possible for productivity growth in period one to exceed the level necessary to accommodate faster demand growth. In this case the unemployment rate falls below u^* in period one and the convergence to equilibrium is cyclical. This case does not change the main implications of this paper. However, estimates of ϕ_1 from Fazzari and González (2023) imply the case described in the text is much more likely.

effect of the unemployment rate on both productivity and labor supply growth that strongly support this requirement. That said, note equation 3 shows that *in steady state*, the unemployment rate is independent of the *level* of demand, it depends only on the steady-state growth rate of demand (g_z) and the supply side parameters (ϕ_0 and ϕ_1). This result follows from the fact that supply accommodates demand. If the level of demand falls permanently, the unemployment rate will rise along the transition path. The higher unemployment lowers labor productivity, which offsets part of the higher initial unemployment rate (given fixed labor supply). This transitional adjustment continues until, in the new steady state, productivity has fallen just enough to accommodate the permanently reduced level of the demand path and the steady-state unemployment rate returns to the level given by equation 3.

The second caveat is that the demand-determined equilibrium unemployment rate implied by equation 3 must be above a minimum unemployment rate determined by the available workforce. That is, there must be some slack in the economy. Therefore, demand growth cannot be accommodated by supply at an arbitrarily high level as discussed further in Fazzari, Ferri, and Variato (2020) and Fazzari and González (2023). We shall proceed with the assumption that in normal times labor supply constraints are not binding.

3. Integrating Interest Rates and Monetary Policy

The results presented in the previous section differ fundamentally from the 'new consensus' or 'new Keynesian' theoretical framework that typically guides mainstream policy recommendations. In most of those models, long-run growth is governed exclusively by the supply side, independent of the dynamic path of demand. From the mainstream perspective, the objective of monetary policy becomes to simply stabilize deviations from the supply determined path that arise from the combination of demand 'shocks' and nominal rigidity assumed to disappear in the long run. Sim (2022, p. 1), following Blanchard (2018), calls this the 'independence hypothesis' and writes that it 'has been at the center of monetary economics and the majority of Keynesian economics have accepted the concept' as an 'unquestionable axiom.' Goodfriend (2007, p. 58) describes part of the mainstream consensus as 'there is a natural rate of unemployment (where output equals its potential) at which wage and price setters perpetuate the going rate of inflation.'[10]

The objective of this paper is to explore what happens if a mainstream monetary policy rule premised on the 'independence hypothesis' is used in an economy that actually

[9]See Fazzari and González (2023) for further development of this point which was also recognized explicitly prior to our work by Setterfield (2011) and Palley (2012).

[10]In the aftermath of the Great Recession some mainstream authors proposed that negative demand shocks can have persistent, even permanent, effects on the supply side, and therefore on output. These models typically employ two features. First, there are hysteresis effects that compromise supply through mechanisms such as reducing worker skills or reducing investment in fixed capital and R&D. Independent of the long-run path of demand, these permanent effects depend on how much a given demand crisis spills over to supply (see Fatás and Summers 2018, for example). Second, these models almost exclusively invoke the zero lower bound for monetary policy so that monetary policy cannot 'fix' the demand side in the short run (see Benigno and Fornaro 2018 and additional references in Fazzari and González 2023). A detailed assessment of this research is beyond the scope of this paper. Briefly, the approach here differs on both of these dimensions. First, the path of demand determines the path of output, which then pulls the supply side along with it. There is no direct effect on supply independent of the long-run demand path. Second, as the subsequent analysis will show, permanent demand shocks will affect the path of supply and actual output regardless of whether monetary policy is constrained by the zero lower bound. Also see Fazzari (2020).

behaves as predicted by the simple demand-led growth model. To generalize the model presented in Section Two for this purpose there must be a channel for the interest rate controlled by monetary policy to affect demand. In a closed economy, the most realistic channel is likely through residential construction, the most interest-sensitive component of aggregate demand. The interest sensitivity of business investment is more questionable, but that channel may also matter for monetary policy. Other post-Keynesian analysis of monetary policy explores the link between the interest rate, income distribution, and aggregate demand.[11] However, the objective here is to illustrate some basic results in the most straightforward way. Therefore, instead of modeling different components of demand separately, assume that the saving rate is time-varying and depends on the interest rate (r_t):

$$s_t = \eta_0 + \eta_1 r_t \tag{4}$$

This specification, while simplistic, is more general than it may appear. One can interpret 'consumption' in this model more broadly as 'induced' demand, that is, demand that depends on the level of output. In a more general model, this demand could include residential construction or business investment.[12] The interest sensitivity of the saving rate, therefore, can be interpreted as related to the cost of credit for various categories of demand. This specification is also qualitatively consistent with a model in which higher interest costs raise debt service and reduce spending for indebted consumers, although this simple approach does not capture the rich dynamics of interest rates and debt as in Barbieri Góes (2023) and Avritzer and Brochier (2022). Again, the objective here is not to model the details of the varied channels through which interest rates affect aggregate demand. Rather, this approach identifies some basic conceptual effects of monetary policy when growth is demand-led beyond the short run.

Imposing a zero lower bound on the policy rate and the possibility of interest rate smoothing, specify monetary policy through a Taylor-like rule[13]:

$$r_t^{\text{targ}} = \max\left[0,\ \gamma_0 - \gamma_1(u_{t-1} - u_t^{\text{targ}})\right] \tag{5}$$

$$r_t = \lambda_r r_{t-1} + (1 - \lambda_r) r_t^{\text{targ}}$$

Goodfriend (2007, p. 59) states the Taylor rule 'became the most common way to model monetary policy.' Rochon and Setterfield (2008) and Levrero (2023) identify mainstream monetary policy with the Taylor rule. For simplicity, this specification suppresses the

[11] See Galbraith (1957), Pivetti (1991), Lavoie (1995), Serrano, Summa, and Moreira (2020), and Docherty (2021). Another channel for interest rate effects on demand could arise through interest rate elasticity of autonomous demand, for example, residential investment and debt-financed consumption. It is worthwhile to explore this channel in more complex models (see Barbieri Góes 2023, for example). However, to the extent that the level of Z_t (and not its growth rate) depends on the level of the interest rate, the main conclusions of the following analysis will remain largely unchanged. In this respect, it is useful to consider the results of Deleidi (2018), Barbieri Góes and Deleidi (2022) that find a statistically significant effect of interest rates on residential investment. Pérez-Montiel and Pariboni (2022) present empirical support for a long-run effect of residential investment on output and therefore conclude that residential investment matters for the trend of output, in addition to the cycle. Many factors may affect the residential investment trend. The key point here is that the level of residential investment, as part of Z_t will depend on the level of the interest rate. Any trend in residential investment related to the interest rate would require a trend in the interest rate itself.

[12] In this simple model, $1/s_t$ is the Keynesian multiplier at any point in time. In a more general model, the supermultiplier contains a term reflecting investment induced by the accelerator principle. If a lower interest rate raises the capital-output ratio, the supermultiplier would rise, a result analogous to the simple specification used here.

[13] Lima, Setterfield, and da Silveira (2023) generalize the concept of a zero lower bound to an 'effective lower bound.'

inflation component of the Taylor rule. But this simplification is easily modified to include a linear inflation effect on the target interest rate along with a linear Phillips Curve. As the appendix shows, adding these features to the model just changes the γ_0 and γ_1 coefficients in the interest rate equation. In particular, the total response of the target interest rate to changes in unemployment will be larger if the policy also targets inflation and there is a negative correlation between inflation and unemployment.

4. Short-Run Demand Shocks and Monetary Stabilization

Mainstream perspectives on monetary policy propose that interest rate adjustments should stabilize demand relative to a supply determined output path. As the discussion above demonstrates, the steady-state output path in this model is demand-led with supply following, as long as slack labor resources exist. However, the model can reproduce some aspects of mainstream results assuming a constant growth rate of autonomous demand (g_z) with a target unemployment rate equal to the steady-state unemployment rate (u^*) from equation 3 that equates supply growth to g_z. If g_z is constant, the economy will follow a steady growth path over time, with what will be interpreted through the lens of mainstream models as a 'natural' or 'neutral' unemployment rate at which supply and demand growth are balanced.

Following a temporary shock to the level of autonomous demand, the simple demand-led growth model delivers results that appear consistent with mainstream models used to guide monetary policy. A temporary demand shock does not change the steady-state path of the economy. Therefore, the demand-led growth model largely mimics the behavior of a mainstream model in which the long-run path of the economy is independent of demand. To illustrate this result, consider a simulation of simple model. Details of the simulation and parameter choices appear in the appendix, but the main qualitative results hold for any sensible parameter choices. Figure 1 presents impulse-response functions from the simulation following a negative shock in quarter 5 to autonomous demand (Z_t). The shock initially equals one quarter per cent of output and then decays with a quarterly autoregressive parameter of 0.80 each quarter. The dashed lines show a baseline case in which there is no monetary policy response, that is, with a constant interest rate. The solid lines are the counter-factual case when an increase in the unemployment rate leads to a policy-induced decline in the interest rate.[14]

Initially, the impulse-response functions correspond to basic mainstream predictions as well as what Rochon and Setterfield (2008, p. 13), similar to Palley (2007), identify as the 'activist' post-Keynesian view of monetary policy. The negative demand shock raises the unemployment rate immediately on impact. Higher unemployment lowers productivity (see equation 2). After the shock, demand growth returns back toward its initial value, the temporary drop in demand decays, and the unemployment rate falls back toward its initial value in both scenarios. However, with activist monetary policy, interest rate cuts initially push down the saving rate compared with the baseline case.[15] A lower saving rate boosts aggregate demand causing the unemployment rate to decline more

[14] Docherty (2021, figure 3) presents similar results from a model in which monetary policy affects demand through a distributional channel.

[15] As discussed earlier, one can think of the effect of the interest rate on saving rate in this simple model as changing the multiplier. In a more general model, if the interest rate changes the accelerator effect due to induced investment, the

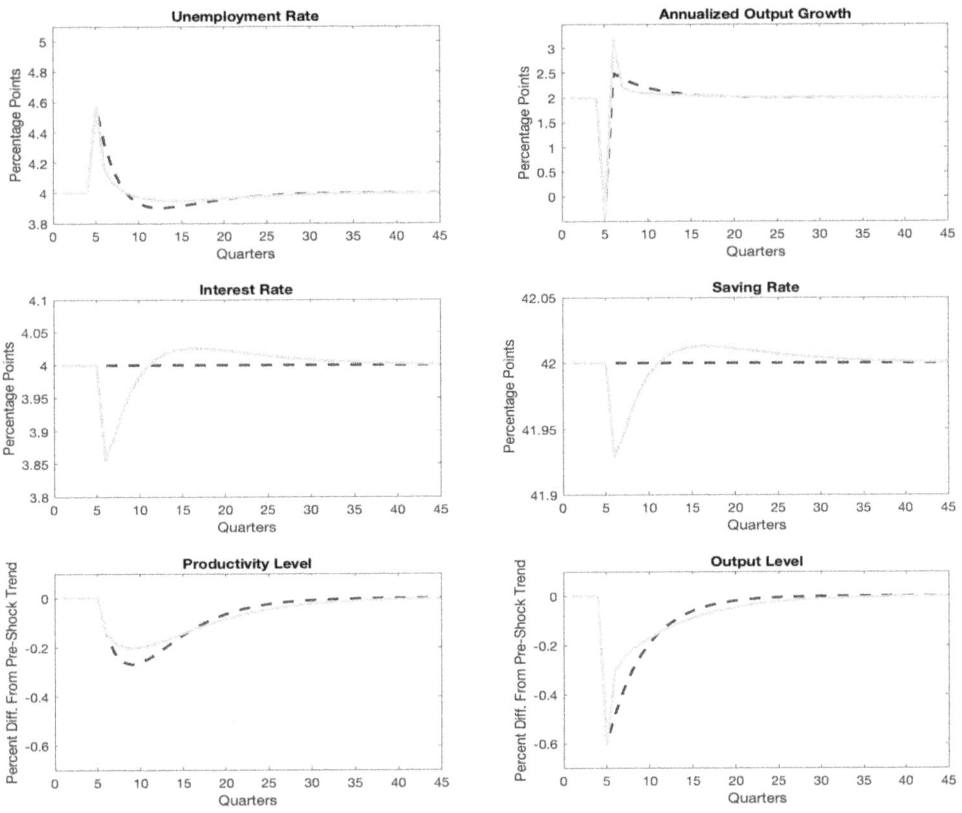

Figure 1. Temporary negative shock to autonomous demand.

Note: Simulation results following a temporary negative demand shock as described in the text and the simulation appendix. Dashed lines are the benchmark scenario with no monetary policy response. Solid lines represent results with Taylor-rule monetary policy.

quickly, output to recover more quickly, and productivity growth to rebound more quickly for a few quarters. Due to the discrete time simulation, the unemployment rate overshoots the long-run equilibrium and falls slightly below its steady-state value, leading the interest rate and the saving rate to temporarily rise slightly above its initial value because of the mechanical Taylor rule. However, the short-run effects of activist monetary policy are stabilizing.

The effects are symmetric. A positive demand shock will have the standard effect of reducing unemployment. Assuming no change in the long-run growth path of autonomous demand, this effect will be temporary. But it could be beneficial if the initial equilibrium unemployment rate is above the minimum level imposed by labor supply. A rigid monetary policy rule that targets an unemployment rate higher than the rate consistent with true full employment reduces the Keynesian benefits of positive demand shocks. This result also implies an asymmetric monetary policy rule with a stronger response to higher unemployment than lower unemployment, may improve economic performance compared with the standard Taylor rule.

decline in the saving rate would also be accompanied by an increase in the investment rate, but with the same dynamics, changing the quantitative effect, but leaving the qualitative results presented by the simulations unchanged.

5. Permanent Shocks to the Level of Demand

Consider the effect of a negative shock to autonomous demand that leads to a permanently lower level of autonomous demand, but, following the shock, demand growth returns to the previous rate of g_z. The level of demand and the level of output are permanently reduced. These results are consistent with the interpretation of the simple theoretical model presented earlier following equation 3. Again, lower demand causes the unemployment rate to rise. With a fixed labor supply, one might guess that the unemployment rate remains permanently higher. However, this is not the case in this model because of the endogenous relationship between the unemployment rate and the supply side. The initial rise in the unemployment rate induces slower productivity growth. This effect mitigates the rise in unemployment. Because neither the long-run growth rate nor the productivity growth parameters have changed, the steady-state unemployment rate does not change (see equation 3). A permanent reduction in the level of the demand path does not raise unemployment, instead it reduces labor productivity as supply adjusts to the lower level of demand.

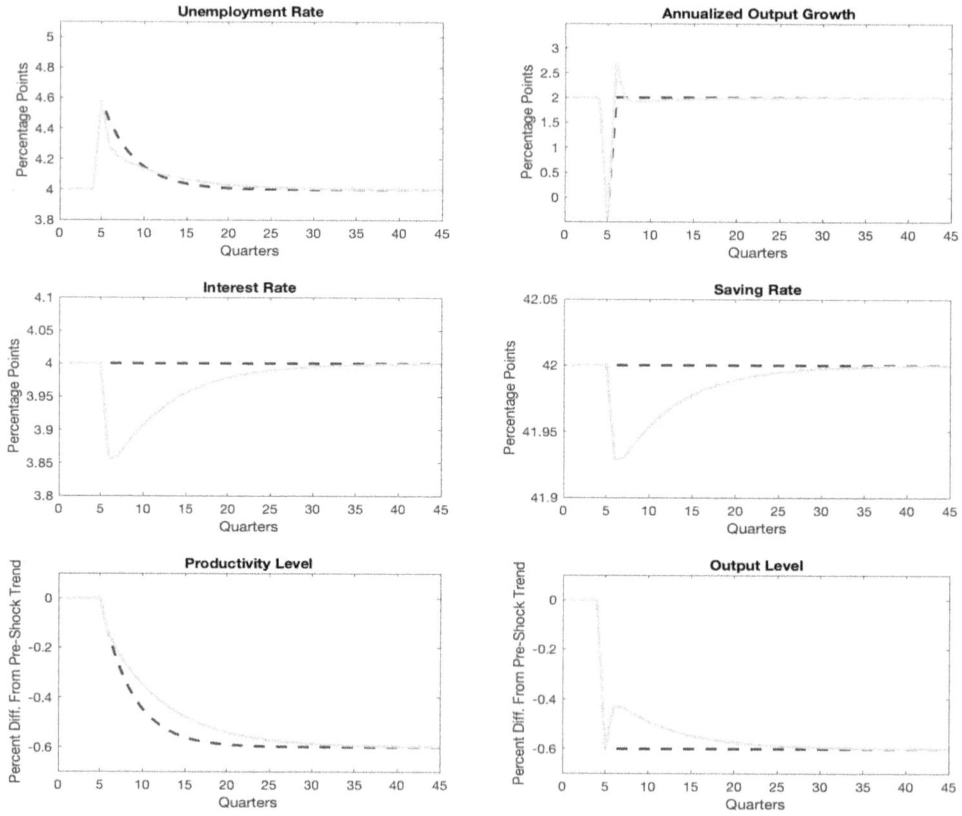

Figure 2. Permanent negative shock to autonomous demand.

Note: Simulation results following a permanent negative demand shock as described in the text and the simulation appendix. Dashed lines are the benchmark scenario with no monetary policy response. Solid lines represent results with Taylor rule monetary policy.

This result has important implications for monetary policy. Figure 2 shows the effect of a negative permanent level shock to autonomous demand equal to a quarter per cent of GDP holding the long-run growth rate of autonomous demand constant. Again, the dashed lines show a base case with a constant interest rate while the solid lines simulate the results when monetary responds to the unemployment rate. The initial impact of the shock is the same as it is following a temporary shock as shown in Figure 1. However, because the shock does not decay, unemployment is more persistent. The monetary policy rule reduces the interest rate by more than in the case of the temporary shock and keeps it lower over for a longer time. Again, activist monetary policy mitigates the effects of the demand shock on output, unemployment, and productivity.

The lower right panel of Figure 2 shows that the output path following a permanent demand shock is not just quantitatively different from the effect of a temporary shock, it is qualitatively different. And this difference is fundamentally inconsistent with mainstream views about monetary policy. Note that the dashed line shows there is no return to the initial output path following the shock. With no monetary accommodation, output remains 0.6 per cent below the pre-shock trend. In the first few quarters following the shock, a lower interest rate offsets part of this output loss. However, monetary policy does not generate convergence back to the pre-shock trend. Indeed, the output path with activist monetary policy converges to the baseline case, permanently below the earlier trend even though the interest rate never comes close to its lower bound.

The reason for this result is demand-driven path dependence of supply. The higher unemployment and weaker economy induced by lower demand reduces productivity growth temporarily during the transition path between the initial and final equilibria. This effect permanently lowers the level of productivity relative to the pre-shock trend. The unemployment rate converges back to its original steady-state value given by equation 3. Mainstream monetary policy would conclude its job is done: the unemployment rate has returned to its initial equilibrium level, what the mainstream would interpret as the 'natural' rate. Targeting the output gap would lead to the same result because, in this model, the output gap and the unemployment rate are identical.[16] According to the mainstream model, the long-run path of the economy is independent of demand. Therefore, this outcome would be interpreted, incorrectly, as a negative 'supply shock,' assumed unrelated to the demand shock, that cannot, and should not, be offset by monetary policy. Policymakers guided by a standard Taylor rule would believe they have successfully restored full employment. They will ratchet down their estimate of potential output. But they would be mistaken. The economy could be restored to its previous higher output path with policies to stimulate autonomous demand (see also Aspromourgos 2007; Serrano, Summa, and Moreira 2020, p. 380).

6. Permanent Shocks to Demand Growth

This section analyzes an even greater inconsistency between the operation of Taylor-rule monetary policy and the predictions of the demand-led growth model. Consider a

[16] This statement would not be strictly true if the minimum unemployment rate is above zero. Then, the output gap would be lower than the unemployment rate by the amount of the minimum unemployment rate. All the results presented here go through, however, with the unemployment rate normalized to zero when all labor resources are fully employed.

permanent reduction in the growth rate of the demand-generating process. In the simple model presented here, as well as in the more developed models in Fazzari, Ferri, and Variato (2020) and Fazzari and González (2023), a permanent reduction in the growth rate of autonomous demand (g_z) causes a permanent reduction in output growth and supply growth along with a permanent increase in the equilibrium level of the unemployment rate (see equation 3).

Figure 3 shows these effects for a one percentage point decline in the annual growth rate of autonomous demand. In the model without a monetary policy response, output growth falls by one percentage point immediately and growth remains one percentage point lower indefinitely. The unemployment rate also rises, but over time the rate of change in the unemployment rate from quarter to quarter declines. Why? Again, a higher unemployment rate reduces productivity growth (equation 2). Therefore, the unemployment rate changes by less each period as time passes, ultimately converging to the new higher equilibrium unemployment rate. At this higher rate, demand and supply converge in both levels and growth rates (see equation 3).

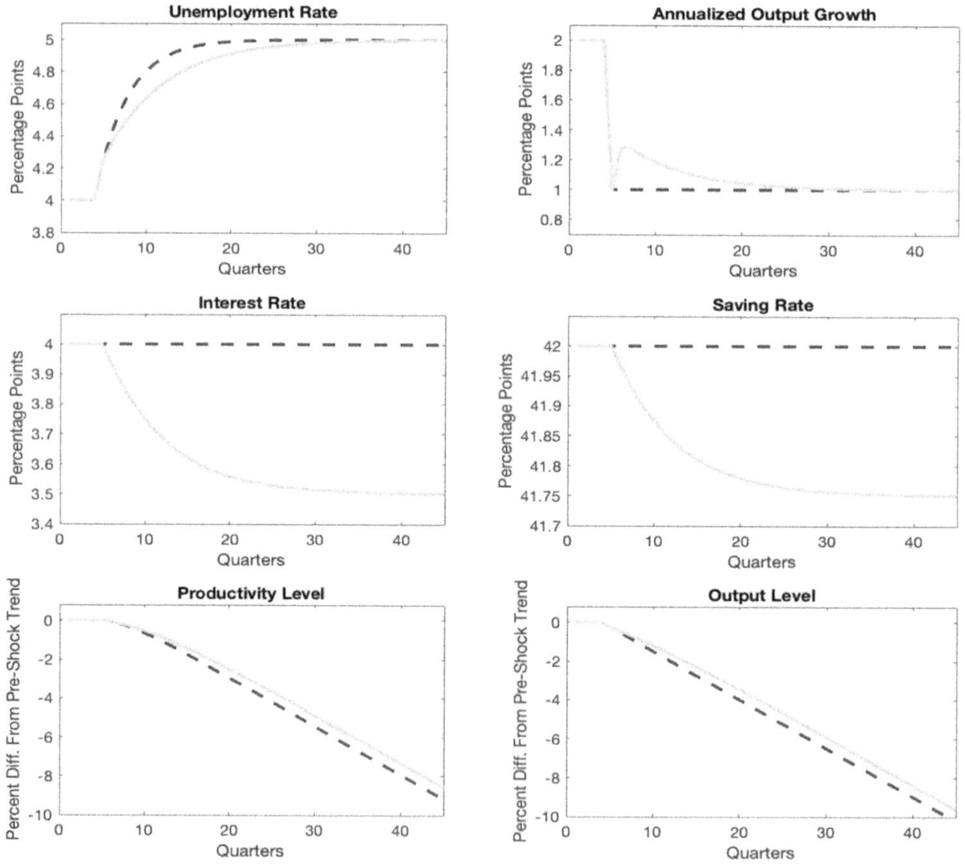

Figure 3. Permanent negative shock to autonomous demand growth.

Note: Simulation results following a permanent negative shock to autonomous demand growth as described in the text and the simulation appendix. Dashed lines are the benchmark scenario with no monetary policy response. Solid lines represent results with Taylor rule monetary policy.

How does mainstream monetary policy affect these dynamics? The higher unemployment rate leads monetary policy to cut interest rates raising the level of demand by reducing the saving rate.[17] This policy offsets some of the output loss along the weaker demand growth path, but the effect on output *growth* is only temporary. In the Taylor rule equation, the long-run level of the interest rate depends linearly on the gap between the current unemployment rate and the target unemployment rate. If the target rate does not change after the permanent reduction in demand growth, the gap does not disappear, but it converges to a constant and monetary policy that follows the Taylor rule no longer cuts the interest rate. This result follows in a straightforward way from equations 3 and 5. In a steady state, assuming the zero lower bound is not binding the interest rate converges to:

$$r^* = \gamma_0 - \gamma_1(u^* - u_t^{targ}) = \gamma_0 - \gamma_1\left(\frac{\phi_0 - g_z}{\phi_1} - u_t^{targ}\right)$$

If u_t^{targ} is set at the equilibrium unemployment rate for a high level of g_z and then g_z falls, the equilibrium interest rate will decline, but it will converge to a constant level despite the fact that the output and employment paths are permanently lower due to slower demand growth. Figure 3 illustrates these effects. Because the interest rate is permanently lower, the saving rate falls permanently. This effect implies both output and productivity levels are somewhat higher with monetary policy that follows the Taylor rule compared with no monetary policy response. But monetary policy has no effect on long-run output growth or the long-run unemployment rate. *Mechanical Taylor rule policy cannot prevent stagnation induced by a permanently lower demand growth rate.*

One can imagine two policy responses to this situation. First, and perhaps most likely for monetary policy guided by mainstream thinking, policymakers would infer that the economy was hit by some kind of negative supply shock that permanently raised the 'natural' unemployment rate and slowed productivity growth. Even though the assumed 'supply shock' would coincide with slower demand growth, mainstream models would interpret the supply effect as independent from the demand side of the economy. Indeed, because supply converges to demand, supply would be lower. But the weaker path for the economy is not the result of exogenous changes in technology, worker preferences, etc. Instead, it is due in this model to the long-run effect of a lower demand path on productivity.

In this case, the monetary authority might raise its unemployment target to the new higher equilibrium rate. The effect of raising the target unemployment rate in the Taylor rule would imply that what previously was perceived as output below potential now becomes defined as the 'new normal' with a zero-output gap. Other things equal, this change could imply raising the interest rate back to the initial level, offsetting any benefit of monetary policy in the face of lower demand. However, as the economy converges to the lower-growth equilibrium, there would be no persistent excess demand, as the mainstream perspective would predict following a negative supply shock, despite the

[17] In a more general model with capital, a permanent reduction in the growth rate of autonomous demand also causes a decrease in the investment share. This accelerator effect would increase the output loss. If the capital-output ratio is sensitive to the interest rate, a monetary policy response would mitigate, to some extent, the decline in the *level* of aggregate demand induced by the lower investment share. However, the growth effects would be the same as those presented in the text from the simple model.

higher equilibrium unemployment rate because there really was no negative supply shock. Therefore, monetary policymakers could conclude that the 'natural' interest rate had fallen and simply leave the lower rate in place, as is the case in the simulation presented in Figure 3. This policy would imply a one-time change in the Taylor rule intercept, γ_0, in equation 5.

However, a second more enlightened and practical approach to monetary policy might be followed. Policymakers might recognize that the stagnant economy and the stubbornly higher unemployment rate signal an under-performing economy, and the stagnation might be interpreted, correctly, as the result of weak demand. Through the mainstream lens, this situation implies that the current 'natural' rate of interest is lower than the current policy rate, inducing policymakers to reduce the intercept of the Taylor rule continuously over time in an attempt to find the 'natural' rate of interest they assume exists. *But there is no 'natural' interest rate that can restore the economy's initial growth path* (also see Lavoie 2014, section 4.2.2 and Cesaratto and Pariboni 2022, along with further references in those sources on this point).

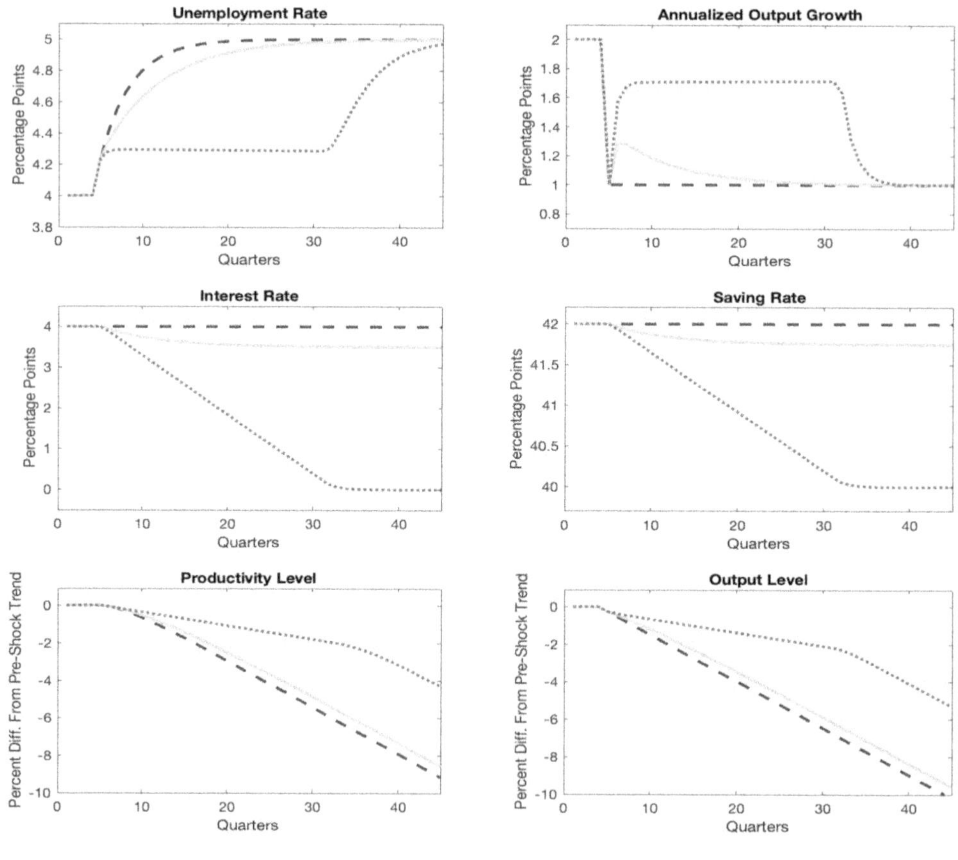

Figure 4. Negative demand growth shock and march to the zero lower bound.

Note: Simulation results following a permanent negative shock to autonomous demand growth as described in the text and the simulation appendix. Dashed lines are the benchmark scenario with no monetary policy response. Solid lines represent results with Taylor rule monetary policy. Dotted lines depict results if monetary policy cuts interest rates as long as the unemployment rate remains above the original level, unless constrained by the lower bound.

Figure 4 shows the result of a policy that attempts to find a natural rate of interest when autonomous demand growth falls. There are now three policy scenarios in the figure: the dashed line shows results with no monetary policy response and the solid line depicts a mechanical Taylor rule policy that simply accepts the higher unemployment rate caused by the demand growth shock as the new normal (as in Figure 3). The dotted lines show what happens if monetary policy abandons strict rule-based policy and embarks on a mission to find a new 'natural' interest rate that restores the former growth path by continuously reducing the intercept of the Taylor rule equation. This dynamic induces a rising multiplier, a source of growth to demand for a while, keeping the unemployment rate below the equilibrium level implied by slower growth of autonomous demand. However, eventually, the interest rate hits the zero lower bound and then the multiplier stops rising. The permanently lower interest rate influences the level of saving and demand, so the output is somewhat higher with the interest rate at zero rather than a positive level dictated by a mechanical Taylor rule. But after the interest rate hits its lower bound, growth converges to the same lower level that was obtained without activist monetary policy, unemployment converges to the new, higher equilibrium level, and the level of output falls continuously away from the initial trend.

The problem with the mainstream view that monetary policy can usually solve problems of insufficient demand is that *monetary policy affects the level rather than the growth rate of demand.*[18] Mainstream, so-called New Keynesian, models do not recognize this problem because demand is assumed to converge back to an equilibrium supply determined path in the long run when wages and prices fully adjust to restore the neoclassical general equilibrium. Monetary policy is mostly a tool to speed that convergence. Therefore, absent a demand shock so large that the zero-lower bound binds, adjusting the level of the interest rate to its 'natural' target seems like it should be sufficient. However, the supermultiplier model with accommodating supply recognizes that demand growth can be permanently lower than a level that induces full utilization of resources. Weak demand pulls supply down with it. Any attempt to address persistent slow demand growth with monetary policy alone results in an inevitable march to the zero lower bound.

7. Supply Shocks and Monetary Policy

Although the main theme of this article is to explore the basic implications of monetary policy on the demand dynamics of supermultiplier models, the simple model here has a supply side and we can consider how Taylor rule monetary policy affects the economic

[18]A possible criticism of the idea that an interest rate set by monetary policy affects just the level, rather than the growth rate, of demand could arise from the neo-Kaleckian growth model if interest rates affect the investment-capital ratio. Among other channels, a lower interest rate could raise the profit share of indebted firms and therefore raise growth as in Hein and Stockhammer (2010, equation 17). However, their full analysis does not recommend that monetary policy target growth. Palley (2007) also specifies growth as a positive function of profits. Pariboni (2016, section 1) surveys several models in which interest payments by workers affect capacity utilization and therefore partially determine the investment-capital ratio and growth in the neo-Kaleckian models. However Pariboni (2016, p. 217) concludes these models do 'not provide a fully satisfactory tool.' In a supermultiplier model, Pariboni (2016) finds, consistent with the results here, that the interest rate affects the long-run level but not the growth rate of output. The debate between the neo-Kaleckian and supermultiplier approaches to demand-led growth is beyond the scope of this paper. In the supermultiplier model presented here, adding effects of the interest rate on either the functional distribution of income or the capital-output ratio would not change the main results.

implications of changes in supply, modeled by shocks to labor productivity (ϕ_0 in equation 2).

A negative productivity shock reduces the unemployment rate in the supermultiplier model because output and employment are driven by demand. If labor is less productive but the demand path does not decline, the unemployment rate falls. Assuming monetary policymakers do not have knowledge about the productivity shock, a falling unemployment rate leads to a higher interest rate which reduces demand. This policy response most likely arises from the fear, or reality, that a lower unemployment rate will raise inflation.

Figure 5 shows the effect of a temporary supply shock initially equal to a quarter percentage point of output that decays with a 0.8 autoregressive coefficient each quarter. Assuming the economy was not initially facing hard supply constraints, there is no need for output to fall, as the dashed lines show, because the path of demand has not been affected. But if monetary policy raises the interest rate, aggregate demand and output fall. In addition, a higher interest rate increases unemployment and reduces productivity (solid lines). Productivity is lower due to the dependence of supply on the path of demand. In the long run, everything comes back to its initial path. But Taylor rule

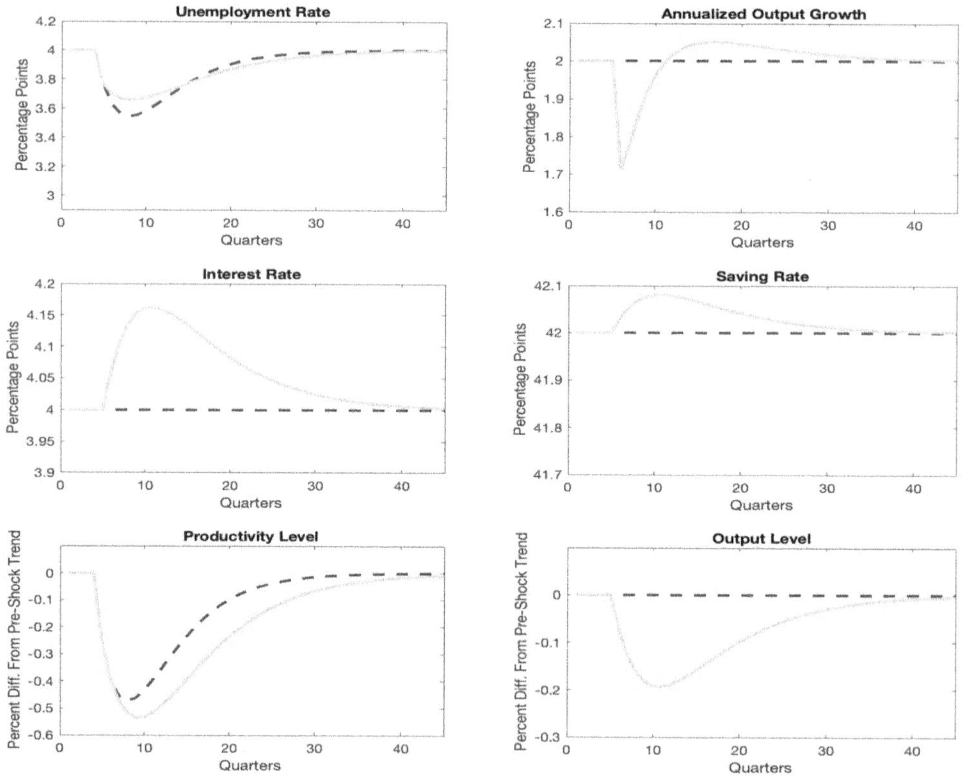

Figure 5. Temporary negative supply shock.

Note: Simulation results following a temporary negative supply shock as described in the text and the simulation appendix. Dashed lines are the benchmark scenario with no monetary policy response. Solid lines represent results with Taylor rule monetary policy.

monetary policy, which in this case is probably best interpreted as fighting the threat of inflation following a negative supply shock, slows recovery.

Now consider a permanent negative shock to productivity growth. The first thing to recognize is that if autonomous demand growth (g_z) remains constant, the equilibrium unemployment rate will fall. This outcome follows from equation 3 because a permanent reduction in productivity growth reduces ϕ_0. Again, the economic intuition is that the path of demand, initially, has not changed so unemployment falls if labor becomes less productive. Without monetary policy intervention, this initial situation prevails in the long run, that is, the demand and output paths are not affected by the productivity shock as long as the new equilibrium unemployment rate does not fall below a minimum level imposed by labor supply.

The outcome without policy intervention is depicted by the dashed lines in Figure 6. The solid lines show the result of the mechanical Taylor rule response if monetary policy continues to target the initial higher unemployment rate, reducing demand and output. In the long run, the unemployment gap in equation 5 converges to a constant and the interest rate ultimately stabilizes. The level of output falls in the long run, but output growth returns to its initial value.

But now suppose monetary policy insists on trying to restore the initial, higher unemployment rate despite the fact that the unemployment gap stabilizes because policy is

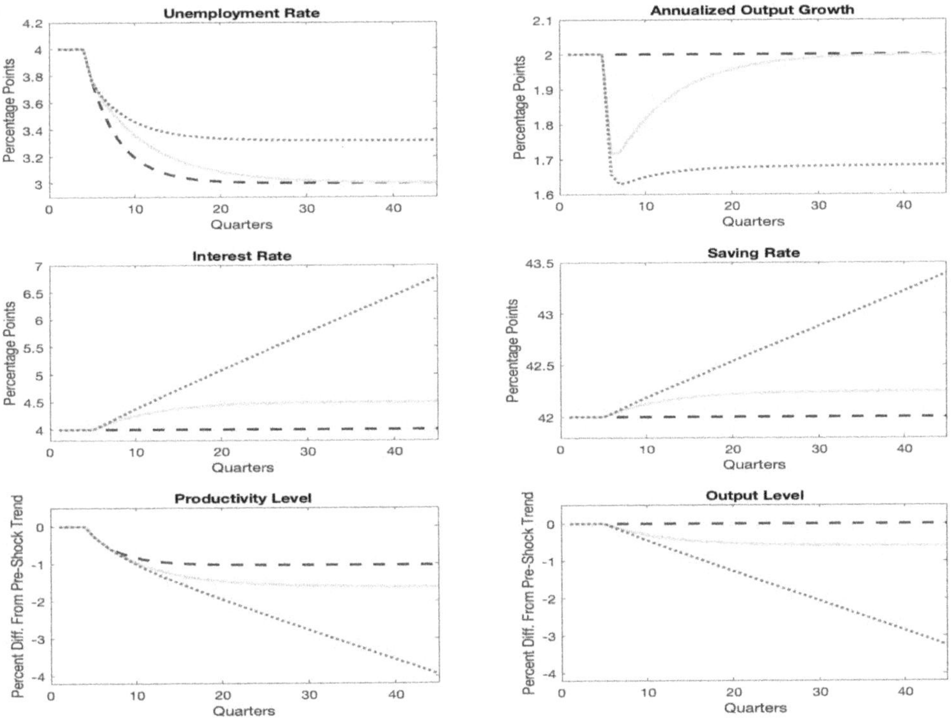

Figure 6. Permanent negative supply shock, two monetary policy responses.

Note: Simulation results following a permanent negative supply shock as described in the text and the simulation appendix. Dashed lines are the benchmark scenario with no monetary policy response. Solid lines represent results with Taylor rule monetary policy. Dotted lines depict results if monetary policy raises interest rates as long as the unemployment rate remains below the original level.

based on the idea that the non-existent 'natural' unemployment rate has not declined. Policy then strives to find a non-existent 'natural' interest rate by continuously raising the policy rate. The outcome is illustrated by the dotted lines in Figure 6. The attempt to raise the unemployment rate back to its initial level is frustrated. Effectively, the continuous rise in the interest rate continuously reduces the multiplier. Aggregate demand growth falls below g_z and the economy converges to a steady-state path with lower output growth, lower productivity growth, and higher unemployment than if monetary policy had not responded to the supply shock. One would suppose that, eventually, the continuous march to higher interest rates would stop despite the inability of monetary policy to return the unemployment rate to its initial level. But this kind of monetary policy could inflict significant economic damage.

Finally, consider how monetary policy operates when there is a permanent *positive* shock to productivity growth. Any growth theory implies faster productivity growth creates the opportunity for higher standards of living and enhanced absolute economic mobility. In the mainstream view, the economy will 'naturally' adjust to a higher growth path in the long run, perhaps with a little help from monetary policy to speed adjustment. According to supermultiplier theory, however, there must be some *independent* stimulus to demand growth if the economy is to exploit the growth opportunity created by the productivity shock. There is no endogenous process that changes the path of demand and therefore higher productivity simply leads to higher unemployment. Monetary policy can fight higher unemployment with lower interest rates which may stimulate demand for a while. But, as in the case discussed previously of a negative demand growth shock, the attempt to restore unemployment to its pre-shock level will lead to an inevitable march to the lower bound for the interest rate because the model requires a continuous decline in the interest rate to raise the growth rate of demand.

8. Monetary Policy, Demand-Led Growth, and Recent US Macro History

This section briefly explores how one can interpret recent monetary policy and macro outcomes using the very simple model developed in this paper. Again, the model is much too stylized for a detailed quantitative analysis, but even in this simple form, it provides useful insights.

Figure 7 presents the US effective federal funds interest rate since 1978 (solid line, left scale). This rate is the key policy variable assumed by mainstream models to keep the economy on an entirely supply determined, full employment path in the long run, at least in the absence of a binding lower bound on the policy rate. The figure also shows an index of US real GDP divided by the working-age population (aged 15–64, dotted line, right scale). The GDP index is scaled to equal 100 in both 1990 and 2007 (dashed line) and can be interpreted as GDP per potential worker relative to the 1990–2007 trend.

Two major features are evident in the figure. First, as implied by the mechanical Taylor rule, interest rates are cut aggressively in recessions, at least beginning in the early 1990s.[19] Second, the Federal Funds rate has been on a long-run downward trend, at least until the pandemic (discussed below).

[19]The interpretation of policy in the 1980s is less clear. The Volcker Fed tried to fight inflation, beginning in 1979, by targeting money supply growth leading to volatile financial conditions and a very deep recession. In the third

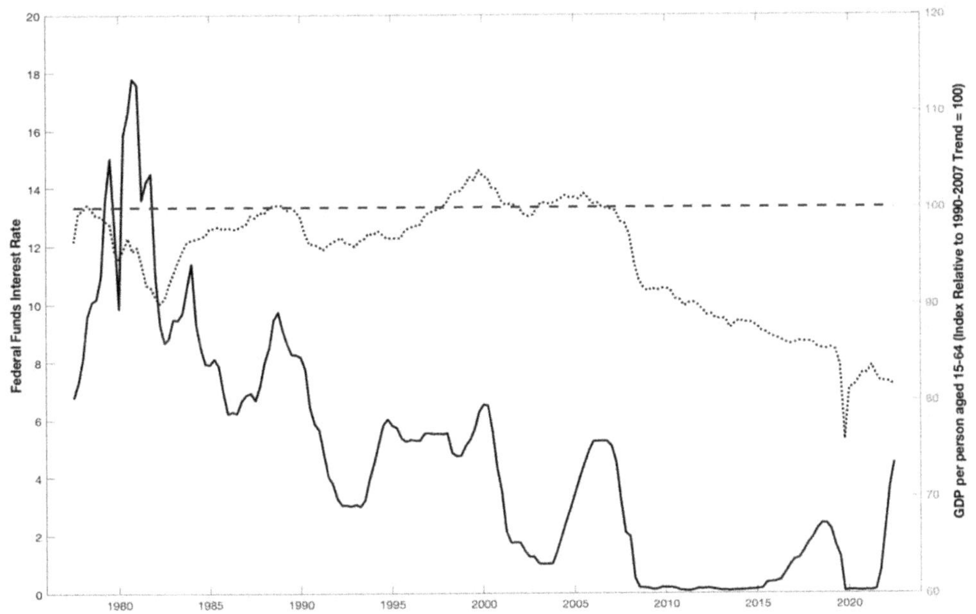

Figure 7. Federal funds rate and GDP per potential worker relative to trend.
Note: Author's calculations using source data from Federal Reserve Economic Data (FRED).

One can argue that the mainstream approach to understanding short-run monetary policy worked reasonably well in the 1990s. The early 1990s recession was shallow. By the late 1990s, the US economy was booming, perhaps the only true 'boom' since the 1960s. It would be reasonable to claim that the US operated close to full employment by 1999. But a good case can also be made that this outcome was not much due to monetary policy. Instead, the strength of the late 1990s US economy can be attributed to the enormous business investment boom associated with what came to be known as the technology bubble, which would be interpreted in the model presented here as a positive shock to autonomous demand. While lower interest rates may have helped pull the economy out of the early 1990s slump, interest rates *rose* in the middle 1990s, well prior to the emergence of the late-decade boom.

Following the recession caused by bursting of the tech bubble, monetary policy was again aggressive in an attempt to restore trend growth and low unemployment. But output and employment under-performed during a period often labeled a 'jobless recovery.' Even with the policy rate pushed down to an unprecedented low by postwar standards of one percentage point, recovery was sluggish. Although the unemployment rate was reasonably low by 2006, this was not a booming economy. The low interest rates helped fuel a housing bubble that surely strengthened the economy through early 2006, but Fed policy did not seem particularly effective. And the low interest rates contributed to the financial fragility that would soon bring the economy to its knees.

quarter of 1982, the Fed relented and allowed interest rates to fall, approximately in line with Taylor rule logic. Perhaps the 1980s can be viewed as a transition to a policy regime by the 1990s in which recessions induced substantial cuts in the policy rate.

Through the lens of the demand-led growth model presented here, even the aggressive monetary policy response to the tech collapse of the early 2000s was not strong enough to restore the booming economy of the late 1990s.

The experience of monetary policy in the Great Recession and its aftermath corresponds most closely with the theoretical perspective presented here. Early in the recession, policymakers believed they could keep the downturn modest with monetary policy.[20] By late 2008, it became clear this was not the case as the policy rate collapsed to zero and the US economy contracted at an alarming rate (−8.5 per cent in the fourth quarter of 2008 and −4.6 per cent in the first quarter of 2009, annualized rates). However, several quarters of zero interest rates do not necessarily contradict the mainstream perspective. A very large demand shock might cause the lower bound on interest rates to bind even though the economy will return to a supply determined growth path, independent of the path of demand, in the long run. Figure 7 shows the policy rate remained at zero for *seven years* (December 2008 through December 2015). In addition, even though the Fed began to raise its rate target in early 2016, Figure 7 also shows that the economy had not recovered anything close to its pre-2007 trend by that time. Consistent with responses to a permanent negative demand shock discussed above, it seems as if the Fed decided that since interest rates had been so low for so long, the economy must have been close to full employment in 2016 and some (unknown) supply shock had pushed the 'natural' trend of the economy well below its path prior to the Great Recession. Annualized labor productivity growth fell from 2.6 per cent (fourth quarter of 2000 to fourth quarter of 2007) to 1.4 per cent (fourth quarter of 2007 to fourth quarter of 2019).

The interpretation of this history is very different using the simple demand-led growth model presented here. The financial crisis that caused the Great Recession led to a permanent negative shock to demand. Figure 8 shows the dramatic drop in a broad measure of real autonomous demand relative to its trend prior to the Great Recession (from Fazzari and González 2023; also see a related autonomous demand definition in Summa, Petrini, and Teixeira 2023). The growth rate of this measure of autonomous demand from 2000 to 2007 was 3.7 per cent at an annual rate; from 2007 to 2019 it was just 2.0 per cent. A narrow definition of autonomous demand growth that includes just real government spending (including government-financed medical care) fell from 4.3 to 1.7 per cent over the same periods. With such a massive decline in autonomous demand growth, the simple model predicts monetary policy will push the policy rate to the zero lower bound and keep it there, which happened from 2009 to 2016. There was no need to begin raising interest rates in 2016; there was certainly no sign of accelerating inflation. It seems the Fed simply decided the economy must be at full employment even though GDP was well below the pre-2008 trend.[21]

Finally, briefly consider the monetary policy response to the dramatic economic disruption caused by the COVID-19 pandemic. The early stages of the pandemic surely

[20] Representative of this view is a statement from Ben Bernanke in the spring 2008 that 'monetary and fiscal policies are in train that should support a return to growth in the second half of this year and next year' (testimony to the Joint Economic Committee of the US Congress, 10 April 2008). At that time, fiscal responses to the weakening economy were trivial, Bernanke's view, consistent with new consensus thinking, had to be that monetary policy would do the job. In reality, the second half of 2008 and early 2009 were disastrous.

[21] The headline unemployment rate in 2016 was close to its level prior to the Great Recession. However, broader measures of unemployment and the employment-population ratio showed persistent slack in the labor market.

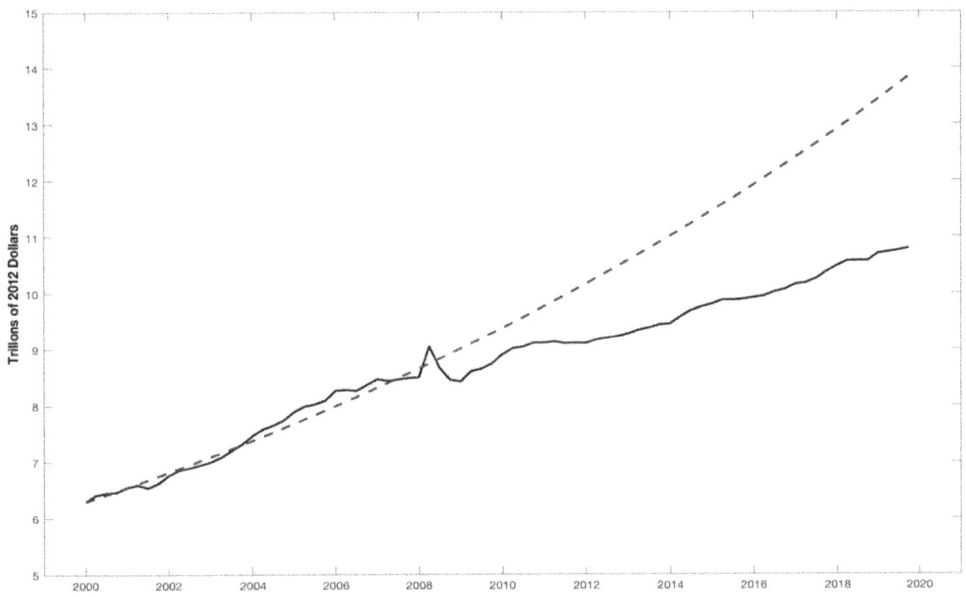

Figure 8. Autonomous demand relative to pre-2007 trend.

Note: Autonomous demand as defined in Fazzari and González (2023) including government consumption and investment (minus some cyclical components such as unemployment insurance), autonomous social spending (primarily government-financed health care), exports, and residential investment. The trend growth rate (dotted line) is the annualized growth from the 2000 average to the 2007 average.

caused enormous contractions in both demand and effective supply. A few months before the pandemic hit, the Fed had already backed off the tentative interest rate increases that started in late 2016. It seems there was a recognition that demand was weak even before the pandemic. When the pandemic hit, monetary policy responds quickly. By late spring of 2020, the federal funds rate was again effectively zero where it would remain for almost two years. While this policy likely was implemented with an eye toward stabilizing demand, perhaps the greater motivation, especially in 2020, was to contain financial instability and prop up asset prices. Clearly, unprecedented fiscal stimulus played a much bigger role in containing a demand collapse due to the pandemic, putting the economy on a surprisingly quick path to recovery (although still not to anything approaching the pre-Great Recession trend). In 2022, monetary policy turned aggressively contractionary because of accelerating inflation. That such an aggressive policy has, as of this writing in mid-2023, not caused much of an economic slowdown raises questions about the effectiveness of monetary policy to affect the demand path, an important issue that lies outside the scope of this article but merits further attention in research.

Although the pandemic macro shocks are complicated, these events bear some resemblance to the negative supply shock analysis in the previous section. If one discounts the severe, but very brief, lockdown contraction in the late spring of 2020, the demand path seems largely maintained, no doubt due to massive fiscal stimulus to counteract what otherwise likely would have been a catastrophic reduction in demand. Therefore, output growth relative to trend remains approximately constant over several years.

Labor productivity swung wildly early in the pandemic, but since the third quarter of 2020, labor productivity has fallen. The supply shock model predicts a fall in the unemployment rate, other things equal. The headline unemployment rate is about the same as prior to the pandemic. A broader measure of unemployment (U-6) is a bit lower than pre-pandemic. The model here provides reasonable support for the view that the Fed's aggressive interest rate policy since the spring of 2022 is unnecessarily fighting the effects of a supply shock.

The more relevant question is how monetary policy will evolve going forward as the unusually disruptive pandemic and Ukraine war effects fade. The mediocre growth trend from the economic peak in 2007 to the pre-pandemic peak, seems likely to return since there is no clear reason to expect a long-run change in autonomous demand generation. Considering the recent inflation experience, the monetary policy stance in the face of what could still be a 'secular stagnation' economy (Summers 2015) is likely to be interest rates above the zero lower bound. But, as the analysis here shows, this outcome does not mean the economy is fully utilizing its potential. Furthermore, if demand falters, a march back toward the zero lower bound is likely.

9. Conclusion

This paper uses a simple demand-led growth model to show that monetary policy that follows a mainstream Taylor rule will be ineffective in addressing permanent negative shocks to the level or, especially, the growth rate of autonomous demand. The basic problem arises from implementing policy guided by a flawed economic model according to which the long-run output path is independent of demand. In a supermultiplier model with accommodating supply, permanent negative shifts in demand permanently lower the output path, but they do not necessarily raise the equilibrium unemployment rate or create long-run 'output gaps.' As Aspromourgos (2007, pp. 532 and 533) writes, interest rate policy depends on the 'belief-systems' of the central bank and '[f]alse beliefs about the actual structure of the world can be validated.' Therefore, mainstream monetary policy will not identify the need for demand stimulus, even though resources are wasted.

Furthermore, if demand *growth* declines, monetary policy could systematically drive the interest rate to the zero lower bound even if the stagnation is correctly identified as a weakness in demand. In this case, the problem is that interest rate management can affect the level of demand rather than its growth rate. Therefore, if growth is persistently below a target level that maximizes production and employment, interest rates must fall continuously if monetary policy is the only tool available to offset suboptimal growth in autonomous demand. The interest rate will eventually hit its lower bound. This result corresponds to 'secular stagnation' as proposed by Summers (2015). Persistently slow growth of aggregate demand leads to a secular downward trend in interest rates. However, there is an important difference between the perspective presented here and the results from a variety of mainstream papers that generate effects of demand dynamics beyond the short run. Summers and related research, such as Benigno and Fornaro (2018), propose that longer run demand constraints arise if and only if monetary policy is constrained by the zero lower bound. By contrast, the results here demonstrate that demand can constrain output and raise unemployment relative to potential even with positive nominal interest rates. This problem arises if monetary policy is based on an underlying economic model that ignores how demand dynamics can affect supply.

These results raise important doubts about the effectiveness of monetary policy as the first line of defense against insufficient demand. This article makes these points with a very simple, stylized model that does not account for many important details through which monetary policy operates through different components of aggregate demand. A much more developed model is required to assess quantitatively how monetary policy affects an economy led by demand, Barbieri Góes (2023) is an important step in this direction. But adding complexity such as explicit models of interest-sensitive sectors is unlikely to change the basic conceptual results presented here as long as the model retains the feature that demand leads supply and monetary policy affects the level, but not the long-run growth rate, of aggregate demand.

The results here reinforce what I believe is the most important policy message of the burgeoning supermultiplier research program. We cannot assume that long-run growth can be understood by looking at the supply side in isolation. To create a strong economy that operates at or near full employment requires structural features to assure adequate aggregate demand growth. Nominal adjustment is not effective, which seems partially recognized in the mainstream by now as new consensus models propose monetary policy as the primary mechanism to close output and unemployment gaps. But the logical results here, along with even a cursory look at recent history, imply monetary policy cannot do the job. It is possible that discretionary monetary policy can help to offset some undesirable effects of negative, temporary demand shocks. But monetary policy is not well suited to address insufficient demand beyond the short run. Good macroeconomic performance in the 21st century requires attention to policies that ensure strong and sustainable growth of autonomous demand over time horizons extending beyond a few quarters.

This goal requires putting the long-run demand growth implications of fiscal and distributional measures front and center in policy analysis and implementation. Lima, Setterfield, and da Silveira (2023) propose fiscal policy as effective explicitly when monetary policy can no longer do the job. It also implies that monetary policy may be more productively directed to objectives of financial stability and income distribution (see Lavoie 2014, pp. 234–238 and further references there).

Acknowledgements

The author thanks Alejandro González for excellent research assistance. Helpful comments from Gilberto Lima and other participants in the 4th Demand-Led growth workshop (Rio de Janeiro, July 2023) and the FMM conference (October 2023) and two anonymous referees are gratefully acknowledged.

Disclosure Statement

No potential conflict of interest was reported by the author(s).

Funding

The author thanks the Weidenbaum Center on the Economy, Government, and Public Policy for financial support.

References

Aspromourgos, T. 2007. 'Interest as an Artefact of Self-Validating Central Bank Beliefs.' *Metroeconomica* 58 (4): 514–535.

Avritzer, J. D., and L. Brochier. 2022. 'Household Credit-Financed Consumption and the Debt Service Ratio: Tackling Endogenous Autonomous Demand in the Supermultiplier Model.' Post-Keynesian Economic Society Working Paper 2219.

Barbieri Góes, M. C. 2023. 'A Tale of Three Prices: Monetary Policy, Autonomous Consumption, and Housing Affordability in the US.' *Structural Change and Economic Dynamics* 67: 115–127.

Barbieri Góes, M. C., and M. Deleidi. 2022. 'Output Determination and Autonomous Demand Multipliers: An Empirical Investigation for the US Economy.' *Economic Modelling* 116: article 106004.

Benigno, G., and L. Fornaro. 2018. 'Stagnation Traps.' *Review of Economic Studies* 85 (3): 1425–1470.

Blanchard, O. J. 2018. 'Should We Reject the Natural Rate Hypothesis?' *Journal of Economic Perspectives* 32 (1): 97–120.

Brown, J., S. M. Fazzari, and B. C. Petersen. 2009. 'Financing Innovation and Growth: Cash Flow, External Equity, and the 1990s R&D Boom.' *Journal of Finance* 64 (1): 151–185.

Cesaratto, S., and R. Pariboni. 2022. 'The Relation Between Keynesian Monetary Theory and Demand-Led Growth: A Sraffian Exploration.' *Review of Keynesian Economics* 10 (3): 291–315.

Deleidi, M. 2018. 'Post Keynesian Endogenous Money Theory: A Theoretical and Empirical Investigation of the Credit Demand Schedule.' *Journal of Post Keynesian Economics* 41 (2): 185–209.

Docherty, P. 2021. 'A Short Period Sraffa-Keynes Model for the Evaluation of Monetary Policy.' University of Technology Sydney Working Paper Series No. 1 / 2021, February.

Dutt, A. 2006. 'Aggregate Demand, Aggregate Supply, and Economic Growth.' *International Review of Applied Economics* 20 (3): 319–336.

Dvoskin, A., and M. T. Landau. 2023. 'Limits to Fiscal and Monetary Policy in Small Open Economies.' Working Paper 109, Banco Central de la Repúplica Argentina, May.

Fatás, A., and L. H. Summers. 2018. 'The Permanent Effects of Fiscal Consolidations.' *Journal of International Economics* 112: 238–250.

Fazzari, S. M. 2020. 'Was Keynesian Economics Ever Dead? If So, Has It Been Resurrected?' *Review of Keynesian Economics* 8 (1): 46–60.

Fazzari, S. M., P. Ferri, and A. Variato. 2020. 'Demand-Led Growth and Accommodating Supply.' *Cambridge Journal of Economics* 44 (3): 583–605.

Fazzari, S. M., and A. González. 2023. 'How Large Are Hysteresis Effects? Estimates from a Keynesian Growth Model.' FMM Working Paper 89, March.

Galbraith, J. K. 1957. 'Market Structure and Stabilization Policy.' *Review of Economics and Statistics* 39 (2): 124–133.

Gallo, E. 2022. 'When Is the Long Run? Historical Time and Adjustment Periods in Demand-Led Growth Models.' *Metroeconomica* 73 (4): 1155–1178.

Goodfriend, M. 2007. 'How the World Achieved Consensus on Monetary Policy.' *Journal of Economic Perspectives* 21 (4): 47–68.

Hein, E., and E. Stockhammer. 2010. 'Macroeconomic Policy Mix, Employment and Inflation in a Post-Keynesian Alternative to the New Consensus Model.' *Review of Political Economy* 22 (3): 317–354.

Lavoie, M. 1995. 'Interest Rates in Post-Keynesian Models of Growth and Distribution.' *Metroeconomica* 46 (2): 146–177.

Lavoie, M. 2014. *Post-Keynesian Economics: New Foundations*. Northampton, MA: Edward Elgar.

Levrero, E. S. 2023. 'The Taylor Rule and Its Aftermath: An Interpretation Along Classical-Keynesian Lines.' *Review of Political Economy*. https://doi.org/10.1080/09538259.2023.2166729.

Lima, G. T., M. Setterfield, and J. J. da Silveira. 2023. 'Achieving Two Policy Targets with One Policy Instrument: Heterogeneous Expectations, Countercyclical Fiscal Policy, and

Macroeconomic Stabilization at the Effective Lower Bound.' Department of Economics, FEA-USP Working Paper 2023-01.
Mason, J. W., and A. Jayadev. 2023. 'Rethinking Supply Constraints.' *Review of Keynesian Economics* 11 (2): 232–251.
Palley, T. I. 2007. 'Macroeconomics and Monetary Policy: Competing Theoretical Frameworks.' *Journal of Post Keynesian Economics* 30 (1): 61–78.
Palley, T. I. 2012. 'Growth, Unemployment and Endogenous Technical Progress: A Hicksian Resolution of Harrod's Knife-Edge.' *Metroeconomica* 63 (3): 512–541.
Pariboni, R. 2016. 'Household Consumer Debt, Endogenous Money and Growth: A Supermultiplier-Based Analysis.' *PSL Quarterly Review* 69 (278): 211–233.
Pérez-Montiel, J. A., and R. Pariboni. 2022. 'Housing is NOT ONLY the Business Cycle: A Luxemburg-Kalecki External Market Empirical Investigation for the United States.' *Review of Political Economy* 34 (1): 1–22.
Pivetti, M. 1991. *An Essay on Money and Distribution*. London: Macmillan.
Rochon, L. P., and M. Setterfield. 2008. 'The Political Economy of Interest-Rate Setting, Inflation, and Income Distribution.' *International Journal of Political Economy* 37 (2): 5–25.
Serrano, F. 1995. 'Long Period Effective Demand and the Sraffian Supermultiplier.' *Contributions to Political Economy* 14 (1): 67–90.
Serrano, F., and R. Summa. 2015. 'Mundell–Fleming Without the LM Curve: The Exogenous Interest Rate in an Open Economy.' *Review of Keynesian Economics* 3 (2): 248–268.
Serrano, F., R. Summa, and F. N. P. Freitas. 2023. 'Autonomous Demand-Led Growth and the Supermultiplier: The Theory, the Model and Some Clarification.' Discussion Paper 003 / 2023, Federal University of Rio de Janeiro Instituto de Economia.
Serrano, F., R. Summa, and V. G. Moreira. 2020. 'Stagnation and Unnaturally Low Interest Rates: A Simple Critique of the Amended New Consensus and the Sraffian Supermultiplier Alternative.' *Review of Keynesian Economics* 8 (3): 365–384.
Setterfield, M. 2011. 'Post-Keynesian Macrodynamics and Path-Dependent Growth.' *Intervention* 8 (2): 299–316.
Sim, J. 2022. *Demand Shocks, Hysteresis and Monetary Policy, Finance and Economics Discussion Series 2022-080*. Washington, DC: Board of Governors of the Federal Reserve System.
Summa, R., G. Petrini, and L. Teixeira. 2023. 'Cycles: Empirics and the Supermultiplier Theory.' *Review of Political Economy*. https://doi.org/10.1080/09538259.2022.2156725.
Summers, L. H. 2015. 'Demand Side Secular Stagnation.' *American Economic Review* 105 (5): 60–65.

Appendix

Inflation in the Taylor rule

Suppose the policy interest rate depends on both an unemployment gap and an inflation (π) gap, abstracting from the zero lower bound:

$$r_t^{\text{targ}} = \gamma_0 - \gamma_1(u_{t-1} - u^*) + \gamma_2(\pi_{t-1} - \pi^*)$$

Add a simple Phillips Curve equation to determine the inflation rate:

$$\pi_t = \beta_0 - \beta_1 u_{t-1}$$

In principle, the intercept β_0 could include a measure of inflation expectations given exogenously. Plug the Phillips Curve into the interest rate rule:

$$\begin{aligned} r_t^{\text{targ}} &= \gamma_0 - \gamma_1(u_{t-1} - u^*) + \gamma_2[\beta_0 - \beta_1 u_{t-1} - \pi^*] \\ &= [\gamma_0 + \gamma_2\beta_0 + \gamma_1 u^* - \gamma_2\pi^*] - (\gamma_1 + \gamma_2)u_{t-1} \end{aligned}$$

Therefore, the specification in the text according to which the target interest rate responds just to the unemployment gap can capture an inflation effect on interest rates as well that magnifies the effective response of interest rates to unemployment. Intuitively, if the economy is hit by a negative demand shock, unemployment tends to rise and inflation tends to fall. Therefore, if the policy rate responds to both unemployment and inflation the response will be larger than if monetary policy targets unemployment only.

A direct of application of this simple inflation model implies that inflation is independent of monetary policy in the long run because the long-run equilibrium unemployment rate is independent of monetary policy. Such a conclusion, however, would need to be explored in a more developed model that better analyzes both the sources of inflation and the dynamics of inflation expectations.

Simulation Details

The simulations presented in the paper begin with the model in steady state with the growth of autonomous demand set at 2 per cent at an annual rate (0.5 per cent quarterly). The initial interest rate and unemployment rate are both set at 4 per cent. The simulation parameter values are:

Parameter	Symbol	Value
Monetary rule intercept	γ_0	0.04
Monetary rule effect of interest rate	γ_1	0.50
Interest rate smoothing parameter	λ_r	0.50
Effect of unemployment rate on quarterly productivity growth	ϕ_1	0.25
Saving rate intercept	η_0	0.40
Effect of interest rate on saving rate	η_1	0.50

The intercept of the productivity equation is set to equate initial productivity growth with the initial growth rate of autonomous demand when the unemployment rate is 4 per cent. The equilibrium value of the saving rate and the effect of unemployment on productivity are approximately the same as those estimated in an expanded model by Fazzari and González (2023). The implied semi-elasticity of output with respect to a one percentage point change in the interest rate is 1.3 per cent, similar to the level estimated from Barbieri Góes (2023) by integrating the impulse-response function for output following a one percentage point shock to the federal funds interest rate.

Shocks are equal to one quarter of 1 per cent of GDP in the fifth simulation quarter. The temporary shock (Figure 1) is assumed autoregressive and decays by 20 per cent per quarter. The permanent level shock (Figure 2) reduces autonomous demand by one quarter per cent of GDP indefinitely. The permanent growth rate shock (Figures 3 and 4) reduces quarterly g_z by one quarter per cent so that annualized growth in autonomous demand falls by one percentage point.

Although the simulation parameters are chosen to reflect plausible values for the US economy, the objective of the simulations is not to provide calibrated quantitative results, but simply to illustrate the broad theoretical predictions from the simple, stylized model. These results are unaffected by parameter choices.

The Supermultiplier-Cum-Finance. An Application to the Credit-Led Boom before the 2008 Crash

Óscar Dejuán Asenjo and Daniel Dejuán-Bitriá

ABSTRACT

The supermultiplier model is gaining momentum. To become a cornerstone of modern macroeconomics, it should explain the dynamics of advanced market economies in a coherent, complete, and simple way. In particular, it is supposed to clarify the possibilities and limits of credit-driven economies, like the one observed in most advanced countries after 1995. This paper contributes to these goals by integrating the Sraffian supermultiplier with the post-Keynesian hypothesis of credit money endogeneity. This hypothesis is somehow modified when *autonomous* banks are able to accelerate credit above output growth, as happened after 2002. The gap between credit and output growth implies that a part of the loans is financing non-output transactions (land, old houses, shares), usually with a speculative bias. The consequences of a persistent gap are demand depression and asset inflation, as we observed after 2008.

1. Introduction

According to Palley (2018), the supermultiplier is the most Keynesian of Keynesian growth models. There are good reasons for such a conclusion. The supermultiplier applies the principle of effective demand to both the equilibrium *level* of income at a given period and its sustainable *rate* of expansion over time. A fully adjusted path of growth implies that firms use efficiently the best available technology. If so, the economy will grow at the warranted or potential rate, resulting from investing the savings corresponding to full capacity (nothing is said about full employment). Notice that such a path continues to be demand-led because it ultimately depends on *the expected growth of persistent autonomous demand.*

To become a cornerstone of modern macroeconomics, the supermultiplier theory should explain the dynamics of advanced market economies in a coherent, complete, and simple way. Such undertaking requires bringing together the spheres of production, distribution, demand, and finance. Our particular approach tries to achieve this goal by mixing the Classical-Sraffian theory of value and distribution[1] and the Keynesian-

[1] Sraffa (1960). Among the Sraffians that look at Keynes in order to rebuild the 'surplus approach' see Pasinetti (1973), Pasinetti (1979), Garegnani (1978-79), and Eatwell (1983).

Kaleckian theory of output and money.[2] Schumpeter [2008] 2012 will be the third leg of our theoretical tripod.

The first goal of this paper is the integration of the Sraffian supermultiplier with the post-Keynesian hypothesis of endogenous credit money. Pariboni (2016), Cesaratto (2017), and Hein & Woodgate (2020) have dared to blaze this trail. From them, we take the baton introducing some novelties. (1) The autonomy of the expected growth of *persistent autonomous demand* is taken so seriously that the alleged instability of the supermultiplier vanishes. (2) Banks are included in the model. Their autonomy makes it possible to accelerate credit above output growth, as it happened after 2002. (3) Our focus on residential investment and mortgage loans connects our model with the credit-led economy dominant in advanced capitalist countries from 1995 to 2008.

The second goal of the paper is to demarcate the limits of a credit-driven economy and the consequences of surpassing them. (Werner, 2005, 2014) has been a source of inspiration.

The paper is structured in four sections, apart from this Introduction. Section 2 analyses the real side of the economy through the supermultiplier model. Our attention focuses on the variables linking the real and monetary circuits. They fix some limits to output growth that eventually check the autonomous credit expansion. Section 3 makes explicit the vertically integrated sector corresponding to banks and connects it with the post-Keynesian hypothesis of credit money endogeneity. Section 4 shows that a persistent gap between the rates of expansion of credit and output transforms credit-driven growth into debt-burdened growth. Demand depression and asset inflation are the logical consequences. Section 5 summarizes our conclusions. The numerical Appendix illustrates the dynamics of the model in the four scenarios that replicate the performance of advanced economies after 1995. It shows that simplicity helps to capture the essentials of the economy. Hopefully, the reader will be able to inspect new hypotheses, scenarios, and techniques.[3]

2. The Real Economy: Demand-Led Growth Underpinned by the Supermultiplier

Our closed and private economy is organized in three vertically integrated sectors (VIS). Their final output consists of consumer goods for households (Y_c produced in VIS_c), capital goods for productive investment (Y_k in VIS_k), and houses for residential investment (Y_z in VIS_Z).[4] According to the Keynesian-Kaleckian principle of effective demand,

[2]See Keynes (1936) (books I to V), and Kalecki (1937). Lavoie (2014) offers a comprehensive study of the post-Keynesian approach. See, in particular, chapters 4, 5, and 6.

[3]Some recent examples: Skott, Santos, and Oreiro (2021) insists on the need of 'fine -tuning' to accelerate the adjustment. Hein & Woodgate (2020) study the formal stability conditions in an economy driven by government expenditure financed with debt. O Dejuán and Dejuán (2018) shows the interaction between financial and real forces by means a predator-prey model. Ó. Dejuán and McCombie (2019) focuses on the role played by the securitization strategy and mortgage-backed derivatives from 1995 till 2008. Dejuán, Portella and Mateo (2020) analyze the impacts of decarbonization using a disaggregate multiplier-accelerator model.

[4]Pasinetti (1973) remarks two traits of economic analysis based on VIS: (1) intermediate consumption and capital consumption are 'transformed' into indirect labor, and indirect fixed capital; (2) The value-added in each VIS (the sum of wages and profits) coincides with the value of final output: $Y_c = VA_c$; $Y_k = VA_k$; $Y_z = VA_z$. A proper multisector economy would require the use of input-output techniques. Here we offer the typical macroeconomic analysis where goods are produced with the same technology but differ in their function.

current output is determined by expected demand *at normal prices* (Keynes, 1936; Kalecki, 1937).[5] Aggregated demand includes households' induced consumption ©, induced capacity creating investment (I), and (proper) autonomous demand (Z), here identified with residential investment.

The following set of equations deliver the equilibrium level of output at t:

$$Y_t = C_t + I_t + Z_t \tag{1}$$

$$C_t = c \cdot Y_t = (1-) \cdot Y_t \tag{2}$$

$$I_t = k \cdot \gamma \cdot Y_t = h \cdot Y_t \tag{3}$$

$$Z_t = Z_{(t-1)}(1 + g_z) \tag{4}$$

Induced consumption (C_t in eq 2) is the aggregate propensity to consume (c), times income. The propensity to consume (c) may be substituted by *(1-σ)*, where σ stands for the income share of aggregate savings. In the Classical - Kaleckian tradition, the expenditure patterns result from the propensities to consume and save out of wages (c_w, s_w) and profits (c_r, s_r). The weights are their shares in income (ω, ρ). We assume that induced consumption out of profits is negligible ($c_r = 0$). If positive, it should be treated as autonomous demand.

Current evidence confirms that the propensity to consume out of wages is high but not unity since workers have to spare a part of their income for unpredicted expenditure and debt service. In our case study, autonomous demand coincides with residential investment financed by mortgage loans. As a first provisional approximation, we can assume that the loans are repaid in one year. If so, borrowers (workers' households) are 'forced' to save $S_{wt} = \sigma_w \cdot Y_t$ These assumptions allow us to write $Z_t = CR_t = S_{wt} = AM_t$. σ_w represents the share in aggregate income of workers' savings. It coincides with the share of residential investment in aggregate demand: $\sigma_w = S_{w,t}/Y_t = Z_t/Y_t = z$. By the same token, σ_r represents the share in aggregate income of the savings out of profits. According to our classical expenditure assumptions, firms retain an amount of profits equivalent to the cost of the new capital. This allows us to write: $\sigma_r = S_{rt}/Y_t = I_t/Y_t = h$.[6]

Equations (5) and (6) summarize these ideas:

$$c = c_w \cdot \omega + c_r \cdot \rho = c_w \cdot \omega \tag{5}$$

$$s = s_w \cdot \omega + s_r \cdot \rho = \sigma_w + \sigma_r = \sigma \tag{6}$$

Productive investment, expansionary investment, or capacity-creating investment is identified with capital accumulation, i.e., the production and purchase of capital goods to enlarge the installed capacity. Entrepreneurs equate total investment (IT_t) to the difference between the expected capital required after period t (KR_{t+1}) (a function of the expected increase in aggregate demand (D_t)), and the capital installed at the beginning

[5]In this sentence, the words in italics signal the Sraffian contribution. Demand expectations are linked to 'normal prices', i.e.. the prices of production forged by competition.

[6]The reader should distinguish between (a) the macroeconomic equilibrium conditions: savings = residential investment + productive investment. After dividing by income, $\sigma = z{+}h$, and (b) the sectoral conditions derived from our particular expenditure assumptions: residential investment is eventually paid with savings out of wages; productive investment, with savings out of profits (or *business savings*): $\sigma_w = z$, $\sigma_r = h$.

of t (KI_t). The first line of equation (7) unfolds in this way.[7]

$$IT_t = KR_{t+1} - KI_t = k \cdot D_t \cdot (1+\gamma) - KI_t = k \cdot \gamma \cdot D_t + (k \cdot D_t - KI_t) = \tag{7}$$

$$= k \cdot \cdot Y_t + (KR_t - KI_t) = \ h \cdot Y_t + (KR_t - KI_t) = I_t + I_{xt}$$

$$h = \frac{I_t}{Y} = k \cdot \gamma = \sigma_r \tag{8}$$

Reading the second line of equation (7) from right to left, we can see that total investment is the sum of the 'extra' investment that fills the initial capacity gap: $I_{xt} = KR_t\text{-}KI_t$, and the 'induced' investment (I_t), a forward-looking concept that depends on the expected growth of demand. According to the *accelerator principle*, to match efficiently aggregate demand expectations, firms are supposed to demand new equipment by an amount: $I_t = k{\cdot}\gamma{\cdot}Y_t = h{\cdot}Y_t$. To remember: '$h$' is the share in income of induced investment and the share in output of the production of capital goods. 'k' stands for the optimal capital/output ratio. It implies a normal degree of capacity utilization that Sraffians normalize at unity ($u^* = 1$). γ is the expected growth of persistent aggregate demand, the key variable of the Keynesian system (Eatwell, 1983).[8] σ_r stands for business savings, i.e., the non-distributed profits that firms retain to fund investment.

The last term of equation (8) states another long-term equilibrium condition for our particular expenditure assumptions: the share of business saving in income ($\sigma_r = S_R/Y$) equals the share of investment ($h = I/Y$). In our Keynesian model, the production of equipment generates a similar amount of profits. They are retained by firms (business savings) to purchase the new equipment.[9]

Autonomous demand (Z) encompasses the elements of aggregate demand that are different from induced consumption and capacity-creating investment. The general model would include modernization investment, residential investment, private autonomous consumption, public expenditure, and exports. In this paper, we identify autonomous demand with residential investment and assume that it is entirely financed with mortgage loans. Equation (4) takes as given the level of expected demand in *t-1* and its expected growth (*the autonomous trend,* so to speak, g_z).

Equations (9) and (10) compute the traditional multiplier (M), which captures induced consumption through c, and the supermultiplier (SM), which captures induced consumption and induced investment through $c + h$.[10] Alternatively, we can

[7]Two advantages of this definition of investment: (1) It is immune to Garegnani's (1978-79) criticism to the marginalist remnants of Keynes' investment function. (2) The separation between two types of investment dilutes Harrod's fear of the extreme instability of the multiplier-accelerator model (Harrod, 1939), (Dejuán, 2017).

[8]In chapter 3 of *The General Theory*, Keynes refers to the 'long-term state of expectations.' Keynes focused on the psychological factors prevailing in an environment of fundamental uncertainty. Following Schumpeter [2008] 2012, we focus on an objective aspect: the potential market of the industries driving the economy. A complete picture should add to building companies and banks, the institutions and policies that favor residential investment.

[9]The assumption that productive investment is financed with business savings was used by Robinson (1962), p. 86, and Shaikh (1991). Of course, such equality does not mean that saving determines investment. To prevent such a conclusion, we could differentiate between *ex-ante investment* (production of machines under the expectation of an increase in aggregate demand), and *ex-post investment* (purchase and installation of the new machines assuming that demand expectations are confirmed).

[10]The first presentations of the supermultiplier, after Serrano (1995), have a Sraffian flavor. See, Bortis (1997), Cesaratto, Serrano, and Stirati (2003), O. Dejuán (2005), White (2009), Aspromourgos (2013), Freitas and Serrano (2015), Girardi and Pariboni (2016), Dejuán (2017), Pérez-Montiel & Manera (2020). Post-Keynesian and neo-Kaleckian contributions to the supermultiplier appear in Allain (2015), Lavoie (2016), and Palley (2018). Critics of the supermultiplier model include Sraffians, post-Keynesian and Marxian economists: Palumbo and Trezzini (2003), Lavoie (2010), Skott et al.

compute these expressions in terms of the corresponding savings patterns that mark tdhe equilibrium condition. In the multiplier model, the production of houses and machines increases income until the savings accruing from wages and profits equal autonomous demand: $(\sigma_w+\sigma_r)\cdot Y_t = Z_t+I_t$. In our supermultiplier model, the production of houses raises income until the savings accruing from wages equal the new autonomous demand: $\sigma_w \cdot Y_t = Z_t$.

$$M = \frac{1}{1-c} = \frac{1}{\sigma} = \frac{1}{\sigma_w + \sigma_r} \tag{9}$$

$$SM = \frac{1}{1-c-\gamma k} = \frac{1}{1-c-h} = \frac{1}{w} \tag{10}$$

After introducing the preceding equations into (1) we obtain the equilibrium level of output in a given period (*t*). Equations (11) and (12) compute It as the multiplier times broad autonomous demand (I_t+Z_t) or the supermultiplier times proper autonomous demand (Z_t). Both results coincide if in (11) we compute the production of capital goods as the *capital* required in the previous year times the expected growth of aggregated demand (γ):

$$Y_t = M \cdot (I_t + Z_t) = M \cdot (\gamma \cdot KR_{t-1} + Z_t) \tag{11}$$

$$Y_t = SM \cdot Z_t \tag{12}$$

Y_t refers to an economy growing along a fully adjusted path of growth. It is a multiple of the expected autonomous trend that drives aggregate demand and output by using capacity in normal conditions. Actual income (Y_t', in (13)) takes into account transient increases in autonomous demand (A'_t). The extra investment that fills the initial gap between actual and required capacity (I_{xt}), is included here. The production of A_t' has an impact on the induced consumption captured by the traditional multiplier. Yet, being a *once and for all expenditure*, it does not alter the *expected growth of aggregate demand* (γ). To repeat, the actual level of output in *t* is driven by demand growing persistently at γ, plus the positive/negative adjustments. From a long-term perspective, these adjustments are supposed to cancel out.

$$Y_t' = SM \cdot Z_t + M \cdot A_t' \;\; SM \cdot Z_t = Y_t \tag{13}$$

The extreme instability associated with the multiplier-accelerator models (the supermultiplier is one of them) disappears when we accept that entrepreneurs-investors are able to identify different types of demand. We are not assuming *perfect foresight*, just *prudence*, the essential virtue of entrepreneurs, according to Adam Smith. Following Dejuan (2017), we distinguish between a *persistent acceleration of expected demand*, a persistent *increase in the level of demand,* and a *transient* increase in the level of demand.[11] Entrepreneurs respond to unexpected increases in demand by raising the degree of capacity utilization. If overutilization continues, they will consider that the increase in the level

(2021). Following Ciccone (1986), the critics argue that normal capacity is not an attractor. The debate appeared in vol. 2 of *Political Economy. The Surplus Approach.*

[11] In this paper, the expression '*persistent* demand' refers to the level or rate of growth of demand that has ruled in the recent past and is expected to last long enoung to justify an increase in capacity. In the expression '*transient* demand' the adjective might be replaced by *transitory ,temporary* or *seasonal.*

of demand is not a seasonal phenomenon; that it urges extra investment (I_{xt}) to fill the gap between installed and required capacity. If overutilization remains despite repeated adjustments in production capacity, entrepreneurs will realize that they face a persistent acceleration of demand. Consequently, they will raise the expected demand growth implicit in the acceleration mechanism ($h = k \cdot \gamma$).

Apart from being *stable*, the supermultiplier is a *stabilizing* mechanism. The investment moved by the accelerator, to meet the increasing demand for Z, shapes the structure of demand and production until the growth rates of expected aggregate demand, output, and capital coincide with the autonomous trend (g_z). Such coincidence implies that the economy is growing at the *warranted* or *potential* rate, the one corresponding to a given technology (k) and a given share of consumer-like expenditure that includes residential investment ($\theta = c + z$).

$$g_w = \frac{1 - c - z}{k} = \frac{1 - \theta}{k} = \frac{\sigma_r}{k} = \frac{h}{k} \tag{14}$$

The warranted or potential rate (g_w) will be fully adapted when γ '$= g_z$' and $\sigma_r = h$'. Remember that γ is a part of h, and σ_r adapts to h. Hicks (1950) called this process *the traverse*.

Our supermultiplier model is necessarily a stable process because the two subsystems we consider are stable *per se* and do not interact between them. The main part of the economy produces to satisfy autonomous and induced demand. It is governed by the supermultiplier whose stability only requires that $(c + h) < 1$. The ancillary part (production of I_x) is governed by the multiplier, also stable for $c < 1$. Contrary to Harrod (1939), the movements of capacity utilization during the traverse do not affect the expected growth of autonomous demand embedded in the accelerator. Otherwise, autonomous demand would not be truly autonomous.

The expected growth of demand and output has obvious limits.

(a) *Limit from the supply side.* The maximum rate of growth ($\hat{\gamma}$) is given by the maximum warranted rate ($\bar{g}_w$). It depends on the maximum business savings rate ($\bar{\sigma}_r$), inversely related to the minimum rate of consumer-like expenditure ($\underline{\theta}$).[12]

$$\hat{\gamma}_1 = \bar{g}_p = \frac{(1 - \underline{\theta})}{k} = \frac{\bar{\sigma}_r}{k} \tag{15}$$

(b) *Limit from the demand side.* When most households own a house, we can assume that the autonomous trend will decelerate and stabilize at $\bar{g}_z < \hat{\gamma}_1$.

$$\hat{\gamma}_2 = \bar{g}_z \tag{16}$$

Figure 1 summarizes the main ideas advanced in this section. Autonomous and aggregate demand are growing at the potential-warranted path ($\gamma_a = g_{za} = g_{wa} = 3\%$). An

[12] From the very formulation of the supermultiplier ($SM = 1/(1-c-k\gamma)$) we can derive a similar limit. By construction, $(c+k\gamma)$ has to be lower than 1, leaving room for proper autonomous demand, the driver of the system. The last statement implies that the maximum rate of growth is related to the minimum propensity to consume in the following way: $\hat{\gamma} < \frac{(1 - \underline{c})}{k}$.

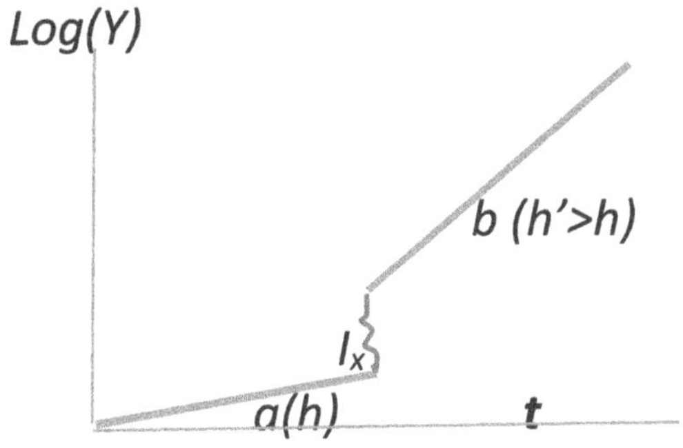

Figure 1. The traverse to a higher rate of growth.

improvement in credit facilities raises the autonomous trend to $g_{zb} = 5\%$. The number of houses built *per year* increases steadily, and so does the induced demand derived from the construction activity. Eventually, firms realize that the expected growth of aggregate demand should be raised from γ_a to γ_b. First, they adjust capacity through extra investment (I_x) to make possible an efficient acceleration of production. The potential or warranted rate adjusts to γ_b via h and σ_r. In Figure 1, the traverse is achieved in one period. In general, it will take longer and follow a smoother path.

To repeat. The multiplier that operates during the *traverse* and the supermultiplier that paves the way for the warranted path are stable and stabilizing mechanisms. This does not imply that capitalism is a stable system. Instability is usually related to the 'multiplicand', in particular when autonomous demand depends strongly on credit. This is the topic to be analyzed in the next sections.

3. Banks and Credit Money in a Monetary Production Economy

3.1. Endogenous Credit Money

Post-Keynesian economics focuses on credit money, the dominant means of payment in advanced economies. The model rests on two pillars: the endogeneity of credit-money[13] and the consistency between financial flows and stocks.[14]

Basil Moore summarizes the first hypothesis in this sentence: 'Money is credit-driven and demand determined' (Moore, 1988, p. 28). Banks create money by the very fact of granting loans. The lender credits the current account of the borrower with a new deposit created *ex nihilo* and accepted as a means of payment. Bank money is *destroyed* when borrowers use their deposits to cancel their outstanding debts. In principle, the supply of loans adapts to firms' and households' demand for means of payment. The Central Bank (CB) could check credit expansion by raising the cash coefficient (bank's

[13]The hypothesis of money endogeneity has been developed by economists in the post-Keynesian and the circuit traditions. Among post-Keynesians, see Kaldor (1981), Moore (1988), Wray (1990), and Rochon and Rossi (2017). Among the 'circuitists' see Graziani (1989), Parguez and Seccareccia (2000), and Lavoie (2016).

[14]The stock-flows consistent model was formally introduced by Godley and Lavoie (2007). See also Nikiforos and Zezza (2017). It is not always easy to find the above identities in the financial accounts and balances. Investment banks transform the nature of the assets and liabilities. An example: the securitization process initiated in 1995 converted mortgage loans into mortgage-backed securities.

liquid reserves over deposits). In practice, it accommodates the monetary base to banks' required reserves. The CB is afraid of aborting a boom and/ or causing a financial crash.

Stock-flow consistent models show the three faces of bank money and explain the identity among the *flows* of credit, deposits, and debt (see eq. 17 where 'Δ' refers to the net variation of the variable during period *t*). The consistency between flows and stocks explains the identity among *outstanding* loans, deposits, and debt (see eq. 18 where angular brackets refer to the level of *stocks* at a given date, say 31/12/t).

$$\Delta CR_t \equiv \Delta DEBT_t \equiv \Delta DEP_t \tag{17}$$

$$[CR]_t \equiv [DEBT]_t \equiv [DEP]_t \tag{18}$$

There are as many financial strategies as agents in need of liquidity. The financial culture of each country also makes a difference. Researchers are supposed to select the key elements for their particular purposes and explain them in a didactical way. At this moment, we are especially interested in finding the links between the hypothesis of credit money endogeneity and the supermultiplier. A brief reference to Schumpeter ([2008] 2012), Graziani (1989), and Cesaratto (2017) will clarify our position.

Schumpeter ([2008] 2012) warns about the tendency of capitalism towards stagnation. In the'circular flow', firms reproduce the same goods (and quantity of goods) in the same way. At the end of each production period, they have the materials and banknotes they need to start a new process. The circular flow is broken by innovative entrepreneurs that foresee new goods and new markets for traditional goods. In our case, the securitization of mortgage loans after 1995 could be considered the innovation that allowed a massive building of houses for low-income groups. The next step for innovators (and their imitators) is to convince banks to finance these projects. No previous savings is required to finance the new undertakings; credit creates the means of payments. –A clear advance of the money endogeneity hypothesis.

Graziani (1989) focuses on the need of any firm to borrow short-term for advancing the wages required in any production process. This is 'initial finance', the 'flux' moment that accounts for the injection of liquidity. The loans will be reflected in new deposits and used by workers to buy the consumer goods as soon as they arrive at the market. At this moment, firms in the consumer goods sector will pay back the loan. This is the 'reflux' moment or 'final finance', in Graziani parlance. It represents the 'money destruction' that closures the circuit.

Cesaratto (2017) alters Graziani's meaning of final finance and connects initial finance with the (super)multiplier process. Initial finance continues to be related to the short-term loans for production. Given the flow of new orders, firms will make up their expectations on the aggregate demand brought about by the (super)multiplier, a mechanism absent in Graziani's analysis. Final finance is not related to the amortization of short-term loans but final demand.

In this paper we focus on the liquidity created in a construction-led economy fueled by long-term mortgage loans. The mortgage loans can be granted directly to the building companies at the beginning of the production period, or to the households which purchase the new houses at the end. In the first case, all the firms in the construction VIS would not need further liquidity. The remaining firms would borrow to advance wages, as Graziani suggests. Cesaratto is right to precise that the amount of short-term loans should be computed taking into account the supermultiplier effect. Our second case refers to the final finance to households buying new homes. In the production of these houses, a similar amount of savings has been created and spared as extra deposits. Yet, banks do not need them to fund mortgage loans. The additional liquidity generated by final demand lubricates the channels of production.

Let us close this section by insisting on the possibility of organizing the provision and absorption of liquidity in different ways. Our suggestions are compatible whith those of Graziani, and Cesaratto. The difference is that we do not search for a specific and stable relationship between liquidity, demand, and production.

3.2. Peculiarities of the Vertically Integrated Sector Corresponding to Banks

In our 'fractional reserve system', bank money (deposits) represents about 95% of the liquid assets. Surprisingly, banks are usually ignored in macroeconomic literature, both orthodox and heterodox. The oblivion could be justified if banks only delivered intermediate services to firms and their interest payments did not alter aggregate demand. None of these assumptions is appropriate in our increasingly financialized economies. It is the moment to bring banks to the foreground of the supermultiplier model by building the corresponding vertically integrated sector (VIS_b). Panico, Pinto, and Puchet (2012) provide a Sraffian approximation to the banking industry that we will complete and adapt to our needs.

Banks' expertise consists in selecting creditworthy borrowers, deciding the amount of the loan, and tailoring the amortization plan. For these services, banks get interest payments (INT_t) that can be computed as the interest rate (i) times the money lent at the beginning of period t (CR_t). The debt service (DS_t) also includes amortization allowances. We compute them by 'a' times the stock of outstanding debt ($[DEBT]_t$). The amortization rate (a) *is* inversely related to the repayment period.[15]

$$DS_t = INT_t + AM_t \tag{19}$$

$$INT_t = i \cdot CR_t \tag{20}$$

$$AM_t = a \cdot [DEBT]_t \tag{21}$$

The nature of both types of financial commitments is different. Only interest payments imply a proper transfer of income from borrowers to lenders. Amortization allowances are the payment for the goods purchased with the loan. The periodical installments of any mortgage loan sum up the cost of the house. If residential investment is fully financed with mortgage loans and repaid in the same year ($a = 1$), we can write '$Z_t = CR_t = AM_t$'. The same result holds for any value of $a < 1$ if we consider a stagnant economy where the yearly flows of output and credit are constant. When both variables are growing, we should write '$Z_t = CR_t = AM_t + \Delta DEP_t$'. The liquidity increase, represented by ΔDEP_t, will pass to the following periods and dry up by the periodical installments.

[15] Alternatively interest payments can be computed as i' times the outstanding debt: $INT_t = i' \cdot [DEBT]_t$. Consistency requires that $i \cdot CR_t = i' \cdot [DEBT]_t$. The second formulation will be used in section 4 to simplify the definition of debt service: $DS_t = (i' + a) \cdot [DEBT]_t$. For the time being we will use the first formulation that locates the financial transfer in the year when each loan is granted.

In our initial presentation, the final income corresponding to final output was distributed between wages and profits, and absorbed by induced consumption (C_t), induced investment (I_t), and residential investment (Z_t). Now a part of wages is transferred to banks as the payment for banks' services (B_t). The accounting scheme will look like this:

$$Y_t = R_t + W_{d,t} + INT_t = I_t + C_t + Z_t + B_t \tag{22}$$

One of the advantages of dealing with vertically integrated sectors is that the value-added generated in each VIS (sum of wages and profits) coincides with the demand for and the supply of the final goods/services it produces. For VIS_b we can write $VA_{bt} = B_t$. Our particular assumption is that banks' value-added can be proxied by the interest payments to banks.[16]

$$B_t = VA_{bt} \approx INT_t \tag{23}$$

Like any other corporation, banks compete for customers searching revenues and profits. Each bank is supposed to offer the standard financial services at the minimum cost. In other words, they are supposed to hire labor and capital (L_b, K_b) at the normal remuneration forged by competition (w^*, r^*). The 'normal' long-term interest payments is given by equation (24), where $\varepsilon^* = INT_t^* / Y_t$

$$INT_t^* = W_{b,t}^* + R_{b,t}^* = w^* \cdot L_b + r^* \cdot K_b = \varepsilon^* \cdot Y_t \tag{24}$$

The actual share of interest payments is $\varepsilon_t = (INT_t/Y_t)$. In section 4 we will analyze the consequences of a persistent positive gap between ε_t and ε^*. Our interest is to emphasize that banks' autonomy allows them to expand credit faster than output, implying that a part of loans finances *non-output transactions*. A good example is the acceleration of mortgage loans after 2002, when the residential market was almost saturated. The new loans were diverted to the purchase of land and old houses.

Banks' thrust to expand credit beyond output can be explained by the following peculiarities of the banking sector.

(1) *Economies of scale*. Bank output is not a 'produced' service in the ordinary sense of the word. A proof is the formidable economies of scale enjoyed by banks. To double output, a construction company may require a couple of years. If technology and wages remain constant during this period, the company's profit rate will remain constant. To double the euros lent in mortgage loans, banks only have to relax the creditworthiness criteria and multiply by two the previous loans, just a keystroke. Banks will get extra interest payments and profits.

(2) *The interest rate is not a proper price* in the ordinary sense of the world. It is a monetary phenomenon since its primary determinant is the official rate (i_o) fixed by the Central Bank (CB) when lending to banks in need of money reserves. Banks add a first mark-up (*mu'*) that covers the normal costs of bank services (profits included). If the borrower or the entire economy is in a risky position, banks add a second mark-up (*mu'*) to cover possible defaults. Neither is the interest rate an efficient

[16] Banks also charge fees for credit card management, direct debiting, currency exchange, and the like. To simplify our presentation, we assume that these revenues roughly match banks' interest payments to depositors and bondholders.

way to equilibrate the demand for and the supply of loans. The price elasticity of credit-demand is quite unpredictable.[17]

(3) *Oligopoly and entry barriers.* At the national and international levels, the credit market is dominated by a handful of big banks. In the Classical-Sraffian tradition, such markets may be exposed to fierce competition provided there is freedom of entry and exit. If the rate of profit is above the general one, new firms will enter and force a reduction of prices and profits. The fact that banks enjoy extra profits during the entire boom period (which implies a constant *mu'*) suggests the presence of entry barriers.

(4) *Financial risks.* A credit boom increases financial risks. They should bring about an increase of *mu'* and a possible reduction of credit demand. Yet, banks have learned how to hide financial risks. The massive securitization of mortgage loans and the creation of mortgage-back derivatives are the best illustrations of this phenomenon. No less important is the moral-hazard problems prompted by messages like 'too big to fall.'

The preceding statements suggest a reformulation of the post-Keynesian hypothesis of credit money endogeneity. It is a condition for long-term financial sustainability more than a description of credit allocation in any place at any time. In principle, we can expect that the bulk of credit finances output transactions and grows in step with output. But we cannot rule out the possibility that a significant part of bank loans finances non-output transactions, usually with a speculative bias. The credit boom launched in 1995 and accelerated in 2002 is the best example. Presumably, in the midst of a recession, banks will be unable to convince firms to expand production and capacity. Households are likely persuaded to borrow by easing the financial conditions. Speculators are eager to get funds for betting in the real estate and the stock exchange markets. High-interest rates will not deter them if the expected capital gains are even higher.

4. Sustainable and Unsustainable Paths of Growth in a Construction-Led Economy Fueled with Credit

4.1. The Interwoven Chain of Real and Financial Variables

The dynamics of our economy can be captured by two interwoven chains, one for the economic circuit, the other for the financial one. The real chain is articulated by the following equations.

$$Z_t = Z_{(t\;\;1)}(1 + g_z) = Z_{(t-1)}(1 + \gamma) \tag{25}$$

RJMP2015817 - Table rule update for Table 1

$$Y_t = R_t + W_t = R_t + W_{dt} + INT_t \tag{27}$$

$$Y_t = (I_{xt}) + I_t + C_t + B_t + Z_t = (KR_t - KI_t) + k \cdot \gamma \cdot Y_t + c \cdot Y_t + INT_t + Z_t \tag{28}$$

[17] For the sake of simplicity, in this paper we assume a constant interest rate. In the numerical exercise of the Appendix there would be no problem to introduce new scenarios with different rates altering the transfer of income. The impact on credit demand it is beyond our reach.

These equations bring to mind some relationships presented in section 2. We take as given the previous level of autonomous demand (Z_{t-1}) and its expected growth (g_z). If this rate persists long enough, it will determine the expected growth of aggregate demand (γ). In a long-run analysis, both variables are interchangeable. Output and income adjust to demand: $Y_t = D_t$. Income is made of wages, profits, and interest payments (in our case, they are a part of wages). Productive investment is computed by the accelerator mechanism. Previously, firms have to fill the inherited gaps of capacity, in particular those that result from an acceleration of expected demand. Final consumption is the propensity to consume times current income. B_t stands for the interest paid to banks in exchange for the financial services received by borrowers. Z_t stands for residential investment that we suppose entirely financed by mortgage loans.

The financial chain is represented by

$$CR_t = CR_{t-1}(1+) \tag{29}$$

$$CR_{n,t} = CR_t - AM_t = CR_t + a \cdot [DEB]_t \tag{30}$$

$$[CR]_t = [CR]_{t-1} + CR_{n,t} = [CR]_{t-1} + \Delta CR_t \tag{31}$$

$$DS_t = INT_t + AM_t = (i' + a)[DEBT]_t \tag{32}$$

Equation (29) admits that banks are autonomous enough to decide, within certain limits, the rate of credit expansion (φ). After subtracting amortization allowances, we get the net credit ($CR_{n,t}$) (eq. 30). It coincides with the new flows of credit, debt, and deposits: $\Delta CR_t = \Delta DEBT_t = \Delta DEP_t$. The stock of outstanding loans (after the last day of t) results from adding the net flow of credit to the previous stock (eq. 31). It coincides with the stocks of outstanding debts and deposits. Equation (32) reminds the reader that the debt service is the sum of interest payments and amortization allowances. At this moment, we compute them by the gross interest rate ($i'+a$) times outstanding debts.

The first link between the real and financial chains is the rate of expansion of output (γ) and credit (φ). Dynamic equilibrium requires that φ is equal to or lower than γ. A persistent positive gap between both rates brings about an increase of the indebtedness ratio ($\beta = [DEBT]_t/Y_t$) and the debt service ratio ($\delta = DS_t/Y_t = (i'+a)\cdot\beta$). Borrowers (workers' households) will be forced to increase their saving propensity ($\sigma_w = S_{wt}/Y_t$) after a persistent increase in δ. Since σ_w is in the denominator of the supermultiplier, we can expect a fall in the income corresponding to a given level of autonomous demand.

The second link between the real and financial chains is the transfer ratio: $\varepsilon = INT_t/Y_t$. We have defined 'normal transfers' as those allowing banks to pay normal wages and profits in VIS_b. Its share in income amounts to $\varepsilon^* = INT_t^*/Y_t$. The difference between these two ratios (ε-ε^*) informs about the extra interest payments (INT_{xt}/Y_t) perceived by banks. Probably, they will be hoarded, increasing the liquidity of the system defined as $\lambda = DEP_t/Y_t$.[18]

Table 1 highlights the key financial variables and identifies the thresholds that should not be overstepped to avoid excessive risks.[19]

[18] An alternative way to measure liquidity includes in the denominator the value of non-liquid assets: $\lambda' = \frac{[DEP]_t}{\bar{X} \cdot P_{xt}}$

[19] The array of financial indicators is not exhaustive. For business students, the most relevant indicator is the *leverage coefficient*: 'borrowed funds over equity'. Table 2 does not mention it because, in our model, firms finance productive investment entirely with equity.

Table 1. Significant financial ratios.

Variables	Definition	Safety thresholds
Transfer ratio	$\varepsilon_t = \frac{INT_t}{Y_t} = \frac{INT_t^* + INT_t}{Y_t}$	$\varepsilon_t^* = \frac{INT_t^*}{Y_t}$
Liquidity ratio	${}_t = \frac{[DEP]_t}{Y_t} = \frac{[DEP]_t^* + [DEP_x]_t}{Y_t}$	${}_t^* = \frac{[DEP]_t^*}{Y_t}$
Debt service ratio	${}_t = \frac{INT_t + AM_t}{Y_t} = (i' + a) \cdot \beta$	$\delta^* = \bar{\sigma}_W$
Indebtedness ratio	$\beta_t = \frac{[DEBT]_t}{Y_t}$	$\beta^* = \frac{\bar{\sigma}_W}{(i' + a)}$

Notes: *INT** allows banks to pay the normal wage (w^*) and profit rate (r^*). *[DEP]** refers to the stocks of deposits for ordinary financial transactions. *[DEP]* includes extra-deposits of non-financial agents and *extra reserves* of banks. δ^* is the maximum sustainable debt service ratio given the maximum propensity to save of workers, $\bar{\sigma}_W$. β^* is the indebtedness ratio whose financial service is δ^*.

4.2. Sustainable and Unsustainable Credit-Driven Paths

Underneath our previous analysis is the credit boom (after 1995) leading to a financial crash and economic recession (after 2008). In the numerical example of the Appendix, we replicate the story of a handful of advanced capitalist economies (the USA, the UK, Spain, Ireland, ...) using the equations of the supermultiplier-cum finance model built in this paper.

The first lesson we have learned from this experience is that credit may drive and sustain a path of economic growth. By 1993 most advanced economies were stuck in a recession with underutilization of capacity and unemployment. Cheap mortgage loans pushed residential investment up. The supermultiplier mechanism spread the impulse through all the industries. For a time, the yearly flows of credit and output stabilized above 4%. This episode is reflected in the first scenario of table A (Appendix) and Figures 2 and 3 (at the end of this section). In quarters 1-5, output expands at the warranted rate, i.e., at full capacity utilization ($u = 1$). Credit expands at the same rate, so the indebtedness and debt-service ratios remain at their initial levels. There are no abnormal transfers of income to the banking sector via interest payments ($INT_x/Y = 0$).

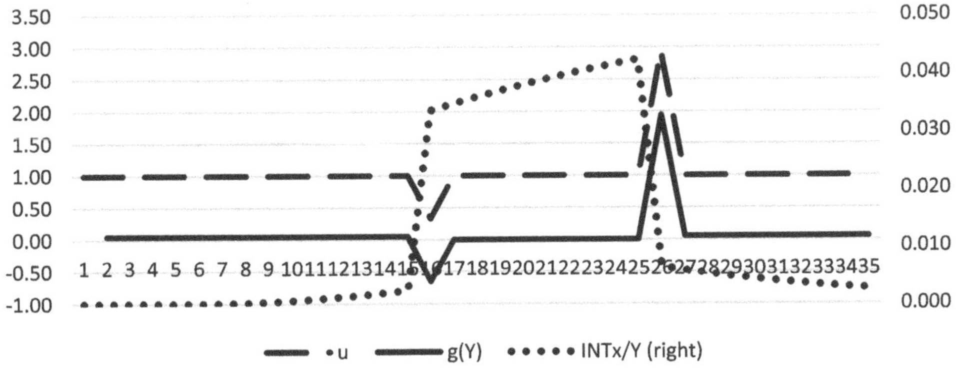

Figure 2. Evolution of the real variables.

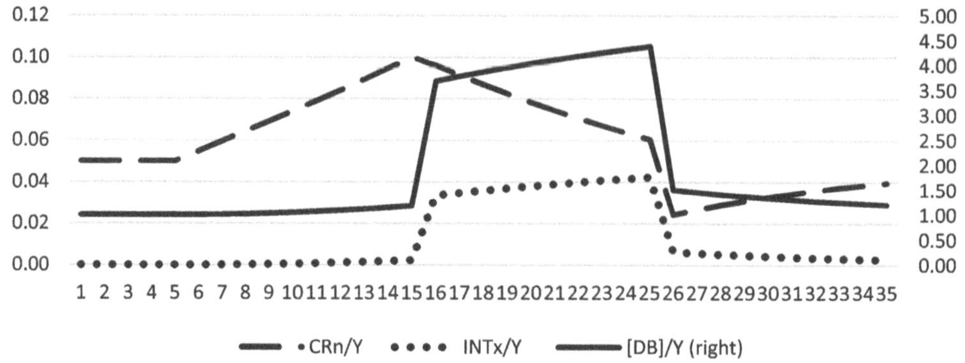

Figure 3. Evolution of the financial variables.

After 2002, the good results of the securitization strategy encouraged banks to accelerate credit to unprecedented levels. This time the real economy did not follow suit. Probably the residential market had tapped the growth limits enunciated at the end of section 2. Scenario 2 (quarter 6-15) simulates that credit grows systematically above output: ($\varphi = 0.10$) > ($\gamma = 0.05$). The consequences are an increase in the key financial ratios: indebtedness (β), debt-service (δ), income-transfer (ε), and liquidity (λ). For a time, the strong growth of output disguised financial disequilibria. When the recession arrived, the disequilibria showed up and caused demand depression and asset inflation.[20] Each imbalance feeds back as we can appreciate in expressions (33) and (34).

4.2.1. Overindebtedness and Demand Depression

The following diagram depicts the vicious circle leading to demand depression. A permanent gap between the growth rates of credit and output conveys higher indebtedness and debt-service ratios ($\Delta\beta$, $\Delta\delta$). To meet their higher financial commitments, debtors are obliged to increase their saving ratio ($\Delta\sigma_w$). This conveys a fall in induced consumption, the supermultiplier, and the equilibrium level of income corresponding to a given autonomous demand. The fall in income automatically raises the indebtedness ratio. At this moment, the credit-driven economy becomes a debt-burdened economy.

$$(\varphi > \gamma) \longrightarrow \Delta\beta = \frac{[DEBT]}{Y} \rightarrow \Delta\delta = \frac{INT + AM}{Y} \rightarrow \Delta\sigma_w, \nabla c \rightarrow \nabla SM = \frac{1}{\sigma_w} \rightarrow \nabla Y \qquad (33)$$

The ‘multiplicand’ (autonomous demand) also falls. After the first layoffs, workers’ households feel vulnerable and refrain from borrowing. After the first defaults, banks realize that they are in a risky position and refuse to lend. The saying holds true: ‘Banks lend you an umbrella on a sunny day and claim it back when the first drops fall’. The engine of our economy (residential investment fueled with mortgage loans) is seized up.

[20]The endogenous deterioration of the structures of debt (Minsky, 1964), is another way to present the issue at stake. Credit for non-output transactions appears directly in Werner (2005, 2014) and indirectly in Schularick and Taylor (2012), and Borio and Lowe (2002).

Scenarios Figres 2 and 3. Sc-1: Quarters 1-5: Long-period equilibrium path, steady growth: $\varphi = \gamma = 0.05$

Sc-2: Quarters 6-15: Credit acceleration financing non-output transactions: $\gamma = 0.05$; $\varphi = 0.1$

Sc-3: Quarters 16-25: Stagnation: $\gamma = 0$; $\varphi = 0$. Sc-4: Quarters 26-35: Recovery: $\gamma = \varphi = 0.05$

Variables: *u:* degree of capacity utilization; *g(Y)*: current rate of output growth; *INTx*: extra interest payments associated with loans for non-output transactions.

Comments: (1) A proof of the stabilizing properties of the supermultiplier model is that output growth adjusts to the autonomous trend (from 0,05–0 in t = 16, and from 0 to 0,05 in t = 26). A second proof is that capacity utilization (u) stays most of the time at its desired level (in our case, 1). If the stocks of inventories were insufficient, the adjustment of u would be slower and smoother. (2) The acceleration of credit and the pile-up of debt brings about extra interest payments (INT_x) that depress aggregate demand.

Variables: (a) INT_x: extra interest payments derived from credit for non-output transactions; they are hoarded as excess reserves, the fuel of speculative bets. (b) *CRn*: net flow of credit in *t*; it increases the stocks of outstanding credit and debt. (c) $[DEBT]/Y = \beta$: indebtedness ratio. The path of the debt-service ratio ($DS/Y = \delta$) replicates that of β at a different level.

Comments. The acceleration of total and net credit after t = 6 does not affect the indebtedness ratio immediately because economic growth continues buoyant. In the recession, the ongoing disequilibria show up and exhibit inertia. β continues growing despite the stagnation of total credit ($\varphi = 0$), and the fall of net credit.

4.2.2. Credit Overexpansion, Excess Liquidity, and Asset Inflation

Given the formidable economies of scale banks enjoy, an acceleration of loans is bound to cause extra interest payments (INT_x) that will be hoarded as extra reserves of banks and extra deposits of rentiers (the shareholders). They are a proxy for the excess liquidity that funds the demand for speculative bets (D_x). Since the supply of these assets is fixed ($\bar{X}$), we can expect an increase in their prices (P_x, initially normalized at one).[21] After realizing the capital gains, speculators will be encouraged to borrow even more. The process feeds back.

$$(\varphi > \gamma) \Longrightarrow \Delta\varepsilon = \frac{INT}{Y} \rightarrow \Delta\lambda = \frac{[DEP]}{Y} \rightarrow \Delta D_x \rightarrow \Delta P_x \tag{34}$$

This is Werner (2005) quantitative theory of credit. Schularick & Taylor (2012) and Borio & Lowe (2002) abound on the credit roots of asset inflation, mainly when rentiers finance their speculative bets with new loans. Tobin's portfolio theory Tobin (1958) suggests that the asset price rally will stop when P_x reaches the desired ratio between liquid assets (deposits) and illiquid ones (equity, land, and so on) (see equation (35) and Figure 4,

[21]Notice the differences between output inflation (P_y) and asset inflation (P_x). During the last boom (1995-2008) credit doubled for both non-produced assets and produced goods. The residential and stock exchange markets experienced important bubbles: their price indexes almost trebled. On the contrary, the adjustment in the industrial market came through quantities: cars' factories simply doubled the output of luxury cars.

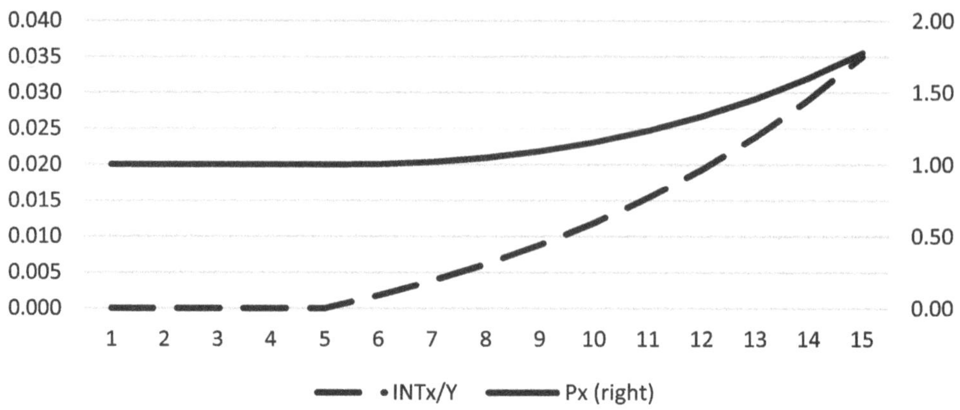

Figure 4. Simulation of the dynamics of extra liquidity and asset bubbles.

where λ^* is the desired liquidity ratio).

$$\Delta P_x = \frac{\Delta[DEP]_t}{\bar{X} \cdot \lambda_t^*} \tag{35}$$

Variables: (1) *INTx*: extra interest payments hoarded as excess liquidity to prepare speculative bets. (2) P_x: asset inflation in the stock exchange market.

Note: For better visualization, we have assumed that after period 6, credit expands at 0.2 (instead of the 0.1 rate indicated in scenario 2).

4.3. Comparison with Earlier Results

After inspecting a comprehensive range of countries and years, theorists and econometricians with different backgrounds have reached conclusions similar to those derived in this section.

- Claessents, Kose, and Terrones (2009): Recessions that coincide with credit crunches, significantly when housing busts last longer and are more severe.
- Mendoza and Terrones (2012): Credit booms are often (though not always) followed by banking crises, currency crises, and 'sudden stops'.
- Schularick and Taylor (2012): Lagged credit growth is the strongest predictor of financial crises. Other variables add little information, especially after WW2.
- Jordà, Schularick, and Taylor (2013): Financial recessions are more costly than normal recessions in terms of lost output. For both types of crises, more credit-intensive expansions tend to be followed by deeper recessions and slower recoveries.
- Borio and Lowe (2002): Sustained rapid credit growth combined with large increases in asset prices appear to increase the probability of an episode of financial instability.
- Pariboni (2016) highlights the responsibility of the unequal distribution in the 2008 crisis. His conclusion: cheap loans for workers' consumption are not a solution to the lack of aggregate demand resulting from falling wages.

- Hein and Woodgate (2020): 'It is necessary to introduce financial variables into models driven by non-capacity creating autonomous demand in order to assess the long-run (in) stability and sustainability of growth'.

Official agencies also insist on taking the financial instability of modern economies seriously and check banks' power on money creation. For half a century, the Basel Committee on Bank Supervision (BCBS) has regulated the capital adequacy ratios for banks engaged in a risky credit expansion. More capital in the banks' balance sheet is supposed to provide a safety cushion against insolvency and reinforce the prudence of financial managers. In case of bankruptcy, they have more to lose.

Adair Turner, the Chairman of Britain's Financial Services Authority when the global financial crisis struck in 2008, stated that the crisis was caused by 'too much debt of the wrong sort'.

> 'The fundamental problem is that modern financial systems left to themselves *inevitably create debt in excessive quantities*, and in particular debt that does not fund new capital investment but rather the purchase of already existing assets, above all real estate. It is that debt creation which drives booms and financial busts: and it is the debt overhang left over by the boom that explains why recovery from the 2007–08 financial crisis has been so anemic'. 'We have neither the science to tell us what the perfect level [of debt] is, nor the policy tools to achieve it.' 'What we lack is any precise science to tell us how much debt is too much and what mix of debt is optimal.' (Turner, 2015, pp. 3-4, 47 and 195).

We agree with the diagnosis, not with the conclusion. Hopefully, our supermultiplier-cum-finance model proves that economics has something to say about these crucial issues.

5. Conclusions

At a given moment, the equilibrium output level can be computed as a multiple of the expected autonomous demand. The condition is that the autonomous trend lasts long enough and is truly autonomous (i.e., independent on the ups and downs of capacity utilization). In that case, we can expect a sustainable path of growth underpinned by a stable supermultiplier. This hypothesis does not mean that the capitalist is a stable system. The roots of stability lie on the multiplicand, most of all when autonomous demand depends strongly on credit.

Banks are integrated into the supermultiplier-cum finance model as financial corporations subject to competition. As autonomous corporations, banks decide, within certain limits, the pace of credit expansion and the allocation of loans. Indeed, banks are interested in credit expansion given the formidable economies of scale they enjoy and their expertise to conceal financial risks to the supervisor. If the gap between credit growth and output growth persists long enough, the key financial ratios will trespass their safety limits, rendering the economy more vulnerable. These facts (clearly illustrated by the 2008 crisis) suggest a reformulation of the money endogeneity hypothesis. It is more a long-term equilibrium condition than a description of the economy's performance in any region at any time. In principle, we can expect that the bulk of credit finances output transactions. But we cannot rule out banks' capability to finance non-output transactions, usually with a speculative bias. The 2008 crash shows that a credit-driven path of growth is limited from the real side of the economy, and it collapses when banks trespass these limits.

The first goal of this paper was the integration of the Sraffian supermultiplier with the post-Keynesian hypothesis of money endogeneity. These are the main links we have found.

- In the multiplicand, the part autonomous demand financed by credit (CR_t/Z_t) and the ratio between the rates expansion of credit and output (φ/γ). The long term sustainability of the system requires that both ratios are equal to or below one.
- In the multiplier, the borrowers propensity to save. In our case, σ_w stands for the savings propensity of workers to fulfill their financial commitments. This ratio is supposed to be at least equal to the ratio of debt service to income (δ_t).
- The link between the real and financial chains is the transfer ratio: $\varepsilon = INT_t/Y_t$. We have defined 'normal transfers' as those allowing banks to pay normal wages and profits in VIS_b. Its share in income amounts to $\varepsilon^* = INT_t^*/Y_t$. The difference between these two ratios (ε-ε^*) informs about the extra interest payments (INT_{xt}/Y_t) perceived by banks. Probably, they will be hoarded, increasing the liquidity of the system defined as $\lambda = DEP_t/Y_t$

The second goal of the paper was the analysis of the consequences of surpassing these limits. The last boom and bust in our financialized economies confirm that a persistent gap between the rates of growth of credit and output ($\varphi>\gamma$) brings about over-indebtedness leading to demand depression and excess of liquidity leading to asset inflation. Expressions (33) and (34) show that they are self-reinforcing processes.

The financial instability of capitalism is an old problem. Surprisingly, it has received scant attention from the leading economists of each era. Keynes is an exception. He was well aware of the importance of credit in a *monetary production economy* and the dangers of granting loans to finance the speculative bets that characterize a 'casino economy'. Two quotes summarize Keynes' thought that our paper has unveiled from a theoretical model that integrates Keynesian, Sraffian, and Schumpeterian ideas.

> 'Credit is the pavement along which production travels and the bankers if they knew their duty, would provide the transport facilities to just the extent it is required in order that the productive powers of the community can be employed at full employment.' Keynes (1973) (CW-6, p. 197).

> 'Speculators may do no harm as bubbles on a steady stream of enterprise. But the position is serious when enterprise becomes a bubble on a whirlpool of speculation. When the capital development of a country becomes a by-product of the activities of a casino, the job is likely to be ill done' (Keynes, 1936, p. 159).

Acknowledgments

During the long preparation of this paper, we received helpful comments from John S. McCombie (University of Cambridge), Richard Werner (University. of Southampton), Gumersindo Ruiz (University of Malaga), and Eladio Febrero (University of Castilla – La Mancha). Our gratitude to all of them Also, to the people attending the seminar in Centro Sraffa (Università Roma Tre) on the 30th May 2018, where a first version of the paper was presented. The detailed and constructive comments of the referees deserve explicit recognition.

Disclosure Statement

No potential conflict of interest was reported by the author(s).

ORCID

Óscar Dejuán http://orcid.org/0000-0002-9319-6609

References

Allain, O. 2015. 'Tackling the Instability of Growth: A Kaleckian-Harrodian Model with an Autonomous Expenditure Component.' *Cambridge Journal of Economics* 39 (5): 1351–1371.

Aspromourgos, T. 2013. 'Sraffa's System in Relation to Some Main Currents in Unorthodox Economics.' In *Sraffa and the Reconstruction of Economic Theory*, edited by E. S. Levrero, A. Palumbo, and A. Stirati, Vol. 3, ch. 1, 15–34. New York: Palgrave Macmillan.

Borio, C., and P. Lowe. 2002. 'Asset Prices, Financial and Monetary Stability: Exploring the Nexus.' *BIS Working Papers* 14: 1–35.

Bortis, H. 1997. *Institutions, Behaviour and Economic Theory: A Contribution to Classical-Keynesian Political Economy*. Cambridge: Cambridge University Press.

Cesaratto, S. 2017. 'Initial and Final Finance in the Monetary Circuit and the Thoery of Effective Demand.' *Metroeconomica* 68 (2): 228–258.

Cesaratto, S., F. Serrano, and A. Stirati. 2003. 'Technical Change, Effective Demand and Employment.' *Review of Political Economy* 15 (1): 33–52.

Ciccone, R. 1986. 'Accumulation and Capacity Utilization: Some Critical Considerations on Joan Robinson's Theory of Distribution.' *Political Economy, Studies in the Surplus Approach* 2: 17–36.

Claessents, S., M. A. Kose, and M. E. Terrones. 2009. 'What Happens During Recessions, Crunches and Busts?' *Economic Policy* 24 (60): 653–700.

Dejuán, O. 2005. 'Paths of Accumulation and Growth: Towards a Keynesian Long-Period Theory of Output.' *Review of Political Economy* 17 (2): 231–252.

Dejuán, Ó. 2017. 'Hidden Links in the Warranted Rate of Growth. The Supermultiplier Way Out.' *European Journal of the History of Economic Thought* 24 (2): 369–394.

Dejuán, O., and D. Dejuán. 2018. 'A Predator-Prey Model in Financial-Driven Economies.' *Review of Keynesian Economics* 6 (2): 159–179.

Dejuán, Ó, and J. McCombie. 2019. 'Economic Limits of the Orignate to Distribute Model of Banking.' In *Finance, Growth and Inequality*, edited by L. P. Rochon, and V. Monvoisin, 36–57. Cheltenham: Edward Elgar.

Dejuán, Ó, F. Portella-Carbó, and M. Ortiz. 2020. 'Economic and Environmental Impacts of Decarbonisation Through a Hybrid MRIO Multiplier-Accelerator Model.' *Economic Systems Research*, doi:10.1080/09535314.2020.1848808.

Eatwell, J. 1983. 'The Long-Period Theory of Unemployment.' *Cambridge Journal of Economics* 7 (3): 269–285.

Freitas, F., and F. Serrano. 2015. 'Growth Rate and Level Effect, the Stability of Adjustment of Capacity to Demand and the Sraffian Super-Multiplier.' *Review of Political Economy* 27 (3): 258–281.

Girardi, D., and R. Pariboni. 2016. 'Long-run Effective Demand in the US Economy: An Empirical Test of the Sraffian Supermultiplier.' *Review of Political Economy* 28: 523–544.

Godley, W., and M. Lavoie. 2007. *Monetary Economics. An Integrated Approach to Credit, Money, Income, Production and Wealth*. New York: Palgrave Macmillan.

Graziani, A. 1989. 'The Theory of the Monetary Circuit.' *Thames Papers in Political Economy* 7: 1–30.

Harrod, R. 1939. 'An Essay in Dynamic Theory.' *Economic Journal* 49: 14–33.

Hein, E., and R. Woodgate. 2020. 'Stability Issues in Kaleckian Models Driven by Autonomous Demand Growht -Harrodian Instability and Debt Dynamics.' *Metroeconomica* 72 (1): 1–36.

Hicks, J. R. 1950. *A Contribution to the Theory of the Trade Cycle*. Oxford: The Clarendom Press.

Jordà, Ò, M. Schularick, and A. M. Taylor. 2013. 'When Credit Bites Back.' *Journal of Money.' Credit and Banking* 45 (2): 3–28.

Kaldor, N. 1981. A Keynesian perspective on money'. Lloyds Bank Review. (Reprinted in Further essays on economic theory and policy, edited by Targetti and Thirlwall 1989, 1-19.).

Kalecki, M. 1937. 'A Theory of the Business Cycle.' *Review of Economic Studies* 4 (2): 77–97.

Keynes, J. M. 1936. *The General Theory of Employment, Interest and Money*. Harcourt Brace Javanovich: London and New York.

Keynes, J. M. 1973. *The Collected Writings of John Maynard Keynes (XXIX Vols*. London: MacMillan.

Lavoie, M. 2010. 'Surveying Short-run and Long-run Stability Issues with the Kaleckian Model of Growth.' In *Handbook of Alternative Theories of Economic Growth*, edited by M. Setterfield, Chapter 6. Cheltenham: Edward Elgar.

Lavoie, M. 2014. *Post-Keynesian Economics. New Foundations*. Cheltenham: Edward Elgar.

Lavoie, M. 2016. 'Convergence Towards the Normal Rate of Capacity Utilization in Kaleckian Models: The Role of non-Capacity Creating Autonomous Expenditures.' *Metroeconomica* 67 (1): 172–201.

Mendoza, E. G., and M. E. Terrones. 2012. An anatomy of credit booms and their demise.' *National Bureau of Economic Research* (Technical report).

Minsky, H. P. 1964. 'Longer Waves in Financial Relations: Financial Factors in the Severe Depressions.' *The American Economic Review* 54 (3): 83–96.

Moore, B. J. 1988. *Horizontalists and Verticalists: The Macroeconomics of Credit Money*. Cambridge: Cambridge University Press.

Nikiforos, M., and G. Zezza. 2017. Stock-flow consistent macroeconomic models'. Levy Economics Institute - Working Papers, 891: 1-70.

Palley, T. J. 2018. 'The Economics of the Super-Multiplier: A Comprehensive Treatment with Labor Markets.' *Metroeconomica*, doi:10.1111/meca.12228.

Palumbo, A., and A. Trezzini. 2003. 'Growth Without Normal Capacity Utilization.' *European Journal of the History of Economic Thought* 10 (1): 109–135.

Panico, C., A. Pinto, and M. Puchet. 2012. 'Income Distribution and the Size of the Financial Sector: A Sraffian Analysis.' *Cambridge Journal of Economics* 36: 1455–1477.

Parguez, A., and M. Seccareccia. 2000. 'The Credit Theory of Money: The Monetary Circuit Approach.' In *What is Money?*, edited by J. Smithin, 101–120. New York: Routledge.

Pariboni, R. 2016. 'Household Consumer Debt, Endogenous Money and Growth: A Supermultiplier-Based Analysis.' *PSL Quaterly Review* 69 (278): 211–233.

Pasinetti, L. 1973. 'The Notion of Vertical Integration in Economic Analysis.' *Metroeconomica* XXV: 1–29.

Pasinetti, L. 1979. *Lectures on the Theory of Production*. London: Palgrave - MacMillan.

Pérez, J. A., and C. Manera. 2020. 'Autonomous Expenditures and Induced Investment: A Panel Test of the Sraffian Supermultiplier Model in European Countries.' *Review of Keynesian Economics* 8 (2): 220–239.

Robinson, J. 1962. *Essays on the Theory of Economic Growth*. London: Macmillan.

Rochon, L. P., and S. Rossi. 2017. *Advances in Endogenous Money Analysis*. Cheltenham: Edward Elgar.

Schularick, M., and A. M. Taylor. 2012. 'Credit Booms Gone Bust: Monetary Policy, Leverage Cycles, and Financial Crises, 1870-2008.' *American Economic Review* 102 (2): 1029–1061.

Schumpeter, J. (2008) 2012. *The Theory of Economic Development: An Inquiry into Profits, Capital, Credit, Interest and the Business Cycle*. Cambridge, MA: Harvard University Press.

Serrano, F. 1995. 'Long Period Effective Demand and the Sraffian Supermultiplier.' *Contributions to Political Economy* 14: 67–90.

Shaikh, A. 1991. 'Wandering Around the Warranted Path: Dynamics non-Linear Solutions to the Harrodian Knife-Edge.' In *Nicholas Kaldor and Mainstream Economics*, edited by E. Nell, and J. Semmler, 320–334. London: Macmillan.

Skott, P., J. F. C. Santos, and J. L. Oreiro. 2021. 'Supermultipliers, 'Endogenous Autonomous Demand' amd Functional Finance.' *Metroeconomica*, doi:10.1111/meca.12360.
Sraffa, P. 1960. *Production of Commodities by Means of Commodities. Prelude to a Critique of Economic Theory*. Cambridge: Cambridge University Press.
Tobin, J. E. 1958. 'Liquidity Preference as Behaviour Toward Risk.' *Review of Economic Stadies* 25: 65–86.
Turner, A. 2015. *Between Debt and The Devil. Money, Credit, and Fixing Global Finance*. Princeton: Princeton University Press.
Werner, R. A. 2005. *New Paradigm in Macroeconomics*. Basingstoke: Palgrave Macmillan.
Werner, R. A. 2014. 'The Quantity Theory of Credit and Some of its Policy Implications.' In *A Flow-of-Funds Perspective on the Financial Crisis*, edited by B. Winkler, A. V. Riet, and B. P. Vol. 1, 22–45. Basingstoke: Palgrave-McMillan.
White, G. 2009. 'Demand-led Growth in a Multi-Commodity Model with Learning: Some Preliminary Results.' *The University of Sydney. Economics Working Paper Series* 2009 (1): 1–35.
Wray, R. 1990. *Money and Credit in Capitalist Economies*. Cheltenham (UK): Edward Elgar.

APPENDIX

Table A: Numerical example of credit-led growth leading to credit-burdened growth.
General notes:

- Figures refer to the initial values taken as data. Some parameters remain constant in all the scenarios.
- An apostrophe (') before a variable refers to the same variable in the previous period.
- Angular brackets refer to stocks.
- Shadow cells in the middle of the table indicate the required adjustment after the change of an autonomous variable.

Definitions of parameters and variables

Name	Formulation	Explanation
PARAMETERS		
Technology		
$l = 0.9$	Data	Labor coefficient (constant in the 4 scenarios)
$k = 2$	Data	Capital coefficient, normal or desired (constant)
u	KR/KI	Capacity utilization. Normal utilization: $u^* = 1$.
Distribution and prices		
$w = 1$	Data	Real wage per worker (constant)
$\omega = 0.9$	$W/Y = w{\cdot}l$	Share of wages in income (constant because constant w & l)
r	R/KI	Actual rate of profit. The normal rate of profit in a long period equilibrium is: $r^* = (1\text{-}w{\cdot}l)/k = 0.05$
ρ	$R/Y = r{\cdot}k = 1\text{-}\omega$	Share of profits. Constant except for the adjustment periods where $u \neq 1$.
Py	A function of the employment rate	Price index of produced goods (constant since employment, L, adapts through migration). This implies a flat Phillips curve
Px	$[DEPx]/[X]{\cdot}\lambda^*$	Price index of fixed non-produced assets [X]. Initially Px = 1.
Demand and savings		
$c_w = 0.88$	Data or $(1\text{-}s_w)$	Propensity to consume out of wages.
$\underline{c}_w$	Data	Minimum consumption rate out of wages (historically given)
$c_r = 0$	Data	Propensity to consume out of profits. 0 in all the scenarios.
c	$C/Y = c_w{\cdot}\omega + c_r{\cdot}\rho = \omega$	Aggregate propensity to consume (weighted average)
θ	$(C + Z)/Y = c + z$	Share in income of consumption type expenditure
$s_w = 0.11$	Data	Propensity to save out of wages. Enough to attend the service of debt in normal circumstances.
σ_w	$s_w{\cdot}\omega$	Share in income of savings out of wages

(*Continued*)

Continued.

Name	Formulation	Explanation
$s_r = 1$	$1\text{-}c_r$	Propensity to save out of profits.
σ_r	$s_r{\cdot}\rho =$ (Y-C-Z)/Y	Share in income of business savings (i.e., savings out of profits)
s	(Y-C)/Y $= s_w{\cdot}\omega + s_r{\cdot}\rho$	Aggregate propensity to save (a weighted average)
h	$k{\cdot}\gamma$	Share in income of productive investment
z	Z/Y = 1-c-h	Share in income of autonomous demand (here, residential inv.)
M	1/(1-c) = 1/s $= 1/(\sigma_w + \sigma_r)$	Multiplier.
SM	1/(1-c-h) $= 1/\sigma_w$	Supermultiplier. It changes when there is a change in s_w and in h
g_j	(J-'J)'J	Rate of growth of any variable J.
γ	Data	Expected rate of growth of persistent aggregated demand. It adjusts to the expected rate of growth of persistent autonomous demand when it lasts long enough. In equilibrium: $g_z = g_d = g_y = g_L = g_K = \gamma$
Finance		
φ	Data	Rate of growth of the flow of credit (mortgage loans)
β	[DEBT]/Y	Ratio of indebtedness. Initially, $\beta_o = 1$
δ	(INT + AM)/Y $= i{\cdot}cr + a{\cdot}\beta$	Ratio of debt-service or burden of debt. When i applies to outstanding debt.
ε^*	INT*/Y	Normal share of banks' value-added in aggregate value-added. Initially: 0.0125
λ^*	[DEP]/[EQ]	Desired liquidity ratio defined as (ordinary deposits and bank reserves) / (equity at the initial unitary price)
i = 0.125	Data	Interest rate (applied to the current credit flow)
a = 0.05	Data	Amortization rate (applied to the current stock of debt)
i'+a = 0,0625	Data	Debt service rate (applied to the current stock of debt); i' = 0,0125 so that 'i·CR = i'·[DEBT]'
ECONOMIC VARIABLES		
Z	'Z(1+γ)	Autonomous demand = residential investment. Initially, Zo = 10
Y	Z·(SM)	Final demand = final output = factor income
KR	Y·k	Required capacity
KI	'KI + I+Ix	Installed capacity. Initially, KI = KR = 200
L	Y·l	Employment. It adjusts through migration.
W	L·w	Wages
R	Y-W	Profits
INT	i·CR	Interest payments
INT*	$\varepsilon^*{\cdot}$Y	'Normal' interest payments
INTx	INT-INT*	Extra interest payments = extra reserves of banks (RESx). They represent an increase in liquidity and a leakage to aggregated demand
C	Y·c	Induced consumption
I	Y·k·γ	Capacity-creating investment to attend expected increases in demand growing persistently at γ
Ix	KR-KI	Extra investment to adjust capacity. If positive, the new machines are taken from inventories. A part of them may be reproduced with the corresponding multiplier effect. Here we suppose the shortcomings and excesses of inventories offset each other.
θ	C + Z	Consumption type expenditure (they do not increase productive capacity)
S	Y-C = Y·s = SW + SR	Savings
SR	$s_r{\cdot}R = \sigma_r{\cdot}Y$	Savings out of profits (equal to business savings)
SW	$s_w{\cdot}W = \sigma_w{\cdot}Y$ = Y-C	Savings out of wages to meet the expected debt-service of mortgage loans
FINANCIAL VARIABLES		
CR	'CR(1+φ)	Total flow of credit
CRy	f(Y) = Z	Loans for output transactions; in our case they coincide with mortgage loans.
CRx	CR-CRy = CR-Z	Loans for non-output transactions; excess credit
AM	[CR]·a	Amortization allowances
CRn	CR-AM = ΔCR	Net flow of credit (ΔCR ≡ ΔDEBT ≡ ΔDEP)
[CR]	'[CR]+'CRn	Stock of credit, outstanding loans. ([CR] ≡ [DEBT] ≡ [DEP])
[DEP]	DEP*+RESx	Total liquidity.
DEP*	SW $= \sigma_w{\cdot}$Y	Normal liquidity. Savings to meet the financial commitments
RESx	INTx	Extra reserves of banks plus extra deposits of households and firms. A source of speculative bets.
[DEBT]	'[DEBT]+'ΔDEBT	Outstanding debt

Table A (g = g(D) = γ; j = g(CR) = φ)

	Scn 1: balanced growth, g=j=0.05					Scn 2: Cred accel: (j=0.1)>(g=0.05)					Scn 3: Recession: j=g=0					Scn 4: Recovery: j=g=0.05				
	1	**2**	**3**	**4**	**5**	**6**	**7**	**8**	**14**	**15**	**16**	**17**	**18**	**24**	**25**	**26**	**27**	**28**	**34**	**35**
KI	200.0	210.0	220.5	231.5	243.1	255.3	268.0	281.4	377.1	396.0	415.8	138.2	138.2	138.2	138.2	138.2	426.5	447.9	600.2	630.2
Z	10.0	10.5	11.0	11.6	12.2	12.8	13.4	14.1	18.9	19.8	19.3	19.3	19.3	19.3	19.3	20.3	21.3	22.4	30.0	31.5
Y	100.0	105.0	110.3	115.8	121.6	127.6	134.0	140.7	188.6	198.0	69.1	69.1	69.1	69.1	69.1	203.1	213.3	223.9	300.1	315.1
KR	200.0	210.0	220.5	231.5	243.1	255.3	268.0	281.4	377.1	396.0	138.2	138.2	138.2	138.2	138.2	406.2	426.5	447.9	600.2	630.2
L	90.0	94.5	99.2	104.2	109.4	114.9	120.6	126.6	169.7	178.2	62.2	62.2	62.2	62.2	62.2	182.8	191.9	201.5	270.1	283.6
W	90.0	94.5	99.2	104.2	109.4	114.9	120.6	126.6	169.7	178.2	62.2	62.2	62.2	62.2	62.2	182.8	191.9	201.5	270.1	283.6
R	10.0	10.5	11.0	11.6	12.2	12.8	13.4	14.1	18.9	19.8	6.9	6.9	6.9	6.9	6.9	20.3	21.3	22.4	30.0	31.5
INT	1.3	1.3	1.4	1.4	1.5	1.6	1.7	1.8	2.7	2.9	3.2	3.3	3.3	3.7	3.8	3.8	3.9	4.0	4.6	4.8
INTx	0.0	0.0	0.0	0.0	0.0	0.0	0.0	0.0	0.4	0.5	2.3	2.4	2.5	2.9	2.9	1.3	1.2	1.2	0.9	0.8
C	80.0	84.0	88.2	92.6	97.2	102.1	107.2	112.6	150.9	158.4	49.7	49.7	49.7	49.7	49.7	162.5	170.6	179.1	240.1	252.1
I	10.0	10.5	11.0	11.6	12.2	12.8	13.4	14.1	18.9	19.8	0.0	0.0	0.0	0.0	0.0	20.3	21.3	22.4	30.0	31.5
Ix	0.0	0.0	0.0	0.0	0.0	0.0	0.0	0.0	0.0	0.0	-277.6	0.0	0.0	0.0	0.0	268.0	0.0	0.0	0.0	0.0
SW	10.0	10.5	11.0	11.6	12.2	12.8	13.4	14.1	18.9	19.8	12.4	12.4	12.4	12.4	12.4	20.3	21.3	22.4	30.0	31.5
SR	10.0	10.5	11.0	11.6	12.2	12.8	13.4	14.1	18.9	19.8	6.9	6.9	6.9	6.9	6.9	20.3	21.3	22.4	30.0	31.5
S	20.0	21.0	22.1	23.2	24.3	25.5	26.8	28.1	37.7	39.6	19.3	19.3	19.3	19.3	19.3	40.6	42.7	44.8	60.0	63.0
u	1.00	1.00	1.00	1.00	1.00	1.00	1.00	1.00	1.00	1.00	0.33	1.00	1.00	1.00	1.00	2.94	1.00	1.00	1.00	1.00
g(Y)		0.05	0.05	0.05	0.05	0.05	0.05	0.05	0.05	0.05	-0.65	0.00	0.00	0.00	0.00	1.94	0.05	0.05	0.05	0.05
tfx	0.00	0.00	0.00	0.00	0.00	0.00	0.00	0.00	0.00	0.00	0.03	0.03	0.04	0.04	0.04	0.01	0.01	0.01	0.00	0.00
c	0.80	0.80	0.80	0.80	0.80	0.80	0.80	0.80	0.80	0.80	0.72	0.72	0.72	0.72	0.72	0.80	0.80	0.80	0.80	0.80
h	0.10	0.10	0.10	0.10	0.10	0.10	0.10	0.10	0.10	0.10	0.00	0.00	0.00	0.00	0.00	0.10	0.10	0.10	0.10	0.10
z	0.10	0.10	0.10	0.10	0.10	0.10	0.10	0.10	0.10	0.10	0.28	0.28	0.28	0.28	0.28	0.10	0.10	0.10	0.10	0.10
yj	0.00	0.00	0.00	0.00	0.00	0.00	0.00	0.00	0.00	0.00	0.00	0.00	0.00	0.00	0.00	0.00	0.00	0.00	0.00	0.00
s	0.20	0.20	0.20	0.20	0.20	0.20	0.20	0.20	0.20	0.20	0.28	0.28	0.28	0.28	0.28	0.20	0.20	0.20	0.20	0.20
CR	10.0	10.5	11.0	11.6	12.2	13.4	14.7	16.2	28.7	31.5	19.3	19.3	19.3	19.3	19.3	20.3	21.3	22.4	30.0	31.5
AM	5.0	5.3	5.5	5.8	6.1	6.4	6.7	7.1	10.8	11.7	12.7	13.0	13.4	14.9	15.2	15.4	15.6	15.9	18.5	19.0
CRn	5.0	5.3	5.5	5.8	6.1	7.0	8.0	9.0	17.8	19.8	6.6	6.3	6.0	4.4	4.2	4.9	5.7	6.5	11.5	12.5
[CR]	100.0	105.0	110.3	115.8	121.6	127.6	134.6	142.6	216.6	234.4	254.2	260.9	267.2	298.9	303.3	307.5	312.4	318.1	369.3	380.9
DS	6.3	6.6	6.9	7.2	7.6	8.0	8.4	8.9	13.5	14.7	15.9	16.3	16.7	18.7	19.0	19.2	19.5	19.9	23.1	23.8
CRx	0.0	0.0	0.0	0.0	0.0	0.6	1.3	2.1	9.8	11.7	0.0	0.0	0.0	0.0	0.0	0.0	0.0	0.0	0.0	0.0
[DEP']	100.0	105.0	110.3	115.8	121.6	127.6	134.6	142.6	217.0	234.9	256.6	263.3	269.7	301.8	306.2	308.8	313.6	319.3	370.2	381.7
Px	1.0	1.0	1.0	1.0	1.0	1.0	1.0	1.0	1.2	1.2	1.2	3.8	3.9	4.4	4.4	4.5	1.5	1.4	1.2	1.2
EQ($)	200.0	210.0	220.5	231.5	243.1	255.3	269.2	285.2	433.9	469.8	513.1	526.5	539.3	603.5	612.4	617.5	627.3	638.6	740.4	763.4
g(CR)		0.05	0.05	0.05	0.05	0.10	0.10	0.10	0.10	0.10	-0.39	0.00	0.00	0.00	0.00	0.05	0.05	0.05	0.05	0.05
CR/Y	0.10	0.10	0.10	0.10	0.10	0.10	0.11	0.11	0.15	0.16	0.28	0.28	0.28	0.28	0.28	0.10	0.10	0.10	0.10	0.10
CRn/Y	0.05	0.05	0.05	0.05	0.05	0.05	0.06	0.06	0.09	0.10	0.10	0.09	0.09	0.06	0.06	0.02	0.03	0.03	0.04	0.04
[DB]/Y	1.00	1.00	1.00	1.00	1.00	1.00	1.00	1.01	1.15	1.18	3.68	3.78	3.87	4.33	4.39	1.51	1.46	1.42	1.23	1.21
(DS)/Y	0.06	0.06	0.06	0.06	0.06	0.06	0.06	0.06	0.07	0.07	0.23	0.24	0.24	0.27	0.27	0.09	0.09	0.09	0.08	0.08
AM/Y	0.05	0.05	0.05	0.05	0.05	0.05	0.05	0.05	0.06	0.06	0.18	0.19	0.19	0.22	0.22	0.08	0.07	0.07	0.06	0.06
INT/Y	0.01	0.01	0.01	0.01	0.01	0.01	0.01	0.01	0.01	0.01	0.05	0.05	0.05	0.05	0.05	0.02	0.02	0.02	0.02	0.02
INTx/Y	0.00	0.00	0.00	0.00	0.00	0.00	0.00	0.00	0.00	0.00	0.03	0.03	0.04	0.04	0.04	0.01	0.01	0.01	0.00	0.00
P']/EQ$	0.50	0.50	0.50	0.50	0.50	0.50	0.50	0.51	0.58	0.59	0.62	1.91	1.95	2.18	2.22	2.23	0.74	0.71	0.62	0.61
	1	2	3	4	5	6	7	8	14	15	16	17	18	24	25	26	27	28	34	35

Pensions as an Engine of Growth. An Approach to the Spanish Case, Based on the Sraffian Supermultiplier

Eladio Febrero and Fernando Bermejo

ABSTRACT

In this paper, following Cesaratto's lead (Cesaratto, [2005]. *Pension Reform and Economic Theory: A Non-Orthodox Analysis.* Cheltenham: Edward Elgar, especially chapters 6-8), we measure the impact of pensioners' spending on output and employment in the Spanish economy in 2021 by means of the Sraffian supermultiplier, taking pensioners' expenditure as a component of autonomous demand. To do so, we follow another lead, from Dejuán (Dejuan, [2023]. *The Supermultiplier. A Cornerstone of the New Macroeconomics.* Cheltenham: Edward Elgar, chapter 10), who suggests using the Leontief inverse of an extended SAM (social accounting matrix) that also includes both induced consumption and expansionary investment as a multisectoral supermultiplier, or multiplier-accelerator. The weight of PAYG pensions to people aged 65 or older in 2021 is 8 per cent of GDP, and their expenditure 'puts in motion' 6,7 per cent of total production and total employment (directly, indirectly, and hyper-indirect or induced). The government recovers 42 cents in taxes for each euro spent on pensions. Pensions in 2050 are sustainable, either raising taxes on profits or if exports grow pari passu with pensions at a rate below historical records.

1. Introduction

The Sraffian supermultiplier model (SSM) extends the Keynesian principle of effective demand to the long-run (Bortis 1997; Cesaratto et al. 2003; Dejuán 2005; Serrano 1995). In this model, the engines of growth are located in the autonomous components of demand that do not create productive capacity (e.g., Freitas and Serrano 2015). That property makes this model useful for studying the role played by different sources of demand in the growth of concrete economies (e.g., Bastos and Porto 2016; Freitas and Dweck 2013; Labat and Summa 2023; Passos and Morlin 2022; or Barbieri Góes 2022, amongst others).

This paper follows this demand-led growth accounting approach, which is applied to the Spanish economy. Yet, we focus on one single source of autonomous demand: pensioners' expenditure on consumer goods and services (on this, we agree with Haluska, Braga, and Summa 2021, who consider this as a component of autonomous demand, independent from the rest of public spending). We study its impact in terms of output and employment in 2021 and also the conditions under which it is expected to operate in 2050.

The SSM allows considering Pay-As-You-Go (PAYG) pensions as a source of growth, contrary to the conventional view (e.g., Feldstein 1974; World Bank 1994), which sees these schemes as a burden that slows down economic growth because they reduce savings and accumulation. On this, we follow the Classical-Keynesian approach to pensions led by Cesaratto 2005. Accordingly, we see the PAYG pension scheme as a tax-transfer system and not a social insurance plan (because the social security budget needs not be balanced either in the short or the long run). Our approach fits well with those assuming public spending as an engine of growth (e.g., Woodgate et al. 2023); however, in this paper, we assume that pensions are merely an ingredient of autonomous demand that helps to keep an economy close to full employment whilst it fulfills its main purpose, which is to provide people with an income when they reach a certain age.

Empirical research adopting the SSM has mostly assumed a highly aggregate economy. By contrast, in this paper, we have used a multisectoral approach, following the lead of Dejuán et al. 2020 and Dejuán 2023. Our supermultiplier is an extended Leontief inverse matrix that includes workers' consumption -excluding civil servants' consumption, as suggested by Serrano and Pimentel 2019- and induced investment. This, combined with the pensioners' consumption vector, gives us a disaggregated measure of the impact of pensions on output, employment, and value added. This approach has also some similarities with Pasinetti's notion of growing vertically hyper-integrated subsystems (Pasinetti 1988).

Endogenous money is embodied in the model through the Monetary Circuit Theory (Graziani 2003), following the insights of Nell 1998 and Febrero 2008.

In short, in a defined benefit PAYG, which is a tax-transfer system, we consider pensioners' consumption as an ingredient of autonomous demand. We then compute its impact on output and employment in the Spanish economy, using a multisectoral supermultiplier, for 2021. Then, we consider two alternative scenarios to make this pension scheme financially sustainable in 2050, when the number of pensioners will almost double the current number.

This paper is organized as follows. Section two contains the Classical Keynesian view of a defined benefit PAYG pension scheme. In Section three, we provide an account of how pensioners' expenditure can be dealt with within the SSM framework. Our empirical research is in Section four, whilst Section five offers our main conclusions.

2. Defined-Benefit Payg Pension Schemes from a Classical-Keynesian Standpoint

There are three arguments that justify treating a defined-benefit PAYG (DB-PAYG onwards) pension scheme following the main tenets of the Classical-Keynesian theoretical standpoint. Firstly, a DB-PAYG pension scheme is a system in which the government pays pension benefits to retired people, in an amount that usually depends on the number of years contributing to the system and the amount of those contributions, usually proportional to wages. This benefit, once calculated, will be paid to the retired person until her death, regardless of whether or not total benefits outstrip total contributions. The

Spanish pension system, under circumstances prevailing in 2023, can be deemed a DB-PAYG (some details of the Social Security in Spain are provided in Section four below).

From a Classical-Keynesian standpoint,[1] this type of pension scheme shows the following features. Firstly, DB-PAYG is a tax-transfer mechanism,[2] not an insurance plan, because (*i*) the benefits paid to retirees are the result of a political decision affected by social and intergenerational conflict, and (*ii*) although the largest part of its revenues come from payroll taxes, the difference between outlays and revenues is covered with general taxation or through the issuance of public debt (payroll taxes are a particular type of taxes).[3] This point is well argued by Cesaratto 2005, who also adds that the fiction of an insurance plan could only be accepted as a social convention and a means to politically legitimate such a pension system.[4]

Secondly, in a tax-transfer system, pension benefits fund some autonomous consumption expenditure, which is an ingredient of autonomous demand. In economic systems that operate below full capacity utilization, the Keynesian principle of effective demand holds in the short and in the long term, as far as investment in productive capacity is an induced component of demand that keeps that capacity at a level that is compatible with the trend output (see, for instance, Dejuán 2023, pp. 3–4). As Cesaratto writes:

> According to the theory of long-period effective demand the engine of growth is represented by *autonomous* or *final* components of aggregate demand [...] Autonomous expenditure [....] includes social transfers from the state which contain PAYG pension payments. [...] It should thus be appreciated that in the [C]lassical-Keynesian approach social spending represents an engine of growth. (Cesaratto 2005, chapter 6, p. 200, italics in the original)

The element that links output to autonomous demand is the supermultiplier (Hicks 1950), also called the Sraffian supermultiplier (Serrano 1995; Bortis 1997, chapter 4) or the multiplier-accelerator (Dejuán, 2023, p. 1).

In that view, pensioners' expenditure can contribute to keeping output, productive capacity, and employment growing at a relatively high level, according to the Keynesian principle of effective demand. As Pivetti writes: 'a generous PAYG system of the defined-benefit type is most likely to raise the community's propensity to consume, thereby strengthening also the demand for capital' (Pivetti 2006, p. 383). That is precisely the context in which a PAYG pension scheme is the most sustainable.

This stands in stark contrast to the conventional view, held by official institutions, like the European Commission (2021), which makes macroeconomic projections assuming that employment tends to gravitate around a NAWRU (non-accelerating wage rate of unemployment), and then output grows depending on the rate of growth of employment, total factor productivity and capital deepening, all exogenous variables (see European Commission 2020 for details and Carnazza et al. 2023 for a critical review). In that account, pensions are a cost as far as output is supply determined and pensions are a portion of output that has to be transferred to agents that did not contribute to its production.

[1]See Eatwell and Milgate 1983, chapter 1. See also Cesaratto, 2021, chapters 1 and 3.

[2]The Spanish system is a rather regressive one, provided that payroll taxes are capped once wages reach a threshold.

[3]In the Spanish case, in 2021, if we take into account only workers' contributions and contributory pensions and leave aside other revenues and outlays, the social security budget would show a deficit of 1.6 per cent of GDP, which would be covered by government resources or by issuing public debt. Government contributions to the Social Security budget amount to 27 per cent of total revenues, and outlays different from contributory pensions are 22 per cent of total outlays. For further details, see Section four below in this paper.

[4]Wray 2005, p. 2, 2006, p. 409, shares this view regarding the American social security system.

And thirdly, the notion of endogenous money (banks create money -bank deposits- when they grant credit) allows agents to spend before collecting savings (which arise after spending takes place). The main implication of this is that payroll taxes do not fund the payment of pensions: the former, like other taxes, are part of the reflux mechanism that allows the government to repay its debts (to banks or bondholders).

In the context of aging societies, due to lower fertility rates and a longer life expectancy, those supporting the Classical-Keynesian view of PAYG pension schemes do not neglect that the viability of PAYG is seen under threat because pension payments are expected to exceed revenues largely. However, conventional solutions like shifting to a funded system are rejected because increasing savings at present to build up a fund to pay future pensions may lead to a problem of effective demand today, and the *conventional* mechanisms to drive an economy to full employment (the interest rate as a real phenomenon) simply do not work (the Sraffa's critique of Neoclassical capital theory -see Cohen and Harcourt 2003- reinforces the Keynesian critique: for instance, Cesaratto, 2005, p. 201). Alternatively, cutting benefits shifts the risks caused by changes in the demography to the elderly, something undesirable, provided that the nature of pension systems is to guarantee some income to people beyond a certain age. Additionally, if what is at risk is the ability of a system to provide the elderly with goods and services in the future, what should be done is to increase the productive capacity today. If savings do not fund investment, but the latter depends on expected demand in the future, a stronger demand at present is more useful than increasing savings today (e.g., Wray 1990–91).

Other 'solutions' to keep the social security budget balanced, consisting of parametric reforms of the PAYG scheme,[5] are seen with some skepticism, not because a demographic shock will make labor scarce,[6] but because the reduction of the reserve army might lead to a redistribution of income in favor of wages (Kalecki 1943). Then, if capitalists see profits (and labor discipline) in jeopardy, they will claim measures to weaken the labor bargaining power (Cesaratto calls them Neo-Malthusian policies, see, for instance, Cesaratto 2005, p. 277): these include those listed in footnote no. 5 in this paper, plus weakening trade unions, cutting wages, reducing investment, practicing tax evasion, *et cetera*. The true problem with those measures is that they drive an economic system towards stagnation.

All-in-all, whilst from a Classical-Keynesian standpoint PAYG pensions can be viewed as an additional tool to bring an economic system closer to full employment (besides providing the elderly with income once they cannot get it by working), this does not mean that pension expenditure can (and should) grow without any limit (beyond full employment). The following critiques can be replied to from this standpoint.

2.1. Generous Pension Benefits May Encourage old Workers to Retire Earlier

Pension systems are conceived for aged people, and they should not be confused with basic or universal income. Although very often pension benefits have been used to

[5]Delaying the retirement age, tightening the access to benefits before the official retirement age, reducing the benefit rate (often shifting to a DC-PAYG: e.g., cutting benefits with the excuse of longer life expectations, introducing notional accounts), not updating nominal pensions when inflation rises, *et cetera*.

[6]Although this might cause problems in some industries in the short run, in the long run, labor demand determines the labor supply.

sort out problems of unemployment of aged people, the incentive to retire earlier could be reduced by the introduction of benefit cuts for those who retire before the official retirement age. Hence, although PAYG pensions can contribute to foster economic growth, they are not a tool designed exclusively for that purpose.

2.2. Public Spending and Public Debt May Become Excessive

Although it is not clear whether there exists a limit for public indebtedness (those sympathetic to the Modern Monetary Theory -see, for instance, Wray 2022- would reject any limit if the government issues its own money and it is not committed to exchange it for anything else), many post-Keynesians (e.g., Sawyer 2021; Woodgate et al. 2023), would argue that what is relevant is the notion of sustainability of debt, given by the stability of the ratio of public debt to GDP: this requires the rate of growth of GDP to be above the interest rate on public debt. The external constraint (given by the rate of growth of exports and the limit for external indebtedness) requires that the rate of growth of domestic expenditure remain moderate (Morlin 2022; Woodgate et al. 2023).

In contrast to the conventional view of sustainability (e.g., Blanchard 2022), Classical-Keynesian authors hold that the Wicksellian concept of *natural interest rate* does not exist (e.g., Dejuán 2007). Then, the interest rate is viewed as an administered variable that is possible (under certain circumstances) to keep under control with the help of the central bank.

In any event, the quotient between public debt and GDP might stabilize at an unacceptable rate (this is particularly relevant in the European Union); in such case, post-Keynesian economists would suggest increasing tax rates (see the last part of Section four in this paper).

2.3. Pension Benefits are an Intergenerational Zero-sum Distributional Measure

If pensions rise and payroll contributions to social security rise as well, to keep its budget balanced, the effect on output is ambiguous according to the supermultiplier: on the one hand, autonomous demand rises with pensions, but the supermultiplier declines if the wage share, net of taxes, falls.

However, keeping pensions relatively high has three positive effects on output: (*i*) a more generous pension does not induce workers to increase their savings when they are near their retirement age if they fear that they have accumulated too little pension fund (e.g., Ghilarducci et al. 2012); (*ii*) PAYG pensions are a stable component of autonomous demand, that behaves anti cyclically in an economic crisis, as it happened in Spain between 2009 and 2013 (e.g., Bermejo et al. 2020; Labat and Summa 2023); and (*iii*) if social security revenues are raised from taxes on income with a low spending propensity (or even on wealth) rather than on wages, aggregate demand would be less affected.[7] And we recall that a DB-PAYG, as a tax-transfer system, does not require keeping contributions equal to pension outlays: social security deficits can be funded

[7]The social security budget is part of the general government budget and, as such, the gap between outlays (pensions benefits) and proceeds (workers' social security contributions) can be covered with general taxes: there is no justification to keep social security outlays balanced with revenues. In the Spanish case, the Government made a 'loan' out of general taxes to the Social Security in 2021 amounting to 8 per cent of its total budget.

with debt (besides with other taxes). In such case, what is required is that indebtedness is sustainable.

3. Pensions, Endogenous Money and the Supermultiplier

Pensioners' expenditure on consumer goods in a DB-PAYG pension scheme can act as an engine of growth of an economic system. They demand consumer goods that are final deliveries of an economic system that, in turn, require the production of other industries as inputs. The Monetary Circuit Theory (e.g., Graziani 2003) and the Classical Theory of Production (as revived by Sraffa 1960) are useful for describing how this engine works. We follow Nell 1998, Part III, and Febrero 2008, to explain how money circulates across an economic system that produces the goods and services that pensioners demand (Figure 1).

Firstly, we need to describe the real side of an economic system.[8] The following figure is useful for this end.

The first line indicates that by combining fixed capital (KF_{KF} with the subindex indicating the industry in which inputs are used), circulating capital (KC_{KF}), and labor (L_{KF}), an industry produces fixed capital and, as a by-product, one-year-older stock fixed capital, $KF_{t+1,}$ is obtained at the end of the production process (therefore, KF_{t+1} is what remains of KF_{KF} after one production process); the symbol Å denotes the combination of different inputs in a production process. The same holds for the second line (which stands for the production of circulating capital, KC) and the third one (the production of consumer goods, C).

Additionally, each production process uses fixed capital of different ages. Hence, after a production process, part of the stock of fixed capital becomes scrap.

This quantity system goes hand-in-hand with a price system:

$$r\mathbf{pK}_t + \mathbf{p}(\mathbf{K}_t - \mathbf{K}_{t-1}) + (1 + r)\mathbf{pA} + w\mathbf{a}_n = \mathbf{p} \qquad (1)$$

where r and w are the profit rate and the nominal wage per unit of labor, respectively.

We assume that competitive conditions hold so that all industries earn a uniform profit rate that is charged on all material inputs except the depreciation of fixed capital, given by the term (KF_i – KF_{t+1}). For simplicity's sake, we shall assume that all wages are spent on consumer goods, C, and part of the profits are saved and invested (the rest is consumed). The system is closed.

3.1. The Monetization of Autonomous Demand

Money is introduced at the end of a production process, making possible the circulation of commodities required for the start of a new production process and the consumption of part of the output. Circulation is described with the help of the following three figures.

In an initial circuit, as the one described in Figure 2, once the level of output to be obtained at the end of the production process that is going to start has been decided according to expected demand, producers of KF and KC borrow short-term from banks (1) to hire workers (2): this is *initial finance* (Graziani 2003). Workers in these

[8] For a description of how money circulates, it is convenient to spell out the structure of production (Nell 2002, p. 529).

$$KF_{KF} \oplus KC_{KF} \oplus L_{KF} \rightarrow KF \oplus KF_{t+1}$$
$$KF_{KC} \oplus KC_{KC} \oplus L_{KC} \rightarrow KC \oplus KF_{t+1}$$
$$KF_{C} \oplus KC_{C} \oplus L_{C} \rightarrow C \oplus KF_{t+1}$$

Figure 1. Quantity system.

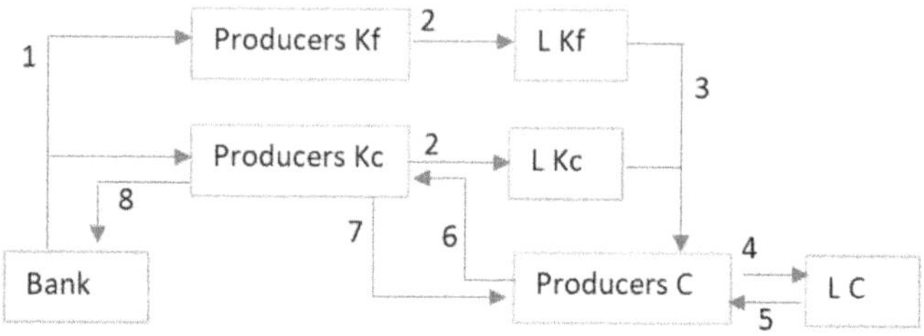

Figure 2. Circulation of money (I).

sectors spend their wages on consumer goods that have already been produced (3); the producer of consumer goods C uses part of those proceeds from the sale of their produce to consume a fraction of its output and the rest is spent on hiring workers (4) that, in turn, spend their wages on consumer goods (5): this is a closed circuit. Next, the producer of C purchases circulating capital KC (6). Then, capitalists of the KC sector spend part of these proceeds on consumer goods (7) and the remaining liquidity is used to repay its short-term debt to the bank, corresponding to its debt for the payment of wages (8). In this circuit, not all the money introduced as initial finance is destroyed: the monetary reflux is incomplete.

In a second circuit (see Figure 3), producers of C and Kc borrow on a long-term basis (1) to fund their investment in new fixed capital (2); then, the producer of Kf uses the proceeds from the sale of its output to purchase Kc (3), to purchase some consumer goods (4) and to repay its short-term debt to the bank (5), corresponding to the payment of wages in the former circuit. The producers of Kc and C use their revenue (6.a, 6.b) to pay part of their long-term loans to fund their investment in the past (we assume that the maturity of the long-term loan matches the lifetime of fixed capital).

After these two circuits, we can introduce the payment of pensions by the government, as in a PAYG scheme, which is illustrated with the help of Figure 4.[9]

In this third circuit, banks lend to the government (1) for the monetization of the payment of pensions (2) that pensioners spend on consumer goods (3), and the producer of consumer goods, therefore, increases its demand for inputs from the rest of the economy; then the rest of the economy pays taxes (4) that the government uses for the cancellation of its debt to the bank (5).

In a PAYG system, workers pay contributions to social security in proportion to their wages (i.e., a payroll tax). Nevertheless, the social security budget needs not to be

[9]In a general case, the funding of autonomous demand, which usually comprises autonomous consumption, residential investment, public consumption and exports, should enter here. In this section, and for simplicity's sake, we have identified autonomous demand with pensioners' consumption.

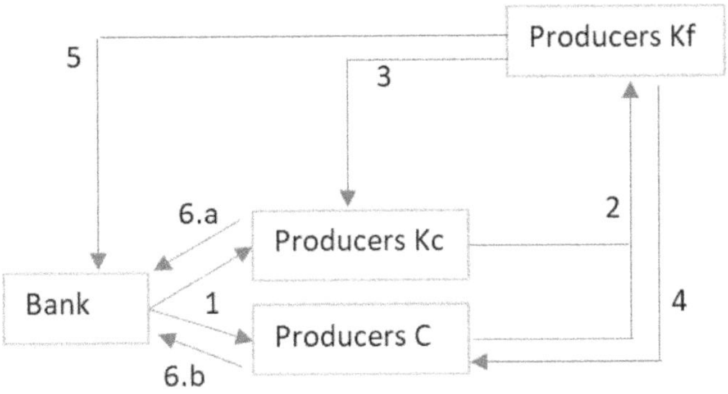

Figure 3. Circulation of money (II).

balanced all the time. Further, we reject the notion of pensions as a 'deferred wage' in favor of a tax-transfer system, with benefits grounded on the notion of conflict, institutions and history (Cesaratto 2005: a summary view in his chapter 9).

In this context, the endogeneity of money arises at three different points in time. In the first circuit, bank lending allows the monetization of the payment of wages. This is initial finance, so that the production process can begin, and provided that this is scarcely controversial, we do not elaborate further on this issue. In the second circuit, banks grant long-term loans to fund investment in productive capacity (the maturity of these loans should match the lifetime of fixed capital to be purchased). In our opinion, banks create money *ex nihilo* when they lend to fund (a fraction of total) investment (Rochon 2005 shares this view).

And the third time that endogenous money arises is when banks lend to the government. This is not initial finance in the proper sense, because it does not fund the production of goods and services but contributes to funding the demand that is required to realize that production in monetary terms.

This third circuit plays a key role in two senses. On the one hand, a demand is funded here that creates additional demand in other sectors (this is contained in expression 3.4

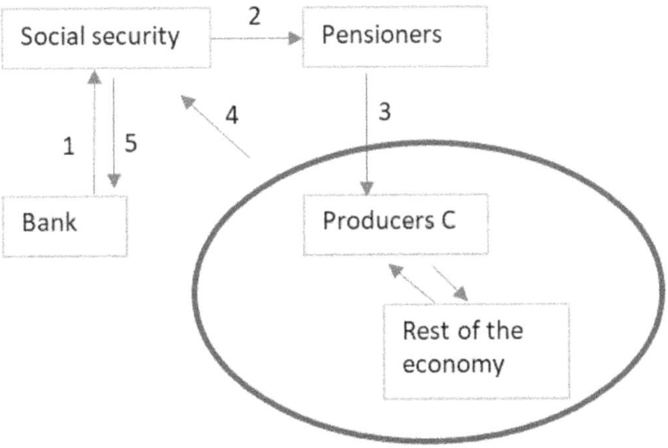

Figure 4. Circulation of money (III): The circuit of pensions.

Central bank		Private bank	
Refinancing operation +100	Deposits gov. +100	Bonds +100	Refinancing operation +100
	Deposits gov. -100 Reserves +100	Reserves +100	Deposits gov. +100
Refinancing operation -100	Reserves -100	Reserves -100	Refinancing operation -100

Figure 5. Banks purchase government bonds and the central bank creates deposits for the government.

below in this section). If this demand is stable, it contributes to stabilizing the whole economic system. On the other hand, in this circuit some liquidity is provided to other sectors (the producer of consumer goods in our model), facilitating the reflux of other circuits. And the liquidity that is not destroyed in the reflux stage in this circuit provides agents with some liquidity that helps to reduce the borrowing from banks in other circuits (this liquidity is a revolving fund of finance: on this concept, see Cesaratto 2017; Cesaratto and Di Bucchianico 2020 or Cesaratto and Pariboni 2022; Davidson 1986).

How do banks lend to the government? In countries like Spain, the central bank acts as the government's banker, though it is forbidden to offer it any lending facility. These two statements are fully compatible. As explained by Lavoie 2022, the central bank is the banker of the government; this means that when the government sells bonds, it obtains deposits at the central bank;[10] however, if the central bank cannot purchase those bonds in primary markets, it has to lend reserves to third agents for that end. Figure 5 describes how a private bank, that misses the required reserves, purchases public bonds in primary markets.

In the first step, the private bank purchases bonds (i.e., it acquires a claim against the government), but if the corresponding government deposits are held on the liability side of the central bank balance sheet (a liability to the government), the latter has to lend to the private bank the required reserves for the purchase of the bonds. This may be done through a refinancing operation. Next, in general, these government deposits are transferred to banks (government spending is managed from accounts held by the government in private banks), leading to an increase in the reserve account held by banks at the central bank. In a third step, banks use these reserves to cancel their debt to the central bank.

Three facts need some clarification: firstly, with the asset purchase programs (particularly the PSPP, an acronym for public sector purchase program) since 2015, the ECB has provided banks with huge amounts of reserves; this makes it unnecessary for banks to borrow from the central bank for the purchase of government bonds. Secondly, with the transfer of government deposits (which are an autonomous liquidity factor) to banks and the subsequent debt repayment to the central bank, central banks avoided unexpected changes in the supply of reserves, something that would have driven the overnight interest rate to the deposit facility rate (see Bindseil 2004, chapter 2, p. 48). However, since 2015, government deposits held at the National Central Banks' (Eurosystem) balance sheet have increased markedly, coinciding with the beginning of the massive purchase of public debt by central banks and the subsequent creation of

[10] In Lavoie 2022, Table 2, banks purchase government bonds first and then they use them as collateral when borrowing reserves from the central bank.

excess reserves, which drove the overnight interest rate to the deposit facility rate. Thirdly, contrary to what is held by some authors sympathetic to the Modern Monetary Theory (e.g., Ehnts 2020), by lending reserves to banks, the central bank is not monetizing public spending: as Lavoie (2022), has argued, if banks (or other private agents) do not wish to purchase government bonds, the willingness of the central bank to lend reserves is not sufficient for the creation of government deposits if it is not allowed to purchase those bonds in primary markets.

3.2. Pensions and the Supermultiplier

An additional point of some interest is the connection between the situation described above, combining the Classical Theory of Production and the Theory of the Monetary Circuit on the one hand, with the supermultiplier, on the other hand. In this economic system, pensioners' consumption expenditure is the unique component of autonomous demand and, provided that the flexible accelerator is a stable mechanism, it is the ultimate determinant of final output through the principle of effective demand. The quantity system represented in Figure 1 above, can be written in matrix form as follows:

$$\mathbf{K^t} \cdot \mathbf{q} + \mathbf{A} \cdot \mathbf{q} + \mathbf{y} = \mathbf{q} + \mathbf{K^{t+1}} \cdot \mathbf{q} \tag{2}$$

Where $\mathbf{K^t}$ is the matrix of t-years old fixed capital per unit of total output, available at the beginning of a production process. Then, $\mathbf{K^t} \cdot \mathbf{q}$ stands for the stock of fixed capital outstanding at the beginning of the production process, and $\mathbf{K^{t+1}} \cdot \mathbf{q}$ in the right hand side of (2) is that stock of fixed capital once the production process has taken place (fixed capital one year older): it is obtained as a by-product of that process, simultaneously with total output $\mathbf{q}$. $\mathbf{A}$ is a matrix of circulating capital per unit of output (the usual Leontief input-output symmetric matrix), so $\mathbf{A} \cdot \mathbf{q}$ is circulating capital, and $\mathbf{y}$ is a vector of (net) final deliveries. Vector $\mathbf{y}$ can be decomposed into workers' consumption, investment and autonomous demand:

$$\mathbf{y} = (\mathbf{b} \cdot \mathbf{a}_n + (\mathbf{K^t} + \mathbf{A}) \cdot g) \cdot \mathbf{q} + \mathbf{Z} \tag{3}$$

Column vector $\mathbf{b}$ stands for the basket of consumer goods purchased by a worker during the production process (e.g., one year), $\mathbf{a_n}$ is the (row) vector of direct labor requirements, scalar g is the rate of growth of fixed and circulating capital, and vector $\mathbf{Z}$ is the vector of autonomous demand, which includes pensioners' consumption and additional elements, like exports, the consumption of civil servants, residential investment, *et cetera*. We can define the matrix of depreciation per unit of output as follows:

$$\mathbf{D} = \mathbf{K^t} - \mathbf{K^{t+1}} = \hat{\mathbf{T}}^{-1} \cdot \mathbf{K^t} \tag{4}$$

Depreciation is given by the difference between the matrix of fixed capital per unit of output t-years old and t + 1-years old or, alternatively, dividing each ingredient of the stock of fixed capital by its litefime, given by diagonal matrix $\mathbf{T}$.

By using (3) and (4), expression (2) can be rearranged in the following manner:

$$[\mathbf{I} - (\mathbf{K^t} + \mathbf{A}) \cdot g - (\mathbf{A} + \mathbf{D}) - \mathbf{b} \cdot \mathbf{a}_n]^{-1} \cdot \mathbf{Z} = \mathbf{q} \tag{5}$$

which can be interpreted as that sectoral output $\mathbf{q}$ depends on autonomous demand $\mathbf{Z}$ through the multisectoral supermultiplier $[\mathbf{I} - (\mathbf{K^t} + \mathbf{A}) \cdot g - (\mathbf{A} + \mathbf{D}) - \mathbf{b} \cdot \mathbf{a}_n]^{-1}$.

This supermultiplier is quite similar to the one suggested in Dejuán et al. 2020, Section three, pp. 6–8.

If we define the vector **Z** of autonomous demand as:

$$\mathbf{Z} = n \cdot \mathbf{z} + \mathbf{Z}' \qquad (6)$$

Where n is the number of pensioners, **z** is the consumption basket of an average pensioner and **Z'** stands for the rest of elements of autonomous demand, the expression that gives us the impact of pensioners' consumption on output is:

$$[\mathbf{I} - (\mathbf{K}^t + \mathbf{A}) \cdot g - (\mathbf{A} + \mathbf{D}) - \mathbf{b} \cdot \mathbf{a}_n]^{-1} \cdot n \cdot \mathbf{z} = \mathbf{q}_p \qquad (7)$$

The reader may observe strong similarities with Pasinetti's notion of growing vertically hyper-integrated subsystems (Pasinetti 1988), although here, subsystems are related to a basket of commodities.[11]

4. An Empirical Estimation of the Supermultiplier of Pensions in Spain.

4.1. Some Aspects of the Spanish Pension System in 2021

Before providing an account of the empirical estimations, we offer a brief description of the main aspects of the Spanish Social Security system as it was in 2021 (and continues to 2024).

The summary global social security budget for 2021 is in Table 1.

Regarding social security revenues, almost 7 per cent is paid by the government (particularly on behalf of unemployed people, 8,5 € billion). Workers' contributions amount to 116.3 € billion.

With respect to the transfers from the government, they mostly fund other items different from contributory pension benefits: non-contributory pensions, minimum guaranteed income, baby caring, some social and health services, and increase some contributory pensions (to reach minimum levels).

Included in 'Other revenues' is also a loan from the government, amounting to 13,83 € billion with the purpose of balancing the global social security budget.

Hence, the government's contribution to the social security budget represents 26,75 per cent of total revenues.

And with respect to the global budget outlays, contributory pensions (including complements) amount to 143,04 € billion, of which retirement pensions of people aged 65 or more are 97 € million euros. Contributory pensions amount to 135,98€ billion, which is 78.87 per cent of the social security budget (here we exclude the complements which are paid with public resources).

Taking these figures into account, if we consider as revenues just the contributions made by workers, and as outlays the contributory pensions without complements, the pension system shows a deficit of 1.6 per cent of GDP in 2021, which is covered with resources from the general government budget, or through issuing public debt.

[11]This supermultiplier goes beyond the traditional multisectoral multipliers because it includes induced investment in productive capacity. For more information about multisectoral multipliers, see Miller and Blair 2009, chapter 6.

Table 1. The Spanish social security system. Some main aspects. Billions of euros. 2021.

Revenues		Outlays	
Contributions to social security	125,14	Pension benefits (contributory pensions excluding complements)	165,77
			135,98
Transfers from the Government	31,18	Health and social services	4,33
Other revenues	16,09	Other outlays	2,31
Total	172,41	Total	172,41

Source: Authors' elaboration from Seguridad Social (www.seg-social.es).

Focusing on retirement pensions, the official age for retirement (in 2021) is 66 years (65 if the worker contributed for 38 years or more). The *de facto* age of retirement in 2024 is 65,1 years. Currently (in 2024), a minimum of 15 years of contributions is required to be eligible for pension benefits, and the (defined) benefit to be obtained after retirement is calculated based on the value of the contributions made in the last 25 years. Generally, workers contribution to social security amounts to 28.3 per cent (23.3 per cent is assumed by the employer and 4.7 per cent by the employee). It is possible to retire earlier than the official age, though in that case, the pension benefit is penalized with some cuts. It is compulsory to be no more than 2 years younger than the age requirement applicable and a minimum of 35 years of effective contributions, accounting for at least 2 of them within the last 15 years preceding the time becoming eligible. The ordinary retirement pension will be downsized according to reduction coefficients depending on the accredited contribution period and the months in advance of the request for early retirement. Thus, applying for retirement 2 years in advance will bear 21 per cent percentage reduction if the worker has contributed less than 38 years and 6 months, but this percentage falls to 13 per cent if the period contributing to the social security is larger than 44 years and 6 months.

Social Security also admits the option of delayed retirement. The pension reform of 2021 improved the economic and compatibility conditions between pension and work to promote this option. Firstly, delayed retirees will gain an additional 4 per cent on the ordinary amount of the initial pension for each full year worked after the corresponding retirement age. Alternatively, they will receive a lump-sum payment depending on the extension of the work period between the legal and the real retirement date. This lump-sum will also increase in case the contribution period of the retiree exceeds 44 years and 6 months.

Once pensions are determined, when people entitled to that benefit retire, they are updated according to the CPI. Hence, *the Spanish pension system can be deemed a defined benefit-PAYG pension scheme.*

In 2013, the government passed a reform through Act 23/2013, dated December 23, regulating the Sustainability Factor and the Revaluation Index of the Social Security Pension System. Whilst the reform aimed to keep the social security budget balanced, it essentially consisted of two types of cuts behind the term 'sustainability factor'. On the one hand, the so called 'factor de equidad intergeneracional' consisted in reducing benefits on the basis of the expected evolution of the life expectancy at the retirement age: the longer the expectancy, the larger the cut. On the other hand, the 'factor de revalorización anual', which gives us the amount (in percentage points) in which pensions increase, is made to depend on the rate of growth of net revenues of the social security system, keeping contributions untouched. Hence, if the number of contributors times their average contribution grows less than the number of pensioners times their average pension benefit, pensions should not grow in nominal terms.

According to the Reform of 2013, there were a floor and a ceiling for upgrading pensions: the minimum was 0.25 per cent (which would apply in the event that the sustainability factor was lower than that value), and the maximum would be the CPI plus 0.5 per cent. Hence with a negative sustainability factor and CPI above 0.25 per cent, inflation would make the adjustment to keep (in the long-run) the social security budget balanced. *These mechanisms made the Spanish pension system closer to a defined contribution-PAYG scheme.*

This Reform was repealed in 2021 through Act 21/2021, dated December 28. In the new situation, pensions are updated according to CPI, contributions have risen and some incentives have been introduced to delay the retirement age.

4.2. The Situation in 2021

We start from expression (7). The vector $\mathbf{q}_p$ gives us the sectoral output which depends on the pensioners' expenditure on consumer goods, $n \cdot \mathbf{z}$ (note that, in the general case, $n \cdot \mathbf{z}$ is only a fraction of the whole autonomous demand). In our calculations, matrices **K**, **A**, **D**, and vectors **b** and **z** only include domestic output. And scalar g stands for the expected average long-term rate of growth of total output.[12]

Table 2 informs about induced domestic consumption and investment in absolute terms and with respect to total consumption and total investment.[13] A detailed description of how induced consumption has been obtained can be found in the Appendix II. We inform that induced consumption does not include the civil servants' consumption, which is considered autonomous spending.[14] Additionally, regarding induced investment, for some commodities, it is larger than the corresponding figure for total gross capital investment. This is because induced investment includes growing circulating capital as well.

Information about pensioners' consumption $n \cdot \mathbf{z}$ is in Table 3.

Once we obtain $\mathbf{q}_p$ from (7), we can obtain the vectors of sectoral employment, value added, and imports, that depend on pensions[15]:

$$\mathbf{L}_p = \mathbf{a}_n \cdot \hat{\mathbf{q}}_\mathbf{p} \tag{8}$$

$$\mathbf{VA}_p = \mathbf{va} \cdot \hat{\mathbf{q}}_\mathbf{p} \tag{9}$$

$$\mathbf{M}_p = \mathbf{m} \cdot \hat{\mathbf{q}}_\mathbf{p} \tag{10}$$

---

[12] This implies that we ignore any feedback from the rest of the world, in the sense that Spanish imports are exports for the rest of the world that, in turn, could cause some imports from Spain. Spain is a small open economy, and we assume that this feedback is negligible.

[13] Calculations have been made adopting a disaggregation at 64 sectors whilst results are offered for a lower disaggregation (15 sectors).

[14] On this, we follow Serrano and Pimentel 2019; see also Labat and Summa 2023.

[15] The conventional (aggregate) supermultiplier (e.g., expression 8 in Bortis 1997, p. 80) corresponds to expression (9) that can be rewritten as: $\mathbf{VA}_p = \mathbf{va} \cdot [\mathbf{I} - (\mathbf{K^t} + \mathbf{A}) \cdot g - (\mathbf{A} + \mathbf{D}) - \mathbf{b} \cdot \mathbf{a}_n]^{-1} \cdot n \cdot \mathbf{z}$. It measures the incomes generated within the production of all material inputs required to obtain the basket of pensioners' consumer goods. This includes direct output, all circulating inputs, workers' consumer goods, the depreciation of fixed capital and inputs required to expand productive capacity, including fixed and circulating capital. See Dejuán 2023, p. 179.

Table 2. Induced consumption and Investment. Spain, 2021.

A-15		Consumption				Investment		
							Induced investment	
		Total private consumption	Induced consumption	Consumption by pensioners	Consumption by civil servants	Total Investment	$A \cdot g \cdot \mathbf{q}$	$(D + g \cdot K) \cdot \mathbf{q}$
S01	Agriculture, forestry and fishing	7,252.0	4,097.6	1,201.4	1,066.8	2,433.5	817.4	2,104.0
S02	Energy supply, water supply and waste management activities	19,521.9	10,631.9	1,364.1	2,768.0	−35.8	2,265.9	0.0
S03	Food, beverages, tobacco and textiles	30,379.4	17,538.0	4,750.2	4,566.1	1,417.7	2,060.3	0.0
S04	Manufacture	20,250.7	12,983.1	2,376.1	3,380.2	37,343.7	6,162.4	35,132.6
S05	Construction	5,473.2	3,074.6	923.9	800.5	109,306.1	1,306.6	58,058.8
S06	Wholesale and retail trade	104,763.4	63,707.1	14,538.7	16,586.3	17,607.5	2,565.8	0.0
S07	Transport	14,913.5	9,759.6	1,528.6	2,540.9	431.0	2,053.5	0.0
S08	Accommodation and food service activities	71,509.4	48,625.9	6,727.0	12,659.9	0.0	343.1	0.0
S09	Information and communication	18,362.3	11,063.9	2,566.2	2,880.5	20,157.5	1,041.5	0.0
S10	Financial and insurance activities	24,756.8	14,254.7	4,033.9	3,711.2	0.0	1,325.1	0.0
S11	Real estate activities	113,645.2	64,866.0	18,874.6	16,888.0	183.0	927.8	0.0
S12	Professional, scientific and technical activities; administrative and support service activities	11,604.0	8,127.6	961.2	2,116.0	14,350.7	3,300.7	0.0
S13	Public administration, defense and education	15,916.4	12,450.3	422.1	3,241.5	0.0	243.9	0.0
S14	Health services and social work activities	26,996.4	15,972.2	4,129.2	4,158.4	0.0	529.7	0.0
S15	Arts, entertainment and recreation; other service activities; activities of household and extra-territorial organizations and bodies	34,983.1	20,596.5	5,274.1	5,362.4	158.4	486.6	0.0
	Total consumption and investment	**520,327.7**	**317,748.9**	**69,671.2**	**82,726.8**	**203,353.2**	**25,430.3**	**95,295.4**
	% on total private consumption and % on total FBK		**61.1%**	**13.4%**	**15.9%**		**12.5%**	**46.9%**

Note: Monetary values in millions of euros. The vector **q** stands for total output.
Source: Own elaboration.

Table 3. Distribution of Social Security spending on retirement pensions, n · z (2021).

A-15		Consumption profile of Pensioner Households	Pensioners' Expenditure
S01	Agriculture, forestry and fishing	1.72%	1,201.4
S02	Energy supply, water supply and waste management activities	1.96%	1,364.1
S03	Food, beverages, tobacco and textiles	6.82%	4,750.2
S04	Manufacture	3.41%	2,376.1
S05	Construction	1.33%	923.9
S06	Wholesale and retail trade	20.87%	14,538.7
S07	Transport	2.19%	1,528.6
S08	Accommodation and food service activities	9.66%	6,727.0
S09	Information and communication	3.68%	2,566.2
S10	Financial and insurance activities	5.79%	4,033.9
S11	Real estate activities	27.09%	18,874.6
S12	Professional, scientific and technical activities; administrative and support service activities	1.38%	961.2
S13	Public administration, defense and education	0.61%	422.1
S14	Health services and social work activities	5.93%	4,129.2
S15	Arts, entertainment and recreation; other service activities; activities of household and extra-territorial organizations and bodies	7.57%	5,274.1
	Total domestic consumption by pensioners (producer prices)		**69,671.2**
	Total imported consumption by pensioners (producer prices)		9,485.3
	Total pensioners' consumption (producer prices)		**79,156.5**
	Indirect tax on products		9,953.4
	Total pensioners' consumption (purchasing prices)		**89,109.9**
	Direct taxes		8,224.8
	Social Security spending on retirement pensions		**97,334.7**
	Number of retirement pensions (thousands)		**5,931**

Note: Monetary values in million euros.
Source: Own elaboration based on 2021 Household Budget Survey elaborated by INE.

Where **va** and **m** are (row) vectors of value added and imports per unit of output, and symbol ^ denotes a diagonal matrix.

The composition of the pensioners' consumer basket (in Table 3) has been obtained from the Household Budget Survey. For our calculations, we had to subtract direct taxes (€ 8,224.8 million) from paid pensions, and then subtract indirect taxes (€ 9,953.4 million), in order to measure pensioners' consumption spending into producer prices (these are the prices in which Input-Ouput figures are computed). Next, we set aside goods and services purchased by pensioners that are not produced in Spain (€ 9,485.3 million). Hence, when Social Security paid € 97,334.7 million in retirement pensions for those aged 65 or older, the latter spent € 69,671.2 million in consumer goods produced in Spain, valued in producer prices. The largest items in the consumer basket are real estate activities and wholesale and retail trade. Followed by accommodation and food service activities.

Next, we premultiply vector $n \cdot \mathbf{z}$ in Table 2 (the consumption of domestic output by pensioners) by matrix $[\mathbf{I} - (\mathbf{K}^{\mathbf{t}} + \mathbf{A})g - (\mathbf{A} + \mathbf{D}) - \mathbf{b} \cdot \mathbf{a}_n]^{-1}$, as described in expression (7). Matrix **A** is a square (64 × 64) symmetric input-output matrix of domestic intermediate inputs; the last input-output matrix published by Spanish Statistics Agency is for 2015, so we have updated it following the method described in Eurostat (Eurostat 2014).

Matrices **D** and **K**, for depreciation of the stock of fixed capital and fixed capital matrices respectively, have been obtained from information about the net stock of productive fixed capital provided by the Fundación BBVA and IVIE (2023) for 2020 (we have assumed that capital coefficients do not change from 2020 to 2021). Matrix **K** has 8

Table 4. Total Output q_p generated by Social Security spending on retirement pensions (2021).

A-15		Total effect on Output		%Output over Total Output in 2021
S01	Agriculture, forestry and fishing	4,666.6	2.91%	7.33%
S02	Energy supply, water supply and waste management activities	7,142.4	4.46%	5.99%
S03	Food, beverages, tobacco and textiles	13,233.4	8.26%	8.36%
S04	Manufacture	16,246.8	10.14%	3.20%
S05	Construction	7,578.8	4.73%	4.43%
S06	Wholesale and retail trade	24,763.2	15.45%	8.72%
S07	Transport	7,153.2	4.46%	5.68%
S08	Accommodation and food service activities	10,774.5	6.72%	11.70%
S09	Information and communication	5,671.0	3.54%	5.71%
S10	Financial and insurance activities	10,521.4	6.56%	12.34%
S11	Real estate activities	26,090.0	16.28%	17.25%
S12	Professional, scientific and technical activities; administrative and support service activities	9,963.5	6.22%	5.32%
S13	Public administration, defense and education	1,892.1	1.18%	1.13%
S14	Health services and social work activities	6,510.3	4.06%	5.09%
S15	Arts, entertainment and recreation; other service activities; activities of household and extra-territorial organizations and bodies	8,059.7	5.03%	11.24%
	Total Output generated by spending on retirement pensions	**160,266.8**	**100.00%**	**6.65%**

Note: Monetary values (producer prices) in million euros.
Source: Own elaboration.

types of fixed capital goods; matrix **D** is calculated by dividing each fixed capital good in matrix **K** by its useful lifetime (this information has been taken from the Spanish Tax Agency). Row vector **b** has been estimated using information from the Household Budget Survey. It includes only domestic goods and services. All consumption funded with wages and mixed-income has been assumed endogenous.[16] Finally, we have assumed $g = 2.5$ per cent.

Vector $\mathbf{q}_p$ of total output needed to produce the pensioners' consumption basket is in Table 4.

Pensioners' expenditure is *responsible* for a little more than 6.6 per cent of total output: at the sectoral level, 17.2 per cent of total real estate activities, 11.2 per cent of arts, entertainment and recreation, 11.7 per cent of accommodation and food services, 12.3 per cent of financial and insurance activities, and 8.7 per cent of trade (wholesale and retail).

Regarding total employment, as measured in expression (8), results are provided in Table 5. Total employment, that is direct, indirect and induced employment in the production of the final deliveries demanded by 5,931 thousand pensioners is 1,222.9 thousand full-time equivalent units, almost 6.7 per cent of total employment (in full-time equivalent units). This is especially relevant in sectors like arts, entertainment and recreation (14.1 per cent of total employment), financial and insurance, real estate activities, and accommodation and food services (around 12 per cent). According to our calculations one full-time equivalent unit of work produces the consumer basket of roughly 4.85 retired pensioners, or alternatively, one retired pensioner puts in motion 0.21 full time working units.

[16]Contrary to what is usual in the literature (e.g., Freitas and Dweck 2013; Pariboni 2016), in our empirical research we have not distinguished between autonomous and induced consumption and, therefore, all household consumption of durable goods is considered induced. We believe that when considering the effects on output, employment and value added of pensioner's expenditure, which does not vary so much in the short run, durable goods can be considered induced expenditure: if induced income is stable, indebtedness related to income should also be stable.

Table 5. Employment sustained by Social Security spending on retirement pensions (2021)

A-15		Direct Effect	Indirect effect	Induced effect	Total Effect		%Total effect over Total Lequiv in 2021
S01	Agriculture, forestry and fishing	13,630.5	27,679.6	10,858.0	52,168.1	4.27%	7.38%
S02	Energy supply, water supply and waste management activities	7,225.8	6,581.4	3,399.9	17,207.1	1.41%	7.33%
S03	Food, beverages, tobacco and textiles	14,819.2	17,255.0	9,275.4	41,349.6	3.38%	8.20%
S04	Manufacture	5,115.6	28,790.2	10,324.1	44,229.8	3.62%	3.28%
S05	Construction	7,099.6	38,324.1	12,815.3	58,239.0	4.76%	4.43%
S06	Wholesale and retail trade	172,058.6	46,734.0	62,458.0	281,250.6	23.00%	9.44%
S07	Transport	11,415.8	25,192.3	12,507.5	49,115.6	4.02%	6.08%
S08	Accommodation and food service activities	89,650.0	8,454.4	45,485.3	143,589.8	11.74%	11.70%
S09	Information and communication	5,415.0	6,578.6	3,720.4	15,714.1	1.28%	2.86%
S10	Financial and insurance activities	16,326.2	20,403.3	9,041.3	45,770.8	3.74%	12.07%
S11	Real estate activities	11,272.5	9,752.7	5,018.0	26,043.2	2.13%	11.95%
S12	Professional, scientific and technical activities; administrative and support service activities	6,811.2	96,180.1	31,468.5	134,459.8	10.99%	5.54%
S13	Public administration, defense and education	6,729.1	8,062.4	15,210.2	30,001.7	2.45%	1.11%
S14	Health services and social work activities	55,079.2	10,944.8	16,571.6	82,595.5	6.75%	5.40%
S15	Arts, entertainment and recreation; other service activities; activities of household and extra-territorial organizations and bodies	146,190.4	17,064.7	37,934.5	201,189.5	16.45%	14.13%
	Total number of jobs	**568,838.6**	**367,997.4**	**286,088.0**	**1,222,924.0**	**100.00%**	**6.66%**

Source: Own elaboration.
Note: Employment measured in number of equivalent jobs.

With respect to the impact of pensioners' spending on value added (expression 4.2), this can be seen in Table 6. Total pensioners' expenditure (total pensions after direct taxes) at producer prices, which amounts to € 79,156.5 million, leads to the generation of an amount of value added (at producer prices) of € 82,313.7 million (it should be noted that only € 69,671.2 million are spent on final domestic goods and services). Hence, we have a multiplier effect of pensions on value added of 1.04.

Finally, an interesting result is that when the government pays € 97,334.7 million in pensions, it ends up recovering € 40,711.5 million in taxes, which means a rate of return of 41.8 per cent. This payback is made through four channels (further explained in appendix II). The first channel would be the direct taxes on income that both pensioners (€ 8,224.8 million) and employees involved in production to meet pensioners' consumption (€ 10,765.6 million) pay to the Government. The second channel involves the net taxes on production from the increase in the level of industrial output sustained by pensioner consumption (€ 2,140.1 million). This increase in production includes all the direct, indirect, and induced impacts previously defined. The third channel comprises

Table 6. Distribution of Income generated by Social Security spending on retirement pensions (2021).

A-15		Total effect on Value Added		%Value Added over Total Value Added in 2021
S01	Agriculture, forestry and fishing	2,306.0	2.80%	7.32%
S02	Energy supply, water supply and waste management activities	2,733.8	3.32%	5.99%
S03	Food, beverages, tobacco and textiles	2,833.4	3.44%	8.18%
S04	Manufacture	3,313.9	4.03%	3.17%
S05	Construction	2,695.0	3.27%	4.43%
S06	Wholesale and retail trade	13,274.6	16.13%	8.91%
S07	Transport	2,493.0	3.03%	5.78%
S08	Accommodation and food service activities	5,621.7	6.83%	11.70%
S09	Information and communication	2,424.1	2.94%	5.61%
S10	Financial and insurance activities	5,454.3	6.63%	11.75%
S11	Real estate activities	22,618.4	27.48%	17.42%
S12	Professional, scientific and technical activities; administrative and support service activities	5,250.1	6.38%	5.30%
S13	Public administration, defense and education	1,574.1	1.91%	1.20%
S14	Health services and social work activities	4,022.0	4.89%	5.11%
S15	Arts, entertainment and recreation; other service activities; activities of household and extra-territorial organizations and bodies	5,699.4	6.92%	12.61%
	Total Value Added generated by spending on retirement pensions	**82,313.7**	**100.00%**	**7.55%**
	Wages	25,666.9	31.18%	
	Payroll taxes	7,777.2	9.45%	
	GOS + mixed income	46,729.5	56.77%	
	Net taxes on production	2,140.1	2.60%	
	Intermediate consumption	62,906.7		
	Indirect tax on products	2,140.1		
	Imports	13,195.9		
	Total Output generated by spending on retirement pensions	**160,266.8**		

Note: Monetary values in million euros.
Source: Own elaboration. N.B. Total Value Added plus intermediate consumption, indirect tax on products and imports yields total output generated by pensions.

the payroll taxes transferred from households to the Government derived from the total wages sustained by pensioners' consumption (€ 7,777.2 million). Lastly, the fourth channel accounts for the indirect tax on goods and services initially purchased by pensioner households (€ 9,953.4 million) plus indirect tax on goods and services derived from the indirect and induced effects on production to meet pensioners' consumption (€ 1,850.5 million). This is detailed in Appendix I.

4.3. Pensions, Output and Employment in Spain in 2050

The demographic projection of people aged 65 or older, and the number of retired pensioners in Spain over 2023–72 is shown in Figure 6.

The rate of growth of the number of retired pensioners lies between 2 per cent and 3 per cent until 2045[17] (in 2022, retired pensioners amounted to 62 per cent of total population aged 65 or more, and that percentage is expected to rise to 75 per cent in 2072 due

[17]Assuming that pensioners expenditure is roughly 20 per cent of autonomous demand, *ceteris paribus*, the contribution of public transfers to the growth of output in the next 20 years would be compatible with the results obtained by Labat and Summa from 1998 to 2019, Labat and Summa, 2023, p. 8, Table 3.

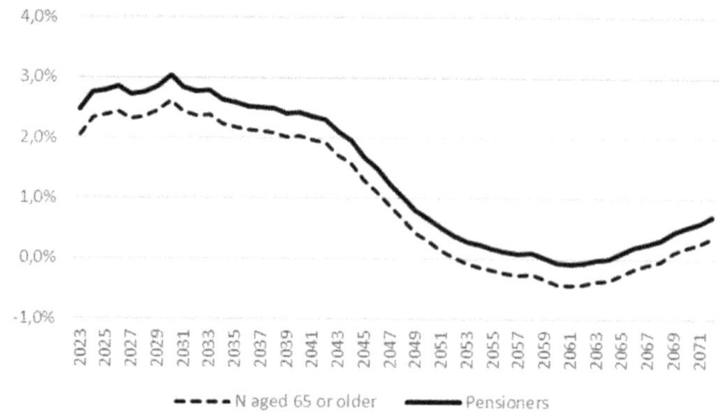

Figure 6. People aged 65 or older and retired persons. Spain 2023–72. Rate of growth. Source: INE (Spanish Statistical Agency) and own elaboration.

to a falling rate of unemployment and the increasing participation of women in the labor market).[18]

In 2050, it is expected that the number of retired pensioners will amount to 11,147 thousand people, almost 90 per cent more than in 2021, and 70 per cent of total population aged 65 or older. Under present circumstances (the same technology, income distribution, pension benefits *et cetera* as in 2021), could the Spanish economy be able to bear the burden of 5.2 additional retired pensioners in 2050 without cutting benefits? This challenge is double: does the Spanish economy count with sufficient labor force to produce the goods demanded by the additional pensioners? And is the additional social security expenditure financially sustainable?

The answer to the first question depends on the answer to the second one. In principle, if the benefit per pensioner remains constant, the cost of paying pensions to the additional retirees in 2050 would amount to € 85,598.3 million, which in turn, after discounting taxes, would generate € 71,978.6 million in value added. The latter can be split into € 22,438.3 million in wages, € 6,797.8 million in payroll taxes, € 40,869.7 million in gross operating surplus plus mixed income, plus € 1,872.9 million in net taxes on production. Further, the additional production depending on pensioners' consumption would require 1,069.1 thousand additional jobs. The payment of pensions would cause a fiscal return of € 35,689.1 million, which would reduce the initial Social Security deficit to € 49,909.2 million. If this deficit is offset with taxes on benefits, the ones to be taxed not only involve the GOS + mixed income due to the increase in consumption by the additional pensioners in 2050 (€ 40,869.7 million) but also € 46,729.5 million in GOS + mixed income generated by pensioners' consumption in 2021. Thus, a 57 per cent tax rate on benefits would be needed to compensate the Social Security deficit.

[18] As it is well known, when the rate of growth of GDP is above the interest rate, public debt is sustainable (see for instance Morlin 2022, pp. 589–590, expressions 23 and 25; Woodgate et al. 2023, pp. 6–7, expressions 17 and 18). In our subsystem, the rate of growth of autonomous demand is given by the pensioners' expenditure that is assumed to grow in proportion to the number of retired people. Hence, public indebtedness due to pension spending should remain sustainable if the rate of interest on public debt remains below the rate of growth of autonomous demand.

Alternatively, we can keep tax rates unchanged. In that case, another component of autonomous demand should grow *pari passu* with pensions, causing output to grow even more, and with it tax revenues, so that the Social Security budget remains balanced. We have considered exports (autonomous investment for the modernization of productive capacity, related for instance to renewable energies could have been considered as an alternative to exports). The outlays corresponding to additional pensioners can be offset by revenues from taxing € 253,392.4 million value added. This additional value added can be generated (expression 4.9 above) if, besides additional pensioners' consumption, exports increase by € 190,013.3 million. In that situation the number of full-time equivalent labor units should rise by 4,031 thousand units.

Is the required volume of employment in this situation feasible? We think so. Creating 4,03 million additional jobs in the next nearly 30 years seems a very large number, though in 2050, according to official demographic projections by the Spanish Statistics Agency (INE) and the European Commission's hypotheses on the labor market (EC 2021), there will be around 7.3 million people aged between 16 and 64 without a job (inactive and unemployed people). Employment should grow from 2022 to 2050 at a rate of 0.68 per cent (we inform that employment grew at 1.08 per cent from 1980 to 2022). If the rate of unemployment in 2050 is 4 per cent, there will be 941.5 thousand people unemployed, so immigration seems to be necessary to cover the gap. And the required rate of growth of pensions plus exports is 0.75 per cent, something that history shows that it is achievable (the rate of growth of exports, on average, between 2001 and 2019 has been higher than 3 per cent).

5. Conclusions

PAYG pensions are a component of autonomous demand in the Sraffian supermultiplier, and as such they can be seen as an engine of growth. In Spain, in 2021, pensions paid to people aged 65 or more amounted to a little more than 8 per cent of GDP, and they demanded goods and services for around 6.7 per cent of total production. 5,9 million pensioners put in motion more than 1,2 million full-time equivalent workers (roughly 7 per cent of the labor supply). For each euro spent in pensions, the government recovered 42 cents in taxes, so when the government pays public pensions for € 97.3 billion it recovers € 40.7 billion.

These figures make us believe that a PAYG pension scheme will be viable in the future: if in 2050, retired pension beneficiaries increase from 5.9 to 11.1 million people, their expenditure will put in motion almost 2,3 million full-time equivalent workers. To have a balanced social security budget, the tax rate on profits should be 57 per cent. Alternatively, if exports (a component of autonomous demand) increase by 190 thousand million euros, the social security budget would remain balanced without changing taxes. In this case, the amount of labor required to produce that final demand should have to increase by more than 4 million full-time equivalent jobs. These are large figures, but the annual rates of growth required to reach them are below historical ones.

All-in-all, it is quite likely that a large percentage of this labor force will have a non-resident origin and that this will come with a decline in the outstanding reserve army so profits might decline. These two factors will make it difficult for pensions to act as a locomotive for the economy, though not impossible.

Acknowledgements

We would like to use this opportunity to acknowledge and thank the reviewers who reviewed this article and aided in its publication.

Disclosure Statement

No potential conflict of interest was reported by the author(s).

ORCID

Eladio Febrero http://orcid.org/0000-0002-0722-9487
Fernando Bermejo http://orcid.org/0000-0003-0792-5674

References

Barbieri Góes, M. 2022. 'An Analysis of the Patterns of Economic Growth in US: Autonomous Demand Components, and Their Divergent Multipliers.' Paper presented at the 26th FMM conference, Berlin.

Bastos, C., and G. Porto. 2016. 'Decomposing the Growth of Portugal: A Case for Increasing Demand, Not Austerity, in a Small European Economy.' Instituto de Economia UFRJ, Working Paper No. 34.

Bermejo, F., E. Febrero, and A. F. T. Avelino. 2020. 'Socioeconomic Effects of Pension Spending: Evidence from Spain.' *International Journal of Social Economics* 47 (5): 599–617.

Bindseil, U. 2004. *Monetary Policy Implementation. Theory, Past and Present*. Oxford: Oxford University Press.

Blanchard, O. 2022. *Fiscal Policy Under Low Interest Rates*. Cambridge, MA: The MIT Press.

Bortis, H. 1997. *Insitutions, Behavior and Economic Theory. A Contribution to Classical-Keynesian Political Economy*. Cambridge: Cambridge University Press.

Carnazza, G., C. Fontanari, P. Liberati, and A. Palumbo. 2023. 'From Potential GDP to Structural Balance: A Theoretical Reassessment and New Evidence for Italy.' *Review of Political Economy* 35 (2): 510–540.

Cesaratto, S. 2005. *Pension Reform and Economic Theory: A Non-Orthodox Analysis*. Cheltenham: Edward Elgar.

Cesaratto, S. 2017. 'Initial and Final Finance in the Monetary Circuit and the Theory of Effective Demand.' *Metroeconomica* 68 (2): 228–258.

Cesaratto, S. 2021. *Seis Lecciones de Economía, Vilassar de Mar*. Barcelona: El Viejo Topo.

Cesaratto, S., and S. Di Bucchianico. 2020. 'Endogenous Money and the Theory of Long-Period Effective Demand.' *Bulletin of Political Economy* 14 (1): 1–38.

Cesaratto, S., and R. Pariboni. 2022. 'The Relation Between Keynesian Monetary Theory and Demand-led Growth: A Sraffian Exploration.' *Review of Keynesian Economics* 10 (3): 291–315.

Cesaratto, S., F. Serrano, and A. Stirati. 2003. 'Technical Change, Effective Demand and Employment.' *Review of Political Economy* 15 (1): 33–52.

Cohen, A., and G. C. Harcourt. 2003. 'Retrospectives Whatever Happened to the Cambridge Capital Theory Controversies?' *Journal of Economic Perspectives* 17 (1): 199–214.

Davidson. 1986. 'Finance, Funding, Saving and Investment.' *Journal of Post Keynesian Economics* 9 (1): 101–110.

Dejuán, Ó. 2005. 'Paths of Accumulation and Growth: Towards a Keynesian Long-Period Theory of Output.' *Review of Political Economy* 17 (2): 231–252.

Dejuán, Ó. 2007. 'The Conventional Versus the Natural Rate of Interest: Implications for Central Bank Autonomy.' *Journal of Post Keynesian Economics* 29 (4): 645–666.

Dejuán, Ó. 2023. *The Supermultiplier. A Cornerstone of the New Macroeconomics*. Cheltenham: Edward Elgar.

Dejuán, Ó., F. Portella-Carbó, and M. Ortiz. 2020. 'Economic and Environmental Impacts of Decarbonisation Through a Hybrid MRIO Multiplier-Accelerator Model.' *Economic Systems Research* 34 (1): 1–21. Published online 27 Nov 2020.
Eatwell, J., and M. Milgate. 1983. 'Introduction.' In *Keynes's Economics and the Theory of Value and Distribution*, edited by J. Eatwell, and M. Milgate. London: Duckworth.
Ehnts, D. 2020. 'The Fiscal-Monetary Nexus in Germany.' Institute for International Political Economy Berlin, Working Paper 138/2020.
European Commission. 2020. *The 2021 Ageing Report. Underlying Assumptions and Projection Methodologies.* European Economy, Economic and Financial Affairs, Institutional Paper 142, November.
European Commission. 2021. *The 2021 Ageing Report. Economic and Budgetary Projections for the EU Member States (2019-2070).* European Economy, Economic and Financial Affairs, Institutional Paper, 148, May.
Eurostat. 2014. *Eurostat Manual of Supply, Use and Input-Output Tables.* Luxemburg: Office for Official Publications of the European Communities.
Febrero, E. 2008. 'The Monetization of Profits in a Monetary Circuit Framework.' *Review of Political Economy* 20 (1): 111–125.
Feldstein, M. 1974. 'Social Security, Induced Retirement, and Aggregate Capital Accumulation.' *Journal of Political Economy* 82: 905–926.
Freitas, F., and E. Dweck. 2013. 'The Pattern of Economic Growth of the Brazilian Economy 1970–2005: A Demand-Led Growth Perspective.' In *Sraffa and the Reconstruction of Economic Theory: Volume Two*, edited by E. S. Levrero, A. Palumbo, and A. Stirati. Basingstoke: Palgrave Macmillan.
Freitas, F., and F. Serrano. 2015. 'Growth Rate and Level Effects, the Stability of the Adjustment of Capacity to Demand and the Sraffian Supermultiplier.' *Review of Political Economy* 27 (3): 258–281.
Fundación BBVA and IVIE (Instituto Valenciano de Investigaciones Económicas). 2023. 'El stock y los servicios del capital en España y su distribución territorial y sectorial', València, March. https://www.fbbva.es/bd/el-stock-y-los-servicios-del-capital-en-espana/.
Ghilarducci, T., J. Saad-Lessler, and E. Fisher. 2012. 'The Macroeconomic Stabilisation Effects of Social Security and 401(k) Plans.' *Cambridge Journal of Economics* 36: 237–251.
Graziani, A. 2003. *The Monetary Theory of Production.* Cambridge: Cambridge University Press.
Haluska, G., J. Braga, and R. Summa. 2021. 'Growth, Investment Share and the Stability of the Sraffian Supermultiplier in the US Economy (1985-2017).' *Metroeconomica* 72 (2): 345–364.
Hicks, J. R. 1950. *A Contribution to the Theory of the Trade Cycle.* Oxford: The Clarendon Press.
Kalecki, M. 1943. 'Political Aspects of Full Employment.' *The Political Quarterly* 14 (4): 322–330.
Labat, H., and R. Summa. 2023. 'A Supermultiplier Demand-Led Growth Accounting Analysis Applied to the Spanish Economy (1998-2019).' *European Journal of Economics and Economic Policies: Intervention* 21 (1): 1–30.
Lavoie, M. 2022. 'MMT, Sovereign Currencies and the Eurozone.' *Review of Political Economy* 34 (4): 633–646.
Miller, R. E., and P. D. Blair. 2009. *Input-output Analysis: Foundations and Extensions.* Cambridge: Cambridge University Press.
Morlin, G. 2022. 'Growth Led by Government Expenditure and Exports: Public and External Debt Stability in a Supermultiplier Model.' *Structural Change and Economic Dynamics* 62: 586–598.
Nell, E. J. 1998. *The General Theory of Transformational Growth. Keynes After Sraffa.* Cambridge: Cambridge University Press.
Nell, E. J. 2002. 'On Realizing Profits in Money.' *Review of Political Economy* 14 (4): 519–530.
Pariboni, R. 2016. 'Household Consumer Debt, Endogenous Money and Growth: A Supermultiplier-Based Analysis.' *PSL Quarterly Review* 69 (278): 211–233.
Pasinetti, L. L. 1988. 'Growing Subsystems, Vertically Hyperintegrated Sectors and the Labour Theory of Value.' *Cambridge Journal of Economics* 12: 125–134.
Passos, N., and G. Morlin. 2022. 'Growth Models and Comparative Political Economy in Latin America.' *Revue de la Régulation* 33 (2nd semester): 1–23.

Pivetti, M. 2006. 'The 'Principle of Scarcity', Pension Policy and Growth.' *Review of Political Economy* 18 (3): 379–390.
Rochon, L. P. 2005. 'The Existence of Monetary Profits Within the Monetary Circuit.' In *The Monetary Theory of Production. Tradition and Perspectives*, edited by G. Fontana, and R. Realfonzo. New York: Palgrave Macmillan.
Sawyer, M. 2021. 'Keep Calm and Carry On: Responding to Higher Public Debt After the Pandemic.' *Academia Letters*, Article 276.
Serrano, F. 1995. 'Long Period Effective Demand and the Sraffian Supermultiplier.' *Contributions to Political Economy* 14 (1): 67–90.
Serrano, F., and K. Pimentel. 2019. 'Super Haavelmo: Balanced and Unbalanced Budget Theorems and the Sraffian Supermultiplier.' Paper presented at the Second Workshop on Demand-led Growth, Rio de Janeiro, Brazil.
Sraffa, P. 1960. *Production of Commodities by Means of Commodities.* Cambridge: Cambridge University Press.
Woodgate, R., E. Hein, and R. Summa. 2023. 'Components of Autonomous Demand Growth and Financial Feedbacks: Implications for Growth Drivers and Growth Regime Analysis.' Post-Keynesian Economics Society, Working paper 2307, May.
World Bank. 1994. *Averting the Old Age Crisis and Promote Growth.* New York: Oxford University Press.
Wray, L. R. 1990–91. 'Can the Social Security Trust Fund Contribute to Savings?' *Journal of Post Keynesian Economics* 13 (2): 155–170.
Wray, L. R. 2005. 'Social Security's 70th Anniversary: Surviving 20 Years of Reform.' *The Levy Institute of Bard College*, Policy Note 2005/6.
Wray, L. R. 2022. *Making Money Work for Us. How MMT Can Save America.* Cambridge: Polity Press.

Appendices

Appendix I: Fiscal return on pensioners' consumption

When the government pays 97,334.7 € million in pensions, it ends up recovering 41.8 per cent in taxes (40,711.5 € million) through the channels as described in Figure A.I.1:

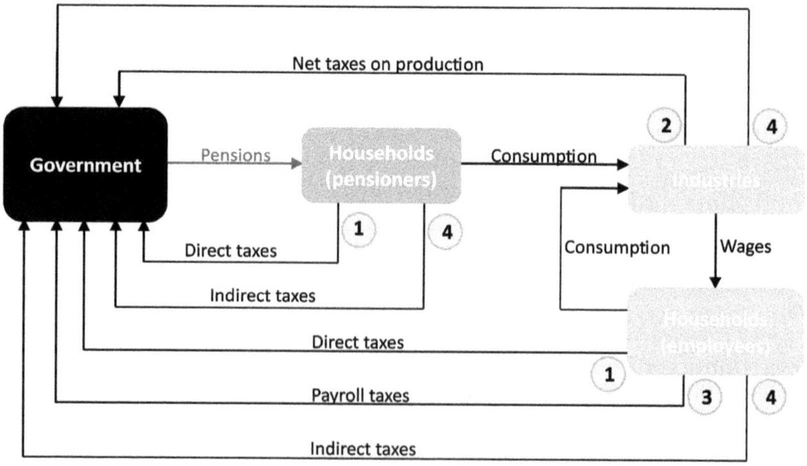

Figure A. I.1.#Fiscal return derived from Social Security spending on retirement pensions. Source: Own elaboration.

- **Channel 1 – Direct taxes on income**

- By pensioners (8,224.8 million euros): 8.45 per cent effective income tax rate for pensioners applied to total pension benefits (97,334.7 million euros). The effective income tax rate has been obtained from Tax Agency records.
- By workers (10,765.6 million euros): 13.43 per cent effective income tax rate on both wages (33,44.1 million euros) and GOS + mixed-income (46,729.5 million euros) sustained by pensioner consumption.

$$\text{effective income tax rate} = \frac{\text{income tax}_{2021}}{\text{wages}_{2021} + (\text{GOS} + \text{mixed income})_{2021}} = \frac{145{,}636}{588{,}325 + 496{,}252}$$

The income tax, wages and GOS + mixed-income for the Spanish economy in 2021 has been obtained from National Accounting by INE.

- **Channel 2 – Net taxes on production**

This is one of the components in the value added generated from the output sustained by pensioners' consumption.

$$\text{NTOP}_\text{p} = \text{NTOP}_\text{d} \cdot \text{q}_\text{p} \quad \text{NTOP}_\text{d} = \text{diag}\left(\frac{\text{NTOP}_{2021}}{\text{q}_{2021}}\right)$$

Where $NTOP_d$ is a diagonalized matrix of coefficients by sector resulting from dividing the (row) vector of sectoral net taxes on production $NTOP_{2021}$ by the total sectoral output q_{2021} for the Spanish economy in 2021.

Both values of net taxes on production and output were obtained from the National Accounting by INE.

- **Channel 3 – Payroll taxes**

As the previous one, this is one of the components in the value added generated from the output sustained by pensioners' consumption.

$$\text{CCSS}_\text{p} = \text{CCSS}_\text{d} \cdot \text{q}_\text{p} \quad \text{CCSS}_\text{d} = \text{diag}\left(\frac{\text{CCSS}_{2021}}{\text{q}_{2021}}\right)$$

Where $CCSS_d$ is a diagonalized matrix of coefficients by sector resulting from dividing the (row) vector of sectoral payroll taxes $CCSS_{2021}$ by the total sectoral output q_{2021} for the Spanish economy in 2021.

Both values of payroll taxes and output were obtained from the National Accounting by INE.

- **Channel 4 – Indirect taxes**

- By pensioners (9,953.4 million euros): 14.3 per cent effective indirect tax rate on domestic consumption by pensioners (69,671.2 million euros).

$$\text{effective indirect tax rate} = \frac{\text{indirect tax}_{2021}}{\text{Domestic household consumption}_{2021}} = \frac{74,\,335}{520,\,327.7}$$

The indirect tax on products and household consumption for the Spanish economy in 2021 has been obtained from National Accounting by INE.

The income tax, wages and GOS + mixed-income for the Spanish economy in 2021 has been obtained from National Accounting by INE

- By workers and industries (1,850.5 million euros): indirect tax on goods and services derived from the indirect and induced effects on production to meet pensioners' consumption.

$$\mathrm{IndTax_p} = \mathrm{IndTax_d} \cdot \mathrm{q_p} \qquad \mathrm{IndTax_d} = \mathrm{diag}\left(\frac{\mathrm{IndTax_{2021}}}{\mathrm{q_{2021}}}\right)$$

Where IndTax_d is a diagonalized matrix of coefficients by sector resulting from dividing the (row) vector of sectoral indirect tax on products $\mathrm{IndTax_{2021}}$ by the total sectoral output $\mathrm{q_{2021}}$ for the Spanish economy in 2021.

Both values of indirect tax on products and output were obtained from the National Accounting by INE.

Appendix II: Estimation of Workers' Induced Consumption

Based on the traditional IO methodology, an increase in exogenous consumption $\mathbf{c_p}$ not only causes a proportional gain in gross output (direct impact), but it is also transmitted to the production system where inter-industrial backward linkages generate a multiplicative effect (indirect impact). Such a multiplicative effect arises from the need of all industrial sectors to be provided with the inputs required in their productive processes. Besides industrial inputs, the economic sectors also demand the additional labor required in the production process resulting from the direct and indirect impacts above described, increasing the total wage in the economy. This rise in income is then spent by the households of workers, generating a second round of induced consumption shocks that increase total output $\mathbf{q_p}$. The (column) vector of workers' induced consumption in such second round is determined as follows:

$$\mathbf{B} = \mathbf{b} \cdot \mathbf{a_n} \cdot \mathbf{q_p}$$

where:

- **b** is the basket of consumer goods purchased by a worker during the production process. This is made up by the (column) vector of consumption propensities for the households where the reference person is employed and the vector of income allocated to the workers' consumption profile.
  - The consumption profile for employed households has been collected from the microdata of the Household Budget Survey (HBS) that is carried out yearly by the Spanish Statistics Institute. This database provides information on the amount and structure of household expenditure based on the COICOP (Classification of Individual Consumption by Purpose). The HBS also contains socioeconomic records about the standard of living, such as income and the professional activity of the household reference person. Thus, by defining specific data filters, we have obtained the composition of the consumption basket for those households where the reference person is employed.

Two important requirements have been considered:

- VAT and trade taxes were deducted from the purchasing prices of goods and services, as long as the exogenous demand must be accounted in producer prices to make it compatible with IO tables.
- Given that HBS data refers to expenditure on goods and services according to the COICOP classification, it has been necessary, therefore, to allocate these commodities to the industrial sectoring scheme adopted by the IO table. This means considering households' consumption by economic sector instead of by products. To our knowledge, there is not an official correspondence between the HBS and the IO tables. Thus, to provide comparable results between consumption purposes and sectoral production, the HBS data were merged according to the standard ISIC (rev. 4) aggregation.

- The vector of income allocated to the workers' consumption profile is mainly based on sectoral wages plus mixed-income. Nevertheless, some additional adjustments need to be made before applying that primary income to the workers' consumption profile. The first modification results from withdrawing payroll taxes plus direct taxes to sectoral wages plus mixed-income in order to obtain the disposable income of worker households. Secondly, savings of worker households have been deducted from the disposable income assuming the same saving rate for the private sector in the Spanish National Accounts for 2021. Finally, imports and indirect taxes have been extracted from total consumption to obtain the (column) vector of consumption domestically produced in producer prices.

Wages, mixed-income, savings of the private sector and the sectoral level of production have been obtained from National Accounting records published by INE.

- $\mathbf{a_n}$ is the (row) vector of direct labor requirements per unit of output $\mathbf{q}$ by sector.
- $\mathbf{q_p}$ is the (column) vector of total output generated by pensioners' consumption.

In view of the above, the consumption by workers needs to be considered endogenous to the extent that it depends on the level of output $\mathbf{q_p}$ that is caused by the initial pensioner consumption shock. Thus, the consumption by workers is simultaneously estimated with output $\mathbf{q_p}$ by extracting $\mathbf{b} \cdot \mathbf{a_n}$ from the exogenous final demand and transferring it to the extended Leontief inverse matrix. This information is encapsulated in Table A.II.1.

Table A.II.1. Induced consumption generated by Social Security spending on retirement pensions (2021).

A-15		$\mathbf{B} = \mathbf{b} \cdot \mathbf{a_n} \cdot \mathbf{q_p}$		% induced consumption over Total consumption in 2021
S01	Agriculture, forestry and fishing	265.0	1.29%	3.65%
S02	Energy supply, water supply and waste management activities	687.6	3.35%	3.52%
S03	Food, beverages, tobacco and textiles	1,134.3	5.52%	3.73%
S04	Manufacture	839.7	4.09%	4.15%
S05	Construction	198.9	0.97%	3.63%
S06	Wholesale and retail trade	4,120.4	20.05%	3.93%
S07	Transport	631.2	3.07%	4.23%
S08	Accommodation and food service activities	3,145.0	15.30%	4.40%
S09	Information and communication	715.6	3.48%	3.90%
S10	Financial and insurance activities	922.0	4.49%	3.72%
S11	Real estate activities	4,195.4	20.41%	3.69%
S12	Professional, scientific and technical activities; administrative and support service activities	525.7	2.56%	4.53%
S13	Public administration, defense and education	805.3	3.92%	5.06%
S14	Health services and social work activities	1,033.0	5.03%	3.83%
S15	Arts, entertainment and recreation; other service activities; activities of household and extra-territorial organizations and bodies	1,332.1	6.48%	3.81%
	Total induced consumption generated by spending on retirement pensions	**20,551.1**	**100.00%**	**3.95%**

Note: Monetary values in million euros.
Source: Own elaboration.

Components of Autonomous Demand Growth and Financial Feedbacks: Implications for Growth Drivers and Growth Regime Analysis

Ryan Woodgate, Eckhard Hein and Ricardo Summa

ABSTRACT

This paper presents a simple closed-economy model that is driven by the growth of two autonomous components of demand, namely government spending and rentiers' consumption out of interest income. Using this model, it seeks to make two contributions. First, by focusing on the financial dynamics that arise from debt-financed government spending, we show that an underlying stock-flow interaction provides an endogenous mechanism which, under certain conditions, aligns the two autonomous growth rates in the long run. Hence, an economy can be driven by two autonomous components of demand, without one dominating the other in the long-run nor without policy changes being required to align the two growth drivers. Second, we prove that if two autonomous demand components are dynamically interdependent, then the relative size of their growth contributions may be misleading as a guide to classify growth regimes, both in the long-run equilibrium as well as during the traverse towards this equilibrium. Furthermore, we show that the relative growth contributions are economic policy contingent. We thus argue that interdependencies between autonomous growth components arising from financial stock-flow interactions should not be ignored in Sraffian supermultiplier growth decomposition exercises that aim to identify underlying growth drivers.

1. Introduction

Initial versions of Sraffian supermultiplier (SSM) autonomous demand-led growth models (Serrano 1995; Freitas and Serrano 2015, 2017) have paid little attention to the monetary and financial requirements and implications of these models. However, as recently pointed out again by Cesaratto and Di Bucchianico (2020) and Cesaratto and Pariboni (2022), the growth of autonomous demand, which by definition is independent of current production, needs to be financed by sources other than income from current production. This necessarily implies the endogenous generation of means of finance, and hence endogenous money and credit, as it has been developed in post-Keynesian monetary theory (Lavoie 2022, ch. 4; Hein 2023a, ch.3). According to Cesaratto and Di Bucchianico (2020, 3–4), two implications arise from this:[1]

> 'From a theoretical point of view, it creates a natural field of convergence between the endogenous money literature and the Sraffian supermultiplier approach. From a substantial point of view, inclusion of the financial side leads us to regard autonomous demand-led as prone to financial crisis due to excess indebtedness, for instance, of households or of peripheral countries (...).'

Starting with Pariboni (2016), the debt dynamics associated with financing autonomous demand have been explored and the long-run stability conditions for autonomous demand-led growth have recently been examined in Freitas and Christianes (2020), Hein and Woodgate (2021), Morlin (2022), and Vieira Mandarino, Dos Santos, and Macedo e Silva (2020), for example.

Morlin (2022) has explicitly focussed on the discussion of two autonomous growth drivers, government spending and exports. As is well known in the autonomous-demand led growth literature, two or more components of autonomous demand require that these components will have to grow at same rate in the long run, if each of them is meant to contribute to growth in long run equilibrium (Allain 2022). Otherwise, the share of the driver(s) with the lower growth rate(s) will converge towards zero. In Morlin (2022), the two autonomous growth drivers, exports and government expenditures, are considered to be independent of each other. The adjustment then takes place via a balance of payments constraint, towards which government policies respond, in order to prevent over-indebtedness, financial fragility and, finally, financial crises. Either governments reduce their expenditure growth or/and they apply industrial policies in order to increase the income elasticities of export (and reduce those of imports). In his general and abstract analysis of two (or more) autonomous growth rates, Allain (2022) discusses three options for their convergence: (1) one (seemingly) autonomous parts still contains an induced element which make it converge to the growth rate of the truly autonomous component, (2) discretionary decisions adjust one rate to the other, (3) changing financial conditions and financial constraints enforce an adjustment through policy change, similar to Morlin's (2022) arguments.[2]

We do not deny the actual and potential relevance of such mechanisms. However, in this paper, we will argue that the explicit inclusion of credit and finance into autonomous demand-led growth models already generates a mechanism, which may align two (or more) autonomous growth rates to each other, under certain conditions. Endogenous credit and finance associated with autonomous demand growth, generate (changes of) financial assets and liabilities, as well as future income flows related to these financial

---

[1] See Cesaratto (2017), Cesaratto and Di Bucchianico (2020), and Cesaratto and Pariboni (2022) for detailed accounts of the close relationship between autonomous demand-led growth and post-Keynesian monetary circuit and endogenous money theory. In this context, Cesaratto and Pariboni (2022, 306) also point out the close relationship of Sraffian supermultiplier models with Kalecki's notion that external markets created by government deficits and export surpluses are drivers of growth: 'The autonomous components of aggregate demand, which in the supermultiplier model drive growth and coincide with Kalecki-Luxemburg's external markets, can be financed by purchasing power creation by banks, by accumulated wealth or foreign income.... By definition, external markets are fueled by debt creation, and the seed of financial instability and crisis can be traced here.'

[2] For a stock-flow supermultiplier model with two debt-financed autonomous expenditures (autonomous government and household consumption), and interrelations between sectoral autonomous demand growth and sectoral indebtedness, with possible emergence of financial fragility processes, see Pedrosa, Brochier, and Freitas (2023).

assets and liabilities, which are independent of production, each potentially generating and funding autonomous demand (consumption, residential investment, exports).[3] Although present in the closed economy autonomous demand-led growth model driven by government expenditures provided by Hein and Woodgate (2021), it has not been made explicit as a mechanism potentially aligning two (or more) autonomous growth rates.[4] To provide a simple theoretical model aligning two autonomous growth rates via the financial stock-flow interaction is hence the first contribution of this paper. For this purpose, we will make use of Allain's (2021) general and abstract distinction between an active and a passive autonomous growth driver, where the latter endogenously adjusts to the former.[5]

We will provide a simplified version of the model proposed by Hein and Woodgate (2021), in which government expenditures growth is the active autonomous growth rate while rentiers' consumption out of interest income becomes the passive autonomous growth rate. The explicit consideration of financing autonomous government demand thus provides the grounds for considering two autonomous growth rates, with the dynamics of the stocks (of debt and thus assets) and income generated from these stocks providing the link through which the growth rate of the passive component endogenously adjusts towards the growth rate of the active component. Such an adjustment thus does not need any external constraint and policy interventions or rules to meet this constraint.

Furthermore, we will discuss the empirical implications of our model regarding the recent research on autonomous growth drivers and growth regimes (Campana et al. 2024; Freitas and Dweck 2013; Girardi and Pariboni 2016; Labat and Summa 2023; Morlin, Passos, and Pariboni 2022; Passos and Morlin 2022). This research has relied on the de-composition of autonomous and induced components of aggregate demand, the calculation of growth contributions of autonomous growth drivers (government expenditures, credit-financed private consumption, residential investment and exports), as well as on growth contributions of the changes in the components of the supermultiplier (the propensities to consume, to invest and to import) (Hein 2023b). However, it has not addressed the (potential) interrelationship between the different components of autonomous demand.

We will use some results of this SSM research on the de-composition of autonomous and induced components of aggregate demand just to illustrate this interrelationship between different components of autonomous demand. We will then show, theoretically,

[3]We do not mention government expenditure here, because we hold that in sovereign money economies, governments do not have to pre-fund their expenditures, although policy makers may have imposed some policy rules (government debt ceilings, debt brakes, balanced budgets etc.) which may impose a constraint on government expenditures, which may then interact with other autonomous expenditure components. In countries without sovereign money, government expenditures would have to be mentioned here, too.

[4]Freitas and Christianes (2020) have two autonomous growth rates (government expenditures and capitalist consumption), but just assume that the two will be equal in the long run, without discussing their interaction. Brochier and Macedo e Silva (2019) have presented an autonomous demand-led stock-flow consistent growth model driven by consumption out of wealth, with wealth being endogenous in the long run. They thus include financial issues, but only have one autonomous growth rate which is endogenous.

[5]In the journal version of his paper, Allain (2022) has abandoned the distinction between 'active' and 'passive' components of autonomous demand in favour of 'autonomous' and 'semi-autonomous' demand components. He thus follows Fiebiger (2018, 2020) and Lavoie and Fiebiger (2019), who have argued that 'semi-autonomous' may be a better terminology to indicate the independence of parts of demand from income generated in current production, which may be, nonetheless, through some other mechanism be related to the dynamics of production in the long run. They refer to Kalecki (1968, 265–269), who is using 'semi-autonomous' for the autonomous part of capitalists' consumption, and the effect of technical change and innovations on investment.

that our model with government expenditures as the active component of autonomous demand may, under certain conditions, including the economic policy regime, generate a regime in which autonomous private consumption expenditures as the passive component of autonomous demand may dominate in terms of the growth contributions. Classifying such an economy as autonomous consumption-led would thus be somewhat misleading. This indicates that the integration of financial flow and stock variables, and their interaction, may establish important links between the autonomous components of aggregate demand and their growth contributions, which should be considered in the growth regime analysis. To point this out clearly is the second contribution of our paper.

The paper is organised as follows. In Section 2 we will present the most basic closed economy model driven by autonomous government expenditures growth, as the active, and the growth of consumption out of interest income, as the passive component of autonomous demand that adjusts towards the growth of the active component in long-run equilibrium. Section 3 then turns to current research on demand-led growth accounting based on the SSM growth model. It argues that classifying countries according to the relative size of the growth contributions of autonomous demand components may be misleading. This is then demonstrated making use of the simple model, both for the long-run growth equilibrium and for the traverse towards this equilibrium. Section 4 summarises and concludes.

2. A Simple Closed Economy Autonomous Demand-led Growth Model with an Active and a Passive Component of Autonomous Demand

Here we develop a simple SSM model that is primarily driven by the growth rate of autonomous government spending. However, since government spending is financed through the issuance of government bonds, the resulting public interest payments induce rentier consumption, which serves as a 'secondary' or 'passive' component of autonomous expenditures. Thus, the growth of autonomous government expenditure enables rentiers' autonomous consumption and, it will be shown, sets the pace for long-run output growth and capital accumulation. Yet, as we shall also show, this does *not* imply that the growth contribution of government spending is necessarily greater than that of autonomous consumption, such that this economy would always be classified as government demand-led. Indeed, despite the causal primacy of government spending in this simple model, we can show that the growth contribution of autonomous consumption may exceed that of government spending in the short run as well as the long run, giving rise to a seemingly autonomous-consumption-led economy.

We develop the model as follows, assuming constant prices and a price level equal to unity such that nominal and real values are the same. Suppose consumption (C) is given by the product of the marginal propensity to consume (c) and disposable income, the latter composed of of income arising from production (Y), that is wages and profits, and interest paid on government debt (iL):[6]

$$C = c(Y + iL),\ 0 < c < 1. \tag{1}$$

[6]For simplifying purposes, we are not considering class distinctions and its consequences for different propensities to consume. Therefore, we also do not explore the possible effect of different propensities to consume out of different income streams.

where L is the stock of government debt and i is the interest rate on government debt. Investment (I) is fully induced by the level of output (Y), where the responsiveness of investment to changes in output is governed by the marginal propensity to invest (h), which is fixed in the short run and variable in the long run in a way that shall be described later:

$$I = hY, 0 < h < 1. \tag{2}$$

To maintain our focus on the matter at hand, we follow Hein (2018) and assume that firms finance investment through issuing equity, bought by rentiers' households, rather than debt, and pay out all their profits as dividends to these households. Supposing that government expenditures (G) are fully autonomous and grow at a constant rate of γ:

$$\hat{G} = \gamma, 0 \leq \gamma, \tag{3}$$

we can solve for the short-run equilibrium (denoted by an asterisk) level of output through equating output with the sum of planned consumption, investment, and government expenditures, which are taken as given in the short run, such that:

$$Y^* = \frac{ciL + G}{1 - c - h} = m\,(C^A + G) = mZ. \tag{4}$$

Equation 4 shows that the short-run equilibrium level of output depends on the supermultiplier, $m = \frac{1}{1 - c - h}$, and on autonomous demand (Z), which in our simple model is made up of two components, autonomous government spending (G) and autonomous consumption out of interest income arising from public debt ($ciL = C^A$). However, these two components are related. Since we ignore taxes, we suppose that new government debt is issued to cover government spending and interest payments on outstanding government debt in any period, as in Hein (2018) and in Hein and Woodgate (2021). Government deficit-financed expenditure thus adds to the stock of government debt held as interest yielding assets by the private households, which then affects autonomous consumption out of interest income.

Based on our assumptions, the time rate of change (denoted by a dot) of public debt is given by:

$$\dot{L} = G + iL. \tag{5}$$

Dividing by the stock of government debt, it follows that the growth rate (denoted by a hat) of government debt is determined by the ratio of government spending to government debt ($\rho \equiv G/L$) and the interest rate:

$$\hat{L} = \rho + i. \tag{6}$$

Making use of the public spending-to-debt ratio ρ, we can express the short-run equilibrium output from Equation 4 as a function of the level of government debt, assuming a given public spending-to-debt ratio in the short run:

$$Y^* = \mu L, \tag{7}$$

with $\mu = \frac{ci + \rho}{1 - c - h}$. It follows, then, that the growth rate of output (g) is given by the sum of the growth rate of μ and the growth rate of public debt:

$$g = \hat{Y} = \hat{\mu} + \hat{L}, \tag{8}$$

where the growth rate of μ is given by:

$$\hat{\mu} = \frac{(\dot{c}i + \dot{i}c + \dot{\rho})(1 - c - h) + (\dot{c} + \dot{h})(ci + \rho)}{(1 - c - h)(ci + \rho)}. \tag{9}$$

For the purposes of the analysis that follows, however, we will assume the overall marginal propensity to consume and interest rate are time invariant, such that $\dot{c} = \dot{i} = 0$.[7] The time rate of change of the public spending-to-debt ratio, on the other hand, is given by:

$$\dot{\rho} = \rho(\gamma - i - \rho). \tag{10}$$

Equations 11 and 12, which follow the usual form seen in the SSM literature, specify the dynamic equations for the marginal propensity to invest and for the rate of capacity utilisation. Capacity utilisation is defined as the ratio of output over the capital stock ($u = Y/K$) assuming, purely for simplicity, a capital-potential output ratio of one. The change in the propensity to invest is dependent upon deviations of the utilisation rate from the firms' target rate, the long-run normal rate (u_n), and the responsiveness (η) of the marginal propensity to invest to deviations of capacity utilisation from the normal rate:

$$\dot{h} = h\eta(u - u_n). \tag{11}$$

The rate of capacity utilisation is determined by the difference between the growth rate of output and the accumulation rate of capital (g_k):

$$\dot{u} = u(g - g_k). \tag{12}$$

Dividing Equation 2 by the capital stock, the accumulation rate is given by the marginal propensity to invest and the rate of capacity utilisation as defined above:

$$g_k = hu. \tag{13}$$

The long-run steady state of our system, where $\dot{\rho} = \dot{h} = \dot{u} = 0$, is captured in Equations 14-17, where double asterisks denote long-run equilibrium values.[8]

$$g^{**} = \hat{L}^{**} = g_k^{**} = \gamma \tag{14}$$

$$u^{**} = u_n \tag{15}$$

$$h^{**} = \gamma/u_n \tag{16}$$

$$\rho^{**} = \gamma - i \tag{17}$$

In the steady state, the growth rates of output, government debt and the capital stock are all equal to the growth rate of government spending, as the active component of

[7] Hence, this paper makes no further claims about the effects of changes of c nor i on demand and output.
[8] We ignore the trivial solutions where the long-run equilibrium values are zero.

autonomous demand (Equation 14). Since in the long-run equilibrium, the growth rate of government debt is equal to the autonomous growth rate of government spending, for a given interest rate and a given propensity to consume out of any income, also the growth rate of consumption out of interest income, the passive component of autonomous demand, converges to the growth rate of government spending. The model is thus ultimately driven by government expenditures, the active component of autonomous demand, and autonomous consumption, the passive component, adjusts towards that growth rate through the adjustment of the growth rate of government debt, and thus interest income, to the growth rate of the active component of autonomous demand.

In long-run equilibrium, capacity utilisation is at its target or normal rate (Equation 15). The marginal propensity to invest also converges to its long-run value, which is determined by γ and u_n (Equation 16). This means that, given some exogenous normal utilisation, there is a positive relation between the propensity to invest (or the business investment share) and the growth rate of government spending (and consequently, the growth rate of autonomous demand and output in the steady state), which is a common property of SSM models.[9]

Equation 17 says the long-run public spending-to-debt ratio is given by the difference between the growth rate of government spending and the interest rate on government debt. Hence, for economically meaningful long-run values, it must be the case that:

$$i < \gamma. \tag{18}$$

This represents a basic stability condition, which can be found elsewhere (e.g., Freitas and Christianes 2020; Hein and Woodgate 2021). It is analogous to the 'Domar condition' (Domar 1944), remembering that in our case there are no taxes and the public sector is permanently in deficit, so the growth rate of output (government spending) must be higher than the interest rate to avoid an explosive trend of the debt-to GDP ratio.

A further stability condition is revealed through analysis of the system's Jacobian evaluated at the long-run equilibrium using the Routh-Hurwitz conditions. This second stability condition is essentially the same as that found in similar SSM models.[10] It can be expressed in terms of a limit on the growth rate of government expenditures:

$$\gamma < (1 - c - \eta)u_n. \tag{19}$$

Since many similar derivations can be found in the literature and since stability analysis is not the focus of this paper, we relegate our derivation to the appendix and assume stability conditions 18 and 19 are fulfilled throughout the analysis that follows.[11]

[9] This has consequences for the level of output in the steady state (Equation 4), as a higher propensity to invest increases the level of output.

[10] See Freitas and Serrano (2015, 14), who also elaborate on the interpretation of this stability condition. A similar stability condition is found in, for example, Hein and Woodgate (2021) and Morlin (2022).

[11] For an assessment of the empirical plausibility of the stability conditions (18) and (19) for the case of the United States, see respectively, Blanchard (2019) and Haluska, Braga, and Summa (2021).

3. Contributions of Components of Autonomous Demand to Growth

3.1 Insights from the Supermultiplier Demand-led Growth Accounting

The simple model with two autonomous growth drivers presented in the previous section provides some interesting insights into the dynamics of the relative importance of the components of autonomous demand growth. Therefore, it can provide some analytical basis to discuss the results of the recent empirical literature on SSM demand-led growth accounting. This literature uses the SSM theory (Serrano 1995; Serrano, Summa, and Freitas 2023) to organise the data and to measure the contribution to growth of several autonomous and induced components of demand (Campana et al. 2024; Freitas and Dweck 2013; Girardi and Pariboni 2016; Labat and Summa 2023; Morlin, Passos, and Pariboni 2022; Passos and Morlin 2022).

The methodology of the SSM demand-led growth accounting consists of developing a 'theoretically informed decomposition' (Morlin, Passos, and Pariboni 2022, 32) of economic growth building upon a distinction of demand between autonomous and induced components. This decomposition gives us the contribution of each of the autonomous and induced components of demand to the growth rate of output. The SSM demand-led growth accounting is thus an alternative to the supply-side growth accounting (Hulten 2010), as the former assumes that growth is driven by aggregate demand, while the latter assumes that growth is supply-led. It is also an alternative to other demand-led growth accounting, such as the national income and financial accounting decomposition approach (Hein 2011a, 2011b, 2012), as it imposes the SSM theory to organise the data into induced and autonomous components of demand (for a comparison, see Campana et al. 2024; Hein 2023b; Morlin, Passos, and Pariboni 2022).

More specifically, the output growth is decomposed into changes in the parameters of the supermultiplier and changes in the components of autonomous demand, like in Equation (4) of our theoretical model above. The contribution to growth of each of these demand components will depend on their respective growth rates and their relative share in aggregate demand. Thus, a component that has a larger share of aggregate demand and is growing slowly can make a larger contribution to growth than a component that has a smaller share but a higher growth rate.

It should be noticed that the empirical exercises based on SSM demand-led growth accounting have some differences with the simple theoretical SSM models, such as the one presented in Section 2. First, the SSM growth accounting uses actual data (in general, annual data), which imply disequilibrium processes according to the theoretical model, as the parameters of the supermultiplier may always be changing and the components of autonomous demand may grow at different rates. However, the results of the theoretical model are in general discussed in terms of steady-state solutions, with autonomous demand components growing at the same rate and an unchanging steady-state supermultiplier, which is compatible with that growth rate.

Second, there is a divergence concerning the level of detail between the theoretical model and the empirical methodology. As the demand-led decomposition should reflect the actual data, it must include all the components of demand present in the data. On the contrary, our theoretical model imposes some simplifying assumptions, such as a closed economy with no taxes and public transfers, and only two autonomous demand components. In the literature on SSM demand-led accounting, both the tax burden and the import coefficient are included into the supermultiplier, alongside the propensities to invest and to consume. Moreover, autonomous demand includes other components, such as residential investment, private consumption out of credit, and exports (Campana et al. 2024; Girardi and Pariboni 2016; Labat and Summa 2023; Morlin, Passos, and Pariboni 2022; Passos and Morlin 2022).[12]

We can use some stylized results from these empirical exercises to illustrate our discussion of active and passive components of autonomous demand and its relative contributions to growth. The Spanish economy experienced a higher average growth rate of output and a real estate boom in the period of 1998-2007. We can consider residential investment as the active autonomous component of demand, and government spending as passive (because Spain has had a target primary government budget surplus).[13] However, the contribution of autonomous demand by the public sector was higher than the contribution by residential investment (Labat and Summa 2023). This result arises from two facts: first, because the housing boom and bubble generated windfall tax revenues and allowed fiscal expansion, given the fiscal rule; second, because the share of autonomous demand financed by the government in aggregate demand is higher than the share of residential investment. So, despite the higher growth rates of residential investment than government spending, the latter made a bigger contribution to growth than the former, while its growth was passively adjusting, via tax revenues and the budget rule, to the active autonomous growth rate given by residential investment.

A similar story can be told for the Brazilian economy in the 2000s. Here we will consider exports as the active autonomous demand driver and government spending as the passive, also because of a primary surplus target.[14] Again, the contribution of autonomous demand financed by the public sector to growth was higher than that of exports (Campana et al. 2024). This result also is the consequence of two facts: first, because the commodity boom and the strengthening of south-south trade increased tax revenues and allowed a public expansion, again given a primary surplus target in the government budget; second, because again the share of autonomous demand financed by the government in aggregate demand is higher than the share of exports.

Similar to the theoretical model by Morlin (2022), in both examples it is a policy rule, which links the two autonomous growth drivers and makes government expenditure growth the passive autonomous growth rate in both cases, while residential investment has been the main active component in the Spanish case and exports in the Brazilian case. However, this hierarchy of autonomous growth drivers may then not be visible

---

[12]The level of disaggregation of autonomous components can be even more detailed, e.g., with the distinction between government consumption and investment, investment by state-owned enterprises, business investment in R&D, and consumption out of public transfers and public wages (Labat and Summa 2023). However, in none of the papers of the SSM demand-led growth accounting literature the consumption out of interest on public debt is included. We believe that empirically estimating this latter effect and including it in demand-led decompositions exercises for different countries, to check its contribution to growth, should be a desirable future development of this research agenda.

[13]We are simplifying the story, because exports can also be included as a second active autonomous driver for the Spanish economy.

[14]This is, of course, just a simplified stylized story, as autonomous consumption out of credit and residential investment can be included as important active autonomous drivers in the Brazilian case, too.

in the calculation of growth contributions in the disequilibrium process. We do not question the relevance of policy rules aligning autonomous growth rates,however, we hold, and have already shown above, that even without any policy rule related to government expenditures and government debt (or to exports and foreign indebtedness as additionally included in Morlin's (2022) model), active and passive autonomous growth drivers can be aligned through 'automatic' stock-flow interactions in a monetary production economy. These are, in a sense, prior to the imposition of policy rules on the economic actors in order to align autonomous growth rates in the long run. The implications of our approach for growth regime analysis and relative growth contributions will also be analysed next.

3.2 The Active and the Passive Components of Autonomous Demand Growth and the Relative Contribution to Growth: The Long-run Steady-State

As already pointed out, active and passive components in our model are clearly linked through the stock-flow effects of deficit-financed government expenditures, taking the interest rate and the propensity to consume out of income as given. This can be shown, first, for the steady state properties. In this steady state, (1) the supermultiplier is not changing, as the propensity to invest has already been adjusted and the propensity to consume is fixed by assumption and (2) government spending and autonomous consumption out of interest income arising from public debt grow at the same rate.

In this steady state, consequently, the relative contribution to growth of these two autonomous components depends only on their relative share in aggregate demand. We can express the relationship between these two components in the steady-state, making use of the solution for the long-run government spending-debt ratio (Equation 17):

$$\frac{C^{A**}}{G^{**}} = \frac{ciL^{**}}{G^{**}} = \frac{ci}{\rho^{**}} = \frac{ci}{\gamma - i} \tag{20}$$

The relative share between autonomous consumption out of interest income and government spending, in the long run, will thus depend on three variables: the propensity to consume, the interest rate and the growth rate of government spending. With the long-run stability condition given, the first two factors increase the autonomous consumption-to-government spending ratio, while the last reduces it.

Since the long-run growth contributions of autonomous consumption and of government expenditures are $C^A_{GC} = \gamma\frac{C^A}{Y}$ and $G_{GC} = \gamma\frac{G}{Y}$, respectively, Equation 20 also reflects the relative size of the two growth contributions. By simplifying, we thus get:

$$C^A_{GC} > G_{GC}, \qquad \text{if} \quad \gamma < i(1 + c). \tag{21}$$

In the long-run growth equilibrium, the growth contribution of the passive component of autonomous demand, C^A_{GC}, is hence greater than the active component, G_{GC}, if the autonomous growth rate of government spending is sufficiently small. A higher rate of interest and a higher propensity to consume make such a case more likely. However, it should be recalled from Conditions 18 and 19 that stability requires that $i < \gamma < (1 - c - \eta)u_n$. Hence, while increases in the interest rate and the propensity to consume make the growth contribution of autonomous consumption greater relative to that of government spending, it should be noted that such increases also pose a threat to systemic stability should these parameters become too large.

The explicit consideration of financing autonomous demand thus, first, provides the grounds for two autonomous growth rates, with the dynamics of the stocks of debt and thus assets and income generated from these stocks providing the link through which the growth rate of the passive component, autonomous consumption, endogenously adjusts towards the growth rate of the active component, government expenditures. Second, the growth contributions of passive and active components are determined by those model parameters, which are related to the conditions of finance, the rate of interest, the propensity to spend out of financial income (equal to the average propensity to consume in our simple model), and by the growth rate of the active component of autonomous demand. The relative growth contributions may hence be affected by economic policies, i.e., monetary policies affecting the long-term rate of interest on government debt, distributional policies related to wealth and income inequality affecting the average propensity to consume, and, finally, the growth rate of government expenditures, of course.

3.3 The Active and the Passive Components of Autonomous Demand Growth and the Relative Contribution to Growth: The Traverse

It is not just in the hypothetical long-run equilibrium of our model that the passive autonomous growth contribution, may be greater than the active autonomous growth contribution. Also in the short-run disequilibrium traverse, we may have such a result. We can define the dynamic disequilibrium condition for the growth contribution of our active component of autonomous demand, government spending, to be smaller than that of the passive component, autonomous consumption:

$$C^A_{GC} > G_{GC}, \text{ if } \hat{L}\frac{ciL}{Y} > \gamma\frac{G}{Y}, \tag{22}$$

which, by inserting Equation 6 for $\hat{L}$ and rearranging, is the same as:

$$\rho < \frac{ci^2}{\gamma - ci}. \tag{23}$$

Note that, since long-run stability requires $\gamma > i$, it follows that the right-hand side of Condition 23 is positive by assumption. This inequality implies that, despite the model being ultimately driven by government spending, C^A_{GC} is greater than G_{GC} when ρ is sufficiently small.

To analyse different cases, we start by inserting the steady state value of ρ into its equation of motion in Equation 10, which yields:

$$\dot{\rho} = \rho(\rho^{**} - \rho). \tag{24}$$

We see that ρ steadily falls (rises) to its steady state value if the initial value (ρ_0) exceeds (falls below) its long-run equilibrium value. Next, we denote the threshold value on the right-hand side of inequality (23), which determines which of the two growth contributions is larger, by:

$$d = \frac{ci^2}{\gamma - ci}. \tag{25}$$

By Inequality 23, the value of ρ_t in any period t relative to this constant determinant, d, tells us which growth contribution is greater. Since we know the evolution of ρ is determined by its initial value (ρ_0) and its steady state value (ρ^{**}), then if, for example, $\rho_0 < \rho^{**} < d$ it must be the case that the growth contribution of autonomous consumption will be greater than that of government spending not just in the long run, *but in every period* in the traverse towards this long-run equilibrium. This situation is shown in Panel 1A of Figure 1. Panel 1B shows the case where $\rho^{**} < d < \rho_0$. Now the growth contribution of autonomous consumption exceeds that of government spending in all periods bar the initial ones. Lastly, Panels 1C and 1D show the cases where the growth contribution

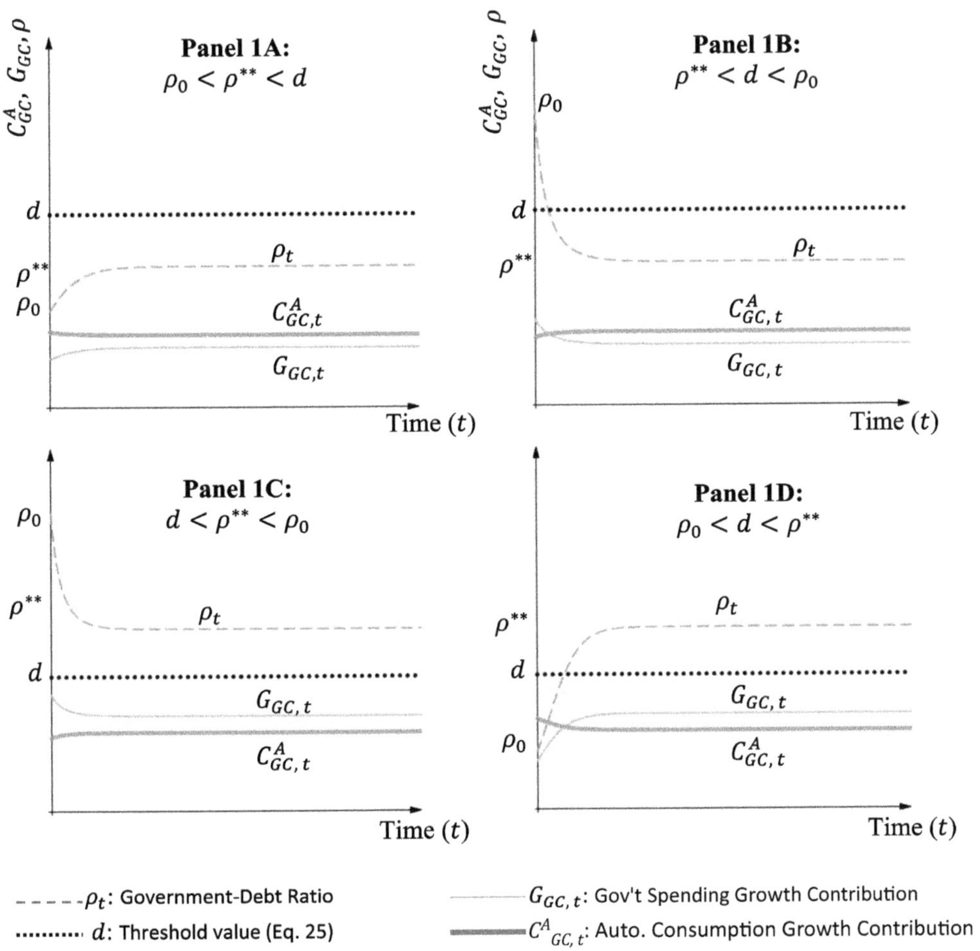

Figure 1. The growth contributions of autonomous consumption (C^A_{GC}) and government spending (G_{GC}) depend on the evolution of the government spending-to-debt ratio (ρ).

of government spending surpasses that of autonomous consumption in all periods in the former and in all periods bar the initial ones in the latter.

Hence, our simple model shows that the analysis of autonomous growth contributions alone is not sufficient to determine the ultimate driver of growth in any given economy, in line with the stylized empirical cases pointed out in Section 3.1. In our example, it is perfectly possible that autonomous consumption contributes more to output growth than autonomous government spending in the long run and the short run, despite government spending being the underlying engine of growth. This result requires an interest rate on government debt that is positive and smaller than but close to the growth rate of government spending, together with a high propensity to consume out of interest income (which is equal to the average propensity to consume in our simple model).

In addition to the endogenous changes in the dominant growth contribution seen above, we can also employ our simple model to analyse the effects of exogenous changes in the policy variables on the disequilibrium traverse. In particular, we can observe what happens to the relative growth contributions at any period in time given a change in the growth rate of government expenditures and a change in the interest rate on government debt.

Figure 2 depicts the evolution of the same key macroeconomic variables over time as Figure 1, but now the economy experiences a policy shock in period T. This gives rise to two periods of analysis: A pre-shock, first policy era where γ is far greater than i and a post-shock, second policy era where γ falls, i rises, or both occur simultaneously. In the first scenario in Panel 2A, γ halves from 5per cent to 2.5per cent and i doubles from 1per cent to 2per cent. In Panel 2B, we have a severe austerity scenario in which i remains constant at 1per cent but γ falls considerably, from 5per cent to 1.2per cent. Lastly, in Panel 2C, γ remains constant at 5per cent but i quadruples from 1per cent to 4per cent.

The qualitative effect of each of these three policy changes is the same in each scenario. The government spending-debt ratio falls in the second policy era while the threshold value rises from d_1 to d_2. As a result, the growth contribution of government spending far surpasses that of autonomous consumption in the pre-shock policy era while autonomous consumption contributes more to demand and output growth in the post-shock era (if not always immediately following any given shock in period T). Hence, we see the various ways by which the dominant growth contribution in our model economy may be determined by policy changes.[15] The economic policy regime thus has an important impact on how the growth regime of an economy may appear according to SSM demand-led growth accounting.

4. Conclusions

Starting from the requirement that autonomous demand-led growth models have to include endogenous money and credit, and hence financial dynamics, because

[15]Though it is, of course, possible that decreases in γ and/or increases in i may not be sufficient in size to change the dominant growth contribution. Though not illustrated here, one could equally examine the opposite cases wherein the policy shock is a rise in γ and/or fall in i. Unsurprisingly, the result in the post-shock period is, in qualitative terms, the mirror image of what is depicted in Figure 2, i.e. a rising government spending-debt ratio ρ, lower threshold value d, higher (and rising) growth contributions of government spending, as well as lower (and falling) growth contribution of autonomous expenditure.

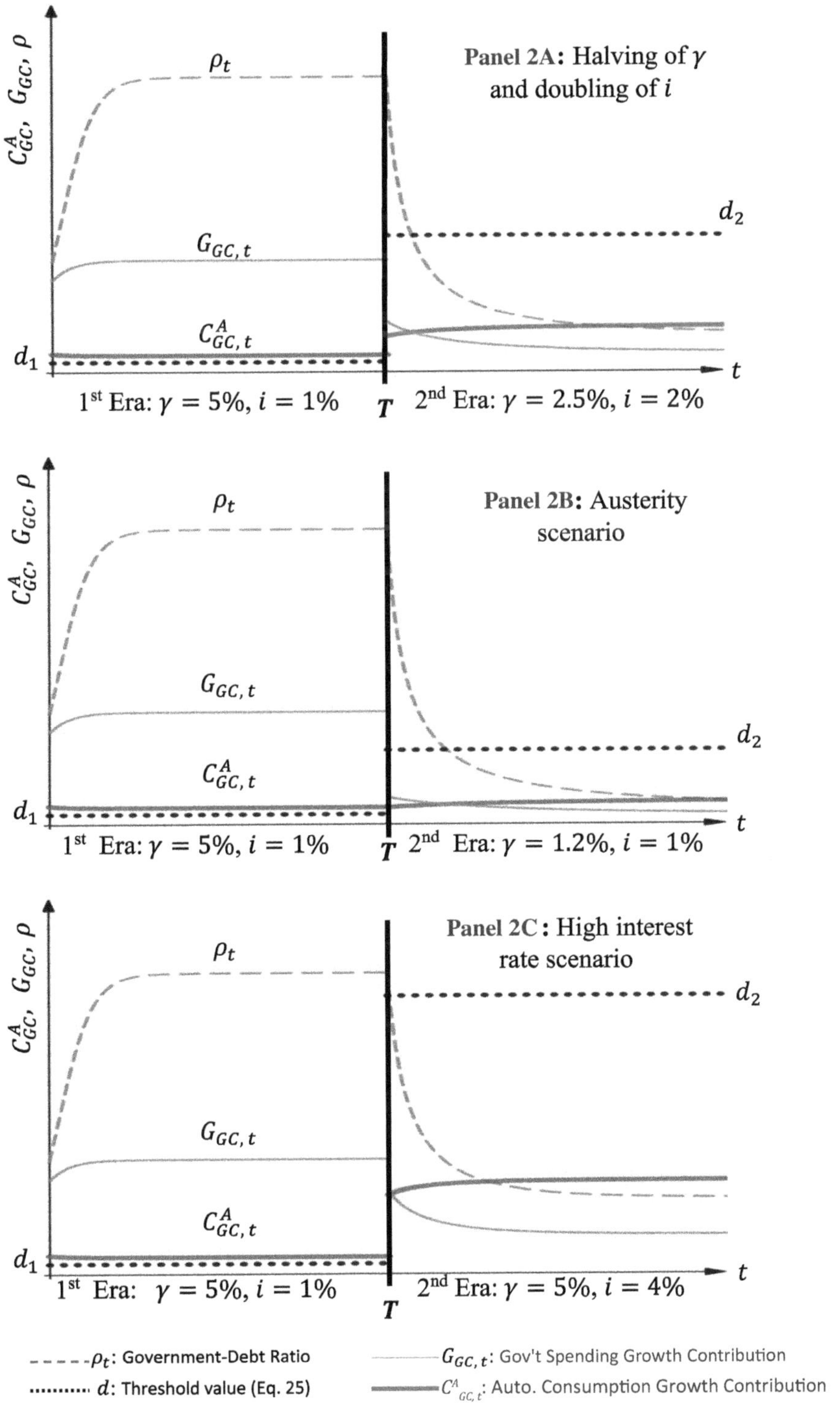

Figure 2. Effect of various policy changes in period T on the growth contributions of government spending and autonomous consumption.

autonomous demand has to be financed independently of income from current production, we have tried to make two contributions in this paper.

First, we have addressed the current debate on the implications of two (or more) autonomous growth rates and the need of adjustment of these two growth rates in long-run equilibrium, if each of the components is meant to contribute to aggregate demand growth. We have shown even for the most basic closed economy autonomous demand-led growth model that the inclusion of some financial stock-flow interaction provides an endogenous mechanism by means of which the passive component of autonomous growth, consumption out of interest income in our model, adjusts towards the active component, government expenditure growth in our model, provided that the general conditions for stability are met. In our view, the inclusion of such an endogenous mechanism, which has been ignored in much of the previous literature, is a more logically fundamental mechanism by means of which two (or more) autonomous growth rates may be aligned, relative to the implementation of exogenous or policy constraints.

Second, our paper has addressed the recent research on demand-led growth accounting based on the SSM growth model. We have started from the consideration that the relative sizes of autonomous growth contributions may be misleading as a guide to classify growth regimes if autonomous growth rates are interdependent. Based on our simple model we have shown that this may indeed be the case, both for the steady state growth equilibrium as well as for the traverse towards this equilibrium. Furthermore, we have shown for our model, that the relative growth contributions are economic policy contingent. This implies that, although the SSM demand-led growth decomposition exercise is an important step, interdependencies between autonomous growth components should not be ignored when growth drivers are supposed to be identified. This seems to be true both for medium- to long-run growth regime analysis, but also for the analysis of the autonomous drivers of short-run cycles. This finding motivates the need for further research on ways of empirically classifying growth regimes that are more robust than simply comparing the relative size of growth contributions, yet do not invoke the complexities that come with a macro-econometric approach given the multitude of possible endogeneity problems.

Acknowledgements

We would like to use this opportunity to acknowledge and thank the reviewers who reviewed this article and aided in its publication.

Disclosure Statement

No potential conflict of interest was reported by the author(s).

ORCID

Ryan Woodgate http://orcid.org/0000-0001-8318-1684

References

Allain, O. 2021. '*A Supermultiplier Model with Two Non-Capacity-Generating Autonomous Demand components*.' Paper Presented at the 25th Conference of the Forum for

Macroeconomics and Macroeconomic Policies (FMM), Berlin, 28-30.10.2021, https://www.boeckler.de/pdf/v_2021_10_29_allain.pdf.

Allain, O. 2022. 'A Supermultiplier Model with Two Non-Capacity-Generating Semi-Autonomous Demand Components.' *Structural Change and Economic Dynamics* 63: 91–103.

Blanchard, O. 2019. 'Public Debt and Low Interest Rates.' *American Economic Review* 109 (4): 1197–1229.

Brochier, L., and A. C. Macedo e Silva. 2019. 'A Supermultiplier Stock-Flow Consistent Model: The "Return" of the Paradoxes of Thrift and Costs in the Long Run?' *Cambridge Journal of Economics* 43 (2): 413–442.

Campana, J., J. Embova Vaz, E. Hein, and B. Jungmann. 2024. 'Demand and Growth Regimes of the BRICs Countries – the National Income and Financial Accounting Decomposition Approach and an Autonomous Demand-led Growth Perspective.' *European Journal of Economics and Economic Policies: Intervention* 21 (1), forthcoming.

Cesaratto, S. 2017. 'Initial and Final Finance in the Monetary Circuit and the Theory of Effective Demand.' *Metroeconomica* 68 (2): 228–258.

Cesaratto, S., and S. Di Bucchianico. 2020. 'Endogenous Money and the Theory of Long Period Effective Demand.' *Bulletin of Political Economy* 14 (1): 1–38.

Cesaratto, S., and R. Pariboni. 2022. 'The Relation Between Keynesian Monetary Theory and Demand-led Growth: A Sraffian Exploration.' *Review of Keynesian Economics* 10 (3): 291–315.

Domar, E. 1944. 'The "Burden of the Debt" and the National Income.' *American Economic Review* 34 (4): 798–827.

Fiebiger, B. 2018. 'Semi-autonomous Household Expenditures as the *Causa Causans* of Postwar US Business Cycles: The Stability and Instability of Luxemburg-Type External Markets.' *Cambridge Journal of Economics* 42 (1): 155–175.

Fiebiger, B., and M. Lavoie. 2019. 'Trend and Business Cycles with External Markets: Non-capacity Generating Semi-autonomous Expenditures and Effective Demand.' *Metroeconomica* 70 (2): 247–262.

Freitas, F., and E. Dweck. 2013. 'The Pattern of Economic Growth of the Brazilian Economy 1970–2005: A Demand-led Growth Perspective.' In *In Sraffa and the Reconstruction of Economic Theory: Volume Two*, edited by E. S. Levrero, A. Palumbo, and A. Stirati. London: Palgrave Macmillan.

Freitas, F., and R. Christianes. 2020. 'A Baseline Supermultiplier Model for the Analysis of Fiscal Policy and Government Debt.' *Review of Keynesian Economics* 8 (3): 313–338.

Freitas, F., and F. Serrano. 2015. 'Growth Rate and Level Effects, the Stability of the Adjustment of Capacity to Demand and the Sraffian Supermultiplier.' *Review of Political Economy* 27 (3): 258–281.

Freitas, F., and F. Serrano. 2017. 'The Sraffian Supermultiplier as an Alternative Closure for Heterodox Growth Theory.' *European Journal of Economics and Economic Policies: Intervention* 14 (1): 70–91.

Girardi, D., and R. Pariboni. 2016. 'Long-Run Effective Demand in the US Economy: An Empirical Test of the Sraffian Supermultiplier Model.' *Review of Political Economy* 28 (4): 523–544.

Haluska, G., J. Braga, and R. Summa. 2021. 'Growth, Investment Share and the Stability of the Sraffian Supermultiplier Model in the U.S. Economy (1985–2017).' *Metroeconomica* 72 (2): 345–364.

Hein, E. 2011a. 'Redistribution, Global Imbalances and the Financial and Economic Crisis – the Case for a Keynesian New Deal.' *International Journal of Labour Research* 3 (1): 51–73.

Hein, E. 2011b. 'Financialisation, Re-Distribution, and the Financial and Economic Crisis – a Kaleckian Perspective.' In *Stabilising an Unequal Economy? Public Debt, Financial Regulation, and Income Distribution*, edited by T. Niechoj, Ö Onaran, E. Stockhammer, A. Truger, and T. van Treeck. Marburg: Metropolis.

Hein, E. 2012. *The Macroeconomics of Finance-Dominated Capitalism – and Its Crisis*. Cheltenham, UK: Edward Elgar Publishing.

Hein, E. 2018. 'Autonomous Government Expenditure Growth, Deficits, Debt, and Distribution in a Neo-Kaleckian Growth Model.' *Journal of Post Keynesian Economics* 41 (2): 316–338.

Hein, E. 2023a. *Macroeconomics After Kalecki and Keynes: Post-Keynesian Foundations.* Cheltenham, UK: Edward Elgar Publishing.

Hein, E. 2023b. 'Varieties of Demand and Growth Regimes - Post-Keynesian Foundations.' *European Journal of Economics and Economic Policies: Intervention* 20 (3), forthcoming.

Hein, E., and R. Woodgate. 2021. 'Stability Issues in Kaleckian Models Driven by Autonomous Demand Growth—Harrodian Instability and Debt Dynamics.' *Metroeconomica* 72 (2): 388–404.

Hulten, C. 2010. 'Growth Accounting.' In *Handbook of the Economics of Innovation, Vol. 2,* edited by B. H. Hall, and N. Rosenberg. Amsterdam: North-Holland.

Kalecki, M. 1968. 'Trend and Business Cycles Reconsidered.' *The Economic Journal* 78 (310): 263–276.

Labat, H., and R. Summa. 2023. 'A Supermultiplier Demand-Led Growth Accounting Analysis Applied to the Spanish Economy (1998-2019).' *European Journal of Economics and Economic Policies: Intervention* 21 (1): forthcoming.

Lavoie, M. 2022. *Post-Keynesian Economics: New Foundations.* Cheltenham, UK: Edward Elgar Publishing.

Morlin, G. 2022. 'Growth Led by Government Expenditure and Exports: Public and External Debt Stability in a Supermultiplier Model.' *Structural Change and Economic Dynamics* 62: 586–598.

Morlin, G., N. Passos, and R. Pariboni. 2022. 'Growth Theory and the Growth Model Perspective: Insights from the Supermultiplier.' *Review of Political Economy*, doi:10.1080/09538259.2022.2092998.

Pariboni, R. 2016. 'Household Consumer Debt, Endogenous Money and Growth: A Supermultiplier-Based Analysis.' *PSL Quarterly Review* 69 (278): 211–233.

Passos, N., and G. Morlin. 2022. 'Growth Models and Comparative Political Economy in Latin America.' *Revue de la Régulation* 33 (2), doi:10.4000/regulation.21444.

Pedrosa, I., L. Brochier, and F. Freitas. 2023. 'Debt Hierarchy: Autonomous Demand Composition, Growth and Indebtedness in a Supermultiplier Model.' *Economic Modelling*, Forthcoming.

Serrano, F. 1995. 'Long Period Effective Demand and the Sraffian Supermultiplier.' *Contributions to Political Economy* 14 (1): 67–90.

Serrano, F., R. Summa, and F. Freitas. 2023. 'Autonomous Demand-Led Growth and the Supermultiplier: The Theory, the Model and Some Clarification.' Working Paper No. 3/2023, IE-UFRJ.

Vieira Mandarino, G., C. H. Dos Santos, and A. C. Macedo e Silva. 2020. 'Workers' Debt-Financed Consumption: A Supermultiplier Stock-Flow Consistent Model.' *Review of Keynesian Economics* 8 (3): 339–364.

Appendix: Proof of Stability Conditions

A system is considered locally stable around its steady state if its Jacobian evaluated at the long-run equilibrium values (J^{**}), which for our model is given by:

$$J^{**} = \begin{pmatrix} \frac{\partial \dot{u}}{\partial u}|_{u^{**},h^{**},\rho^{**}} & \frac{\partial \dot{u}}{\partial h}|_{u^{**},h^{**},\rho^{**}} & \frac{\partial \dot{u}}{\partial \rho}|_{u^{**},h^{**},\rho^{**}} \\ \frac{\partial \dot{h}}{\partial u}|_{u^{**},h^{**},\rho^{**}} & \frac{\partial \dot{h}}{\partial h}|_{u^{**},h^{**},\rho^{**}} & \frac{\partial \dot{h}}{\partial \rho}|_{u^{**},h^{**},\rho^{**}} \\ \frac{\partial \dot{\rho}}{\partial u}|_{u^{**},h^{**},\rho^{**}} & \frac{\partial \dot{\rho}}{\partial h}|_{u^{**},h^{**},\rho^{**}} & \frac{\partial \dot{\rho}}{\partial \rho}|_{u^{**},h^{**},\rho^{**}} \end{pmatrix} =$$

$$\begin{pmatrix} \gamma\left[\frac{\eta}{1-c-\frac{\gamma}{u_n}}-1\right] & -u_n^2 & \frac{u_n ci}{ci+\gamma-i} \\ \gamma\eta/u_n & 0 & 0 \\ 0 & 0 & -(\gamma-i) \end{pmatrix}, \tag{A1}$$

fulfils the following three Routh-Hurwitz (RH) conditions:

1. $Det(J^{**}) < 0$,
2. $Tr(J^{**}) < 0$, and
3. $-Tr(J^{**})[Det(J_1^{**}) + Det(J_2^{**}) + Det(J_3^{**})] + Det(J^{**}) > 0$.

While some authors in the related literature mention a fourth RH condition, it is easy to show this extra condition is in fact redundant, as pointed out by Hein and Woodgate (2021).

It can be shown that:

$$Det(J^{**}) = -u_n\gamma\eta(\gamma - i) \tag{A2}$$

$$Tr(J^{**}) = \gamma\left[\frac{\eta}{1-c-\gamma/u_n} - 1\right] - (\gamma - i) \tag{A3}$$

$$\begin{aligned} &- Tr(J^{**})[Det(J_1^{**}) + Det(J_2^{**}) + Det(J_3^{**})] + Det(J^{**}) \\ &= v\left[\frac{\eta}{1-c-\gamma/u_n} - 1\right]\{(\gamma - i)Tr(J^{**}) - \eta u_n\gamma\} \end{aligned} \tag{A4}$$

The first RH condition is fulfilled when:

$$\gamma > i, \tag{A5}$$

which is the aforementioned basic requirement for an economically meaningful long-run value of the government spending-to-debt ratio ($\rho^{**} = \gamma - i$). RH conditions 2 and 3 are fulfilled if and only if the term in square brackets in Equations A3 and A4 are negative, i.e., when:

$$\eta + c + \gamma/u_n < 1. \tag{A6}$$

Rearranging this yields inequality (20) in the main text.

Debt-credit Flows and Stocks in a Supermultiplier Model with Two Autonomous Demand Components: Consequences for Growth

Stefano Di Bucchianico, Ettore Gallo and Antonino Lofaro

ABSTRACT

Allain [2022. 'A Supermultiplier Model with Two Non-Capacity-Generating Semi-autonomous Demand Components.' *Structural Change and Economic Dynamics* 63: 91–103] raised the question of how two or more non-capacity-generating autonomous demand components growing at different rates may coexist in the supermultiplier, avoiding that one component absorbs all the others in the long-run steady-state. To date, the theoretical shortcut adopted in the literature has been to assume that, at least as long-term averages, the different components grow at the same rate or that institutional elements kick in to tackle this issue. Differently, we propose a solution that resorts to endogenous feedback effects and stock-flow consistent relations to solve such issues. More specifically, we build a simple supermultiplier model in which growth is driven by workers' debt accumulation as well as rentiers' consumption out of interest. We show that, according to specific conditions, there is a steady-state solution in which growth ultimately converges towards that of the fastest growing component, but the other does not disappear due to the presence of the mentioned endogenous stock-flow relations. This provides a way out of the two-component issue, with endogenous money creation surrounding this process of growth driven by credit provided to households.

1. Introduction

The literature on long run growth driven by autonomous demand has been seeing lately intense debates touching upon several points (Serrano, Summa, and Freitas 2023). Among the several fields for discussion, two are of interest to our contribution: the need to incorporate financial elements into this framework and the quest for solving the issue created by the contemporaneous presence of more than one autonomous component of demand. Starting with the former, we find the attempts of Pariboni (2016) and Mandarino, Dos Santos, and e Silva (2020) of including credit-financed debt demanded by workers, and also a very recent contribution stressing the possibility to include

Supplemental data for this article can be accessed online at https://doi.org/10.1080/09538259.2024.2375298

different types of debt (Pedrosa, Brochier, and Freitas 2023). Endogenous money (Rochon 2023; Rochon and Rossi 2017) is another element to be included more extensively. Such an avenue for research has been singled out by Cesaratto (2017) at first, and it can eventually give rise to what has been called a 'monetary theory of demand-led growth' (Cesaratto and Pariboni 2022).[1] This theory recovers Keynes' concept of finance, places it in an endogenous money framework, uses the monetary circuit clues about money creation and destruction, as well as those of initial and final finance, and links them to the financing process of the several autonomous components of aggregate demand (Cesaratto and Di Bucchianico 2020).

In our view, the scenario involving the accumulation of private debt by workers' provides one of the most natural cases for bringing together growth driven by autonomous credit-financed consumption (as in the Supermultiplier literature) and the ability of the financial system to accompany such a process by endogenously providing means of payments without resorting to previously deposited savings (as in the endogenous money literature).[2] Related to this aspect, we recall the important point stressed by Nikiforos (2018), who questions whether autonomous expenditure can be taken as independent from income in the long run (on a similar footing, see also Skott 2019). For instance, the author considers the case of the US, where households had been piling up debt over an extended period, but they eventually had to curb that autonomous part of expenditure due to a mounting debt-to-income ratio. Although such kind of concern is undoubtedly valid particularly in the case of household debt accumulation, our contention is for the stylised analysis we propose to have the 'more limited ambition to help explaining specific periods, episodes or modes of accumulation (and the seeds of forthcoming crises within them) as, for instance, the consumer debt-led growth of the "Great Moderation" era that preceded the "Great Recession"' (Pariboni 2016). Hence, we do not rule out the likely possibility for this kind of accumulation mode to run into a 'Minsky moment', but we abstain from modelling it.

In the simple model, we will set up, analyse, and simulate, there will be the presence of two autonomous components of demand: workers' credit-financed autonomous consumption and rentiers' autonomous consumption out of interest income accruing on the accumulated debt. This brings into play the second point, namely the issue of how to handle the presence of more than one autonomous component of demand, each having its features (Allain 2022). As is commonplace in the literature, a working hypothesis can be that of having the two autonomous components grow, at least on a long run average, at the same pace, thereby avoiding the undesirable steady-state situation in which the component growing at the quickest pace would absorb the entire autonomous demand. Examples of this can be found in Freitas and Christianes (2020), Pedrosa, Brochier, and Freitas (2023). Another route can be that of bringing into the picture institutional elements and deliberate policimaker' decisions that actively prevent that outcome, as in the cases of Morlin (2022) and Dvoskin and Landau (2023) when handling

[1] This strand of research is connected to both circuitist visions such as those of Graziani (2003), but also to 'heretic' mainstream authors as Borio and Disyatat (2011). With a different concern, Dejuán and Dejuán-Bitriá (2018, 2022) show that in a Supermultiplier framework with endogenous money it is possible to analyse a speculative motive for excessive credit creation by banks.

[2] Given the very complex general picture that such a case involves, we will not formally include a well-developed banking system. For a full treatment, see Mandarino, Dos Santos, and e Silva (2020).

the presence of government expenditure and exports. A third option, the one that we will explore, is to resort to purely economic relations, stock-flow relationship to be more specific, that permit keeping together two autonomous components without having to resort to peculiar assumptions. An example of this can be found in Di Bucchianico (2021), who, following the suggestion of Hein and Woodgate (2021) to include financial stocks and flows in a Supermultiplier model, devised an endogenous mechanism setting autonomous credit-financed consumption and capitalists' autonomous consumption on the same growth rate in the long run. More recently, Woodgate, Hein, and Summa (2023) also provide a model in which government expenditure and capitalists' autonomous consumption can coexist in the long term.

We will see that in our model it is possible to keep together workers' autonomous credit-financed consumption and rentiers' autonomous consumption in the long term by simply relying on the stock-flow connection tying the two. Workers let private debt grow to finance their consumption and in so doing they accumulate debt that is kept in rentiers' hands. The flow of interest on accumulating debt in turn feed into rentiers' autonomous consumption. According to specific conditions, the model can be driven by either component, whereas the other endogenously adjusts to the predominant growth rate. Therefore, the fundamental message we aim to convey using our model is that there is the possibility to solve the 'two-autonomous-components-conundrum' without necessarily imposing peculiar hypotheses on their relative behaviour. Rather, stock-flow relations provide a solution, which can be integrated and complemented by institutional elements as well as political crackdowns.

The paper is structured in this way. Section Two reviews the literature in which more than one autonomous component of demand is present, and what are the implications for the models at hand, highlighting the possibility of a new solution to this issue. Section Three sets forth a simple Supermultiplier model in which the two autonomous components of demand are workers' credit-financed consumption and rentiers' consumption out of interest on accumulated debt. The model is simulated in Section Four, also adding a sensitivity analysis for a few parameters. Section Five concludes.

2. Literature Review

The supermultiplier model focuses on the dynamics of the non-capacity-generating autonomous demand components to explain long-run economic growth (Cesaratto, Serrano, and Stirati 2003; Serrano 1995). Most articles in the literature are based on models in which there is only one autonomous component. However, recently, some papers have increased the degree of analytical complexity by introducing a second component. At the same time, Allain (2022) raised some important issues in these new formulations, especially in the case where the two components have different growth rates. Indeed, starting from a model with two generic autonomous demand variables, Z_1 and Z_2, with the same share in total autonomous demand (Z) and equal growth rates, g_1 and g_2, what happens to the steady state equilibrium if, for example, g_1 increases following an exogenous shock while g_2 remains stable? Allain (2022) highlights three different scenarios in which the supermultiplier model might evolve. In the first scenario, the gap between the two rates would be permanent and, inevitably, as periods pass the share in autonomous demand of the component with the higher growth rate (by assumption Z_1)

would increase. Although it is not possible to determine how long this divergent dynamic will last, the component with the highest growth rate would absorb all the autonomous demand and attract the economy's growth rate: in this case, we would return to a supermultiplier with only one autonomous component. However, in the other two scenarios, through discretionary decisions and financial constraints, adjustment mechanisms would be created that would lead to convergence of growth rates, and neither component would disappear. In fact, in a second scenario, after the initial increase, the divergence between g_1 and g_2 would not be sustainable due to limits on the funding of Z_1, such as in the following cases: 'For example, since public spending increases faster than taxes, public debt rises, prompting the government to reduce g_1; or, as the growth of credit-financed residential investment exceeds that of household income, the risk exposure of banks increases, leading them to decide on a cut in g_1. From this shift, g_1 converges back gradually to g_Y' (Allain 2022, p. 98). Thus, g_1 would converge to the GDP growth rate g_Y also equal to the growth rate of the second autonomous component g_2, and the system would stabilise back to the steady state while maintaining a role for both components. Symmetrically, with the latter scenario, the increase in the growth rate of Z_1 would result in new financing opportunities for the second autonomous component, Z_2, such as, 'for example, the decrease in government debt and deficit induces an increase in the growth rate of government spending; or, the improvement in the financial situation of households encourages banks to accelerate lending' (Allain 2022, p. 98). In this case, both g_2 and the economy's growth rate g_Y will converge to the new value of g_1 and once again prevent one of the two autonomous components from absorbing the other. However, for Allain (2022, p. 98) the first scenario, consisting of the disappearance of one of the two autonomous components, 'is not what is usually observed, indicating that some mechanism lead to a readjustment of g_1, g_2 or both' which 'could be due either to discretionary decisions, or to the fact that Z_1 and Z_2 still contain an induced part (besides their autonomous part), or to changing financial conditions'.

The need for such readjustment can be identified in several works in the literature based on the assumption that the growth rates of the autonomous components are equal in the long run. For example, Morlin (2022) focuses on a model with government spending and exports considering the dynamics of the external constraint. The author proposes two adjustment mechanisms. The first is based on the case where excessive growth of government spending, relative to that of exports, may lead to balance of payments stability problems and 'therefore, fiscal policy management can prevent the convergence of the debt-to-exports ratio towards an excessively high ratio' (Morlin 2022, p. 592). In this case, the growth rate of government spending will have to converge to the lower growth rate of exports (as in the second scenario described by Allain 2022). Alternatively, the government could implement industrial policies that would improve the elasticities of exports to income and decrease those of imports, generating a permanent increase in the growth rate of exports. As in Allain's last scenario (2022), this would reduce the foreign constraint and increase fiscal space to allow the government to peg the growth rate of government spending to that of exports. Depending on the case, the direction of adjustment of growth rates may vary; what does not vary is their equality in the long run. A supermultiplier model applied to the open economy is also that of Dvoskin and Landau (2023) in which the dynamics of exports and government spending are again analysed. Also, in this work, the equality of the growth rates of the autonomous components in the long run is assumed if government spending grows more than exports there will be balance-of-payments problems; on the other hand, in the opposite case the government is not maximising income and employment, and it could lead to an unrealistic scenario in which the share of government spending would be insignificant in aggregate demand.

Differently from the last two papers, Freitas and Christianes (2020) present a supermultiplier model for the analysis of government fiscal policy and debt in closed economies. They introduce two sources of autonomous demand: capitalists' autonomous consumption and government consumption. Again, they assume that 'the rates of growth of the two autonomous demand components are related in a way that, although they can be different, there is a tendency for them to be equal on average over time', to avoid the 'implausible situation in which the total autonomous demand share of one of the two autonomous expenditures tends towards 100 percent, while its complement tends to zero' (Freitas and Christianes 2020, p. 319). However, they do not propose a mechanism that can justify the adjustment of growth rates, the latter being beyond the scope of their article. Pedrosa, Brochier, and Freitas (2023) focus again on a closed economy building a stock-flow consistent Supermultiplier model with two sources of debt-financed autonomous demand (government and household consumption), stressing the interplay between households, firms, government indebtedness, and growth. One of the main results of their model concerns the possibility of fiscal policy to stabilise household debt. To demonstrate this, they assume 'the same average autonomous demand growth rate in the long run' (Pedrosa, Brochier, and Freitas 2023, pp. 7–8), without justifying this specific assumption.

So far, therefore, in all these works the theoretical shortcut adopted has been to assume that, at least as a long-run average, all the different components grow at the same rate due to the existence of discretionary choices or financial constraints. However, this assumption is contradicted by the empirical literature, which shows significant differences in the effect of each component on the growth process (Barbieri Góes and Deleidi 2022). Therefore, while not denying the importance of such discretionary mechanisms and financial factors, another strand of literature has attempted to highlight the interplay between financial flows and stocks as an important element to be tackled within a supermultiplier perspective. While also assessing the effect of personal income inequality and income taxes, Barbieri Góes (2019) builds a supermultiplier model by incorporating financial features and real estate prices in the autonomous component of aggregate consumption. Similarly, Brochier and Silva (2019) show how important it is to include financial interactions in a stock-flow supermultiplier model. Then, Hein and Woodgate (2021) developed this approach by explicitly adding a financial element to autonomous demand-led models. In this case, the novelty rests in the insertion of both interest payments on government debt and consumption out of wealth. According to the authors, such shortcut engenders new conditions for long-run stability as well, thereby reinforcing the need to address these points more in-depth. These insights have been then used to show how it is possible, under certain assumptions, to align the growth rates of multiple autonomous components. In particular, Di Bucchianico (2021) sets up a supermultiplier model with workers' autonomous credit-financed consumption and capitalists' autonomous consumption out of interest income accruing from accumulated debt. The author shows how, provided that the emulative response of workers concerning to divergences between their consumption pattern and that of capitalists is sufficiently strong, autonomous credit-financed consumption growth sets the pace of autonomous demand expansion. Otherwise, the growth rate converges to that of the autonomous demand generated by capitalists. Along these lines, Woodgate, Hein, and Summa (2023) construct a supermultiplier model with two components (government spending and rentiers' consumption out interest income) to show a stock-flow mechanism that can align them. Increases in deficit-financed government spending will result in an interest flow to rentiers that will affect their autonomous consumption. Hence, in the long run, the growth rate of consumption out of interest income, the passive component of autonomous demand, will have to align with the growth rate of government spending (Woodgate, Hein, and Summa (2023, p. 6).

Grounding on the approach that relies on endogenous stock-flow interactions to determine the growth path of autonomous demand, in the next sections we will show how the same endogenous feedback effects and relations could be extended to the case where private debt is considered, in a supermultiplier model based on household debt accumulation (Avritzer 2022; Avritzer and Brochier 2022; Mandarino, Dos Santos, and e Silva 2020; Pariboni 2016) and rentiers' consumption out of interest accruing from such debt (Hein and Woodgate 2021).

3. The Model

The Sraffian supermultiplier modelling strategy (Cesaratto, Serrano, and Stirati 2003; Serrano 1995) is enjoying a remarkable deal of theoretical discussion (Allain 2022; Cesaratto 2015; Lavoie 2016). In this section we shall try to build on it to obtain a simple mechanism linking flows and stocks of private debt that generate growth dynamics in which two autonomous components have a tight, intertwined connection.

Grounding on Freitas and Serrano (2015), Serrano and Freitas (2017), we start from a closed economy without a government and an external sector. There is a one fixed-coefficients technique and only one product is produced by combining homogeneous labour with homogeneous fixed capital. We suppose constant returns to scale. Natural resources and labour are overabundant; income distribution is fixed exogenously. All variables are expressed in real terms and the price level does not change; hence, we do not account for inflation. Accordingly, full capacity output Y_{Kt} depends on the capital-to-capacity-output ratio v and the capital stock K_t as in (1):

$$Y_{Kt} = \frac{1}{v} K_t \tag{1}$$

Actual output Y is simply the sum of consumption and investment as in (2).

$$Y = C + I \tag{2}$$

We can now turn to the block constituted by consumption. Aggregate consumption C in (3) is the sum of workers' (C^w) and rentiers' (C^π) consumption. Workers' autonomous consumption is equal to C^c, hence, to the amount of credit financed consumption; we suppose it to be wholly consumed, therefore the marginal propensity to consume out of this component is implicitly equal to one. In addition, their disposable income is made up of their share of income $s_w Y$ (equal to total wages W^w paid to them) minus the expenses due to the payment of interests on their outstanding debt (iD_w) plus the amortisation of outstanding debt (at rate φ), and they consume out of it with a marginal propensity c_W. The rate of interest on banks' loans is proxied by the central bank's policy rate. Rentiers consume, with a marginal propensity c_π, the earnings given by the interest rate calculated to extant debt accumulated by workers[3] D_w and their share of income $s_\pi Y$ (equal to firms' profits Π).

$$C = C^w + C^\pi = C^c + c_w[s_w Y - (i + \varphi)D_w] + c_\pi(iD_w + s_\pi Y) \tag{3}$$

$$I = hY \tag{4}$$

$$Z = C^c - [c_w(i + \varphi) + c_\pi i]D_w \tag{5}$$

$$Y^* = \frac{Z}{1 - [(c_w s_w + c_\pi s_\pi) + h]} = \frac{Z}{s - h} \tag{6}$$

Investment follows the usual pattern as in (4) according to which firms invest a given share h out of aggregate income Y. It is treated as fully endogenous and serves to equip firms, having a marginal propensity to invest h, with the amount of capacity needed to produce at a normal level of utilisation u_n. Firms and banks are highly stylised economic units. Firms collect funding by issuing equities but do not resort to borrowing. Banks only collect interests on debt and do not pay interests on deposits; they transfer interests collected to rentiers and do not accumulate net worth. The balance sheet and the transaction flow matrices are shown in Appendix 1.

In (5) we isolate the autonomous components of consumption Z from the consumption equation 3 and we lump them together. From these equations we can then derive the equilibrium level of output Y^* in (6) which is the product of the supermultiplier, where both the marginal propensities weighted by the shares out of income (whose complement to one is s) and the marginal propensity to invest enter, and the autonomous part of consumption Z. To ensure stability, the denominator of the supermultiplier must be lower than one.

From the level of autonomous demand, in (5), we then move to its time rate of change, in (7). In (8), workers' credit-financed consumption varies according to a law of motion in which they positively increase the amount of credit-financed consumption C^c by a given percentage α. Indeed, workers are supposed to earn enough so that they can save ($c_w < 1$) but not enough so that they must borrow.[4] The parameter α can stand for various factors; in particular, we suppose it to represent the attempt of workers to preserve acquired consumption standards despite an unfavourable pattern of the labour share of income (Barba and Pivetti 2009), and the willingness to pursue consumption standards set by richer households (Cynamon and Fazzari 2016). For the sake of

---

[3]We suppose both workers and rentiers to accumulate deposits in a single bank. Under the hypothesis of a zero rate of interest on bank deposits i_d, the rate of interest times accumulated workers' debt is equal to bank profits. To keep things simple, we do not include formally the bank system in the model but the presence of deposits is shown in Table 4.

[4]Two aspects can be brought up to explain such behaviour (Setterfield and Kim 2016, p. 24). First, aggregate working households' behaviour conceals noticeable differences. While a share of working households save, the other consumes more than they earn and, hence, must resort to borrowing. Second, saving and borrowing at the same time is rational in the presence of uncertainty (engendering precautionary savings) and credit market imperfections (households cannot simply use up borrowed funds as they could do with accumulated savings).

simplicity, we do not further specify it, but it is possible to find in the literature several contributions exploiting it to endogenize the desire to 'keep up with the Joneses', as in Setterfield and Kim (2016), Setterfield, Kim, and Rees (2016). On the other hand, the rate of interest i discourages the accumulation of further consumption-related debt, and it does so being mediated by the parameter β, representing all the elements that concur to make the obtainment of credit more difficult (such as bank stringency over guarantees, the state of confidence in the ability to repay outstanding debt, and so on).[5] In line with Barbieri Goes (2022, Appendix 2), the accumulation of private debt is tracked in equation 9 using an equation in which the time rate of change of private debt $\dot{D}_w$ depends positively on the flow of credit-financed consumption C^c in each period and negatively on amortisation of extant debt (φD_w).

$$\dot{Z} = \dot{C}^c - [c_w(i + \varphi) + c_\pi i]\, \dot{D}_w \tag{7}$$

$$\dot{C}^c = (\alpha - \beta i)C^c \tag{8}$$

$$\dot{D}_w = C^c - \varphi D_w \tag{9}$$

Then we describe household debt accumulation following the intuition offered by Mason and Jayadev (2014, 2015): to use an equation akin to that utilised to describe public debt evolution, adapted to the private debt case. However, to simplify the analysis we omit a list of elements that can be taken into account: for example, defaults on accumulated debt, the presence of inflation eroding the real value of debt, and so forth.

Then, the growth rate of autonomous demand g_z in (11) is derived by rewriting Z as the product of two terms, D_w and (d–q) (10):

$$Z = D_w(d - q),\ d = C^c/D_w, \quad q = c_w(i + \varphi) - c_\pi i \tag{10}$$

$$g_z = g_{D_w} + g_{d-q} = (d - \varphi) + \frac{d(\alpha - \beta i - d + \varphi)}{d - q} \tag{11}$$

To obtain the expression in (11), first, we calculate g_{D_w} by reformulating (9) dividing it through by the absolute level of debt so as to obtain (12):

$$g_{D_w} = \frac{C^c - \varphi D_w}{D_w} = d - \varphi \tag{12}$$

Hence, the growth rate of workers' debt g_{D_w} is given by the ratio d between the flow of credit-finance consumption and the stock of debt minus the amortisation rate φ.

Second, to calculate g_{d-q} as in (14) we need to consider that the rate of change of q is zero, given that it encompasses only given parameters. Then, we need to separately derive the rate of change of d as in (13). To track the evolution of the ratio d, we consider its rate of variation as the difference between that of workers' credit-financed consumption and

[5]Obviously, given that we fully accept the money endogeneity principle, this supply element is constrained by riskiness and profitability evaluations, not by prior saving. We do not consider the possibility for a higher interest rate to affect also functional income distribution. For some evidence about this topic, see Di Bucchianico and Lofaro (2023).

that of workers' private debt.

$$\dot{d} = \dot{C}^{c} - \dot{D}_w = d(\alpha - \beta i - d + \varphi) \tag{13}$$

$$g_{D_w} = \frac{(d \dot{-} q)}{d - q} = \frac{d(\alpha - \beta i - d + \varphi)}{d - q} \tag{14}$$

We now add also the usual list of equations describing capital accumulation, the time rate of change of capacity utilisation and of the propensity to invest, and output growth as we move to the dynamically growing version of the model.

$$g_K = \left(\frac{I/Y}{v}\right)u - \delta \tag{15}$$

$$\dot{u} = u(g - g_K) \tag{16}$$

$$\dot{h} = h\gamma(u - u_n) \tag{17}$$

Capital accumulation g_K, driving the expansion of capacity output, is defined in (15) as a function of the investment share I/Y, the rate of capacity utilisation u, the given v, and the exogenous depreciation rate δ. In (16), the rate of capacity utilisation changes subject to the discrepancy between output growth g and capital accumulation. The marginal propensity to invest is liable to change, according to a flexible accelerator as in (17) and with with responsiveness given by $\gamma > 0$, when the actual rate of capacity utilisation persistently deviates from its normal level.

$$g = g_Z + \frac{h\gamma(u - u_n)}{1 - [(c_w s_w + c_\pi s_\pi) + h]} \tag{18}$$

In (18) output grows over time at a pace g given by the sum of autonomous demand growth g_Z and, when actual and normal utilisation differs, the growth of investment needed to bring capacity utilisation towards its normal value (Serrano and Freitas 2017, p. 75).

Given that the economy is supposed to grow at a pace g_Z set by autonomous demand in the long-run steady state, and that autonomous demand in our case is composed of two elements, we must isolate the dominant component. Indeed, Pariboni (2016, p. 227) points out that 'the economy's growth rate slowly converges to the growth rate of the fastest growing autonomous component'. We exploit this clue by finding a condition according to which one component sets the growth rate of autonomous demand. However, in this case, we also consider that growing workers' debt feeds on rentiers' consumption via interests (as in Hein and Woodgate 2021).

$$g_{zw} \gtreqless g_{z\pi} \rightarrow (\alpha - \beta i)d - c_w(i + \varphi)(d - \varphi) \gtreqless c_\pi i(d - \varphi) \tag{19}$$

$$\alpha \gtreqless (1 - \theta)[c_w(i + \varphi) + c_\pi i] + \beta i, \qquad \theta = \varphi/d \tag{20}$$

$$\frac{\bar{C}^{w}}{\bar{C}^{\pi}} = \frac{d - c_w(i + \varphi)}{c_\pi i} \tag{21}$$

The inequality in (19) compares the growth rates of workers' and rentiers' autonomous consumption. Given that they share the same denominator, to assess their respective sizes we simply compare the elements in (7), rearranged to sort out the autonomous demand of the two groups. Read in terms of the strength of workers' desire to finance via credit additional consumption, we can see in (20) that the dominance of the growth rate of workers' autonomous demand or rentiers' autonomous demand depends on the parameter α being higher or lower than what we find to the right-hand side. For instance, we can suppose the parameter α has been sufficiently high during the period prior to the Great Recession in the US to generate a regime in which workers' debt accumulation drove growth through that phase (Barba and Pivetti 2009; Cynamon and Fazzari 2016). Moreover, in (21) we see how the ratio between workers' and rentiers' autonomous consumption is an increasing function of d. Hence, a rise in the latter ratio results in a rise in the ratio between the two autonomous consumption levels.

Using this analysis, it is possible to highlight how, given that workers' debt accumulation generates also interest payments accruing to rentiers who hold that debt, there emerges the possibility to analyse the long-run pattern of accumulation without resorting to peculiar hypotheses regarding the respective behaviour of the two autonomous components present in the model. Rather, the stock-flow relationship that ties the two components together allows us to avoid the undesirable asymptotic situation in which one autonomous component absorbs all autonomous demand without *ad hoc* hypotheses meant to prevent that scenario.

At this point, we address the stability of the model using the following system composed of three differential equations.[6]

$$\dot{h} = h\gamma(u - u_n) \tag{22}$$

$$\dot{u} = u\left((d - \varphi) + \frac{d(\alpha - \beta i - d + \varphi)}{d - q} + \frac{h\gamma(u - u_n)}{1 - [(c_w s_w + c_\pi s_\pi) + h]} - \frac{h}{v}u + \delta\right) \tag{23}$$

$$\dot{d} = d[\alpha - \beta i - d + \varphi] \tag{24}$$

The dynamic system is composed of three differential equations in three variables h, u, and d. Equation 22 describes the variation of the marginal propensity to invest. Equation 23 describes the variation of the rate of capacity utilisation, in which we substituted (18) and (11) in g and (15) in g_K. Equation 24 simply recalls (13). As in Freitas and Serrano (2015, pp. 263–269), we proceed to find the steady-state solutions of the three-equation

[6]The structure of the system is analogous to that of Freitas and Christianes (2020, pp. 321–323) way of analysing stability, but in our case the system is driven by workers' private debt accumulation instead of public debt, and we treat the system as a three-equation system rather than a two-equation system plus an auxiliary equation as they did.

system:[7]

$$g_Z^* = \alpha - \beta i \tag{25}$$

$$\dot{h} = 0 \rightarrow \; u^* = u_n \tag{26}$$

$$\dot{u} = 0 \rightarrow h^* = (\alpha - \beta i + \delta)\frac{v}{u_n} \tag{27}$$

$$\dot{d} = 0 \rightarrow d^* = \; \alpha - \beta i + \varphi \tag{28}$$

At this point, the analysis of local stability of the system requires the derivation of a 3×3 Jacobian matrix whose partial derivatives are then evaluated considering the parameters h, u, and d at long run equilibrium. Here we report the two fundamental conditions for stability (29) and (30). Their full derivation can be found in Appendix 2.

$$\alpha > \beta i \tag{29}$$

$$\frac{\gamma}{s \; - (\alpha - \beta i + \delta)\frac{v}{u_n}} < \frac{1}{v} \tag{30}$$

The stability conditions are akin to those usually found in the literature. As an example, a similar analysis has been carried out by Woodgate, Hein, and Summa (2023). In the next section, we calibrate and numerically simulate the model.

4. Model Simulation

4.1. Parameter Calibration

Parameter values are set in accordance with the empirical evidence for the US. The model is calibrated at an annual frequency. It is important to stress that the calibration exercise is purely illustrative, as proper evaluation of the model would require further empirical and econometric investigation.

Few well-identified parameters are in line with the macroeconomic performances of the US economy following the 2007–2008 crisis. In particular, the values for the wage share are obtained by averaging the adjusted wage share in the US for the period 2007–2022, yielding a value of 61 per cent — thus implying a profit share of 39 per cent. The consumption propensities out of wages and out of profits are set to 0.7 and 0.2, respectively, to match a tax-adjusted propensity to consume of about 50 per cent, as discussed by Fazzari, Ferri, and Variato (2020), Blecker, Cauvel, and Kim (2022), and Gallo (2022, 2023). The depreciation rate and the capital-capacity ratio are set to 8.4 per cent and 0.989 (on an annual basis), respectively, in line with Fazzari, Ferri, and Variato (2020).

The interest rate is set equal to 1 per cent, obtained by averaging the effective federal funds rate over the period 2007–2022 (before the rate hikes from February 2022 onwards). In Section 4.3, we will see what happens to the model's stability and traverse path when the discount rate increases. Out of the four remaining parameters, the value of

[7] We obviously neglect the solutions involving all the variables of interest to be zero in a steady state.

Table 1. Parameter calibration.

Par.	Description	Value	Source
π	Profit share	0.39	Authors' calculation, based on AMECO (2023)
c_w	Propensity to consume out of wages	0.7	Authors' calculation, based on Fazzari, Ferri, and Variato (2020)
c_π	Propensity to consume out of profits	0.2	Authors' calculation, based on Fazzari, Ferri, and Variato (2020)
u_n	Normal rate of capacity utilisation	0.8242	Setterfield and Budd (2011), Gallo (2022)
v	Capital-capacity ratio (annual)	0.989	Gallo (2022), Fazzari, Ferri, and Variato (2020)
δ	Depreciation rate (annual)	0.084	Fazzari, Ferri, and Variato (2020)
i	Federal funds rate	0.01 (0.02)	Authors' calculation, based on FRED (2023)
γ	Sensitivity of the investment share to $u_t - u_n$	0.15	Nomaler, Spinola, and Verspagen (2021), Gallo (2022)
α	Incompressible credit-financed consumption growth	0.03 (0.035)	Authors' calculation, moments to match
β	Sensitivity of credit-financed consumption to i	0.1	Authors' calculation, moments to match
φ	Amortisation rate	0.01	Svensson (2016)

Source: authors' calculation.

Table 2. Initial conditions.

Variable	Description	Value
u_0	Capacity utilisation rate	0.8242
d_0	Credit-financed consumption-to-debt ratio	0.049
$g_{z,0}$	Autonomous demand (annual) growth rate	0.039
h_0	Investment share	0.148

Source: authors' calculation.

γ is taken from Nomaler, Spinola, and Verspagen (2021) and it is equal to the one adopted by Gallo (2022), who also conducts a sensitivity analysis to assess the effect of a change in the parameter in a simpler version of the supermultiplier model. The amortisation rate is taken from the work of Svensson (2016). Last, α and β are set to match an annual growth rate of autonomous demand of about 3 per cent, in line with Girardi and Pariboni (2016), and Fazzari, Ferri, and Variato (2020). Parameter values are summarised in Table 1.

For the sake of comparability, the model's initial conditions are the same as the ones discussed by Gallo (2022). The only novelty is the initial conditions for the credit-financed consumption-to-debt ratio (d_0) — absent in the cited contribution. Its value is set to be 1 per cent above its steady-state value, in a similar fashion to the growth rate of autonomous demand (set to be $g_{z,0} = g_Z^* + 0.01 = .029 + .01 = 3.9\%$). Broadly speaking, this set of initial conditions represents a situation where the economy is experiencing a credit-fuelled injection of purchasing power, that raises at the same time the credit-financed consumption-to-debt ratio and the growth rate of autonomous demand. Table 2 summarises the model's initial conditions.

4.2. Simulation Results

As mentioned in Section Three, for the sake of simplicity, we do not solve our 3×3 model analytically, focusing on stability and traverse properties by merely adopting the method of numerical integration. Under the parameter constellation discussed in the previous section, the model converges to its long-run equilibrium through damped oscillations, thus constituting a 3D spiral sink. Figure 1 shows the three-dimensional representation of the phase plane of the system.

Let us now look at the behaviour of each of the endogenous variables in the system. First, let us account for the time dimension of our model. More specifically, Figures 2–4 confirm a property of supermultiplier models already observed in Gallo (2022) and Allain (2022), i.e., their slow pace of convergence to the fully- adjusted position. As can be observed from the figures, the model takes about 100 years to settle in its long-run equilibrium following a 1 per cent shock in autonomous demand growth. These simulation results are hence supportive of the view put forward by Gallo and Setterfield (2023), according to which supermultiplier models of both Sraffian and Kaleckian fashion ought to be interpreted as 'traverse models', thus bearing in mind that disequilibrium in the model is the norm rather than the exception. Impact effects and movements over the traverse are to be taken with greater care the stability properties of an equilibrium that might never be reached.

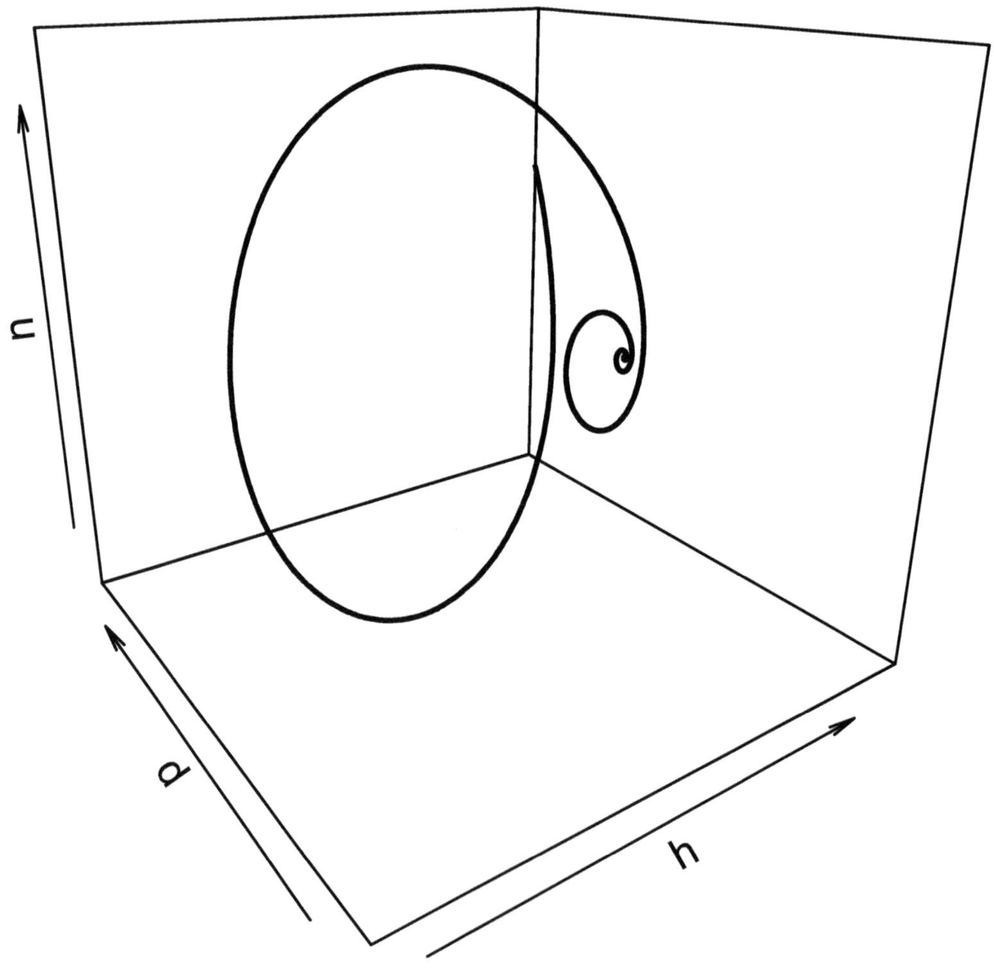

Figure 1. 3D phase plane of the model. Source: authors' representation.

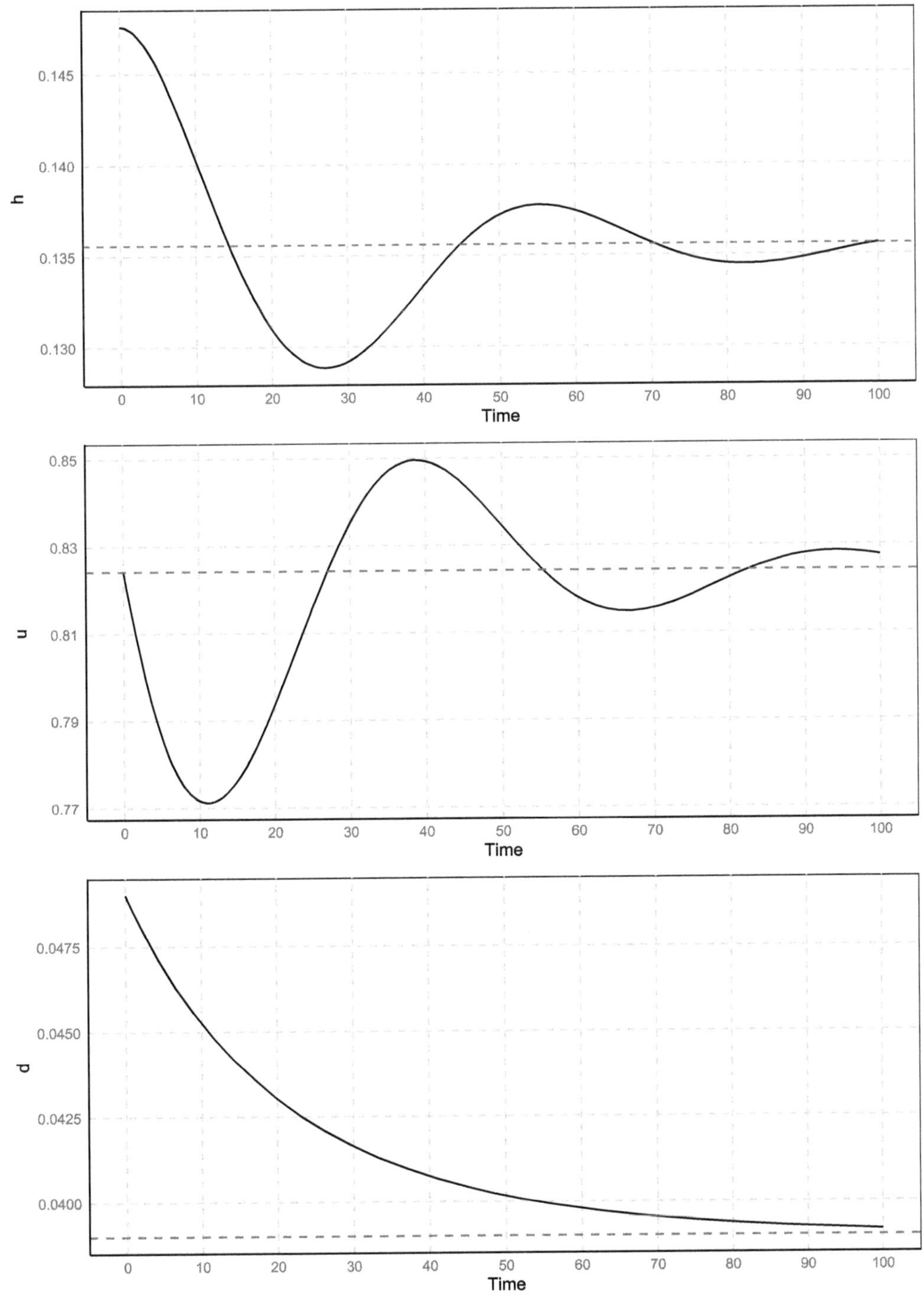

Figure 2. The model's long-run traverse. Source: authors' representation.

The first two panels of Figure 2 show the dynamics of the model in the conventional $h - u$ plane of Sraffian supermultiplier models. Since the investment share at time

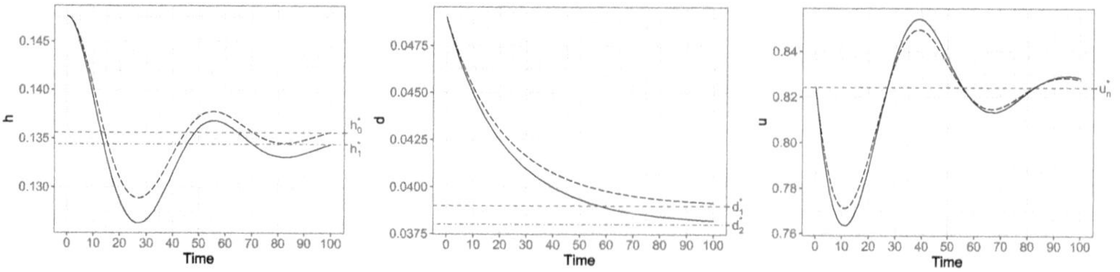

Figure 3. The long-run traverse in the model with changing *i*. Source: authors' representation.

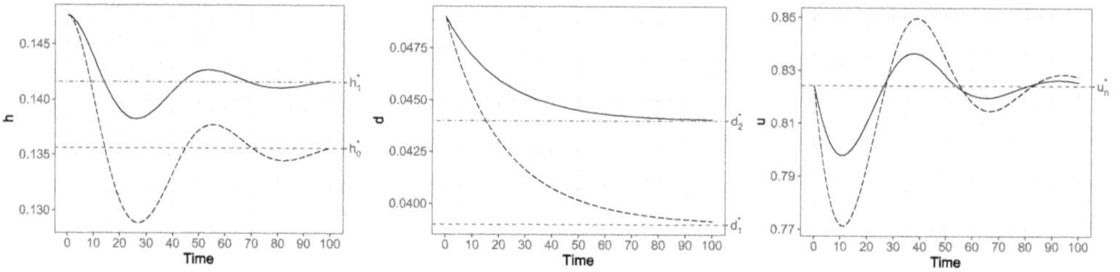

Figure 4. The long-run traverse in the model with changing α. Source: authors' representation.

$t = 0$ is above the one of long-run equilibrium, capacity utilisation will initially decrease (approximately in the first 10 years of the traverse). The damped cycles in the capacity utilisation rate and in the investment share will last until the steady-state position corresponding to a higher level of autonomous demand is achieved.

The last panel shows the monotonic convergence of the credit-financed consumption-to-debt ratio d to its long-run value (equal to 3.9 per cent in the baseline calibration) following a relatively small divergence from the steady-state conditions prevailing prior to $t = 0$. Summarising, a credit-financed consumption shock has long-lasting effects on growth and credit-debt relations, supporting the idea of the interrelation of growth and finance widespread in the post-Keynesian — and particularly Minskyan literature.

4.3. Sensitivity Analysis

This section will assess the sensitivity of the models' results and speed of adjustment when the parameter space is modified. For the sake of simplicity, we do not compute eigenvalues for the model, and thus we cannot assess whether the speed of convergence is affected by looking at changes in the dominant eigenvalues — as e.g., in Gabaix et al. (2016). Therefore, the sensitivity analysis would need to rely on numerical methods only. To do that, a convenient visualisation tool is provided in the Online Appendix of this paper (see Appendix 3). With the aid of a web app, the interested reader could easily perform a re-parametrization of the models.

For the sake of the argument, let us only focus on two changes in the parameter space, by looking first at what happens when the discount rate increases and then, by assessing how the system responds to a change in the parameter α. First, let us assume an increase in the interest rate from 0.1 to 1 per cent. The effect of the change is shown in Figure 3.

The dashed line corresponds to the previous traverse path (as in Figure 2), while the new adjustment process corresponds to the solid line. An increase in the interest rate alters both the long-run steady-state and the model's traverse path. More specifically, the simulation shows that a restrictive monetary policy has a negative effect both on the investment share (because of the negative effect that i has on g_z) and on capacity utilisation in the first phase of the traverse, making the downturn sharper. At the same time, the d ratio increases from one steady-state to the other, because of the increased burden of interest payments. Moreover, the change in i also has the effect of making the adjustment to the new long-run position slightly slower.

Second, let us assess the effect of a change in the growth rate of the incompressible component of credit-financed consumption, i.e., α. More specifically, we assume a shift in the parameter from the baseline calibration of 3 to 3.5 per cent. The result is shown in Figure 4. As before, the dashed lines correspond to the baseline calibration, and the solid ones to the new parameter space. Because of the positive effect of α on g_z, the increase in the former will boost growth and, in turn, the investment share, thus leading the system to converge to a higher value of h^*. Quite intuitively, the equilibrium value of the credit-financed consumption-to-debt ratio will increase. Last, the doubling of α slightly shortens the time of adjustment to the new steady-state position.

5. Conclusion

The need to incorporate financial elements into the Supermultiplier and to solve the steady-state puzzle posed by the presence of more than one autonomous demand component prominently features in current debates. To provide a stylised answer to both issues, we built a simple model in which workers accumulate private debt in the hands of rentiers to sustain spending through credit-financed consumption. In turn, rentiers' autonomous consumption is fed by interest flows accruing from accumulating debt. As we have shown, it is possible to keep together workers' autonomous credit-financed consumption and rentiers' autonomous consumption in the long-term by simply relying on the stock-flow connection tying the two. According to specific conditions, the model can be driven by either component, whereas the other endogenously adjusts to the predominant growth rate.

The stability of the long-run equilibrium as well as the traverse path of the model has been studied by numerically solving the nonlinear system of differential equations underlying the model's adjustment process. To do that, the model has been calibrated at annual frequency using empirical evidence for the US and past studies. The simulation shows that, in line with other supermultiplier models, our system is also characterised by a slow pace of adjustment to the long-run fully adjusted position. Changes in credit-debt relations affect the model by affecting autonomous demand growth, thus having growth effects both during and after the traverse. The robustness of the model to changes in the parameter space has also been assessed by performing a sensitivity analysis.

In conclusion, the main message refers to the possibility to solve the 'two-autonomous-components-conundrum' by accounting for stock-flow relations that provide a purely economic solution to the issue. Hence, there is no inescapable need to impose peculiar hypotheses on the relative behaviour of the autonomous components involved in the model. Further research is needed to uncover additional avenues of application for this principle, as well as to integrate it with institutional elements as well as political crackdowns.

Acknowledgements

We would like to acknowledge and thank the reviewers for their valuable comments and criticism, which greatly improved the quality of the paper and facilitated its publication.

Disclosure Statement

No potential conflict of interest was reported by the author(s).

ORCID

Stefano di Bucchianico http://orcid.org/0000-0002-6688-5994
Ettore Gallo http://orcid.org/0000-0002-4642-4779
Antonino Lofaro http://orcid.org/0009-0003-2149-0643

References

Allain, O. 2022. 'A Supermultiplier Model with Two Non-Capacity-Generating Semi-autonomous Demand Components.' *Structural Change and Economic Dynamics* 63: 91–103.

AMECO. 2023. 'Adjusted Wage Share, Percentage of GDP at Current Factor Cost (ALCD2), United States, United States.' Accessed June 12, 2023. https://economy-finance.ec.europa.eu/economic-research-and-databases/economic-databases/ameco-database_en.

Avritzer, J. D. 2022. 'Debt-led Growth and its Financial Fragility: An Investigation into the Dynamics of a Supermultiplier Model.' *PSL Quarterly Review* 75 (302): 241–262.

Avritzer, J. D., and L. Brochier. 2022. 'Credit-Financed Household Consumption and the Debt Service Ratio: Tackling Endogenous Autonomous Demand in the Supermultiplier Model.' *SSRN*. https://ssrn.com/abstract=4192546.

Barba, A., and M. Pivetti. 2009. 'Rising Household Debt: Its Causes and Macroeconomic Implications—a Long-period Analysis.' *Cambridge Journal of Economics* 33 (1): 113–137.

Barbieri Góes, M. C. 2019. 'Why Fiscal and Distributive Policies Should Rule the Game.' Personal Income Inequality, Taxation and Financial Instability in the Sraffian (Hyper) multiplier Model, FMM Conference Paper.

Barbieri Góes, M. C. 2022. 'Why Fiscal and Distributive Policies Should Rule the Game: Personal Income Inequality, Taxation and Financial Instability in the Sraffian (Hyper)multiplier Model.' PhD thesis.

Barbieri Góes, M. C., and M. Deleidi. 2022. 'Output Determination and Autonomous Demand Multipliers: An Empirical Investigation for the US Economy.' *Economic Modelling* 116: 106004.

Blecker, R. A., M. Cauvel, and Y. K. Kim. 2022. 'Systems Estimation of a Structural Model of Distribution and Demand in the US Economy.' *Cambridge Journal of Economics* 46 (2): 391–420.

Borio, C., and P. Disyatat. 2011. 'Global Imbalances and the Financial Crisis: Link or no Link?' BIS Working Papers No. 346.

Brochier, L., and A. C. M. E. Silva. 2019. 'A Supermultiplier Stock-Flow Consistent Model: The "Return" of the Paradoxes of Thrift and Costs in the Long Run?' *Cambridge Journal of Economics* 43 (2): 413–442.

Cesaratto, S. 2015. 'Neo-Kaleckian and Sraffian Controversies on the Theory of Accumulation.' *Review of Political Economy* 27 (2): 154–182.

Cesaratto, S. 2017. 'Initial and Final Finance in the Monetary Circuit and the Theory of Effective Demand.' *Metroeconomica* 68 (2): 228–258.

Cesaratto, S., and S. Di Bucchianico. 2020. 'Endogenous Money and the Theory of Long-period Effective Demand.' *Bulletin of Political Economy* 14 (1): 1–38.

Cesaratto, S., and R. Pariboni. 2022. 'The Relation Between Keynesian Monetary Theory and Demand-led Growth: a Sraffian Exploration.' *Review of Keynesian Economics* 10 (3): 291–315.

Cesaratto, S., F. Serrano, and A. Stirati. 2003. 'Technical Change, Effective Demand and Employment.' *Review of political economy* 15 (1): 33–52.

Cynamon, B. Z., and S. M. Fazzari. 2016. 'Inequality, the Great Recession and Slow Recovery.' *Cambridge Journal of Economics* 40 (2): 373–399.

Dejuán, Ó., and D. Dejuán-Bitriá. 2018. 'A Predator–prey Model to Explain Cycles in Credit-led Economies.' *Review of Keynesian Economics* 6(2): 159–179.

Dejuán, Ó., and D. Dejuán-Bitriá. 2022. 'The Supermultiplier-Cum-Finance. An Application to the Credit-Led Boom Before the 2008 Crash.' *Review of Political Economy* 1–23.

Di Bucchianico, S. 2021. 'Inequality, Household Debt, Ageing and Bubbles: A Model of Demand-side Secular Stagnation.' IPE Working Paper Series, No. 160/2021.

Di Bucchianico, S., and A. Lofaro. 2023. 'The Impact of Monetary Policy on Functional Income Distribution: a Panel SVAR Analysis (1970–2019).' DEPS Working Paper Series, University of Siena, No. 900.

Dvoskin, A., and M. T. Landau. 2023. 'Income Distribution and Economic Cycles in an Open-economy Supermultiplier Model.' *Structural Change and Economic Dynamics* 64: 273–291.

Fazzari, S. M., P. Ferri, and A. M. Variato. 2020. 'Demand-led Growth and Accommodating Supply.' *Cambridge Journal of Economics* 44 (3): 583–605.

FRED. 2023. 'Federal Funds Effective Rate (DFF), Board of Governors of the Federal Reserve System (US) United States, United States.' Accessed June 12, 2023. https://fred.stlouisfed.org/series/DFF#0.

Freitas, F., and R. Christianes. 2020. 'A Baseline Supermultiplier Model for the Analysis of Fiscal Policy and Government Debt.' *Review of Keynesian Economics* 8 (3): 313–338.

Freitas, F., and F. Serrano. 2015. 'Growth Rate and Level Effects, the Stability of the Adjustment of Capacity to Demand and the Sraffian Supermultiplier.' *Review of Political Economy* 27 (3): 258–281.

Gabaix, X., J. M. Lasry, P. L. Lions, and B. Moll. 2016. 'The Dynamics of Inequality.' *Econometrica* 84 (6): 2071–2111.

Gallo, E. 2022. 'When is the Long Run?—Historical Time and Adjustment Periods in Demand-led Growth Models.' *Metroeconomica* 73 (4): 1155–1178.

Gallo, E. 2023. 'How short is the short run in the Neo-Kaleckian growth model?' *Review of Political Economy* 35 (3): 687–701.

Gallo, E., and M. Setterfield. 2023. 'Joan Robinson's Historical Time and the Current State of Post-Keynesian Growth Theory.' *Cambridge Journal of Economics* 47 (5): 965–984.

Girardi, D., and R. Pariboni. 2016. 'Long-run Effective Demand in the US Economy: an Empirical Test of the Sraffian Supermultiplier Model.' *Review of Political Economy* 28 (4): 523–544.

Graziani, A. 2003. *The Monetary Theory of Production.* Cambridge: Cambridge University Press.

Hein, E., and R. Woodgate. 2021. 'Stability Issues in Kaleckian Models Driven by Autonomous Demand Growth—Harrodian Instability and Debt Dynamics.' *Metroeconomica* 72 (2): 388–404.

Lavoie, M. 2016. 'Convergence Towards the Normal Rate of Capacity Utilization in Neo-K aleckian Models: The Role of Non-Capacity Creating Autonomous Expenditures.' *Metroeconomica* 67 (1): 172–201.

Mandarino, G. V., C. H. Dos Santos, and A. C. M. e Silva. 2020. 'Workers' Debt-financed Consumption: A Supermultiplier Stock–flow Consistent Model.' *Review of Keynesian Economics* 8(3): 339–364.

Mason, J. W., and A. Jayadev. 2014. '"Fisher Dynamics" in US Household Debt, 1929–2011.' *American Economic Journal: Macroeconomics* 6 (3): 214–234.

Mason, J. W., and A. Jayadev. 2015. 'The Post-1980 Debt Disinflation: An Exercise in Historical Accounting.' *Review of Keynesian Economics* 3 (3): 314–335.

Morlin, G. S. 2022. 'Growth Led by Government Expenditure and Exports: Public and External Debt Stability in a Supermultiplier Model.' *Structural Change and Economic Dynamics* 62: 586–598.

Nikiforos, M. 2018. 'Some Comments on the Sraffian Supermultiplier Approach to Growth and Distribution.' *Journal of Post Keynesian Economics* 41 (4): 659–675.

Nomaler, Ö, D. Spinola, and B. Verspagen. 2021. 'R&D-based Economic Growth in a Supermultiplier Model.' *Structural Change and Economic Dynamics* 59: 1–19.
Pariboni, R. 2016. 'Household Consumer Debt, Endogenous Money and Growth: A Supermultiplier-based Analysis.' *PSL Quarterly Review* 69 (278): 211–233.
Pedrosa, Í, L. Brochier, and F. Freitas. 2023. 'Debt Hierarchy: Autonomous Demand Composition, Growth and Indebtedness in a Supermultiplier Model.' *Economic Modelling* 106369.
Rochon, L. P. 2023. 'Endogenous Money.' In *Elgar Encyclopedia of Post-Keynesian Economics.* Cheltenam: Edward Elgar Publishing Limited.
Rochon, L. P., and S. Rossi, eds. 2017. *Advances in Endogenous Money Analysis.* Cheltenam: Edward Elgar Publishing.
Serrano, F. 1995. 'Long Period Effective Demand and the Sraffian Supermultiplier.' *Contributions to Political Economy* 14 (1): 67–90.
Serrano, F., and F. Freitas. 2017. 'The Sraffian Supermultiplier as an Alternative Closure for Heterodox Growth Theory*.' *European Journal of Economics and Economic Policies: Intervention* 14 (1): 70–91.
Serrano, F., R. Summa, and F. Freitas. 2023. 'Autonomous Demand-led Growth and the Supermultiplier: The Theory, the Model and Some Clarification.' IE-UFRJ Discussion Paper, No. 003.
Setterfield, M., and A. Budd. 2011. 'A Keynes-Kalecki Model of Cyclical Growth With Agent-Based Features.' In *Microeconomics, Macroeconomics and Economic Policy: Essays in Honour of Malcolm Sawyer*, edited by P. Arestis, 228–250. London: Palgrave Macmillan.
Setterfield, M., and Y. K. Kim. 2016. 'Debt Servicing, Aggregate Consumption, and Growth.' *Structural Change and Economic Dynamics* 36: 22–33.
Setterfield, M., Y. K. Kim, and J. Rees. 2016. 'Inequality, Debt Servicing and the Sustainability of Steady State Growth.' *Review of Political Economy* 28 (1): 45–63.
Skott, P. 2019. 'Autonomous Demand, Harrodian Instability and the Supply Side.' *Metroeconomica* 70 (2): 233–246.
Svensson, M. L. E. 2016. 'Amortization Requirements may Increase Household Debt: A Simple Example.' International Monetary Fund, WP/16/83.
Woodgate, R., E. Hein, and R. Summa. 2023. 'Components of Autonomous Demand Growth and Financial Feedbacks: Implications for Growth Drivers and Growth Regime Analysis.' *Review of Political Economy* 1–18.

Appendices

Appendix 1. Social accounting matrices

Table A1. Balance sheet matrix.

	Workers	Rentiers	Firms	Banks	Sum
Deposits	D^w_{ep}	D^π_{ep}		$-(D^w_{ep} + D^\pi_{ep})$	0
Loans	$-D^w$			D^w	0
Capital			K		K
Equity		E	$-E$		0
Net worth	$D^w_{ep} - D^w$	$D^\pi_{ep} + E$	$K - E$	$D^w - (D^w_{ep} + D^\pi_{ep})$	K

Table A2. Transaction flow matrix.

			Firms		Banks		
	Workers	Rentiers	Current	Capital	Current	Capital	Sum
Consumption	$-C^w$	$-C^\pi$	$C^w + C^\pi$				0
Wages	W^w		$-W^w$				0
Investment			I	$-I$			0
Profits		$\Pi + [iD^w - i_d(D^w_{ep} + D^\pi_{ep})]$	$-\Pi$		$-[iD^w - i_d(D^w_{ep} + D^\pi_{ep})]$		0
Loan flow	$C^c - \phi D^w$					$-C^c + \phi D^w$	0

(Continued)

Table A2. Continued.

			Firms		Banks		
	Workers	Rentiers	Current	Capital	Current	Capital	Sum
Loan interest	$-iD^W$				iD^W		0
Deposit flow	$-\Delta D^W_{ep}$	$-\Delta D^{\pi}_{ep}$				$\Delta D^W_{ep} + \Delta D^{\pi}_{ep}$	0
Deposit interest	$i_d D^W_{ep}$	$i_d D^{\pi}_{ep}$			$-i_d(D^W_{ep} + D^{\pi}_{ep})$		0
Equity issues		$-\Delta E$		ΔE			0
Sum	0	0	0	0	0	0	

Appendix 2. Stability analysis

We proceed to derive the Jacobian for the three-equation system (22)–(24) and then we evaluate it at the steady-state by means of the solutions (25)–(28).

$$J = \begin{pmatrix} \frac{\partial \dot{u}}{\partial u} & \frac{\partial \dot{u}}{\partial h} & \frac{\partial \dot{u}}{\partial d} \\ \frac{\partial \dot{h}}{\partial u} & \frac{\partial \dot{h}}{\partial h} & \frac{\partial \dot{h}}{\partial d} \\ \frac{\partial \dot{d}}{\partial u} & \frac{\partial \dot{d}}{\partial h} & \frac{\partial \dot{d}}{\partial d} \end{pmatrix} \rightarrow$$

$$J_{u^*,\ h^*,\ d^*} = \begin{pmatrix} (\alpha - \beta i + \delta)\left(\dfrac{v\gamma}{s - \left[(\alpha - \beta i + \delta)\dfrac{v}{u_n} \right]} - 1 \right) & -\dfrac{u_n^2}{v} & -\dfrac{u_n q}{\alpha - \beta i + \varphi - q} \\ (\alpha - \beta i + \delta)\dfrac{v\gamma}{u_n} & 0 & 0 \\ 0 & 0 & -(\alpha - \beta i + \varphi) \end{pmatrix}$$

The Routh-Hurwitz conditions imply:

1. $Det(J^*) < 0$
2. $Tr(J^*) < 0$
3. $-Tr(J^*)[Det(J_1^*) + Det(J_2^*) + Det(J_3^*)] + Det(J^*) > 0$

Let us calculate the determinant and the trace:

$$Det(J^*) = -[u_n \gamma (\alpha - \beta i + \delta)(\alpha - \beta i + \varphi)] < 0$$

$$Tr(J^*) = (\alpha - \beta i + \delta)\left(\frac{v\gamma}{s - (\alpha - \beta i + \delta)\dfrac{v}{u_n}} - 1 \right) - (\alpha - \beta i + \varphi) < 0$$

The determinants of the three second-order principal submatrices of $J_{u^*,\ h^*,\ d^*}$ are:

$$Det(J_1^*) = 0$$

$$Det(J_2^*) = (\alpha - \beta i + \delta)\left(\frac{v\gamma}{s - \left[(\alpha - \beta i + \delta)\dfrac{v}{u_n} \right]} - 1 \right)$$

$$Det(J_3^*) = (\alpha - \beta i + \delta)\gamma u_n$$

Hence, the third Routh-Hurwitz condition becomes

$$- Tr(J^*)[Det(J_1^*) + Det(J_2^*) + Det(J_3^*)] + Det(J^*) =$$

$$= -\left[(\alpha - \beta i + \delta)\left(\frac{v\gamma}{s - (\alpha - \beta i + \delta)\frac{v}{u_n}} - 1\right) - (\alpha - \beta i + \varphi)\right] =$$

$$\left[(\alpha - \beta i + \delta)\left(\frac{v\gamma}{s - \left[(\alpha - \beta i + \delta)\frac{v}{u_n}\right]} - 1\right) + (\alpha - \beta i + \delta)\gamma u_n\right] =$$

$$= -[u_n\gamma(\alpha - \beta i + \delta)(\alpha - \beta i + \varphi)] > 0$$

The determinant is always negative for positive values of the long-run growth rate of autonomous demand, hence

$$\alpha > \beta i \tag{A1}$$

To be verified, the other two Routh-Hurwitz conditions also require

$$\frac{\gamma}{s - (\alpha - \beta i + \delta)\frac{v}{u_n}} < \frac{1}{v} \tag{A2}$$

Limits to Fiscal and Monetary Policy in Small Open Economies

Ariel Dvoskin and Matías Torchinsky Landau

ABSTRACT

In this paper we investigate the impact of the balance-of-payments constraint on output, income distribution and policy space in a small economy open to both commercial and financial flows. We do so by extending a Sraffian supermultiplier growth model to consider current and capital accounts and endogenous money. Expansionary fiscal policies increase output and its long run growth rate but have a negative impact on the balance-of-payments. Based on these results, we derive the value of government spending that maximises output while maintaining external equilibrium.

Monetary policy also influences the balance-of-payments by attracting foreign financial flows through higher interest rates. This relationship is non-monotonic, since these flows can finance the external deficit resulting from a high output level but can also lead to a greater interest burden. This trade off allows us to find the level of the interest rate that maximises external space. It also implies that, with limits, raising interest rates might allow for higher real wages.

Lastly, we examine the effects of the currency denomination of debt. We find that, in case of a depreciation, debt in domestic currency allows for a less contractionary adjustment than foreign currency-denominated debt but does not lead to higher economic growth.

1. Introduction

According to the mainstream, in a small open economy fiscal and monetary policies face a trilemma: they cannot maintain an open capital account, a fixed exchange rate and an independent monetary policy (Mundell 1963).[1] Following this result, the macroeconomic consensus favoured a policy mix of an open economy (assuming that integration promotes growth), an independent monetary policy (which avoids potential 'fiscal dominance', harmful in the long run) and a flexible exchange rate (based on the idea that exchange rate flexibility would allow to absorb shocks).

However, the transmission mechanisms on which the trilemma is based have been criticised from alternative standpoints. Lavoie (2001), based on what is known as the

[1] By 'small' we mean a price taker country, which need not imply that the economy faces an infinitely elastic demand curve for its exports. It only means that the technical and distributive conditions of the economy do not affect international prices (Dvoskin, Feldman, and Ianni 2020).

compensation principle, which extends money endogeneity to open economies (something that is currently also accepted by the mainstream),[2] argues that it is possible to simultaneously maintain a fixed exchange rate and determine the domestic interest rates, even with an open capital account. The only limit to economic policies would be the sustainability of the balance-of-payments, since excessively low interest rate differentials (or excessively high growth rates) could lead to permanent balance-of-payments deficits that would deplete international reserves, breaking the exchange rate parity. According to this perspective, there is an 'asymmetric' trilemma, which becomes operational only when there is a loss of reserves.

Modern Monetary Theory (MMT) adopted the compensation principle to develop a policy programme based on increasing public spending to reach full employment, while keeping low or zero interest rates to maintain low debt ratios and improve income distribution. While they accept that these policies are not compatible with maintaining a fixed exchange rate, MMT supporters share with the trilemma the confidence in the exchange rate as a tool to stabilise the external sector expansively, through export promotion and import substitution.

Nevertheless, there is significant empirical evidence proving that exchange rate depreciations in small open economies, rather than absorbing shocks by increasing net exports, stabilise the balance-of-payments in a contractionary way by reducing real wages and output (Krugman and Taylor 1978). This means that the external sector, rather than promoting economic activity, sets a limit to growth, frequently defined by Thirlwall's law (1979). However, the existence of a limit does not mean that public policy lacks any margin, since nothing guarantees that this limit is reached. Additionally, these analyses have not paid proper attention to the potential role of monetary policy to increase external space by attracting financial flows through positive interest rate differentials, or to reduce it by generating unsustainable debt dynamics.

This article explores the limits for fiscal and monetary policies in a small open economy where a) the compensation principle applies, b) the economy is open to capital flows, and c) the external sector imposes a limit to growth and income distribution. To do so, we build a model of economic growth based on the Sraffian supermultiplier with two sources of autonomous demand (government expenditure and exports) and that considers financial flows.

By doing so, the article contributes to a growing literature that studies balance-of-payments stability in open economy Sraffian supermultiplier models. The paper has four main findings. First, while fiscal policy is constrained by the balance-of-payments, it can affect output levels, although not its growth rate. Second, monetary policy can be used to increase interest rate differentials and attract financial flows that allow for higher output levels, although excessively high interest rates can have the opposite effect by leading to capital outflows due to perceived debt instability and the weight of interest payments. Third, a higher interest rate, or a lower government expenditure, could allow for higher real wages in a balance-of-payments constrained economy. Fourth, issuing debt in domestic currency does not necessarily allow for higher output growth rates, but can facilitate adjustment processes when the economy is in an unsustainable position by reducing the debt burden through depreciations.

[2]See for example McLeay, Radia, and Thomas (2014), from the Bank of England.

The article is organised as follows. As an introduction to the presentation of the growth model, section two discusses the compensation principle, to then critically analyse some non-mainstream positions regarding the degree of freedom for fiscal and monetary policies in open economies, as well as previous contributions to open economy Sraffian supermultiplier models. These limits are then discussed based on the growth model, first excluding capital flows (section three) and then considering them (section four), to examine the capacity of monetary policy to influence these flows and therefore extend (or limit) fiscal and distributive policies effectiveness. Section five considers the impact of the currency denomination of debt. Finally, section six summarises and provides some policy conclusions.

2. Open-Economy Macroeconomics under Endogenous Money

2.1. The Trilemma and the Compensation Principle

The analysis of the economic policy space in open economies is usually based on the monetary policy trilemma, which holds that it is not possible to simultaneously maintain free capital mobility, a fixed exchange rate, and an autonomous monetary policy, understood as its capacity to define the domestic interest rate. This is because, for a given exchange rate, any increase in local interest rates with respect to international rates leads to an inflow of financial flows which, through its positive effect on the quantity of money in the economy, ends up counteracting the increase in the initial interest rate (and vice versa).[3,4]

In the policy scheme proposed by the mainstream — which can be summarised in what is known as the 'new macroeconomic consensus' (Arestis 2009) — the independence of monetary policy is considered as the main tool for managing inflation and output. According to the trilemma, this requires exchange rate flexibility, which is not a disadvantage since it is conceived as the most efficient regime to absorb external shocks.

[3]The trilemma results from the Mundell-Fleming model, an extension of the IS-LM model to open economies (Mundell 1963). Some modern versions consider the possibility of temporary deviations of the interest rate from the international one, as long as the balance-of-payments is sustainable (Romer 2018).

[4]In recent contributions, Rey (2015, 2016) argues that the trilemma is actually a dilemma, since even in a flexible exchange rate framework the monetary authority would lack full freedom to manage the interest rate. She considers the case of a reduction in the international interest rate. In that case, a) there would be more domestic credit available given the role of the dollar as a global currency, and b) the value of domestic financial assets would grow, raising the value of collateral and boosting the demand for credit. Under these conditions, and in order to avoid this expansionary effect, the Central Bank would be forced to reduce the benchmark interest rate to moderate the gap with the international rate. Alternatively (or complementarily), c) the Central Bank could also intervene in the foreign exchange market to prevent currency appreciation as a result of capital inflows — a Central Bank behaviour that the literature has termed 'fear of floating' (Calvo and Relnhart 2002) — which would also imply adjusting the domestic interest rate to maintain yield parity. The argument shows some weaknesses. First, while conditions (a) and (b) are possible, they are not necessary. There is no reason to assume that an increase in private sector financial wealth will have the effect of increasing the demand for credit. And if this does not happen, the increased supply of credit will have to be endogenously sterilised, as the compensation principle holds, at the prevailing rate. Second, if credit does indeed increase, the author does not explain why this effect could not be offset by an eventual exchange rate depreciation, as a consequence of the trade deficit caused by the expansion of the level of activity. Third, case c) ultimately implies the acceptance of the trilemma, since it is the goal, of maintaining a fixed exchange rate what explains the loss of degrees of freedom in the management of the interest rate. Note finally that, ultimately, with her conditions a) and b), what Rey actually denies is the role traditionally assigned to the exchange rate as a shock absorber, since the appreciation associated with capital inflows is expansionary and not contractionary as the Mundell-Fleming model assumes.

However, it has been extensively studied that the quantity of money in an economy does not depend directly on the monetary base created by the Central Bank through a 'bank multiplier'. This is because banks do not need to have reserves to meet the solvent (or effective) credit demand at the prevailing market interest rate, since, after they grant a loan, they can always borrow from the Central Bank to meet the minimum reserve requirements, paying the interest rate set by the monetary authority. Thus, by granting a loan, banks create money *ex nihilo*. This implies that the monetary authority has no control over the quantity of money in the economy, but can determine the risk-free interest rate and, with it, influence the entire interest rate structure.

For an economy open to trade and capital flows, these results regarding the endogeneity of the quantity of money (and the exogeneity of the interest rate) are expressed in what is known as the compensation principle (Lavoie 2001). This mechanism can be briefly illustrated as follows. Assume again a fixed exchange rate regime, and that there is an inflow of foreign exchange, for example, because the monetary authority decides to increase domestic interest rates and attracts capital inflows, or because exports have increased. After the foreign currency is sold in the foreign exchange market, there is an increase in international reserves, since the monetary authority must acquire the foreign currency surplus to keep the exchange rate parity.[5] The reserves purchased by the monetary authority lead to an increase in the monetary base and, subsequently, in commercial banks' reserves. However, contrary to what the trilemma maintains, the increase in bank reserves does not necessarily have any effect on the volume of supplied credit and, therefore, on the interest rate.[6] The reason is that, as in a closed economy, commercial banks have already met all solvent credit demand at the prevailing rate.[7]

Thus, instead of keeping these unwanted reserves without yield, commercial entities will find it more convenient to cancel their debts with the Central Bank or to acquire the securities it issues, obtaining an interest. That is to say, the 'sterilisation' of 'surplus' money is not the result of the monetary authority's willingness to keep fixed the quantity of money (as it occurs, for example, with open market operations) but results automatically from its policy of fixing interest rates.[8]

Symmetrically, when the economy experiences foreign exchange loss, either due to a trade deficit, or because the Central Bank sets a domestic interest rate lower than the international rate, a contraction of the net indebtedness of commercial banks with the

[5]For the sake of simplicity, we assume that all foreign exchange is purchased by the monetary authority. This assumption is irrelevant for the analysis. What matters is that some agent in the economy is willing to acquire the foreign exchange at the price set by the monetary authority. When part of these currency is acquired by private agents, reserves increase to a lower extent, but the sequence described by the clearing principle does not change.

[6]This also implies that trade surpluses do not need to generate an increase in domestic prices as in the monetary approach to the balance-of-payments, since the quantity of money is not affected (Lavoie 2001).

[7]Naturally, this does not exclude the possibility that, if the foreign currency inflow is due to a change in macroeconomic conditions that reduces the aggregate risk perception, banks may modify their credit analysis and consider previously uncreditworthy agents as solvent, expanding credit at the prevailing rate. The important fact is that this phenomenon is not necessary.

[8]Several empirical studies have examined the empirical validity of the compensation principle. Aizenman and Glick (2009) study six Asian and three Latin American economies to find that sterilisation occurred at 100per cent. Lavoie and Wang (2011) illustrate the compensation principle by studying the People's Bank of China balance sheet. Angrick (2018) econometrically verifies the compensation principle in three Asian countries, finding that sterilisation occurs systematically and endogenously. Gerioni et al. (2022) find, based on an econometric analysis, that the compensation principle holds for Brazil.

Central Bank should take place, but this does not necessarily generate pressure on the interest rate. In other words, both when foreign exchange inflows and outflows occur, the monetary authority can still determine the interest rate, even in an open economy with a fixed exchange rate.

The difference in this second case is that, while there is no given limit to the possibility of accumulating international reserves,[9] the continuous loss of foreign currency should eventually lead to the abandonment of the exchange rate parity and the adoption of a flexible exchange rate regime. There is an asymmetric trilemma, which operates in the case of a balance-of-payments deficit, but not when there is a surplus.

Note that, following this approach, the balance-of-payments also imposes constraints on fiscal policy. In a demand-led economy, an increase in public spending boosts economic activity, which leads to higher imports. Thus, an expansionary fiscal policy has similar effects on the balance-of-payments than a reduction in interest rates and can also disrupt a fixed exchange rate regime.

Therefore, when a government faces a balance-of-payments deficit, it has two alternatives: the first is to abandon the exchange rate peg. The second is to resort to capital flows to finance external deficits. We examine both in the following subsections.

2.2. An Exchange Rate Adjustment

Modern Monetary Theory (MMT) is perhaps the most illustrative case for those who advocate for the alternative of devaluating the currency. This view argues that, since monetary surpluses do not necessarily generate inflation (precisely because, as endogenous money theory argues, they are deposited in commercial banks), the State can freely use monetary financing to implement expansionary policies and achieve full employment, being the 'employer of last resort' scheme one of their main proposals (Tcherneva 2012; Wray 2012). In order to limit public debt growth, and also for distributional considerations, they argue that fiscal policy should be accompanied by low (or zero) interest rates (Wray 1997; Forstater and Mosler 2005).

MMT does not ignore that the fixed exchange rate will eventually have to be abandoned if this combination of expansionary policies and low rates is adopted. But exchange rate flexibility is not seen as a problem, since, similarly to what is argued in the Mundell-Fleming model, a sufficiently high exchange rate would, through its positive effect on net exports, allow to offset the trade deficit caused by growth, leaving output unaffected (Wray, Mitchell, and Watts 2019, p. 325).

The fact that monetary autonomy faces no limits is based on the idea that, for any level of income, there is a real exchange rate able to balance the current account by increasing net exports. But this assumption seems to ignore the solid empirical evidence and theoretical arguments that show that a depreciation is an ineffective tool to expand the level of activity and exports in small open economies with a low or null import substitution elasticity due to their incomplete productive matrix ('technological dependence'), and a low price elasticity of exports, which consist mostly of raw materials; and whose dollar price,

[9]Some authors consider as an additional limit the quasi-fiscal cost of the interest from the securities issued by the monetary authority (Frenkel 2007). This should not be problematic if the money created by such interest payments is invested in domestic assets, but it could be an issue if it is used to acquire foreign assets (or if the sterilization is carried out issuing foreign currency securities), putting pressure on the balance-of-payments.

moreover, is not affected by depreciation because these economies are international price takers.[10]

In these economies, a depreciation improves the balance-of-payments only through output contraction, that is, by increasing domestic prices relative to monetary wages, which reduces demand, output, employment and imports, rendering this policy ineffective to reach full employment (Díaz Alejandro 1963; Krugman and Taylor 1978). This implies that there are potential limits to the use of expansionary fiscal and monetary policies, since they affect the balance-of-payments and may force depreciations that reduce output and employment. The model developed in sections three, four and five examines the extent to which these constraints can limit fiscal and monetary policies.

2.3. The Limits of the Interest Rate to peg the Exchange Rate

Given the evidence of the recessionary effects of a devaluation, an alternative would be to resort to increasing interest rates which, by attracting capital inflows and increasing international reserves, would allow to fix the exchange rate even with a trade deficit resulting from high output levels. In the extreme case — represented by the Mundell-Fleming model — any exchange rate would be sustainable if there is a willingness to raise interest rates to the level required to make the necessary foreign exchange available through the financial channel[11] (Obstfeld and Rogoff 1995).

However, if doubts arise about debt sustainability as indebtedness increases, maintaining the same risk-adjusted return between domestic and foreign financial assets requires an increasing interest rate. Assuming that any current account deficit of any size can be financed with external funds is the same than arguing that there is always a sufficiently high interest rate capable of attracting foreign capital. It seems very unrealistic to think of this alternative, being more plausible to assume that, beyond a certain level of indebtedness, foreign capital will stop financing the economy's external deficit (Serrano and Summa 2015, p. 255).

In addition, the determinants of financial flows are far from automatically compensating trade surpluses or deficits, but instead tend to show an autonomous dynamic (Borio and Disyatat 2015). Their determinants include both domestic (or 'pull') factors, such as output growth, the level of indebtedness and interest rate differentials, as well as external (or 'push') factors, mostly linked to the global economic cycle and the international interest rate (Fratzscher 2011).

In view of this limitation, part of the literature has given special importance to the type of domestic assets acquired by capital inflows. If inflows are used to purchase local-currency denominated assets, greater financial and external stability is to be expected, since domestic currency can always be issued to avoid default, which cannot be done with debt denominated in foreign currency (Eichengreen, Hausmann, and Panizza 2002). Indeed, one of

[10] For evidence on the low export elasticities, see Reinhart (1995), Bahmani, Harvey, and Hegerty (2013) and Bernat (2015). Crespo, Dvoskin, and Ianni (2020) prove that, under certain conditions, there is no exchange rate that allows a country to export. Evidence on imports' output elasticity can be found in McCombie and Thirlwall (2004), Crane, Crowley, and Quayyum (2007), Bussière et al. (2011) and Abeles and Cherkasky (2020).

[11] That is the conclusion drawn from the Mundell-Fleming model with a fixed exchange rate and perfect capital mobility. But it is also a generally accepted conclusion in the literature. See for example Rapetti (2013, p. 12), who states that the interest rate parity 'implies that the capital account of the balance-of-payments adjusts to compensate the result of the current account'.

the prerequisites MMT defines for a country to be 'monetary sovereign' is to issue all its debt in domestic currency (Wray 2012, p. 42; Tymoigne and Wray 2013). However, more recent research has shown that borrowing in domestic currency does not completely prevent instability, since the flows from debt repayment can be used to acquire foreign assets, raising spreads and compromising the balance-of-payments (Bertaut, Bruno, and Shin 2022).

Considering these factors, sections three, four and five develop a growth model based on the Sraffian supermultiplier which, in addition to considering the principle of compensation and the recessionary impacts of a devaluation, incorporates the existence of transnational capital flows, recognising that these are sensitive to the interest rate, but also to debt sustainability. A distinction is also made between domestic and foreign currency borrowing to identify the extent to which issuing debt in domestic currency is beneficial.

2.4. The Supermultiplier in an Open Economy

This paper builds on a growing literature that adapts the Sraffian supermultiplier to study open economies. The Sraffian supermultiplier, originally developed by Serrano (1995) and Bortis (1997), has some advantages over alternative heterodox growth models, such as considering the tendency of capacity utilisation to tend to *normal* levels, the positive relationship between the investment share of output and growth, and the fact that autonomous spending tends to determine output (Fagundes, da, and Freitas 2017).

An alleged problem of the supermultiplier, pointed by Nikiforos (2018), is that when more than one source of autonomous demand is considered, if these have different growth rates the sector with higher demand growth will display unsustainable financial positions, since autonomous demand, given that it is not a result of prior income, must necessarily be financed. This would curtail a source of autonomous demand, limiting the degree of 'autonomy' of these expenditures.

This argument has been reframed by Allain (2022) and Woodgate, Hein, and Summa (2023) who have shown that in supermultiplier models with several sources of autonomous demand, they can all be autonomous (in the sense that they do not respond to current output) but some of them will have to adjust to other sources of autonomous demand endogenously to maintain financial stability. Several studies have discussed the interplay of financial factors in supermultiplier models with more than one source of autonomous demand, such as Freitas and Christianes (2020), Hein and Woodgate (2021) or Pedrosa, Brochier, and Freitas (2023).

An open economy can be thought of as a specific case of the more general problem of multiple autonomous demand sources in a Sraffian supermultiplier model. If domestic autonomous spending grows faster than exports, this will lead to a growing current account deficit, implying an unsustainable scenario. Oreiro and Costa Santos (2022), based on this limitation, argue that there is an 'impossible quartet' for supermultiplier models, since they cannot simultaneously have growth led by autonomous demand, exogenous income distribution, induced investment and external equilibrium.

However, some models have extended the supermultiplier model to an open economy setting, showing that domestic autonomous demand can play a role for output determination even if it is constrained by exports. Morlin (2022) developed a model with two sources of autonomous demand, government expenditures and exports, and derives the stability conditions of public and external debt, as well as developing a fiscal rule to ensure sustainability. Dvoskin and Torchinsky Landau (2023), based on the former, adapt this model to consider conflict over income distribution. In both cases, government expenditures cannot affect the growth rate of the economy but have an impact on its level.

While these models consider external debt, they calculate it as a 'mirror' of the current account, and define an exogenous debt limit. This implies that financial flows, which actually have their own determinants, cannot be treated properly, leaving no role for policies that influence them such as the determination of the interest rate by the monetary authority. In the following sections, we build a model that considers the financial side of a Sraffian supermultiplier model with two sources of autonomous demand, government expenditure and exports, and analyse its implications for growth and income distribution.

3. Fiscal Policy in An Open Economy: The Sraffian Supermultiplier

Thirlwall's (1979) canonical model assumes that, in the long run, imports and exports must balance. However, in its search for simplicity, the model does not consider that imports can be paid not only with export proceedings but also with international reserves or by issuing external debt.

Therefore, instead of focusing on the balance of trade equilibrium, we analyse external sustainability through the dynamic of gross international reserves. Temporarily, we assume away financial flows, since we will study their determinants and impacts in the following section. The change in reserves in each period, $\dot{R}$, can be expressed as:

$$\dot{R} = X - M - iD + i_f R \tag{3.1}$$

International reserves grow when the sum of the current and the financial account is positive, implying that a trade surplus, when exports X exceed imports M, has a positive impact on reserves. Conversely, reserves decline with interest payments, which depend on previous debt D and the domestic interest rate i (Cline and Vernengo 2016). In this section, we assume that there are no new capital flows (an assumption that will be abandoned in section four) and that existing debt is denominated in foreign currency (the case of domestic currency denominated debt is discussed in section five). We assume all debt to be indexed at the rate i, to prevent our results from depending on debt maturity. We also assume away other international flows such as foreign direct investment, other income flows, remittances, etc. Finally, reserves are usually not kept in cash but in foreign assets that pay the foreign interest rate i_f.

Imports, in a small open economy, increase in line with output due to the need for foreign intermediate inputs and capital and consumption goods. This 'technological dependency' (Dvoskin and Feldman 2018), a key aspect of developing economies highlighted by structuralist authors, implies that imports can be modelled as a percentage m of output, so $M = mY$ (Fajnzylber 1990). Therefore, reserves growth is defined as:

$$\dot{R} = X - mY - iD + i_f R \tag{3.2}$$

How do we know if reserves are sustainable? Most studies focus on the ratio of external debt or reserves to GDP as an indicator of the external sustainability of an economy's trajectory (McCombie and Thirlwall 1997; Barbosa-Filho 2001; Moreno-Brid 2003). However, as Bhering, Freitas, and Serrano (2019) argue, this can be misleading, since GDP implies production in domestic currency, while imports and interest must be paid with foreign currency, which is obtained through exports. In fact, a growing GDP tends to decrease international reserves and/or increase indebtedness, as this leads to higher imports without necessarily affecting exports. Consequently, Bhering, Freitas, and Serrano (2019) propose to study the debt/exports ratio, since foreign currency is obtained through the latter. Following this approach, we adopt the relation between international reserves and exports r as a measure of external sustainability, since without capital flows the dynamics of international reserves imply an equivalent decrease in net external indebtedness:[12]

$$r = R/X \tag{3.3}$$

Focusing on international reserves as a percentage of exports allows us to study, in section four, the determinants of capital flows explicitly, and hence external debt. These determinants could not be analysed if one assumes that net external debt accommodates automatically and endogenously to the current account result, as Bhering, Freitas, and Serrano (2019) do.[13] If this ratio is derived, its growth is equal to:

$$\dot{r} = \frac{\dot{R}X - R\dot{X}}{X^2} \tag{3.4}$$

By replacing $\dot{R}$ with equation (3.2), we obtain:

$$\dot{r} = 1 - \frac{mY}{X} - i\frac{D}{X} + (i_f - g_X)r \tag{3.5}$$

Equation (3.5) provides insights into the dynamics of international reserves, measured as a share of exports. A higher import coefficient m will reduce reserves because imports are paid with foreign currency. Increasing the interest rate i will also lead to a fall in international reserves, since it increases the burden of interest payments, although interest rate hikes could also attract foreign capital; we deal with this in the next section. In contrast, a higher foreign interest rate i_f favours reserve accumulation by providing higher interest payments on current reserves. Again, this could also lead to foreign outflows, an effect that we discuss in the following section. Exports X provide more foreign currency and consequently increase international reserves, while their growth g_X reduces the reserves-exports ratio by increasing the denominator.

If the country has a current account surplus — so the sum of the first three components of equation (3.5) is higher than one — r can only be stable if exports growth g_X is higher than the rate of return on reserves i_f. Otherwise, the reserves/exports ratio (r) would be ever-growing. Conversely, a country with a current account deficit could have a stable reserves/ratio only if it sustains itself with the yield of its international

[12]Since international reserves are an external asset, its accumulation reduces net external debt and vice versa. We focus on international reserves since in section four the determinants of capital flows and, therefore, external debt are studied explicitly, which could not be done if it is assumed that external debt accommodates to the current account as Bhering, Freitas, and Serrano (2019) do.

[13]Bhering, Freitas, and Serrano (2019), in a following section, study the impact of capital flows, but consider them exogenous, without analysing their determinants.

reserves, which requires $i_f > g_X$. Since this case requires low export growth (which, in the long run, implies low long run output growth, as we will see in the following sections) we will focus on the case of current account surpluses where $g_X > i_f$, which is also more relevant for emerging economies.

Note also that there is a negative relationship between output Y and international reserves. This is because an increase in output requires more imports. Therefore, the determinants of output also influence international reserves, so we need to provide an account of these factors. We do so by building a Sraffian supermultiplier model (Serrano 1995), which has the advantages of displaying long run demand-led growth, a tendency towards a normal rate of capacity utilisation, exogenous income distribution, and a positive relation between growth rates and the investment rate (Fagundes, da, and Freitas 2017).

We build our model based on the one developed by Morlin (2022) and its extension by Dvoskin and Torchinsky Landau (2023). From a Keynesian perspective, we assume that aggregate demand determines output, both in the short and long run. Output equals consumption — both private (C) and public (G) — plus investment I and net exports $X - M$:

$$Y = C + I + G + X - M \tag{3.6}$$

For simplicity, we assume that workers consume all their disposable income, while capitalists do not engage in consumption.[14] Therefore, consumption equals the wage share of output ωY, minus the tax rate τ. The wage share can be calculated as the real wage, $\frac{w}{p}$, multiplied by the labour requirement per unit of output v_l. If we assume international price parity, so domestic prices equal international ones multiplied by the exchange rate e, and we normalise international prices to 1, we obtain that consumption is:

$$C = \omega Y(1-\tau) = \frac{w}{p} v_l Y(1-\tau) = \frac{w}{e} v_l Y(1-\tau) \tag{3.7}$$

Investment is determined by the accelerator mechanism, since a higher output requires more capital goods to be produced, which incentivises capitalists to invest in new machinery to avoid excess use of installed capacity (Samuelson 1939; Serrano 1995). If we assume away capital depreciation, investment I equals a share h of output:

$$I = hY \tag{3.8}$$

Finally, we assume that government spending and exports are autonomous from current income, and together they add up to Z, the total autonomous spending, which is exogenous:

$$Z = G + X \tag{3.9}$$

[14] It would be possible to assume that capitalists consume independently of their income, leading to an additional source of autonomous demand, as in Freitas and Christianes (2020). However, since the model already considers more than one source of autonomous demand, this would not provide any insights while making algebra more complex.

We can define α as the share of autonomous spending represented by government spending; thus, $1 - \alpha$ equals the weight of exports on total autonomous spending.

$$G = \alpha Z \wedge X = (1 - \alpha)Z \tag{3.10}$$

Substituting (3.7), (3.8), (3.9) and $M = mY$ into equation (3.6), we obtain a new equation for output:

$$Y = \frac{w}{e} v_l Y + hY + Z - mY \tag{3.11}$$

And solving for Y:

$$Y = \frac{1}{1 - \frac{w}{e} v_l (1 - \tau) - h + m} Z \tag{3.12}$$

Equation (3.12) represents the action of the Sraffian supermultiplier. Output is determined by autonomous demand Z, 'supermultiplied' by consumption and investment, which are induced by output levels. A higher import coefficient reduces output, because it implies that production takes place abroad rather than domestically. In the long run, the parameters of the supermultiplier cannot increase or decrease indefinitely, so output growth is determined by the growth of autonomous demand components, exports and government spending. However, a change in the parameters that determine the supermultiplier can affect output *levels*, which, as we will see later, is not innocuous (Nah and Lavoie 2019).

Up to now, we defined investment as a fixed share of output h. However, investment is not rigid, but reacts to the gap between capacity utilisation and its desired or normal level. Therefore, we can define a 'flexible' accelerator mechanism (Freitas and Serrano 2015), where h is a parameter indicating the speed of adjustment of investment to capacity utilisation.

$$\dot{h} = h\gamma(u - u_n) \tag{3.13}$$

In equilibrium, where $\dot{h} = 0$, capacity utilisation will tend towards its normal level so $u^* = u_n$. Capacity utilisation u, on its turn, depends on the difference between the growth rate of the economy g_t and the growth rate of the capital stock g_k:

$$\dot{u} = u(g - g_k) \tag{3.14}$$

The growth rate of the economy can be derived from expression (3.12). By applying natural logarithms and then deriving with respect to time, we get:

$$g = \frac{h\gamma(u - u_n)}{1 - \frac{w}{e} v_l (1 - \tau) - h + m} + g_z \tag{3.15}$$

Where g_z is the growth rate of the autonomous components of demand Z. In equilibrium, where $u = u_n$, we get that the autonomous components of demand drive growth, so $g = g_z$. The growth rate of the capital stock, on its turn, is:

$$g_k = \frac{hu}{v} \tag{3.16}$$

Where v is the units of capital required to produce one unit of output. Therefore, substituting (3.15) and (3.16) in (3.14), we get that in equilibrium:

$$h^* = \frac{g_z v}{u_n} \tag{3.17}$$

We can now return to our reserves' equation (3.5) and replace output with equation (3.12), exports with equation (3.10), and the ratio of international reserves to exports by r:

$$\dot{r} = 1 - \frac{m}{(1-\alpha)\left(1 - \frac{w}{e}v_l(1-\tau) - h + m\right)} - id + (i_f - g_X)r \tag{3.18}$$

Equation (3.18) clarifies the connection between fiscal policy and international reserves. A one-off increase in government spending increases α, the weight of government expenditures in total autonomous spending, and boosts output level, which has a direct impact on imports, dampening reserve accumulation.

In a fully adjusted position, the relation between international reserves and exports must reach a constant level r^*. We find that value by defining $\dot{r} = \dot{h} = \dot{u} = 0$:

$$r^* = \left[1 - \frac{m}{(1-\alpha)\left(1 - \frac{w}{e}v_l(1-\tau) - \frac{g_z v}{u_n} + m\right)} - id_t\right]\left[\frac{1}{g_X - i_f}\right] \tag{3.19}$$

The importance of r^* is caused by the fact that this variable has a minimum threshold (equal or higher than zero), which we can call $\bar{r}$, which allows the monetary authority to intervene in the foreign exchange market and avoid a currency depreciation.[15] If r^* is higher than $\bar{r}$, the economy would be accumulating more reserves than the necessary amount to maintain the exchange rate at the expense of the level of output. In that case, there is room for the public sector to expand output to its maximum level compatible with the external constraint on growth, where $r^* = \bar{r}$. This would be equivalent to defining a maximum level of α equal to:

$$\alpha^{max} = 1 - \frac{m}{[1 - id + (i_f - g_X)\bar{r}]\left[1 - \frac{w}{e}v_l - \frac{g_z v}{u_n} + m\right]} \tag{3.20}$$

This equation shows that the limit to government spending is not necessarily given by the need for fiscal equilibrium but by the external sector, since government spending

[15]Note that, when capital flows are assumed away, defining a maximum value $\bar{r}$ is the same than setting a maximum value for the debt/exports ratio as Bhering, Freitas, and Serrano (2019) do. Also, while m is fixed for simplicity, it should be noted that a higher growth rate could increase the import coefficient for two reasons. First, in the short run, lags in the incorporation of new productive capacity could be replaced with imports. But also, both in the short and in the long runs, the investment coefficient h depends positively on the growth rate. If the import propensity of investment is higher than that of other components of demand, a feature of developing economies, a higher growth rate will increase m and reduce r^*.

is a key determinant of output and, therefore, of the balance-of-payments. If this limit is breached and α exceeds α^{max}, increasing indebtedness will eventually deplete Central Bank reserves and force a devaluation. This, by increasing domestic prices, reduces the real wage and the supermultiplier, shrinks demand and imports, and restores the balance-of-payments equilibrium. The external balance is re-established by a devaluation, but instead of acting through an increase in exports as is often assumed, it does so by affecting income distribution and reducing output, as structuralist authors argue. Therefore, it is a recessive rather than an expansionary devaluation (Díaz Alejandro 1963; Krugman and Taylor 1978).[16] Figure 1 shows the effect on reserves of increasing α so it equals α^{max}.

In the long term, there is an additional constraint on government spending. If the growth rate of public spending is higher than that of exports, then the weight of the former on total autonomous spending will increase progressively, and α will tend to 1. If this is the case, the result of equation (3.18) will decrease indefinitely, implying a continuous loss of international reserves, which is an unsustainable result. Therefore, for reserves to be stable, government spending must not grow faster than exports in the long run. Again, we find both a constraint for public activity as well as an important role for it, since nothing precludes government spending from growing more slowly than exports, leading to a decreasing α and therefore to a lower growth rate than the maximum achievable. Fiscal policy can affect output *levels* (by a one-off increase in spending that raises α), although with certain constraints, but it cannot determine the output growth rate, which is limited by exports growth. Henceforth, since we are interested in equilibrium results, we assume that in the long run government spending grows at the same rate than exports, meaning that when equations include α, its value is constant.

What is the impact of income distribution on external sustainability? Equation (3.19) shows that a higher real wage $\frac{w}{e}$ also reduces the reserves ratio by increasing output. Therefore, analogously to government spending, there is a maximum real wage compatible with external equilibrium, given by:

$$\left(\frac{w}{e}\right)^{max} = \left[1 - \frac{g_z v}{u_n} + m - \frac{m}{(1-\alpha)[1 - id_t + (i_f - g_X)\bar{r}]}\right]\left[\frac{1}{v_l(1-\tau)}\right] \tag{3.21}$$

Note that the higher the government spending share of autonomous spending α, the lower the maximum real wage, since the available foreign currency is spent on imports induced by government consumption. Therefore, for a given level of international reserves, there might be a trade-off between government spending and real wages, *ceteris paribus* (Canitrot 1983). However, if there is external space both variables can expand simultaneously. Similarly, the higher the import coefficient, the lower the maximum real wage, implying that import substitution policies can allow for higher wages and output, as argued by Cruz, Gahn, and Morlin (2022). On the financial side, a higher interest rate increases outflows and therefore leads to a lower equilibrium real wage.

[16]For simplicity, we do not include this feature in our model, but it could be considered by making *e* endogenous and inversely related to *r*. For example, see Dvoskin and Torchinsky Landau (2023).

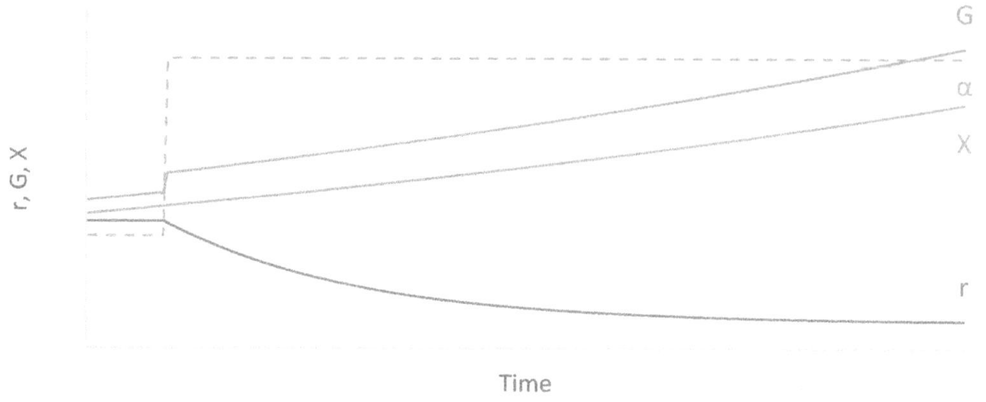

Figure 1. A one-off increase in α.

Up to now, we have assumed that domestic interest rates only play a negative role in the external position and economic growth, a result consistent, for instance, with the MMT approach. However, we are overlooking the fact that higher domestic interest rates can also attract external capital flows, which can finance the trade deficits resulting from higher output if debt is sustainable. This is what we deal with in the next section, finding that the role of domestic interest rates on output and the BOP is not defined *a priori*, and can be positive or negative depending on the current conditions.

4. Fiscal and Monetary Policy with Foreign Financial Flows

The model from section 3 concludes that increasing domestic interest rates reduces international reserves. If they become negative, imports will have to be reduced through a compression of aggregate demand and output, which might happen through lower government spending or a reduction in real wages. However, in the previous section we did not consider the use of the domestic interest rate as a tool to attract foreign capitals, increasing reserves and potentially allowing for a higher level of output.

Equation (4.1) provides an account of the determinants of net foreign debt D. Debt will not necessarily match the current account result in an automatic form, as often assumed, but displays its own determinants. The key issue is if its dynamics, combined with that of the current account, is sustainable (Aguiar de Medeiros 2008; Borio and Disyatat 2015; Kohler 2022). If debt is issued in foreign currency, what determines financial flows[17] is the difference between domestic and foreign interest rates (i and i_f), scaled by the size of the economy (since larger economies tend to attract more capital flows), plus the perceived risk of default, which we assume to depend on the growth of net indebtedness, that is, the foreign debt net of international reserves (Bortz 2014). δ represents the elasticity of financial flows to these factors[18]:

$$\dot{D} = \delta[(i - i_f)Y - (\dot{D} - \dot{R})] \tag{4.1}$$

[17]These financial flows do not only consider foreign capital, but also transactions by domestic agents in foreign currency.
[18]We could add a parameter representing idiosyncratic 'country risk'. We avoid this for simplicity, and consider it as included in the default risk. In countries where returns on domestic assets are persistently lower than on foreign

There is an additional rationale for including Y in equation (4.1). Financial flows $\dot{D}$ do not only include foreign capital, but also transactions by domestic agents in foreign currency. Several peripheral countries display *bimonetary economies* where residents, usually due to past or current experiences of high inflation rates, invest part of their savings in foreign assets. A purchase of foreign currency by a domestic agent is therefore a financial outflow, which reduces $\dot{D}$. Therefore, a higher output implies that there is a larger private surplus that might be used to purchase foreign assets, implying that indebtedness will be more sensible to interest rate differentials.

Analogously to the previous section, we examine the dynamics of gross international reserves. But since these are affected by debt dynamics, which in the previous section were considered exogenous, it is necessary to first define the sustainability of debt in relation to exports. Its dynamic is given by:

$$\dot{d} = \frac{\dot{D}X - D\dot{X}}{X^2} = \frac{\delta[(i - i_f)Y - (\dot{D} - \dot{R})]}{X} - dg_x \tag{4.2}$$

Substituting output and exports with equations (3.10) and (3.12), we obtain an equation for the growth rate of capital flows (as a percentage of exports).

$$\dot{d} = \left[\frac{\delta(i - i_f)}{(1 - \alpha)\left(1 - \frac{w}{e}v_l(1 - \tau) - h + m\right)} + \delta\dot{r} - g_x d \right] \left[\frac{1}{1 + \delta} \right] \tag{4.3}$$

Equation (4.3) shows that a positive interest rate differential favours capital inflows by providing higher returns to investors. A positive reserve accumulation rate also attracts capital flows by improving debt sustainability, and the same happens with a higher output. Finally, the higher the rate of growth of exports the lower the indebtedness ratio because the denominator increases.

In a fully adjusted position, capital flows as a percentage of exports should not grow or decrease indefinitely, and the same applies to international reserves, so $\dot{d} = \dot{r} = \dot{h} = \dot{u} = 0$. Therefore, we can solve for the equilibrium level d^*:

$$d^* = \frac{\delta(i - i_f)}{g_x(1 - \alpha)\left(1 - \frac{w}{e}v_l(1 - \tau) - \frac{g_z v}{u_n} + m\right)} \tag{4.4}$$

Having defined the indebtedness dynamics, we can return to the international reserves, now considering financial flows. By including them in equation (3.2) we obtain[19]:

$$\dot{R} = X - mY - iD + i_f R + \delta[(i - i_f)Y - (\dot{D} - \dot{R})] \tag{4.5}$$

---

ones (usually due inflationary processes caused by external deficits that force currency depreciation) domestic agents tend to invest part of their savings in assets nominated in foreign currency (Sturzenegger 1997; Levy Yeyati and Ize 2003). A purchase of foreign debt by a domestic agent is a capital outflow, which reduces $\dot{D}$. These investment decisions are affected by the same determinants as the ones by foreigners, although there are some differences. A larger interest differential will reduce foreign assets acquisition, while a higher output will have the opposite effect by increasing the available surplus, and the same will do a high default risk. The fact that domestic investors do not only purchase domestic assets but also foreign ones leads to a lower δ for a net debtor country.

[19]Note that the model in section three can be thought of as a special case of the one presented here, where $\dot{D} = 0$.

Therefore, we also need to redefine their growth rate as a percentage of exports $\dot{r}$:

$$\dot{r} = \left[1 - \frac{m - \delta(i - i_f)}{(1-\alpha)\left(1 - \frac{w}{e}v_l(1-\tau) - h + m\right)} - id + (i_f - g_x)r - \delta\dot{d}\right]\left[\frac{1}{1-\delta}\right] \quad (4.6)$$

Again, the ratio r^* can be interpreted as a measure of the capacity of the monetary authority to maintain a certain exchange rate e, while d^* is the equilibrium position of external indebtedness. International reserves depend, in addition to the aforementioned factors, on financial inflows, which are related to the interest rate differential and the growth rate of indebtedness. As mentioned earlier, depreciation can boost reserve accumulation by compressing real wages and demand, reducing imports.

We therefore have a dynamic system with four equations, representing reserves as a share of exports $\dot{r}$, debt as a share of exports $\dot{d}$, the investment share $\dot{h}$ and capacity utilisation $\dot{u}$. To start solving our system, we need to replace $\dot{d}$ on equation (4.6) to study the relationship of international reserves to the model parameters:

$$\dot{r} = (1+\delta)\left[1 - \frac{m - \delta(i - i_f)\left(1 - \frac{\delta}{1+\delta}\right)}{(1-\alpha)\left(1 - \frac{w}{e}v_l(1-\tau) - h + m\right)} - id + (i_f - g_x)r\right] + \delta g_x d \quad (4.7)$$

This equation allows us to determine the equilibrium position of the model. In equilibrium, the indebtedness ratio must be equal to d^* from equation (4.4). By replacing and solving, we obtain the equilibrium value for r^*:

$$r^* = \left[1 - \frac{m - \delta(i - i_f)\left(1 - \frac{i}{g_x}\right)}{(1-\alpha)\left(1 - \frac{w}{e}v_l(1-\tau) - \frac{g_z v}{u_n} + m\right)}\right]\left[\frac{1}{g_x - i_f}\right] \quad (4.8)$$

If the impact of economic growth on imports is higher than its effect on financial inflows,[20] an increase in public spending (α), real wages (w/e) or the investment coefficient (h) will reduce r^* by increasing output. In addition, and independently of that condition, a higher international interest rate i_f or a worsening of global financial conditions (which can be represented by a reduction of δ for a debtor economy) reduces r^*, since the same interest rate differential will lead to lower financial inflows.

The value of r^* cannot be lower than its limit $\bar{r}$ without leading to a currency depreciation. The government has three tools at its disposal to improve the equilibrium value of reserves, being the first the already mentioned option of depreciating the domestic currency, which reduces imports through an economic contraction. The second, also discussed, is to reduce government spending, leading to a lower α. This also reduces demand and imports. Finally, a third strategy that becomes relevant when the economy is open to financial flows is to increase the interest rate differential to attract

[20]That is, if $m > \delta(i - i_f)\left(1 - \frac{i}{g_x}\right)$ a condition that is easily fulfilled given the range of values the parameters can adopt.

foreign capital. Interestingly, the result of such a policy will be ambiguous since a higher interest rate leads to financial inflows but also raises interest payments in the future and might casts doubts on debt sustainability, potentially offsetting the former effect. The results of a contractive monetary policy on international reserves are non-linear, and depend on the result of the following equation:

$$\frac{\partial r^*}{\partial i} = \left[\frac{\delta\left(1 - \frac{2i - i_f}{g_x}\right)}{(1-\alpha)\left(1 - \frac{w}{e}v_l(1-\tau) - \frac{g_z v}{u_n} + m\right)} \right] \left[\frac{1}{g_x - i_f} \right] \lesssim 0 \tag{4.9}$$

Figure 2 shows how the equilibrium ratio of gross reserves to exports reacts to changes in the interest rate in simulated case, assuming the case of a current account surplus country where $g_x > i_f$. Increasing the interest rate favours international reserves up to a point where inflows are exceeded by interest payments and the capital outflows due to the increased default risk. When that point is reached, raising the interest rate reduces international reserves instead of increasing them.

The value of the interest rate that maximises reserves is given by:

$$i^* = \frac{g_x + i_f}{2} \tag{4.10}$$

The value of i^* depends positively on the growth rate of exports g_x and the international interest rate with which domestic assets must compete, i_f. These results may justify why central banks, besides inflationary considerations, avoid setting interest rates too low to minimise interest payments or too high to attract foreign inflows, since, in the long run, both strategies dampen reserve accumulation$i_f > g_x$. This also implies a constraint for monetary policy: in the presence of international financial flows, the interest rate cannot be defined in a fully autonomous fashion since an excessively low rate would lead to capital outflows and an external crisis. Therefore, while there is not a *trilemma* in which monetary policy is completely endogenous for a given exchange rate, it becomes evident that the setting of the interest rate faces much more severe constraints in a financially globalised world.

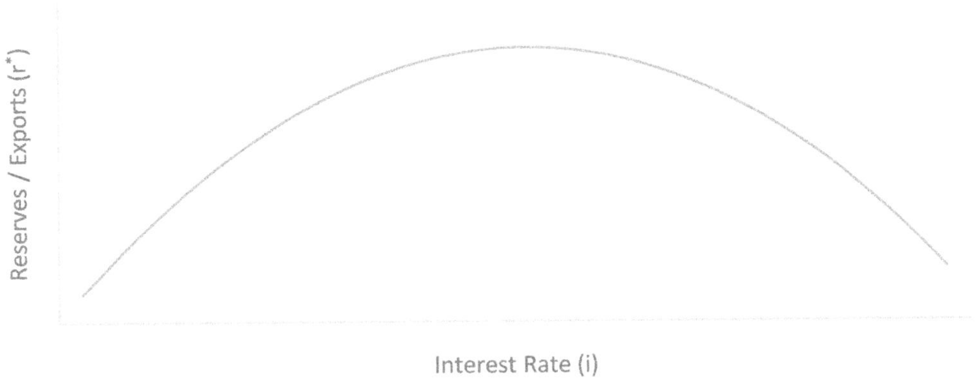

Figure 2. Equilibrium reserves and interest rate.

We can make a similar argument regarding fiscal policy. Increasing the government share of autonomous spending α boosts demand and output, affecting imports and reducing international reserves. Therefore, there is a maximum level of government spending α^{max} which allows for maintaining the exchange rate ($r^* = \bar{r}$), given by equation (4.11). A higher interest rate differential can provide more external space, thus allowing for an increase in government spending. Indeed, this is what usually happens, as evidence points to government spending being procyclical to capital flows (Kaminsky, Reinhart, and Végh 2004).

$$\alpha^{max} = 1 - \frac{m - \delta(i - i_f)\left(1 - \frac{i}{g_x}\right)}{[1 - \bar{r}(g_x - i_f)]\left[1 - \frac{w}{e}v_l(1 - \tau) - \frac{g_z v}{u_n} + m\right]} \tag{4.11}$$

As in the previous section, fiscal, monetary, and exchange rate policies can help improve income distribution by increasing the external space. Since higher real wages increase demand and output, their improvement has a toll on international reserves. Consequently, the same set of tools that increases external space allows for improvements in real wages. Equation (4.12) shows the value of the maximum real wage compatible with balance-of-payments equilibrium, displaying the same determinants as international reserves in equation (4.9).

$$\left(\frac{w}{e}\right)^{max} = \left[1 - \frac{m - \delta(i - i_f)\left(1 - \frac{i}{g_x}\right)}{(1 - \alpha)[1 - \bar{r}(g_x - i_f)]} - \frac{g_z v}{u_n} + m\right]\left[\frac{1}{v_l(1 - \tau)}\right] \tag{4.12}$$

This also applies to the domestic interest rate. Up to a certain point, increasing interest rates can provide international reserves, allowing for a higher real wage and its consequent effect on imports. This result contrasts with the claims of MMT, which call for low interest rates (even if this leads to negative interest rate differentials) in favour of employment and income distribution. In a small open economy, increasing the interest rate can help improve real wages.

In summary, for a small open economy with a stable balance-of-payments, setting $i = i^*$ can be seen as the 'optimal' policy for the Central Bank, because it provides the maximum amount of foreign currency that allows for increasing government spending, output and/or real wages without leading to an unsustainable indebtedness process. However, it is important to note that while the maximum interest rate i^* allows the maximisation of foreign currency availability, nothing guarantees that this external space will be used, since wages and government spending are determined exogenously. This opens the door to an active fiscal stance or the implementation of labour policies that strengthen the bargaining power of workers to maximise output.

Therefore, the interest rate could be used as a tool to allow compatibility between wage demands that lead to a balance-of-payments deficit and a sustainable external position. However, there is a limit for this tool: if wage demands exceed their maximum value compatible with the interest rate that optimises financial flows, as presented in equation (4.13) and which results from replacing in i^* in equation (4.12), then monetary policy lacks capacity to generate external equilibrium. This might be the case of countries with high labour bargaining power and frequent balance-of-payments crises, as was the case in most economies up to the seventies and still is the case in some developing economies (Dvoskin and Torchinsky Landau 2023; Morlin 2023).

$$\left(\frac{w}{e}\right)^{max} = \left[1 - \frac{m - \frac{\delta}{2}(i - i_f)\left(1 - \frac{i_f}{g_x}\right)}{(1-\alpha)[1 - \bar{r}(g_x - i_f)]} - \frac{g_z v}{u_n} + m\right]\left[\frac{1}{v_l(1-\tau)}\right] \tag{4.13}$$

The fact that not all real wages are attainable by increasing the interest rate is shown in Figure 3. Raising the interest rate, up to a certain point, can increase international reserves which can be used to increase real wages and therefore imports. In Figure 3, real wage $(w/e)_1$, given all the other variables, is attainable by raising the interest rate to i_1. On the contrary, there is no interest rate that provides the required reserves to finance the imports induced by real wage $(w/e)_2$. In that case, reaching that real wage would require a fiscal contraction and, therefore, a reduction in output, which would move the curve in Figure 3 upwards.

In sum, the use of the interest rate by the Central Bank can be a powerful tool to address external instability by attracting capital flows that provide relief in the external sector. However, this policy faces limitations, since an excessively high interest rate differential makes the burden of interest payments excessive. This might be worsened by the fact that foreign investors, aware of this instability, can withdraw from the domestic market, making the lack of reserves more acute. Therefore, debt sustainability becomes crucial for maintaining a certain level of the exchange rate, and, consequently, of real wages and economic activity, giving investors a 'veto power' over real wages and output levels (Canitrot 1983).

Finally, we can add commercial and industrial policies to the toolbox, since they can reduce the coefficient m, which allows to reach a higher level of output without increasing imports, or boost exports, raising g_x. As a matter of fact, while fiscal, exchange rate, and monetary policies can manage output levels, they do not allow for raising the maximum

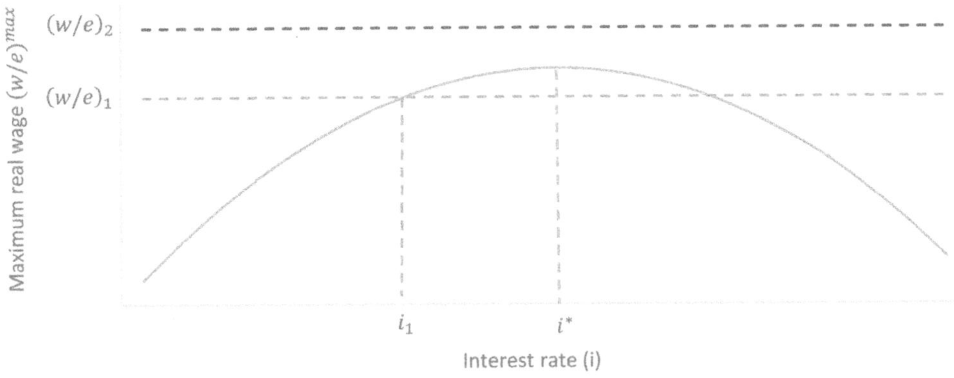

Figure 3. Maximum real wage and interest rate.

output growth rate, which is ultimately defined by exports' growth. Therefore, export promotion becomes a key policy to boost output growth in the long run.

5. The Case of Domestic Currency Denominated Debt

In the 1990s, a series of developing countries experienced a wave of external crises due to a lack of foreign exchange. Eichengreen, Hausmann, and Panizza (2002) linked these crises to the 'original sin' that these economies committed: borrowing significantly in foreign currency. According to these authors, foreign currency debt, as opposed to domestic currency debt, is the source of developing economies' external problems. This is because domestic currency debt can always be repaid through Central Bank action, which is not the case for foreign currency denominated debt. In addition, in times of crisis, the exchange rate tends to depreciate, raising the burden of these liabilities, and limiting the Central Bank's ability to implement expansionary policies, given their potential impact on the exchange rate.

Based on this argument, some proponents of MMT have argued that for a country to be sovereign, in addition to issuing its own currency, it must have its debt denominated in it (Wray 2012; Tymoigne and Wray 2013, p. 40). And many of these economies attempted — often successfully — to develop a market of domestic currency denominated debt, open to international investors, therefore replacing foreign currency denominated debt. This has the additional advantage of providing an additional source of foreign currency for the country: if a non-resident buys a domestic currency denominated asset, it must purchase domestic currency first, increasing financial inflows. Also, in *bimonetary* economies where residents save partially in foreign currency, purchasing domestic currency denominated bonds will reduce their demand for foreign currency.

However, this does not imply that there are no limits for indebtedness when it is denominated in domestic currency. If investors perceive debt to be too high, concerns may be raised that, if they decide to liquidate their positions and acquire foreign currency, they will not be able to do so at the current exchange rate, or that the government will have to default or renegotiate its debt. This will reduce foreign inflows and increase residents' demand for foreign assets, and, in a fixed exchange regime, international reserves, possibly forcing the monetary authority to implement corrective measures. Bertaut, Bruno, and Shin (2022) call this phenomenon the *original sin redux*.

The occurrence of the *original sin redux* is more likely if there is a significant participation of foreigners in the domestic debt market as it has been the case since the financial crisis in many developing economies, since they will switch more promptly to foreign financial assets (Onen, Shin, and Von Goetz 2023). Hofmann, Shim, and Shin (2020) show that issuing debt in domestic currency did not insulate countries from the impact of the 'flight to quality' process in the beginning of the COVID-19 pandemic, and that countries with higher participation of non-residents in their debt markets experienced stronger interest rate increases.

In addition to that, recurring to devaluation to reduce the value of liabilities denominated in domestic currency reduces capital inflows (or increases their financing cost) by increasing risk perception and reducing creditors' capital (Hofmann, Shim, and Shin

2022). Therefore, the advantage of issuing debt in domestic currency might not be as large as initially thought.

To consider how the possibility of issuing debt in domestic currency affects the balance-of-payments constraint, in this section we redefine our model to consider this type of debt. We still consider the debt/exports ratio, since what matters for investors is if the government will be able to maintain the exchange rate (or avoid default) by providing the foreign currency required if they decide to sell their domestic assets to acquire foreign ones. The difference is that now this ratio must be divided by the exchange rate:

$$\frac{\dot{d}}{e} = \left[\frac{\delta(i - i_f)}{(1-\alpha)\left(1 - \frac{w}{e}v_l(1-\tau) - h + m\right)} + \delta\dot{r} - g_x\frac{d}{e} \right]\left[\frac{1}{1+\delta}\right] \tag{4.14}$$

When debt is issued in domestic currency, the positive relation between foreign inflows and net reserves growth is not because the latter provide insurance against default but because their use can avoid a currency depreciation that would reduce the investment return. This implies that parameter δ could display a different value in the case of domestic currency-denominated debt, since it represents the elasticity to a different kind of risk. The difference between debt in domestic and foreign currency is that, in the latter case, the depreciation risk is transferred from the debt issuer to the creditor (Kaltenbrunner and Painceira 2015). Considering the change in the debt equation, the dynamics of reserves as a share of exports become:

$$\dot{r} = \left[1 - \frac{m - \delta(i - i_f)}{(1-\alpha)\left(1 - \frac{w}{e}v_l(1-\tau) - h + m\right)} - i\frac{d}{e} + (i_f - g_x)r - \delta\frac{\dot{d}}{e} \right]\left[\frac{1}{1-\delta}\right] \tag{4.15}$$

Reserves are boosted by depreciation, but now not only because real wages decrease (as in the case of foreign currency-denominated debt), reducing demand and imports, but also because the interest payments from previous debt shrink due to the reduction in interest payments measured in foreign currency, while previous indebtedness (also measured in dollars) is also reduced, increasing net reserves and attracting new capital inflows.[21]

This implies that when debt is issued in domestic currency, depreciation allows for a faster accumulation of reserves than in the case of foreign currency-denominated debt, where the only channel for affecting output is through the reduction of real wages. In a disequilibrium situation where reserves are too low, depreciation can favour reserve accumulation with less cost in terms of output and income distribution if debt is denominated in domestic currency, making the case for trying to issue that type of liabilities instead of foreign-currency denominated ones, a strategy that several emerging markets have been applying.[22]

[21] This happens if the depreciation has a persistent effect over the real exchange rate. If instead it is interpreted by investors as a strategy to reduce liabilities, leading to the expectation of future devaluations, the increase in net reserves might not have significant effects in capital inflows, and even lead to higher outflows.

[22] This is possible if a certain degree of stability is expected in the country, which implies that the interest rate paid on domestic and foreign-denominated debt is similar. If this was not the case, the interest rate on domestic denominated debt would have to be higher, potentially offsetting the advantages of issuing debt in domestic currency. Indeed, the

This does not imply that, in the long run, issuing debt in domestic currency will necessarily lead to higher output levels or growth rates. If we calculate the fully adjusted position for reserves based on (4.14) and (4.15), we find that:

$$r^* = \left[1 - \frac{m - \delta(i - i_f)\left(1 - \frac{i}{g_x}\right)}{(1-\alpha)\left(1 - \frac{w}{e}v_l(1-\tau) - \frac{g_z v}{u_n} + m\right)}\right]\left[\frac{1}{g_x - i_f}\right] \tag{4.16}$$

In equilibrium, reserves are only affected by the exchange rate due to the distributive channel, but not by affecting previous indebtedness. This makes sense, since in equilibrium the exchange rate is expected to be stable. Therefore, the advantages of issuing debt in domestic currency are mostly related to the possibility of restoring external balance more rapidly after a depreciation, rather than increasing the margin for increasing output levels and/or real wages. This does not preclude the possibility that domestic currency denominated debt leads to a higher δ, implying a caveat to this conclusion and leading to an impact on the maximum output attainable (but not on its growth rate).

6. Conclusions

In order to study the dynamics of external indebtedness in small open economies, in this paper we built a simple demand-led economic growth model where the principle of compensation applies, and the balance-of-payments imposes a limit to economic activity. The model allows us to evaluate the limits that the external sector imposes on fiscal and monetary policies and the functional distribution of income, as well as to evaluate the importance of the currency in which the indebtedness is carried out.

Results show that fiscal and monetary policies can alter output and the external conditions of the economy, more widely than in the Mundell-Fleming model. But at the same time, and contrary to what non-conventional approaches such as modern monetary theory (MMT) argue, not only fiscal and monetary policies, but also income distribution, can be constrained by the balance-of-payments, even in economies with 'monetary sovereignty'.

Fiscal policy can be effective, since the government can increase output through higher public spending, an effect that is enhanced by the multiplier effect of consumption and the investment accelerator (together, the Sraffian 'supermultiplier'). However, the increase in output also requires more imports, which, if they exceed exports, must be financed with international reserves or external indebtedness. Since this situation cannot continue indefinitely, an objective limit to fiscal policy is established. Therefore, there is a 'maximum' level of public expenditure which allows for the larger level of output compatible with external sustainability.

In the long run, fiscal policy faces an additional constraint: government spending cannot grow faster than exports, since this would lead to ever-growing external indebtedness. However, nothing guarantees that this limit will be reached, and scenarios with low output and indebtedness, paired with excessive international reserves accumulation,

higher the debt distress, the harder it is to issue domestic currency-denominated debt, so this tool is less available when it is needed the most.

are feasible. This opens the way for an active fiscal policy that exploits the external space, avoiding unnecessary reserve accumulation.

Regarding monetary policy, the model shows that the Central Bank cannot determine the interest rate in a completely autonomous fashion, even when the compensation principle overrides the general validity of the monetary trilemma. If the interest rate differential is too low, capital outflows can lead to a balance-of-payments deficit and cause to an external crisis, forcing an interest rate hike or a devaluation. But an excessively high interest rate also generates negative effects by giving rise to unsustainable indebtedness processes, even in contexts of low economic growth, since financial flows do not depend directly on the current account result but have their own determinants. Therefore, there is an asymmetric trilemma, where the monetary authority can determine the interest rate, but within certain margins, often quite narrow. And that margin can be altered by external conditions: increases in the global interest rate, a greater perception of risk, or a worsening of the terms of trade can reduce foreign exchange inflows and require more contractionary monetary policies.

Even considering these limitations, a positive differential between domestic and international interest rates can attract financial flows, providing the foreign exchange needed to finance output growth caused by an increase in spending and/or real wages. However, if the interest rate is excessively high, the interest burden may become unsustainable, conspiring against its original purpose of raising the foreign exchange availability. There is therefore an 'optimal' interest rate that maximises external space. Even so, nothing guarantees that this greater space will be used to increase output, which requires expansionary fiscal policies or an improvement in real wages, two elements that are, *a priori*, 'exogenous'.

In fact, the interest rate, by attracting foreign exchange, can alleviate distributive tensions by making real wage increases feasible, but this policy also faces constraints: excessively high wages or public spending give rise to an unsustainable demand for foreign exchange, regardless of the prevailing interest rate. In that case, the growing indebtedness will lead to an external crisis and a currency depreciation, affecting prices and real wages, and re-establishing the external balance through a recession. If wage resistance persists, there is a risk of entering an inflationary spiral.

A final takeaway from the model is that, if debt is issued in domestic currency, the recession caused by the devaluation will be smaller than if it is denominated in foreign currency. This is because devaluation reduces the amount of foreign currency commitments, making it easier to restore external equilibrium. But in the long run, borrowing in domestic currency does not necessarily imply higher economic growth.

In summary, this paper shows that fiscal and monetary policies are severely constrained by the balance-of-payments in small open economies; and that, while they can affect output levels, long run output growth rates remain constrained by exports growth. However, within these limits, they are also powerful tools to widen and exploit the external space the economy has to maximise growth and reach a better income distribution while avoiding harmful balance-of-payments crises.

Acknowledgements

The authors would like to use this opportunity to acknowledge and thank Germán Feldman, Esteban Pérez Caldentey, and the reviewers who reviewed this article and aided in its publication.

Disclosure Statement

No potential conflict of interest was reported by the author(s).

ORCID

Ariel Dvoskin http://orcid.org/0000-0001-6603-6012
Matías Torchinsky Landau http://orcid.org/0000-0003-0043-6042

References

Abeles M. and M. Cherkasky. 2020. 'Revisiting Balance-of-Payments Constrained Growth 70 Years After ECLAC's Manifesto: The Case of South America.' *Revista de Economia Contemporanea* 24 (1): 1–24.

Aguiar de Medeiros C. 2008. 'Financial Dependency and Growth Cycles in Latin American Countries.' *Journal of Post Keynesian Economics* 31 (1): 79–99.

Aizenman J. and R. Glick. 2009. 'Sterilization Monetary Policy and Global Financial Integration.' *Review of International Economics* 17 (4): 777–801.

Allain O. 2022. 'A Supermultiplier Model with Two Non-Capacity-Generating Semi-Autonomous Demand Components.' *Structural Change and Economic Dynamics* 63 (September): 91–103. doi:10.1016/j.strueco.2022.09.008.

Angrick S. 2018. 'Global Liquidity and Monetary Policy Autonomy: An Examination of Open-Economy Policy Constraints.' *Cambridge Journal of Economics* 42 (1): 117–135.

Arestis P. 2009. 'The New Consensus in Macroeconomics: A Critical Appraisal.' In *Macroeconomic Theory and Macroeconomic Pedagogy* edited by G. in Fontana and M. Setterfield. London: Palgrave Macmillan.

Bahmani M. H. Harvey and S. W. Hegerty. 2013. 'Empirical Tests of the Marshall-Lerner Condition: A Literature Review.' *Journal of Economic Studies* 40 (3): 411–443.

Barbosa-Filho N. H. 2001. 'The Balance-of-Payments Constraint: From Balanced Trade to Sustainable Debt.' *PSL Quarterly Review* 54 (219): 381–400.

Bernat G. 2015. *Tipo de cambio real y diversificación productiva en América del Sur Estudios y Perspectivas*. 43. Buenos Aires, Argentina: Oficina de la CEPAL en Argentina.

Bertaut C. C. V. G. Bruno and H. S. Shin. 2022. '*Original Sin Redux*.' *SSRN Electronic Journal* doi:10.2139/ssrn.3820755.

Bhering G. F. Freitas and F. Serrano. 2019. 'Thirlwall's Law External Debt Sustainability and the Balance-of-Payments-Constrained Level and Growth Rates of Output.' *Review of Keynesian Economics* 7 (4): 486–497.

Borio C. and P. Disyatat. 2015. 'Capital Flows and the Current Account: Taking Financing (More) Seriously.' *BIS Working Papers* (525) p. 50.

Bortis H. 1997. *Institutions Behaviour and Economic Theory: A Contribution to Classical-Keynesian Political Economy*. Cambridge: Cambridge University Press.

Bortz P. G. 2014. 'Foreign Debt Distribution Inflation and Growth in an SFC model.' *European Journal of Economics and Economic Policies: Intervention* 11 (3): 269–299.

Bussière M. G. Callegari F. Ghironi G. Sestieri and N. Yamano. 2011. 'Estimating Trade Elasticities : Demand Composition and the Trade Collapse of 2008-09.' *American Economic Journal* 5 (3): 118–151.

Calvo G. A. and C. M. Reinhart. 2002. 'Fear of Floating.' *The Quarterly Journal of Economics* 117 (2): 379–408.

Canitrot A. 1983. 'El salario real y la restricción externa de la economía.' *Desarrollo Económico* 23 (91): 423–427.

Cline N. and M. Vernengo. 2016. 'Interest Rates Terms of Trade and Currency Crises: Are We on the Verge of a New Crisis in the Periphery?' In *Financial Deepening and Post-Crisis Development in Emerging Market* edited by A. V. Gevorkyan and O. Canuto. New York: Palgrave Macmillan.

Crane L. D. M. Crowley and S. Quayyum. 2007. 'Understanding the Evolution of Trade Deficits: Trade Elasticities of Industrialized Countries.' *Federal Reserve Bank of Chicago Economic Perspectives* 31 (4): 2–17.

Crespo E. A. Dvoskin and G. Ianni. 2020. 'Exclusion in "Ricardian" Trade Models.' *Review of Political Economy* 39: 194–211.

Cruz M. M. S. J. Gahn and G. S. Morlin. 2022. 'State-owned and Multinational Enterprises Partnership as an Import Substitution Strategy: A Narrative ARDL Approach to the Case of oil Contracts in Argentina (1958–1962).' *Structural Change and Economic Dynamics* 63: 213–223.

Díaz Alejandro C. F. 1963. 'A Note on the Impact of Devaluation and the Redistributive Effect.' *Journal of Political Economy* 71 (6): 577–580.

Dvoskin A. and G. D. Feldman. 2018. 'Income Distribution and the Balance of Payments: A Formal Reconstruction of Some Argentinian Structuralist Contributions Part I: Technical Dependency.' *Review of Keynesian Economics* 6 (3): 352–368.

Dvoskin A. G. D. Feldman and G. Ianni. 2020. 'New-Structuralist Exchange-Rate Policy and the Pattern of Specialization in Latin American Countries.' *Metroeconomica* 71 (1): 22–48.

Dvoskin A. and M. Torchinsky Landau. 2023. 'Income Distribution and Economic Cycles in an Open-Economy Supermultiplier Model.' *Structural Change and Economic Dynamics* 64: 273–291.

Eichengreen B. R. Hausmann and U. Panizza. 2002. 'Original Sin: The Pain the Mystery and the Road to Redemption.' In *Currency and Maturity Matchmaking: Redeeming Debt from Original Sin*. Washington D.C.: Inter-American Development Bank.

Fagundes L. S. da and F. Freitas. 2017. *The Role of Autonomous Non - Capacity Creating Expenditures in Recent Kaleckian Growth Models: an Assessment from the Perspective of the Sraffian Supermultiplier Model.*

Fajnzylber F. 1990. *Industrialización en América Latina: de la caja negra" al 'casillero vacío'.* Santiago de Chile: CEPAL.

Forstater M. and W. Mosler. 2005. 'The Natural Rate of Interest is Zero.' *Journal of Economic Issues* 39 (2): 535–542.

Fratzscher M. 2011. *Capital flows push versus pull factors and the global financial crisis.* 1364.

Freitas F. and R. Christianes. 2020. 'A Baseline Supermultiplier Model for the Analysis of Fiscal Policy and Government Debt.' *Review of Keynesian Economics* 8 (3): 313–338.

Freitas F. and F. Serrano. 2015. 'Growth Rate and Level Effects the Stability of the Adjustment of Capacity to Demand and the Sraffian Supermultiplier.' *Review of Political Economy* 27 (3): 258–281.

Frenkel R. 2007. 'The Sustainability of Monetary Sterilization Policies.' *CEPAL Review* 93: 29–36.

Gerioni E. M. L. N. Rolim J. A. Omizzolo and N. A. V. D. B. Schiozer. 2022. 'Monetary Policy Autonomy and Foreign Reserves Accumulation in Brazil: A Compensation View.' *Cambridge Journal of Economics* doi:10.1093/cje/beac035.

Hein E. and R. Woodgate. 2021. 'Stability Issues in Kaleckian Models Driven by Autonomous Demand Growth — Harrodian Instability and Debt Dynamics.' *Metroeconomica* 72 (2): 388–404.

Hofmann B. I. Shim and H. S. Shin. 2020. *Emerging Market Economy Exchange Rates and Local Currency Bond Markets Amid the Covid-19 Pandemic.* 5. Available at: https://www.bis.org/publ/bisbull07.pdf.

Hofmann B. I. Shim and H. S. Shin. 2022. *Risk Capacity Portfolio Choice and Exchange Rates BIS Working Papers.* 1031.

Kaltenbrunner A. and J. P. Painceira. 2015. 'Developing Countries' Changing Nature of Financial Integration and New Forms of External Vulnerability: The Brazilian Experience.' *Cambridge Journal of Economics* 39 (5): 1281–1306.

Kaminsky G. L. C. M. Reinhart and C. A. Végh. 2004. 'When it Rains it Pours: Procyclical Capital Flows and Macroeconomic Policies.' *NBER Macroeconomics Annual* 19: 11–53.

Kohler K. 2022. 'Capital Flows and Geographically Uneven Economic Dynamics: A Monetary Perspective.' *Environment and Planning A: Economy and Space* doi: 10.1177/0308518(221120823.

Krugman P. and L. Taylor. 1978. 'Contractionary Effects of Devaluation.' *Journal of International Economics* 8 (3): 445–456.

Lavoie M. 2001. 'The Reflux Mechanism and the Open Economy.' In *Credit Interest Rates and the Open Economy: Essays on Horizontalism* edited by M. Vernengo and L. P. Rochon. Cheltenham: Eldward Elgar.

Lavoie M. and P. Wang. 2011. 'The 'Compensation' Thesis as Exemplified by the Case of the Chinese Central Bank.' *International Review of Applied Economics* 26 (3): 287–301.

Levy Yeyati E. and A. Ize. 2003. 'Financial Dollarization.' *Journal of International Economics* 59 (2): 323–347.

McCombie J. S. L. and A. P. Thirlwall. 1997. 'Economic Growth and the Balance-of-Payments Constraint revisited.' In *Markets Unemployment and Economic Policy: Essays in Honour of Geoff Harcourt vol. 2* edited by P. Arestis G. Palma and M. Sawyer. London: Routledge.

McCombie J. S. L. and A. P. Thirlwall eds. 2004. *Essays on Balance of Payments Constrained Growth: Theory and Evidence.* London: Routledge.

McLeay M. A. Radia and R. Thomas. 2014. *Money creation in the modern economy.*

Moreno-Brid J. C. 2003. 'Capital Flows Interest Payments and the Balance-of-Payments Constrained Growth Model: A Theoretical and Empirical Analysis.' *Metroeconomica* 54 (2–3): 346–365.

Morlin G. S. 2022. 'Growth Led by Government Expenditure and Exports : Public and External Debt Stability in a Supermultiplier Model.' *Structural Change and Economic Dynamics* 62: 586–598.

Morlin G. S. 2023. 'Inflation and Conflicting Claims in the Open Economy.' *Review of Political Economy* 35 (3): 762–790.

Mundell R. A. 1963. 'Capital Mobility and Stabilization Policy Under Fixed and Flexible Exchange Rates.' *Canadian Journal of Economics and Political Science* 29 (4): 475–485.

Nah W. J. and M. Lavoie. 2019. 'Convergence in a Neo-Kaleckian Model with Endogenous Technical Progress and Autonomous Demand Growth.' *Review of Keynesian Economics* 7 (3): 275–291.

Nikiforos M. 2018. 'Some Comments on the Sraffian Supermultiplier Approach to Growth and Distribution.' *Journal of Post Keynesian Economics* 41 (4): 659–675.

Obstfeld M. and K. Rogoff. 1995. 'The Mirage of Fixed Exchange Rates.' *Journal of Economic Perspectives* 9 (4): 73–96.

Onen M. H. S. Shin and P. Von Goetz. 2023. *Overcoming Original Sin: Insights from a New Dataset.* 1075.

Oreiro J. L. and Costa Santos J. F. (2022) The Impossible Quartet in a Demand Led Growth-Supermultiplier Model for a Small Open Economy. 2215.

Pedrosa Í L. Brochier and F. Freitas. 2023. 'Debt Hierarchy: Autonomous Demand Composition Growth and Indebtedness in a Supermultiplier Model.' *Economic Modelling* 126. https://www.sciencedirect.com/science/article/abs/pii/S0264999323001815.

Rapetti M. 2013. 'Macroeconomic Policy Coordination in a Competitive Real Exchange Rate Strategy for Development.' *Journal of Globalization and Development* 3 (2): 1–31.

Reinhart C. 1995. 'Devaluation Relative Prices and International Trade: Evidence from Developing Countries.' *Staff Papers — International Monetary Fund* 42 (2): 290–312.

Rey H. 2015. '*Dilemma not Trilemma: The Global Financial Cycle and Monetary Policy Independence.*' *NBER Working Papers* 21162.

Rey H. 2016. 'International Channels of Transmission of Monetary Policy and the Mundellian Trilemma.' *IMF Economic Review* 64: 6–35.

Romer D. 2018. *Short-run Fluctuations.* Berkeley. Available at: https://eml.berkeley.edu/~dromer/papers/Romer%20Short-Run%20Fluctuations%20January2018.pdf.

Samuelson P. A. 1939. 'Interactions Between the Multiplier Analysis and the Principle of Acceleration.' *The Review of Economics and Statistics* 21 (2): 75–78.

Serrano F. 1995. 'Long Period Effective Demand and the Sraffian Supermultiplier.' *Contributions to Political Economy* 14 (1): 67–90.

Serrano F. and R. Summa. 2015. 'Mundell–Fleming Without the LM Curve: The Exogenous Interest Rate in an Open Economy.' *Review of Keynesian Economics* 3 (2): 248–268.

Sturzenegger F. 1997. 'Understanding the Welfare Implications of Currency substitution.' *Journal of Economic Dynamics and Control* 21 (2–3): 391–416.
Tcherneva P. R. 2012. *Beyond Full Employment: The Employer of Last Resort as an Institution for Change*. 732.
Thirlwall A. P. 1979. 'The Balance of Payments Constraint as an Explanation of International Growth Rate Differences.' *BNL Quarterly Review* 64: 45–53.
Tymoigne É and L. R. Wray. 2013. *Modern Monetary Theory 101: A Reply to Critics The Levy Economics Institute Working Paper Collection*. 778.
Woodgate R. E. Hein and R. Summa. 2023. *Components of autonomous demand growth and financial feedbacks: growth regime analysis*. 2307.
Wray R. L. 1997. 'Deficits Inflation and Monetary Policy.' *Journal of Post Keynesian Economics* 19 (4): 543–571.
Wray R. L. 2012. *Modern Money Theory*. Basingstoke: Palgrave Macmillan.
Wray R. L. L. Mitchell and M. Watts. 2019. *Macroeconomics*. London: Springer Nature.

7. Annex. Model stability

To analyse stability, we need to define the four dynamic equations of the model as depending only on the variables and parameters of the model instead of their rate of change. First, we have the two equations representing the supermultiplier, which already meet this condition:

$$\dot{h} = h\gamma(u - u_n) \tag{7.1}$$

$$\dot{u} = u\left[\frac{h\gamma(u-u_n)}{1-\frac{w}{e}v_l(1-\tau)-h+m} + g_z - \frac{hu}{v}\right] \tag{7.2}$$

Second, we have the two equations dealing with reserves and debt. Since these equations depend on $\dot{d}$ and $\dot{r}$, we need to replace their values and solve:

$$\dot{d} = \delta\left[1 - \frac{m-(i-i_f)\left(1+\frac{\delta}{1-\delta}\right)}{(1-\alpha)\left(1-\frac{w}{e}v_l(1-\tau)-h+m\right)} - id + (i_f - g_x)r\right] - g_x d(1-\delta) \tag{7.3}$$

$$\dot{r} = (1+\delta)\left[1 - \frac{m-\delta(i-i_f)\left(1-\frac{\delta}{1+\delta}\right)}{(1-\alpha)\left(1-\frac{w}{e}v_l(1-\tau)-h+m\right)} - id + (i_f - g_x)r\right] + \delta g_x d \tag{7.4}$$

Note that we have two systems of equations, one composed by (7.1) and (7.2), and another of (7.3) and (7.4). The first system is independent of the second one, while the second does depend on the result of the first. This allows us to first resolve the first system and then apply its result to the second. To do so, we calculate the Jacobian in the equilibrium where $h^* = \frac{g_z v}{u_n}$ and $u^* = u_n$.

$$J = \begin{bmatrix} 0 & \frac{g_z v}{u_n}\gamma \\ -\frac{u_n^2}{v} & g_z\left[\frac{v\gamma}{1-\frac{w}{e}v_l(1-\tau)-\frac{g_z v}{u_n}+m} - 1\right] \end{bmatrix} \tag{7.5}$$

The determinant is necessarily positive given the values of the parameters. For the trace to be negative, we need that:

$$v\gamma + \frac{w}{e} v_l(1-\tau) + \frac{g_z v}{u_n} - m < 1 \tag{7.6}$$

Following Freitas and Serrano (2015) this can be interpreted as the need for the marginal spending propensity to be lower to one (the Keynesian stability condition), 'expanded' by the behaviour of investment outside equilibrium. If (7.6) is met, then we can analyse the second system. In that case, the Jacobian will be:

$$J = \begin{bmatrix} -\delta i - g_x(1-\delta) & \delta(i_f - g_x) \\ -i(1+\delta) + \delta g_x & (i_f - g_x)(1+\delta) \end{bmatrix} \tag{7.7}$$

The trace will be negative if:

$$i_f(1+\delta) - \delta i - 2g_x < 0 \tag{7.8}$$

The determinant will be positive if:

$$g_x(g_x - i_f) > 0 \tag{7.9}$$

Which requires $g_x > i_f$. The model will be stable if (7.6), (7.8) and (7.9) are fulfilled.

Impacts of US Interest Rates on Growth, Income Distribution, and Macroeconomic Policy Space in Developing Countries: A SFC Supermultiplier Model

João Emboava Vaz

ABSTRACT
This paper presents a stock-flow-consistent model in which growth is led by exports, government consumption, and consumption out of interest. It considers domestic and external debt dynamics and gross capital flows. The balance of payments constraint serves as a ceiling but not a floor for growth. Countries may choose to not fully use their external space to decrease public debts or accumulate international reserves. The model is applied to a comparative dynamics exercise to explore how a hike in foreign interest rates may impact growth and income distribution in a developing country under different policy responses. The shock forces the country to apply at least one contractionary macroeconomic policy or lose its reserves. Contractionary monetary policy may be the only tool to avoid external disequilibrium after the shock for countries with open capital accounts. Financial flows may impose trade-offs between short and long run policy objectives. Accumulated international reserves helps maintain expansionary policies and higher average growth rates after external shocks by providing liquidity in foreign currency.

1. Introduction

In 2022, the US Fed responded to inflation pressures with the most rapid interest rate hike since the 1979–1982 Volcker's disinflation. At the beginning of the 1980s, the hike was followed by harsh external crises in the developing world. The current hike happens in a new environment. Since the 2000s, developing countries have received large financial flows and accumulated record international reserve stocks.[1] This paper aims to understand how a shock in benchmark interest rates may impact growth, income distribution, and macroeconomic policy space in financially integrated developing countries. Diving into the rationale behind the reserve accumulation pursued by these countries.

[1] According to the IMF, total foreign exchange reserves held by emerging and developing countries went from 714 billion US dollars in 2000 to 7.9 trillion US dollars in 2013.

The empirical literature on determinants of financial flows finds the US interest rate as the primary driver of global financial cycles (Rey 2015; Aidar and Braga 2020). This undermines the results of conventional models on open-economy constraints and external crisis (Krugman 1979) which point to monetary or fiscal policy mismanagement as a main cause of balance-of-payments (BoP) crises. On the other hand, it endorses the findings of post-Keynesian Structuralist authors which point to the opposite causality: external shocks lead to macroeconomic constraints and crises in developing countries (Nikiforos, Carvalho, and Schoder 2015; Cline and Vernengo 2016).

To explore these economic relations theoretically, a stock-flow-consistent (SFC) open-economy supermultiplier model is presented. It builds on the recent integration of balance-of-payments-constrained growth (BPCG) theory in supermultiplier models led by government and exports (Morlin 2022; Dvoskin and Torchinsky Landau 2023).

This paper thus aims to look at the effect of an external shock on macroeconomic policy space through the BoP channel. Linking the Compensation Thesis, the literature on the external dilemma, and the Structuralist literature on external constraints to macroeconomic policy. The growth model is thus used to look at how policymaking directed at increasing growth and decreasing inequality may be affected by a hike in benchmark international interest rates.

Section Two presents the discussion on growth and macroeconomic policymaking in open economies. Section Three develops the SFC model. Section Four presents the comparative dynamics exercise on policy responses to the external shock. Section Five concludes.

2. Open Economy Demand-Led Growth

Most macroeconomists now agree that in capitalist economies money is created in most part by commercial bank's loans (McLeay, Radia, and Thomas 2014, p. 444) with canonical models highlighting Central Bank interest setting instead of 'exogenous money supply' interventions (Carlin and Soskice 2005). However, when open-economy macroeconomics is considered, many economists still follow the canonical Mundell-Fleming model, whose results intrinsically depend on exogenous money (Serrano and Summa 2015). Post-Keynesian economists, on the other hand, have extended endogenous money theory to open economies. Finding that an increase in money supply from the rest of the world can be compensated by changes in the Central Bank's balance sheet (an operation often called 'sterilization'), without necessarily leading to a change in domestic money supply. What has been called the 'Compensation Thesis' (Lavoie 2022, Ch 7.2).

After the 2008 Global Financial Crisis, economists have given greater attention to the determinants of financial flows, criticizing the conventional Mundell-Fleming results (Rey 2015; Borio and Disyatat 2015; Aidar and Braga 2020). This literature finds empirical evidence that capital flows to developing countries mainly follow international conditions, with the US interest rate being the main determinant of global financial cycles. Rey (2015) argues that there is a policy dilemma (instead of Mundell-Fleming's trilemma) between capital openness and monetary policy independence, because the latter has to follow international financial movements when capital accounts are open.

However, when endogenous money is considered, there is no mechanical adjustment from capital flows to interest rates, which depend on a policy choice by the monetary authority (Lavoie 2022, Ch 7.2). Capital *inflows* may be sterilized by central banks, but capital *outflows* can impose a balance-of-payment-constraint — the lack of access to foreign currency necessary to sustain international transactions. On one hand, this may explain how emerging countries accumulated record levels of international reserves in the 2000s while keeping managed exchange rate regimes through interest rate differentials (Ilzetzki, Reinhart, and Rogoff 2022). On the other hand, it points to capital outflows restricting domestic policy through the balance-of-payments-constraint.

These findings undermine the role of fiscal mismanagement in causing external crisis, as presented in conventional models (Krugman 1979) and reinforces the empirical and theoretical findings on the opposite causality: external shocks lead to fiscal crises (Nikiforos, Carvalho, and Schoder 2015; Cline and Vernengo 2016) or at least impose developing countries to a narrower external space for domestic policy (Vernengo and Pérez-Caldentey 2020; Porcile and Yajima 2021).

There is an extensive literature on balance-of-payments-constrained growth (BPCG) (Thirlwall 2012), recently linked to the Sraffian supermultiplier tradition (Serrano 1995; Freitas and Serrano 2015) in models where growth is led by government expenditure and exports (Morlin 2022; Dvoskin and Torchinsky Landau 2023). A neo-Kaleckian version of the supermultiplier model has been presented for open-economies by Nah and Lavoie (2017), but it does not incorporate the public sector nor the balance-of-payments-constraint. The neo-Kaleckian tradition has drawn influence from the New Cambridge School's argument of the importance of stock-flow relations on expenditures (Cripps and Godley 1976) highlighting the relevance of stock-flow-consistent (SFC) modelling (Godley and Lavoie 2007; Nikiforos and Zezza 2018). Some SFC models have been developed to look at debt relations in supermultiplier models (Brochier and Silva 2019; Pedrosa, Brochier, and Freitas 2023) and to look at financial aspects of developing countries (Nalin and Yajima 2022). However, SFC methodologies have not yet been extended to supermultiplier models of small open-economies. This extension might provide new insights to the role of BoP and international reserves in growth trajectories of developing countries and more generally in the relationship between 'semi-autonomous' expenditures (Allain 2022). Next section presents a model with this extension.

3. A Stock-Flow Consistent Supermultiplier Growth Model Led by Public Expenditure and Exports

This paper contributes to the open-economy demand-led growth literature by presenting a supermultiplier model in which growth is led by public expenditure and exports. It builds upon the neo-Kaleckian open-economy supermultiplier model by Nah and Lavoie (2017) while including the public sector as in Hein (2018). Its consideration of domestic and external debt is inspired by the works of Morlin (2022) and Dvoskin and Torchinsky Landau (2023), with different specifications and further considering stock-flow dynamics in line with the SFC tradition after Godley and Lavoie (2007).

3.1. Economic Environment

As in Nah and Lavoie (2017), the modelled economy imports intermediate (and capital) goods, cannot affect its import and export prices, and is too small to affect its own export demand. Tables 1 and 2 present the balance sheet and transaction matrices that synthesize the environment of the economy. Real exchange rates are defined as $e_R = \frac{ep_f}{p}$, in which p and p_f are the domestic and foreign price levels, respectively, and e is the nominal exchange rate. Nominal exchange rates are taken exogenously and as a policy variable, assuming the country is in a fixed or managed exchange rate regime.[2] Exports and imports are partially dependent on short-run variations in the real exchange rate ($X_1(e_R)$ and $M_1(e_R)$), with $\frac{dX_1}{de_R} > 0$ and $\frac{dM_1}{de_R} < 0$, while the rest of exports are exogenous (X_0) and of imports are dependent on domestic income (M_0). International financial flows' dynamics are introduced in Section 'Long run Equilibrium'.

The public sector is introduced by including government consumption[3] (G_C) and interest payments on domestic debt (iB), which may be financed by taxation or by issuing new debt. Tax shares of income are the same for all forms of income, therefore taxes do not have a redistributive role. The government can issue both domestic debt (B) and foreign currency denominated (net) external debt (D). All transactions in dollars are assumed to go through the Central Bank, such that only the public sector holds external assets and liabilities.[4] This simplification gives attention to government action, the focus of this investigation.

The private sector is kept simple. Portfolio flows and private debt are not considered. Investment does not depend on previous savings, and all profits go to rentiers as dividends. Domestic rentiers' savings are held in domestic bonds or equity. They consume the same share of profits and interest receipts. Consumption out of wealth is not considered, for simplicity. Workers are assumed to consume all their after-tax income. Tables 1 and 2 summarize the economic environment.

As in Hein (2018), total disposable domestic income (Y) is composed of productive income (Y_P) and financial income (Y_F), with Ψ representing the ratio of financial to productive income ($\Psi = \frac{Y_F}{Y_P} = \frac{ib}{u}$). Total income distribution can be expressed as: $Y = Y_P + Y_F = W + \Pi + iB$. The wage-share of income is defined as:

$$\omega = \frac{W}{Y} = \frac{(1-\pi)Y_P}{(1+\Psi)Y_P} = \frac{1-\pi}{1+\Psi} \tag{1}$$

Productive wages depend on the exogenous profit share of productive income (π), defined exogenously. Distribution depends on the domestic debt to capital ratio (b) and the utilization of installed capacity ($u = \frac{Y_P}{K}$)[5] because of their impact on Ψ.

[2]In the 2000s, most developing countries assumed some degree of managed floating regime with interest rate arbitrage, reserve intervention, or capital controls (Ilzetzki, Reinhart, and Rogoff (2022)). Exchange rates are taken exogenously as a simplification to focus on volume changes. Section Four considers the case of fully flexible rates.

[3]For matters of simplicity, government consumption and investment were not distinguished. See Deleidi and Mazzucato (2019) for a supermultiplier model which distinguishes public investment.

[4]See Dvoskin and Torchinsky Landau (2023) for the consideration of private external debt in a similar model.

[5]For simplicity the proportion of installed capital to potential output is assumed to remain constant and equal to unit.

Table 1. Balance sheet matrix.

	Workers	Rentiers	Firms	Government	Central Bank	RoW	Σ
Domestic Loans		$+B$		$-B$			0
Foreign Loans				$-D$	$+R$	$+D-R$	0
Equities		$+E$	$-E$				0
Capital			K				K
Σ	0	$+B+E$	0	$-B-D$	$+R$	$+D-R$	$K=E$

Notes: Variables: domestic public debt (B), net external debt (D), international reserves (R), equities (E), and capital stocks (K).

Table 2. Transaction flow matrix.

	Workers	Rentiers	Firms		Treasury		Central Bank	RoW	Σ
			Current	Capital	Domestic	Foreign			
Private domestic consumption	$-C_w$	$-C_r$	$+(C_w+C_r)$						0
Private investment expenditure			$+I$	$-I$					0
Imports			$-M$					$+M$	0
Exports			$+X$					$-X$	0
Government expenditures			$+G_c$		$-G_C$		0		
Taxation	$-\tau W$	$-\tau(\Pi+iB)$			$+T$				0
Wages	$+W$		$-W$						0
Profits		$+\Pi$	$-\Pi$						0
Domestic interest payments		$+iB$			$+iB$				0
Foreign internet payments						$-i_xD$	$+i_fR$	$+i_xD-i_fR$	0
Change in equity				$+E$					0
Change in Domestic loans		$-\Delta B$			$+\Delta B$				0
Change in foreign loans						$+\Delta D$		$-\Delta D$	0
Change in international reserves							$-\Delta R$	$+\Delta R$	0
Σ	0	0	0	0	0	0	0	0	0

Notes: Variables: worker's consumption (C_w), rentier's consumption (C_r), investment (I), imports (M), exports (X), government consumption (G_C), tax revenue (T), wages (W), profits (Π), domestic public debt (B), net external debt (D), international reserves (R), equity (E), tax rate (τ), domestic interest rates (i), US Fed interest rates (i_f), interest rates on external debt (i_x).

3.2. Dynamics of the Model

The dynamics of the model follows Nah and Lavoie (2017), with the introduction of Equation (4) for the government:

$$g = \frac{I}{K} = \gamma + \gamma_u(u - u_n) \tag{2}$$

$$tb = \frac{TB}{K} = x + \phi_e e_R - \phi_u u \tag{3}$$

$$gov = \frac{Gov}{K} = \vartheta - \tau u + ib \tag{4}$$

$$\sigma = \frac{S}{K} = s_r(\pi u + ib) \tag{5}$$

Capital accumulation (g) depends positively on the difference between u and u_n — the current and normal rates of capacity utilization — and on the expected growth of sales (γ), or 'animal spirits'. tb is the trade-balance-to-capital ratio. It depends positively on $x = \frac{X_0}{K}$ and on the effect of an exchange rate depreciation on net exports ($\phi_e e_R$), and negatively on activity-induced imports ($\phi_u u$). Following the canonical neo-Kaleckian open-economy models, the value of ϕ_e is assumed positive in the short-run, although this assumption is relaxed in Section Four. ϕ_u represents the propensity to import out of productive income, which is assumed constant.

gov is the net government expenditure to capital ratio. $\vartheta = \frac{G}{K}$ is assumed to be autonomous from current income and a policy variable. τ is the tax rate on income.[6] σ is the savings-to-capital ratio, which depends on the share of profits on productive income (π) and on the interest on domestic public bonds received by rentiers (ib). s_r is the tax-adjusted savings rate of the rentiers, such that $s_r = s(1-\tau)$, where s is the general propensity to save of the rentiers. Workers as a group do not save.

With the macroeconomic fundamental savings-investment identity, Equations (2)–(5) can be combined:

$$s_r \pi u = \gamma + \gamma_u (u - u_n) + x + \phi_e e_R - \phi_u u + \vartheta - \tau u + (1 - s_r) ib \tag{6}$$

3.3. Short-Run Equilibrium

The short-run equilibrium represents the adjustment of capacity utilization to the given aggregate demand. Combining Equations (1), (2), and (6), the short-term equilibrium rates of capacity utilization (u^*), of accumulation (g^*), and of the wage-share (ω^*) can be presented:

$$u^* = \frac{\gamma + x + \phi_e e_R + \vartheta + (1 - s_r) ib - \gamma_u u_n}{s_r \pi + \phi_u + \tau - \gamma_u} \tag{7}$$

$$g^* = \gamma + \gamma_u \left(\frac{\gamma + x + \phi_e e_R + \vartheta + (1 - s_r) ib - (s_r \pi + \phi_u)\, u_n}{s_r \pi + \phi_u + \tau - \gamma_u} \right) \tag{8}$$

$$\omega^* = \frac{1 - \pi}{1 + \frac{ib}{u^*}} \tag{9}$$

Short-term stability is guaranteed when the Keynesian stability condition, $s_r \pi + \phi_u + \tau > \gamma_u$, holds. When savings (with imports and tax revenue) respond more strongly to changes in capacity utilization than investment. The paradox of savings — the notion that the savings rate has a negative effect on aggregate income — is maintained under the same condition. The paradox of profits[7] — the notion that the profit share has a negative effect on aggregate income — holds when $\frac{\partial e_R}{\partial \pi} < \frac{s_r u^*}{\phi_e}$,

[6] All income is taxed proportionally. A progressive taxation could imply higher aggregate demand levels, while the opposite applies for regressive taxation. This is not considered for simplicity.

[7] Here the paradox of profits is taken with the profit-share in productive income and not in total income, following Hein (2018).

when the positive effect of higher productive profit shares on net exports through higher exchange rates is smaller than the negative effect on domestic demand. Sustaining canonical neo-Kaleckian open-economy model results in the short-run (Blecker 1989; Nah and Lavoie 2017).

3.4. Long Run Equilibrium

3.4.1. Aggregate Demand and Capacity

In the short-run x, ϑ, b and foreign asset positions were assumed given. Right after this quick short-run adjustment, it is expected that these variables start changing. In the long run, it is assumed that γ changes and adjusts to the growth rate of the autonomous components as expressed by Dutt (2019)[8] and that exchange rate effects fade away,[9] represented by $\phi_e = 0$ in the dynamic equations. The model is left with three autonomous non-capacity-creating components of demand (Z):

$$Z = G_C + (1 - s_r)iB + X_0 \tag{10}$$

With Equation (10), Equation (7) can be rewritten in terms of the supermultiplier $\left(\frac{1}{s_r\pi + \phi_u + \tau - \gamma_u}\right)$, the autonomous non-capacity-creating (excluding $\phi_e e_R$), and the autonomous capacity-creating autonomous component of demand (I_A):

$$u'^{*} = \left(\frac{Y_P}{K}\right)^{*} = \frac{I_A + Z}{K(s_r\pi + \phi_u + \tau - \gamma_u)} = \frac{\gamma - \gamma_u\, u_n + z}{s_r\pi + \phi_u + \tau - \gamma_u} \tag{11}$$

In which $z = \frac{Z}{K}$ and Equation (11) corresponds to an alternative short-run equilibrium in which $\phi_e = 0$.

Consumption out of interests on domestic debt, $(1 - s_r)iB$, depends on the government current interest payments, thus representing part of the effect government expenditure has on current aggregate demand. Thus, government expenditure in autonomous demand can be defined as $G = \alpha Z = G_C + (1 - s_r)iB$. The growth rate of this flow ($\overline{g_G}$) is taken exogenously and as a policy variable set by the government, such that government consumption growth (g_{G_C}) accommodates the growth rate of domestic public debt and possible changes in domestic interest rates and rentiers' savings rate. Exports (now only composed of X_0) are also assumed to grow at an exogenously given rate $\overline{g_X}$. A bar above a variable means it is exogenously given and constant, a dot above a variable represents the rate of change of that variable in time, a hat represents the rate of growth of ratio variables, to avoid confusion, and g variables with subscripts represent the growth rate of variables in the subscripts (g with no subscripts representing the rate of accumulation). Long-run dynamics can be described:

$$g_Z = \alpha\bar{g}_G + (1 - \alpha)\bar{g}_X \tag{12}$$

[8]That 'the expected long-run growth is equal to the known rate of growth of the exogenous component [the autonomous demand]' (Dutt 2019, p.17). This assumes Harrodian instability out. Nah and Lavoie (2017) propose an adjustment in two different periods with Harrodian instability, this is not done here for matters of simplicity.

[9]This is in line with the BPCG literature and its empirical findings that relative price changes explain little to none of the long-run movement of trade (Kaldor 1978; Thirlwall 2012).

$$\dot{\alpha} = \alpha(1 - \alpha)(g_G - g_X) \tag{13}$$

$$\left(\widehat{\frac{Z}{K}}\right) = \hat{z} = g_Z - g^* = g_Z - \gamma - \gamma_u\left(\frac{\gamma + z - (s_r\pi + \phi_u)\, u_n}{s_r\pi + \phi_u + \tau - \gamma_u}\right) \tag{14}$$

The condition for the stability and conversion to equilibrium of the ratio z is $\frac{\partial\hat{z}}{\partial z} = -\frac{\gamma_u}{s_r\pi + \phi_u + \tau - \gamma_u} < 0$, which holds given the Keynesian stability condition. The condition points out that g_Z and g converge leading to $\dot{z} = 0$. The long-run equilibrium position also requires that $\dot{\alpha} = 0$. Which is attained when $g_G = g_x$, as in Morlin (2022). α^{**} can assume any level between 0 and 1 in equilibrium as long as the different (semi)autonomous non-capacity-creating components grow at the same rate.

The long-run equilibrium rates of growth (g^{**}), capacity utilization (u^{**}), and autonomous non-capacity-creating-demand-to-capital ratio (z^{**}) can be derived from Equations (12)(14) when $\dot{\gamma} = \dot{\alpha} = \dot{z} = 0$:[10]

$$g^{**} = g_z = g_G = g_x = \gamma^{**} \tag{15}$$

$$u^{**} = u_n \tag{16}$$

$$z^{**} = (s_r\pi + \phi_u)u_n - g_z \tag{17}$$

Long-run growth is determined by the growth rate of the autonomous non-capacity-creating components of demand and the economy converges to a normal level of capacity utilization, in line with the Supermultiplier tradition (Serrano 1995).

3.4.2. Public Domestic Debt Dynamics

The domestic public debt increases with government consumption and interest payments and decreases with tax revenues.:

$$\dot{B} = G_C - T + iB \tag{18}$$

The relevant domestic debt is the ratio of public debt to domestic production or to installed capital, as in Hein (2018). The dynamics of $b = \frac{B}{K}$ shall be considered remembering that $T = \tau Y = \tau(Y_P + iB)$ and that $\vartheta = \alpha z - (1 - s_r)ib$:

$$\dot{b} = \frac{\dot{B}K - B\dot{K}}{K^2} = \alpha z - \tau u + [i(s_r - \tau) - g]b \tag{19}$$

The ratio b will be stable when $\frac{\partial\dot{b}}{\partial b} = i(s_r - \tau) - g < 0$ holds, which imposes the stability condition $g > i(s_r - \tau)$. The condition is less restrictive than Domar's (1944) debt stability hypothesis of $g > i$, in line with the literature that considers private consumption and taxation out of interest on public debt (Godley and Lavoie 2007, Ch. 11; Lavoie 2022, Ch. 5.6.3).

---

[10]With Dutt's (2019) argument, .$\dot{\gamma} = 0$. is reached when $g_Z = \gamma^{**}$.

The equilibrium long-run domestic public debt level of the economy is found by equalizing Equation (19) to zero:

$$b^{**} = \frac{\alpha z^{**} - \tau u_n}{g - i(s_r - \tau)} \tag{20}$$

The long-run wage-share can be described as:

$$\omega^{**} = \frac{1 - \pi}{1 + \frac{ib^{**}}{u_n}} \tag{21}$$

A higher public-debt-to-capital ratio is compatible with lower wage-share in the long-run, as it increases equilibrium financial income. Public debt becomes the only endogenous variable with a distributive role in the long-run.

3.4.3. External Debt and International Reserves Dynamics

The balance of payments (BoP) of the model is based on Morlin (2022) and Dvoskin and Torchinsky Landau (2023), with modifications. The model considers that current account imbalances do not mechanically determine financial flows in an economy with open capital accounts. This implies that the variation in international reserves (R) is the element that accommodates changes in the BoP as a whole. The relevant liability becomes the net external debt (D), which excludes international reserve movements and varies with the results of the capital and financial accounts (F). This can be seen in the dynamics of both stocks:

$$\dot{R} = X - M - i_x D + i_f R + F(i,\ i_f,\ \epsilon) \tag{22}$$

$$\dot{D} = F(i,\ i_f,\ \epsilon) = \delta[(i - i_f)Y_P - \ \epsilon] \tag{23}$$

i_x and i_f are the interest rates on external debt and on international reserves, respectively, such that $i_x = i_f + \mu$, in which $\mu \geq 0$ represents a risk premium of lending to the country. Such that interest on external debt is indexed to or directly affected by the benchmark interest rate (taken to be the US Fed interest rate) while being higher than it.[11] R is the international reserve stock assumed to be held in US Fed treasury bonds to not incur into opportunity costs of holding currency. It is assumed there is high liquidity for these bonds, such that the reserve stocks vary with the BoP result.[12] The net external debt stocks (D) are assumed to be held by the public sector in foreign currency (see Table 1). $\dot{D} = F$, in which F is the net financial inflows and represents the total result of the capital and financial accounts.[13] Financial inflows depend on

[11]This generally points to the returns on the safest assets, Fed bonds, affecting the rentability of assets competiting internationally and captures the usual consideration that interest rates on a country's external debt are not under its control (Cline and Vernengo 2016). One limitation of the definition, however, is that i_x is assumed completely independent from i, which would not be the case if part of the external debt is held on domestic bonds bought by foreigners. A consideration left for further research.

[12]Implicitly this also means that the Central Bank intervenes to sustain exchange rates by reserve intervention, such that all changes in BoP are taken in volumes and not in prices. This is partially relaxed in Section 'Case 1: Exchange Rate Policy'.

[13]Different forms of capital flows are not distinguished, but composition should matter. If the financial account holds more volatile flows, the country will be more sensitive to external shocks. This is captured by δ.

the interest rate differential (between domestic and US rates), on the country's domestic production (assuming larger economies receive more flows), and negatively on the risk assessment by the market (ϵ), assumed exogenous for matters of simplicity.[14] The parameter δ is positive and indicates how much financial inflows are affected by the other variables.

The model follows Bhering, Serrano, and Freitas (2019) in the consideration that the external debt to exports is the relevant variable for external indebtedness. Following Dvoskin and Torchinsky Landau (2023), that is also extended to international reserve stocks:[15]

$$\dot{r} = \left(\frac{\dot{R}}{X}\right) = \frac{\dot{R}X - R\dot{X}}{X^2} = 1 + \frac{Y_P}{X}(\delta(i - i_f) - \phi_u) - i_x d + (i_f - g_x)r - \delta\varepsilon \tag{24}$$

$$\dot{d} = \left(\frac{\dot{D}}{X}\right) = \frac{\dot{D}X - D\dot{X}}{X^2} = \frac{Y_P}{X}\delta(i - i_f) - \delta\varepsilon - g_x d \tag{25}$$

In which $\varepsilon = \frac{\epsilon}{X}$, and r and d are the international reserves and net external debt to export ratios. The individual stabilities of the international reserves and net external debt to exports ratios will then depend on the inequalities $\frac{\partial \dot{r}}{\partial r} = i_f - g_x < 0$ and $\frac{\partial \dot{d}}{\partial d} = -g_x < 0$. Although the net external debt has a less restrictive stability condition of $g_x > 0$ when taken individually, both equations as a dynamic system will only converge to equilibrium if $g_x > i_f \geq 0$ (see Appendix).

The long-run equilibrium positions can be derived when $\dot{r} = \dot{d} = 0$:

$$r^{**} = \frac{1 + \frac{Y_P}{X}(\delta(i - i_f) - \phi_u) - i_x d^{**} - \delta\varepsilon}{g_x - i_f} \tag{26}$$

$$d^{**} = \frac{\frac{Y_P}{X}\delta(i - i_f) - \delta\varepsilon}{g_x} \tag{27}$$

3.4.4. A Limit to External Indebtedness

Until now it was assumed the trade imbalance can be always financed by financial flows, with no limit to r or d. Following Bhering, Serrano, and Freitas (2019), the more plausible situation is considered in which international creditors will not undefinedly finance the country's indebtedness, imposing a maximum level of external debt to exports ratio $\bar{d}$. This level can be associated with a minimum level of international reserve stocks $\bar{r}$ through Equation (26), also necessary for the maintenance of a fixed or managed exchange rate regime (Dvoskin and Torchinsky Landau 2023). The minimum level of international reserves can be described as the one that allows the country to serve

[14]Dvoskin and Torchinsky Landau (2023) use the dynamics of the net external debt to international reserves as a proxy for the risk assessment.

[15]In the model the ratio represents the BoP result to exports.

both needs. Below this level, the country would enter a BoP crisis. Equations (11) and (26) can be used to write this level in terms of all parameters:

$$\bar{r} = \frac{1 + \dfrac{(\gamma^{**} - \gamma_u\, u_n + z^{**})}{(1-\alpha)z^{**}(s_r\pi + \phi_u + \tau - \gamma_u)}(\delta(i - i_f) - \phi_u) - i_x\bar{d} - \delta\varepsilon}{g_x - i_f} \tag{28}$$

Equation (28) shows that the balance-of-payments-constraint depends negatively on the supermultiplier, the limit of acceptable external debt ($\bar{d}$), the interest rate on this debt (i_x), and the size of government expenditure in autonomous demand (α).

3.5. Main Results of the Model and Implications

The neo-Kaleckian open-economy supermultiplier model presented here follows Nah and Lavoie (2017) and extends their model by including four features: the public sector, domestic and foreign assets and liabilities, international gross capital flows, and a balance-of-payments-constraint. For the latter inclusion the model had to disregard long-run effects of exchange rate movements on the rate of accumulation, leaving them to only short-run or traverse effects. This result is in line with the empirical evidence to which BPCG literature builds upon (Kaldor 1978; Thirlwall 2012) and with neo-Kaleckian authors which highlight expansionary effects of devaluation should be stronger in the short-run (Blecker 2016).

The model also sustains the canonical results of the Supermultiplier literature (Freitas and Serrano 2015; Lavoie 2016). The rate of accumulation converges to the growth rate of the autonomous components of demand and utilization converges to normal levels. As in Morlin (2022), the long-run — or maximum — rate of growth is the same as defined by Thirlwall's Law (Thirlwall 2012).[16] Which highlights the role of structural change — and industrial and commercial policy — as the determinants of maximum growth rates. In line with Kaldorian and Latin American Structuralist traditions (Thirlwall 2012).

On the other hand, the introduction of another autonomous demand component — government expenditure — sheds light on the role of the BoP as a ceiling, but not as a floor nor the only determinant of growth. When government expenditure (or domestic autonomous demand more generally) grows faster than exports the economy continually accumulates external debt. This would characterize an unsustainable process (Godley 2012). On the opposite case, however, when government expenditure grows less than exports, the economy accumulates foreign assets and diminishes domestic public debt, a sustainable process. This would impose lower growth than potential, but it would be feasible for long periods of time.

The model concludes that the economy would follow either a balance-of-payments-constrained growth regime or a policy-constrained (or pure) demand-led growth regime.[17] A finding present in the BPCG literature (McCombie and Thirlwall 1999) and highlighted by authors in the Sraffian supermultiplier tradition (Freitas and Dweck 2013; Morlin 2022). However, this conclusion differs from Dvoskin and

---

[16]Thirlwall's Law can be written as $g_b = \dfrac{g_x}{\eta}$. Where η is the income elasticity of imports, which is equal to unit in the model the propensity to import is assumed constant. From Equation (15), $g^{**} = g_z = g_x = g_b$.

[17]'Policy constrained' can also be interpreted as 'politically constrained' as in Kalecki (1943 [1984]).

Torchinsky Landau (2023), which downplays the relevance of the policy-constrained regime as it is not an equilibrium result of the model. Although a 'traverse case' and not a 'long-run case', the policy-constrained regime remains relevant to explain the growth pattern of economies because it is a sustainable process that may be maintained for long periods of time. This conclusion follows the analysis of stock-flow relations proposed by the New Cambridge School (Cripps and Godley 1976), presenting a similar argument to the one made by Godley's trade performance for a static model (Lavoie 2022, Ch.4).

Lastly, the tradition of SFC modelling has also highlighted the role of *stock-flow norms* (Godley and Lavoie 2007, 13). The idea that expenditures may be influenced by desired levels of wealth stocks related to them. In the model, low public expenditures could be explained by the desire to reach lower levels of public debt or higher levels of international reserve stocks. Relating the role of financial variables to the relationship between 'semi-autonomous' components of demand (Allain 2022). Which may provide an economic rationale to the record accumulation of reserves seen in the 2000s following the Asian Financial Crisis of 1997-1998.

4. Impacts of an External Shock on Developing Countries

4.1. Exercise: Policy Reactions to a Hike in the Benchmark Interest Rate

Inspired by the empirical literature that finds that capital outflows from developing countries are usually led by increases in the interest rates in the US, the paper looks at how a rise in the Fed Funds rate — assumed to be the benchmark foreign interest rate i_f — may impact developing countries in the model. This is done through an exercise of comparative dynamics exploring different policy responses to the shock.

This approach may be seen as somehow innovative, as it applies a long-run growth model to a medium-run policy response environment. This is inspired by the insight of Lavoie (2016) about the importance of the traverse (the adjustment path between short-term and long-term equilibriums) in economic dynamics. The dynamic equations let us analyse effects out of the initial position while the long-run equations show all accumulated results between equilibriums.

To focus on developing countries some considerations must be made. Exchange rates were assumed to have no effect in the long-run but have a positive effect in the short-run. An important literature after Krugman and Taylor (1978) finds that exchange rate devaluations have mainly contractionary effects also in the short-run, bringing the BoP to equilibrium through lower income not through higher net exports, especially in developing countries.[18] Following this view, the dominant effect of a nominal exchange rate devaluation is considered to be a decrease of the productive wage-share through an increase in prices, such that $\frac{\partial \pi}{\partial e} > 0$ and $\phi_e = 0$. It is also assumed that the country is a net debtors with the rest of the world, such that $d > r$ and that it has a level of international reserves equal or above the level necessary not to enter a BoP crisis ($r \geq \bar{r}$).

[18]Developing countries are often primary good exporters, so their exports have low exchange rate elasticity (Bernat 2015) and due the absence of capital and intermediary goods industries domestically makes the decrease in imports unlikely (Dvoskin and Torchinsky Landau 2023).

This exercise is constructed under the conditions in which the model presents stable dynamics, that is: when the Keynesian stability condition, $s_r\pi > \gamma_u - \phi_u - \tau$, the domestic debt stability condition, $g > i(s_r - \tau)$, and the external debt system stability condition, $g_x > i_f \geq 0$, all hold. Economic scenarios in which these conditions do not hold will already lead to crises if persistent.

The focus of the exercise is on the dynamic of international reserves as they express the result of the BoP. The immediate effect of the shock on dynamic equations is interpreted as the 'medium-run dynamics', while on the long-run a full adjustment of all stocks to their long-run positions can be already assumed. The impact of a variation in i_f on both the dynamic (medium-run) and the long-run equations of reserves-to-exports ratio can be expressed as:

$$\frac{\partial \dot{r}}{\partial i_f} = (r - d) - \frac{Y_P}{X}\delta < 0 \tag{29}$$

$$\frac{\partial r^{**}}{\partial i_f} = \left[(r^{**} - d^{**}) - \frac{Y_P}{X}\delta\left(1 - \frac{i_x}{g_x}\right)\right]\frac{1}{g_x - i_f} < 0 \tag{30}$$

The foreign interest rate has a negative impact on reserves-to-exports ratio in the period after the shock but the effect on the long-run is ambiguous. The increase on interest rates paid and received on liabilities and assets and the decrease in capital inflows are felt immediately. But lower inflows slowly decrease net external debts decreasing interest payments. For this reason, lower financial inflows may have a positive effect on the long-run external constraint when $i_x > g_x$.[19]

This result is in line with the BPCG literature that incorporates financial flows (Moreno-Brid 2003; Bhering, Serrano, and Freitas 2019). It reflects the dual role of financial flows: as short-term liquidity and long-term liability. When $i_x > g_x$ any positive level of capital inflows tightens the external constraint in the long-run because external debt created by these flows impose interest payments that grow faster than exports. However, even when $i_x > g_x$, higher US interest rates will increase reserves-to-exports ($\frac{\partial r^{**}}{\partial i_f} > 0$) only when the positive impact of decreasing the long-run volume of liabilities is stronger than the price effect of higher interest rates on those liabilities. That is, only when $\frac{i_x}{g_x} > 1 + \frac{D^{**} - R^{**}}{\delta Y_P}$.

The result shows that an increase in benchmark interest rates lead to a deterioration in the BoP which may be temporary or persistent, depending on initial external financial stocks and interest rates on the country's external debts. If the country is running close to the external constraint ($\bar{r}$), already in the first periods after the shock the economy must choose between selling reserves or bringing BoP to equilibrium through macroeconomic policy. The modelled government has 3 macroeconomic tools to do so: the nominal exchange rate (e), domestic interest rate (i), and government expenditure (g_G).

[19] Note that Equation (26) can be written as $r^{**} = \frac{X - M + (g_x - i_x)d^{**}}{g_x - i_f}$, which highlights that when $i_x > g_x > i_f$, $\frac{\partial r^{**}}{\partial d^{**}} = \frac{g_x - i_x}{g_x - i_f} < 0$. For stability $g_x > i_f$ was assumed. Since $i_x > i_f$, $i_x > g_x > i_f$ is possible.

Impacts of each policy tool are considered on short-run capacity utilization and wage-share, the BoP dynamics, and the long-run equilibrium variables. Table 3 summarizes these effects, while each subsection next goes through them.

4.1.1. Case 1: Exchange Rate Policy (↑ e)

The government may let the currency take the whole shock of capital outflows, which would be correspondent to a case of fully flexible exchange rates. As described, the effect that dominates for developing countries is the shock of nominal exchange rates on distribution, through increased domestic prices. In the short-run, the currency devaluation decreases both the equilibrium capacity utilization and the wage-share. In the long-run, the currency devaluation also decreases equilibrium wage-share by increasing the equilibrium autonomous demand level and the public domestic debt stock. The effect on BoP, on the other hand, depends on the parameters:

Medium-run dynamics:

$$\frac{d\dot{r}}{de} = \frac{\partial\left(\frac{Y_P}{X}\right)^{**}}{\partial e} * (\delta(i - i_f) - \phi_u) \tag{31}$$

Long-run:

$$\frac{\partial r^{**}}{\partial e} = \left[\frac{\partial\left(\frac{Y_P}{X}\right)^{**}}{\partial e} * \frac{\left[\delta(i - i_f)\left(1 - \frac{i_x}{g_x}\right) - \phi_u\right]}{(g_x - i_f)}\right] \tag{32}$$

Since $\frac{\partial\left(\frac{Y_P}{X}\right)}{\partial e} < 0$,[20] the sign of Equation (38) will depend on $(\delta(i - i_f) - \phi_u)$. If the effect of the devaluation on capital inflows is stronger than the effect on diminishing imports, $\delta(i - i_f) > \phi_u$, then the devaluation has a negative effect on the BoP the traverse. This result is in line with the empirical literature after Rey (2015), which finds that global financial cycles commanded by US monetary policy cannot be offset by exchange rate movements in developing countries. Indeed, Rey's dilemma between monetary policy independence and capital openness can be seen in the model as higher δ imposes weaker the possibilities of positive effects of nominal exchange rates on the reserves-to-exports ratio in the medium-run.

The devaluation leads to lower GDP which decreases capital attraction, leading to lower levels of net external debt. Those levels, however, are expressed in dollar terms, because of the devaluation their value in domestic currency could have significantly

---

20 $$\frac{\partial\left(\frac{Y_P}{X}\right)^{*}}{\partial e} = \frac{\partial \pi}{\partial e} * \frac{\partial\left(\frac{Y_P}{X}\right)^{*}}{\partial \pi} = \frac{\partial \pi}{\partial e} * \frac{\partial\left(\frac{\gamma - \gamma_u u_n + z}{(1-\alpha)z(s_r\pi + \phi_u + \tau - \gamma_u)}\right)}{\partial \pi} = \frac{\partial \pi}{\partial e} * \frac{-s_r(\gamma - \gamma_u u_n + z)}{(1-\alpha)z(s_r\pi + \phi_u + \tau - \gamma_u)^2} < 0,$$

since it was defined that $\frac{\partial \pi}{\partial e} > 0$. In the long-run, the effect on z^{**} must be considered.-

$$\frac{\partial\left(\frac{Y_P}{X}\right)^{**}}{\partial e} = \frac{\partial \pi}{\partial e} * \left[\frac{-s_r(\gamma^{**} - \gamma_u u_n + z^{**})}{(1-\alpha)z^{**}(s_r\pi + \phi_u + \tau - \gamma_u)^2} + \frac{\partial z^{**}}{\partial e}\right] =$$

$$\frac{\partial \pi}{\partial e} * \left[\frac{-s_r(\gamma - \gamma_u u_n + z)}{(1-\alpha)z(s_r\pi + \phi_u + \tau - \gamma_u)^2} - \frac{s_r u_n(\gamma^{**} - \gamma_u u_n)}{(1-\alpha)z^{**2}(s_r\pi + \phi_u + \tau - \gamma_u)}\right] < 0.$$

Table 3. Effects of macroeconomic policy responses on key endogenous variables.

Policy variables	Short-run equilibrium		Medium-run dynamics	Long-run equilibrium					
								$i_x \geq g_x$	$i_x < g_x$
	u^*	w^*	$\dot{r}$	z^{**}	b^{**}	w^{**}	d^{**}	r^{**}	
$\uparrow e$	–	–	+/–	+	+	–	–	+	+/–
$\uparrow i$	+	+/–	+	0	+	–	+	–	+
$\downarrow \alpha$	–	0	+/–	0	–	+	–	+	+/–

Notes: + and – represent positive or negative partial derivatives from the change in the variable on equilibrium values. +/– means the effect is ambiguous. 0 means there is no effect. Variables: capacity utilization (u), wage share (w), international reserves to exports (r), autonomous non-capacity creating demand to capital (z), domestic debt to capital (b), external debt to exports (d), nominal exchange rates (e), nominal interest rate (i), share of government demand on autonomous demand (α), interest rate on net external debt (i_x), growth rate of exports (g_x).

increased. In the long-run, this leads to a new positive effect on reserves (in dollars) through lower levels of interest payments. When $i_x > g_x$, this effect is dominant, and reserves increase in the long-term. On the other hand, depreciation also increases the volume of domestic public debt through an increase in z.

4.1.2. Case 2: Monetary Policy (↑ i)

As an alternative to devaluing the currency, the government could choose to attract capitals by increasing domestic interest rates. This increases short-term capacity utilization but decreases wage-share under realistic assumptions.[21] In the long-run, an interest rate hike decreases the wage-share directly and through its increase of domestic public debt. It can also lead to a debt instability if the stability condition $g > i(s_r - \tau)$, is broken. The effects on the BoP are described:

Medium-run dynamics:

$$\frac{\partial \dot{r}}{\partial i} = \frac{Y_P}{X} \delta > 0 \tag{33}$$

Long-run:

$$\frac{\partial r^{**}}{\partial i} = \frac{Y_P}{X} \left[\frac{\delta \left(1 - \frac{i_x}{g_x}\right)}{(g_x - i_f)} \right] \tag{34}$$

An increase in domestic rates will increase international reserves in the short/medium-run. However, its positive effects on long-run BoP depend on $i_x < g_x$. When $i_x > g_x$, the increase in capital inflows is offset in the long-run by a greater increase in debt services payment, the opposite effect of what was shown with the hike of i_f.

Given the structure of the model, an increase in domestic interest rates has expansionary effects on output/capacity utilization. This result must be taken cautiously. The model only presents one channel from interest rates to activity, the consumption out of interest. While it leaves out credit-based expenditures (consumption and investment), for

[21]Fromm Equations (7) and (9), the condition is that the autonomous demand excluding consumption out of interest is positive, $\gamma + x + \vartheta - \gamma_u u_n > 0$. A condition that should be easily met by all economies.

simplicity. The latter are usually higher than the former which point out the possibility that higher interest rates can also dampen GDP in the short-run.

4.1.3. Case 3: Fiscal Policy ($\downarrow \alpha$)

The last case is the one in which the government directly responds to the worsening of the external conditions decreasing the share of government expenditure in demand-(α).[22] While α is endogenous in the long-run in the model, the fact that it can assume any value between 0 and 1 means the government may diminish temporarily its demand growth (g_G) to decrease α.

In the short-run, a decrease in government expenditure decreases capacity utilization which decreases the wage-share. However, in the long-run it increases the wage-share by decreasing the level of public domestic debt to GDP. This is a formal implication of the specification of the model but should be taken with attention. It is often the case that government expenditure has redistributive roles decreasing inequality, when that is the case cuts in public expenditure may increase inequality in the real world (Lavoie 2022, Ch.5). Effects on BoP are described:

Medium-run dynamics:

$$\frac{\partial \dot{r}}{\partial \alpha} = \frac{(\gamma^{**} - \gamma_u\, u_n + z^{**})(\delta(i - i_f) - \phi_u)}{(1-\alpha)^2 z^{**}(s_r \pi + \phi_u + \tau - \gamma_u)} \tag{35}$$

Long-run:

$$\frac{\partial r^{**}}{\partial \alpha} = \frac{\partial \left(\frac{Y_P}{X}\right)^{**}}{\partial \alpha} \left[\frac{\left(\delta(i - i_f)\left(1 - \frac{i_x}{g_x}\right) - \phi_u\right)}{g_x - i_f} \right] \tag{36}$$

Since $\frac{\partial \left(\frac{Y_P}{X}\right)^{*}}{\partial \alpha} = \frac{\partial \left(\frac{Y_P}{X}\right)^{**}}{\partial \alpha} > 0$,[23] a decrease in government expenditure has similar effects on BoP that an increase in nominal exchange rates. Further supporting the policy dilemma.

4.2. Policy Takeaways

The exercise concludes that an increase in foreign interest rates constrains developing countries' macroeconomic policy space. Already after the shock the country must choose whether selling its reserves or implementing at least one form of contractionary macroeconomic policy. Fiscal, monetary, and exchange rate policies were the tools considered here.

---

[22] The possibility of change in the tax rate is not considered, assuming changing tax rate policy takes longer time. Generally, the tax rate affects BoP negatively in the medium-run, while long-run results would depend on the parameters.

[23] $$\frac{\partial \left(\frac{Y_P}{X}\right)^{*}}{\partial \alpha} = \frac{\partial \left(\frac{Y_P}{X}\right)^{**}}{\partial \alpha} = \frac{\partial \left(\frac{(\gamma^{**} - \gamma_u\, u_n + z^{**})}{(1-\alpha) z^{**}(s_r \pi + \phi_u + \tau - \gamma_u)} \right)}{\partial \alpha} = \frac{(\gamma^{**} - \gamma_u\, u_n + z^{**})}{(1-\alpha)^2 z^{**}(s_r \pi + \phi_u + \tau - \gamma_u)} > 0$$

For the first periods after the shock, higher domestic interest rates ease the external constraint by attracting capital flows. While exchange rate devaluations and fiscal contraction may ease the BoP disequilibrium only through contractionary effects on aggregate demand, leading to lower average growth. A devaluation increases long-run inequality and may increase external debt in domestic prices. However, devaluation and austerity might not even be effective in bringing BoP to equilibrium.

When $\delta(i - i_f) > \phi_u$, that is, when the response of financial flows to changes in output is stronger than the response of imports, neither devaluation nor austerity have any positive effect on the BoP and might even aggravate the loss of reserves. This is the dilemma observed by the literature following Rey (2015). With greater capital account openness (high value of δ) only monetary policy would be able to prevent a BoP disequilibrium after a negative external shock. The dilemma holds as a short-to-medium-run trade-off for the contractionary phase of the global financial cycle.

In the long-run, impacts on financial flows are offset by an (opposite) effect on interest payments on the new volume of external debt. When $i_X < g_X$, the effect is just partially offset and the sign of the effect of the medium-run dynamics still holds in the long-run. However, when $i_X > g_X$, the immediate effect on financial flows is reversed in the long-run for all policies. Higher interest rates tighten the long-run constraint, while devaluation and austerity loosen it. This result highlights the dual role of financial flows: providing short-term liquidity but increasing long-term liability. Which is in line with the BPCG literature that considers capital flows (Moreno-Brid 2003; Bhering, Serrano, and Freitas 2019) and points to a possible policy trade-off between short and long run results. In terms of income distribution, higher interest or nominal exchange rates lead to lower wage-shares in the long-run. While lower government expenditures have a positive effect on the wage-share through lower public debt.

As seen, a negative shock caused by interest rate hikes could be temporary depending on the parameters. The shock could also be temporary depending on US monetary policymaking. In both cases, the country would be able to sustain expansionary policies if it has international reserves to spend. The massive accumulation of reserves by emerging countries since 1997 and their partial expenditure by some countries in 2015 and 2022 may be strategies in this direction. Not making use of full external space allows countries to have external liquidity to maintain expansionary policies and higher growth rates in times of tighter external conditions. This goes in the opposite direction of interpretations (and empirical studies) on reserve accumulation which only looks at the effect of reserves on growth through the direct opportunity cost of not using the whole external space (Cruz and Walters 2008).

The findings presented here are based on a balance-of-payments-constraint which has in its core the necessity to access a currency not issued domestically to trade. This would not be the case for countries trading in their own currency. The paper has also not dealt in depth with capital flows management policies. They could help diminish the magnitude of external shocks on the BoP (through lower δ).[24]

[24]See Botta et al. (2023) for more on this.

5. Conclusion

This paper presents two main contributions to the field of open-economy macroeconomics of distribution and growth. First, it presents a stock-flow-consistent supermultiplier model in which growth is led by exports, government consumption and consumption out of interest. Traditional supermultiplier model results are maintained even when SFC relations are considered in an open-economy context. Domestic debt stability conditions are less restrictive under SFC considerations. The neo-Kaleckian supermultiplier model may be conciliated with the balance-of-payments-constraint when the exchange rate effect fades away in the long-run. Structural change determines the maximum long-run growth rates, in line with Kaldorian and Structuralist traditions, but average growth rates are affected by macroeconomic policies. Domestic expenditures may be kept below balance-of-payments-constrained growth rates for a long time (although not indefinitely) to pursue lower levels of public debt or higher levels of international reserves. Which highlights the role *stock-flow-norms* (Godley and Lavoie 2007) may have in the relationship between semi-autonomous expenditures (Allain 2022).

Secondly, the paper contributes to the understanding of external constraints to macroeconomic policymaking in developing countries with a comparative dynamics exercise of different domestic policy responses to a hike in benchmark interest rates (US Fed rates). The exercise explores short, medium, and long-run effects in the model. It finds that the shock forces a country to immediately spend reserves or apply some contractionary macroeconomic measure. Rey's (2015) dilemma arises in the short-to-medium-run as currency devaluation and fiscal contraction may be unable to bring BoP to equilibrium because of its effects on capital attraction. Monetary policy being the only tool able to do so. In the long-run, initial effects may be reversed as financial inflows provide short-term liquidity but represent long-run liabilities. Possibly imposing a policy trade-off between short and long-run goals. Expansionary macroeconomic policies and higher growth rates can be maintained if countries have enough reserves to spend. Presenting a rationale for the accumulation of reserve stocks.

The results point to the BoP as a possible constraint to macroeconomic policy space in developing countries not only in the long-run, but in all periods. Which becomes more complex with large capital flows to these countries, possibly imposing trade-offs between short and long-run objectives. It also provides a possible explanation for historical facts observed in the 2000s. In the period, high external liquidity may have supported emerging countries to conciliate high growth rates (way above developed countries) with the accumulation of large reserve stocks, which now provide some liquidity against future external shocks.

Acknowledgments

This paper was first written as a master's Thesis supervised by professors Eckhard Hein, Marc Lavoie, and Bruno Tinel. I am grateful to them for instigating discussions and thoughtful advice. It also draws on fruitful discussions with Ricardo Summa, Guilherme Morlin, and Matias Torchinsky. I also thank two anonymous reviewers and the colleagues at the 4th Workshop on Demand-led Growth in IE-UFRJ and at the 16th EAEPE Summer School in Roma Tre for their comments. All remaining errors are my own, of course.

Disclosure Statement

No potential conflict of interest was reported by the author(s).

ORCID

João Emboava Vaz http://orcid.org/0009-0007-1449-3060

References

Aidar, G., and J. Braga. 2020. 'Country-risk Premium in the Periphery and the International Financial Cycle 1999-2019.' *Investigación económica* 79 (313): 78–111.

Allain, O. 2022. 'A Supermultiplier Model with Two Non-Capacity-Generating Semi-Autonomous Demand Components.' *Structural Change and Economic Dynamics* 63: 91–103.

Bernat, G. 2015. 'Tipo de Cambio Real y Diversificación Productiva en América del Sur.' *Oficina de la Cepal en Buenos Aires, Estudios y perspectivas series* 43: 1–49.

Bhering, G., F. Serrano, and F. Freitas. 2019. 'Thirlwall's law, External Debt Sustainability, and the Balance-of-Payments-Constrained Level and Growth Rates of Output.' *Review of Keynesian Economics* 7 (4): 486–497.

Blecker, R. 1989. 'International Competition, Income Distribution and Economic Growth.' *Cambridge Journal of Economics* 13 (3): 395–412.

Blecker, R. 2016. 'Wage-led Versus Profit-led Demand Regimes: The Long and the Short of It.' *Review of Keynesian Economics* 4 (4): 373–390.

Borio, C., and P. Disyatat. 2015. 'Capital Flows and the Current Account: Taking Financing (more) Seriously.' BIS Working Papers, 525.

Botta, A., G. Porcile, D. Spinola, and G. T. Yajima. 2023. 'Financial Integration, Productive Development and Fiscal Policy Space in Developing Countries.' *Structural Change and Economic Dynamics* 66: 175–188.

Brochier, L., and A. C. M. E. Silva. 2019. 'A Supermultiplier Stock-Flow Consistent Model: The "Return" of the Paradoxes of Thrift and Costs in the Long Run?' *Cambridge Journal of Economics* 43 (2): 413–442.

Carlin, W., and D. Soskice. 2005. 'The 3-Equation New Keynesian Model — A Graphical Exposition.' *Topics in Macroeconomics* 5 (1): 1–36.

Cline, N., and M. Vernengo. 2016. 'Interest Rates, Terms of Trade, and Currency Crises: Are We on the Verge of a New Crisis in the Periphery?' In *Financial Deepening and Post-Crisis Development in Emerging Markets, Gevorkyan*, edited by A. Canuto, 41–62. New York: Palgrave Macmillan.

Cripps, F., and W. Godley. 1976. 'A Formal Analysis of the Cambridge Economic Policy Group Model.' *Economica* 43 (172): 335–348.

Cruz, M., and B. Walters. 2008. 'Is the Accumulation of International Reserves Good for Development?' *Cambridge Journal of Economics* 32 (5): 665–681.

Deleidi, M., and M. Mazzucato. 2019. 'Putting Austerity to bed: Technical Progress, Aggregate Demand and the Supermultiplier.' *Review of Political Economy* 31 (3): 315–335.

Domar, E. 1944. 'The "Burden of the Debt" and the National Income.' *The American Economic Review* 34 (4): 798–827.

Dutt, A. 2019. 'Some Observations on Models of Growth and Distribution with Autonomous Demand Growth.' *Metroeconomica* 70 (2): 288–301.

Dvoskin, A., and M. Torchinsky Landau. 2023. 'Limits to Fiscal and Monetary Policy in Small Open Economies.' *Review of Political Economy*. 1–28. Advance online publication. https://doi.org/10.1080/09538259.2023.2279162.

Freitas, F., and E. Dweck. 2013. 'The Pattern of Economic Growth of the Brazilian Economy 1970–2005: A Demand-led Growth Perspective.' In *Sraffa and the Reconstruction of Economic Theory: Volume Two*, edited by E. S. Levrero, A. Palumbo, and A. Stirati, 158–191. London: Palgrave Macmillan.

Freitas, F., and F. Serrano. 2015. 'Growth Rate and Level Effects, the Stability of the Adjustment of Capacity to Demand and the Sraffian Supermultiplier.' *Review of Political Economy* 27 (3): 258–281.

Godley, W. 2012. 'Seven Unsustainable Processes: Medium-Term Prospects and Policies for the United States and the World.' In *The Stock-Flow Consistent Approach*, edited by M. Lavoie, and G. Zezza, 216–254. London: Palgrave Macmillan UK.

Godley, W., and M. Lavoie. 2007. *Monetary Economics: An Integrated Approach to Credit, Money, Income, Production and Wealth.* London: Palgrave Macmillan UK.

Hein, E. 2018. 'Autonomous Government Expenditure Growth, Deficits, Debt, and Distribution in a neo-Kaleckian Growth Model.' *Journal of Post Keynesian Economics* 41 (2): 316–338.

Ilzetzki, E., C. M. Reinhart, and K. S. Rogoff. 2022. 'Rethinking Exchange Rate Regimes.' In *Handbook of International Economics (Vol. 6)*, edited by G. Gobinath, E. Helpman, and K. Rogoff. North Holland: Elsevier.

Kaldor, N. 1978. *Further Essays on Applied Economics.* London: Duckworth.

Kalecki, M. 1943 [1984]. 'Political Aspects of Full Employment.' In *The Political Economy: Readings in the Politics and Economics of American Public Policy*, edited by T. Ferguson, and J. Rogers. New York: Routledge.

Krugman, P. 1979. 'A Model of Balance-of-Payments Crises.' *Journal of Money, Credit and Banking* 11 (3): 311–325.

Krugman, P., and L. Taylor. 1978. 'Contractionary Effects of Devaluation.' *Journal of International Economics* 8 (3): 445–456.

Lavoie, M. 2016. 'Convergence Towards the Normal Rate of Capacity Utilization in neo-Kaleckian Models: The Role of non-Capacity Creating Autonomous Expenditures.' *Metroeconomica* 67 (1): 172–201.

Lavoie, M. 2022. *Post-Keynesian Economics: New Foundations.* Northampton: Edward Elgar Publishing USA.

McCombie, J., and A. Thirlwall. 1999. 'Growth in an International Context: A Post Keynesian View.' In *Foundations of International Economics*, edited by J. Deprez, and J. Harvey. London: Routledge.

McLeay, M., A. Radia, and R. Thomas. 2014. 'Money Creation in the Modern Economy'. Bank of England Quarterly Bulletin 2014 Q1. https://ssrn.com/abstract=2416234.

Moreno-Brid, J. 2003. 'Capital Flows, Interest Payments and the Balance-of-Payments Constrained Growth Model: A Theoretical and Empirical Analysis.' *Metroeconomica* 54 (2–3): 346–365.

Morlin, G. 2022. 'Growth led by Government Expenditure and Exports: Public and External Debt Stability in a Supermultiplier Model.' *Structural Change and Economic Dynamics* 62: 586–598.

Nah, W., and M. Lavoie. 2017. 'Long-run Convergence in a neo-Kaleckian Open-Economy Model with Autonomous Export Growth.' *Journal of Post Keynesian Economics* 40 (2): 223–238.

Nalin, L., and G. T. Yajima. 2022. 'Balance Sheet Effects in a Financialized Environment: A Stock-Flow Consistent Framework for Mexico.' *Review of Political Economy* 1–21.

Nikiforos, M., and G. Zezza. 2018. 'Stock-Flow Consistent Macroeconomic Models: A Survey.' *Journal of Economic Surveys* 31: 1204–1239. https://doi.org/10.1111/joes.12221.

Nikiforos, M., L. Carvalho, and C. Schoder. 2015. '"Twin Deficits" in Greece: In Search of Causality.' *Journal of Post Keynesian Economics* 38 (2): 302–330.

Pedrosa, Í, L. Brochier, and F. Freitas. 2023. 'Debt Hierarchy: Autonomous Demand Composition, Growth and Indebtedness in a Supermultiplier Model.' *Economic Modelling* 126: 1–15.

Porcile, G., and G. Yajima. 2021. 'New Structuralism and the Balance-of Payments Constraint.' In *Thirlwall's Law at 40*, edited by T. Palley, E. Pérez-Caldentey, and M. Vernengo. London: Edward Elgar Publishing.

Rey, H. 2015. 'Dilemma Not Trilemma: The Global Financial Cycle and Monetary Policy Independence.' NBER Working Paper Series No. 21162.

Serrano, F. 1995. 'Long Period Effective Demand and the Sraffian Supermultiplier.' *Contributions to Political Economy* 14: 67–90.

Serrano, F., and R. Summa. 2015. 'Mundell–Fleming Without the LM Curve: The Exogenous Interest Rate in an Open Economy.' *Review of Keynesian Economics* 3 (2): 248–268.

Thirlwall, A. P. 2012. 'Balance of Payments Constrained Growth Models: History and Overview.' In *Models of Balance of Payments Constrained Growth*, edited by E. Soukiazis, and P. A. Cerqueira, 11–49. London: Palgrave Macmillan.

Vernengo, M., and E. Pérez-Caldentey. 2020. 'Modern Money Theory (MMT) in the Tropics: Functional Finance in Developing Countries.' *Challenge* 63 (6): 332–348.

Appendix

The local stability of the long-run equilibrium depends on a negative trace and a positive determinant of the following Jacobian matrix:

$$J = \begin{pmatrix} \frac{\partial \dot{r}}{\partial r} & \frac{\partial \dot{r}}{\partial d} \\ \frac{\partial \dot{d}}{\partial r} & \frac{\partial \dot{d}}{\partial d} \end{pmatrix}$$

Which impose the inequalities:

$$Det_J = \frac{\partial \dot{r}}{\partial r} * \frac{\partial \dot{d}}{\partial d} - \frac{\partial \dot{r}}{\partial d} * \frac{\partial \dot{d}}{\partial r} = -g_x(i_f - g_x) > 0$$

$$Tr_J = \frac{\partial \dot{r}}{\partial r} + \frac{\partial \dot{d}}{\partial d} = i_f - 2g_x < 0$$

The first inequality holds when $i_f \langle g_x \rangle 0$ or $i_f > g_x < 0$. The second inequality holds when $\frac{i_f}{2} < g_x$, which imposes $g_x > 0$, since $i_f \geq 0$. Both inequalities will then only hold when $g_x > i_f \geq 0$.

Index

Note: Figures are indicated by *italics*. Tables are indicated by **bold**.

For Product Safety Concerns and Information please contact our EU representative GPSR@taylorandfrancis.com
Taylor & Francis Verlag GmbH, Kaufingerstraße 24, 80331 München, Germany

www.ingramcontent.com/pod-product-compliance
Ingram Content Group UK Ltd.
Pitfield, Milton Keynes, MK11 3LW, UK
UKHW050351071126
477531UK00011B/565
* 9 7 8 1 0 4 1 0 5 3 8 0 4 *